Windows NT®
Server 4
Security
Handbook

WINDOWS NT®
SERVER 4
SECURITY
HANDBOOK

Lee Hadfield • Dave Hatter • Dave Bixler

Windows NT Server 4 Security Handbook

Library of Congress Catalog No.: 97-67039

ISBN: 0-7897-1213-x

99 98 97   6 5 4 3 2 1

Interpretation of the printing code: the rightmost double-digit number is the year of the book's printing; the rightmost single-digit number, the number of the book's printing. For example, a printing code of 97-1 shows that the first printing of the book occurred in 1997.

Screen reproductions in this book were created using Collage Plus from Inner Media, Inc., Hollis, NH.

Contents at a Glance

Table of Contents

Credits

PRESIDENT
Roland Elgey

SENIOR PRESIDENT/PUBLISHING
Don Fowley

PUBLISHER
Stacy Hiquet

GENERAL MANAGER
Joe Muldoon

MANAGER OF PUBLISHING OPERATIONS
Linda H. Buehler

PUBLISHING MANAGER
Fred Slone

TITLE MANAGER
Al Valvano

EDITORIAL SERVICES DIRECTOR
Carla Hall

MANAGING EDITOR
Caroline D. Roop

ACQUISITIONS EDITOR
Tracy Dunkelberger

PRODUCTION EDITOR
Sherri L. Fugit

PRODUCT MARKETING MANAGER
Kourtnaye Sturgeon

ASSISTANT PRODUCT MARKETING MANAGER
Gretchen Schlesinger

WEB MASTER
Thomas H. Bennett

TECHNICAL EDITORS
Bob Chronister
John Piraino

SOFTWARE SPECIALIST
Brandon K. Penticuff

TECHNICAL SUPPORT SPECIALIST
Nadeem Muhammed

ACQUISITIONS COORDINATOR
Carmen Krikorian

SOFTWARE RELATIONS COORDINATOR
Susan D. Gallagher

SOFTWARE COORDINATOR
Andrea Duvall

EDITORIAL ASSISTANT
Jennifer Chisholm

BOOK DESIGNER
Ruth Harvey

COVER DESIGNER
Jay Corpus

PRODUCTION TEAM
Kay Hoskin
Laura A. Knox
Staci Somers
Lisa Stumpf

INDEXER
Tim Wright

Composed in *Century Old Style* and *ITC Franklin Gothic* by Que Corporation.

To my wife Leslee and my son Samuel, my two favorite people.

—DH

About the Authors

Lee Hadfield is a Senior Systems Engineer for Ikon Office Solutions, a Microsoft Solution Provider and software developer. He has over ten years of PC networking experience, and currently heads up the Network Integration Group for Integra's Solution Services Division located in Tucson, Arizona. Experienced with Novell, LAN Manager, and Windows NT, his work is currently focused around the Microsoft BackOffice family of server products, most notably Systems Management Server and its integration into new or existing network environments. He holds both Microsoft Certified System Engineer and Novell Certified NetWare Engineer certifications. Lee is the author of *Special Edition Using SMS 1.2*.

Dave Hatter has contributed to *Special Edition Using Lotus Notes and Domino 4.5*, *Using Lotus Notes 4.5*, and *Special Edition Using Lotus Notes 4*. He also has done technical editing for Que's sister imprints, Sam and Waite. Dave is a Principal of Definiti where he specializes in Lotus Notes, Microsoft Exchange, and Inter/intranet development. Dave holds the following certifications: Certified Lotus Professional developer (CLPAD) and System Administrator (CLPSA), and Microsoft Certified Product Specialist (MCPS) for Windows NT Workstation and Server 3.51. He has a B.S. in Information Systems from Northern Kentucky University, where he teaches a number of technology related community education courses. Dave stays busy outside of work by appearing monthly on "Northern Kentucky Magazine" to discuss current technology and trends (catch it on WTKR Channel A6) and by writing columns for *The NKUpdate* and *The Cincinnati Business Courier*. He lives in Fort Wright, Kentucky with his wife Leslee and his son Samuel. Dave can be reached via e-mail at **dhatter@definiti.com** or on the Web at **w3.one.net/~dhatter**.

Dave Bixler is an Enterprise Network Consultant with Entex Information Services, the largest PC systems integrator in the United States. He has been working in the networking arena for the last nine years on network designs, server implementations, and network management, as well as Internet Security. Dave's industry certifications include Novell's CNE for NetWare versions 3.x and 4.x, ECNE, MCNE, as well as Microsoft's MCPS and MCSE. He also has IBM's PSE, Check Point Software's CCSE, and 3Com's 3Wizard Master certifications. Dave is finishing up his B.S. in Computer Science, which was put on hold by four years of military service in the U.S. Army. Dave lives in Cincinnati, Ohio with his wife Sarah, son Marty, and two Keeshonds, Zeus and Arcus. Dave can be reached via e-mail at **dbixler@art-deco.net**.

Acknowledgments

I thank God for talent, Dave Bixler at Entex, also Carl Danowski and Nik Kalyani at Definiti for their help and guidance.

—DH

We'd Like to Hear from You!

As part of our continuing effort to produce books of the highest possible quality, Que would like to hear your comments. To stay competitive, we *really* want you, as a computer book reader and user, to let us know what you like or dislike most about this book or other Que products.

Please send your comments, ideas, and suggestions for improvement to:

The Expert User Team

E-mail: **euteam@que.mcp.com**
CompuServe: 105527,745
Fax: (317) 581-4663

Our mailing address is:

Expert User Team
Que Corporation
201 W. 103rd Street
Indianapolis, IN 46290-1097

You can also visit our Team's home page on the World Wide Web at the following address:

http://www.mcp.com/que/developer_expert

Thank you. Your comments will help us to continue publishing the best books available in today's market.

Thank you,

The Expert User Team

Introduction

Journeying into the realm of networking in 1985, Microsoft had meager beginnings with the networking enhancements made to MS-DOS 3.1. Another, more significant step was taken with the release of Windows for Workgroups 3.11 (WFW) in 1991. However, it was the 1993 release of a new 32-bit operating system with built-in networking capabilities and a graphical user interface (GUI) that set Microsoft on a course for dominance in the networking arena. This new operating system was called Windows New Technology (Windows NT, for short) and showed promise, although its reception by industry analysts and business users was lukewarm at best.

Since the introduction of Windows NT, a lot has happened in the world of networking. Of all these many advancements and changes, there are two things that have had the most significant impact on networking with Windows NT and consequently, network security. The first is the maturation of Windows NT into a world-class network operating system (NOS). The second is the growth of wide area networks (WAN's), internetworking, and the explosion of the Internet. ■

Enter the *Windows NT Server Security Handbook.* This book follows the premise that the best offense is a good defense. While no system that is plugged in is 100 percent secure, if you can make your systems much more difficult to break into than average, you can wear most hackers down and they'll move on to easier targets. The *Windows NT Server Security Handbook* helps you bolster your defenses by introducing you to the security threats your networks face (this can be frightening if it's your responsibility to protect these systems). It shows you the powerful security model of Windows NT and teaches you the techniques and procedures you need for implementation to protect your Windows NT networks, and the mission critical information they contain.

Microsoft works at a frenzied pace to continually increase the functionality and performance of Windows NT. Some of the many enhancements include the following:

- The Windows 95 user interface replaces the old Windows 3.*x* interface.
- The operating system architecture has been rewritten to provide quantifiably better performance.
- The inclusion of Internet Information Server (IIS) which includes HTTP, FTP, and Gopher services.
- Native TCP/IP filtering, enabling you to create a basic, inexpensive firewall.
- Gateway Services for NetWare now includes support for NetWare Directory Services (NDS).
- The new Point-to-Point Tunneling Protocol enables you to send non-TCP/IP data through TCP/IP networks.
- Improved usage and security of the Registry.
- The addition of the System Policy Editor that grants more control over the user's network environment.
- The incorporation of a Domain Name Service (DNS) server service makes it easy to add DNS services to your network.
- The inclusion of Administrative Wizards that can significantly simplify administration, especially for new administrators.
- A vastly improved and more useful Task Manager.
- The inclusion of a Multi-Protocol Router (MPR) service.

Although the significant enhancements to Windows NT included in version 3.51 helped it shed its reputation as being a "niche" product, it's only in version 4.0 that the fruition of this effort is truly realized. Windows NT 4.0 is a scalable, robust, feature laden, secure operating system, and it is rapidly becoming the operating system of choice for both high-end clients and servers because it delivers the best "bang-for-the-buck" of any high-end operating system.

Maintaining Security

This claim easily is backed-up by Windows NT's impressive sales figures. Windows NT Server sales grew 86 percent in 1995, and according to 1996 sales results published by International Data Corporation (IDC), Windows NT Server outsold Novell's NetWare 3.*x*, 4.*x*, and NetWare Loadable Modules combined! There were 732,000 new units of Windows NT Server sold compared to 669,000 new units of NetWare 3.*x*, 4.*x*, and NetWare Loadable Modules (NLMs).

However, as functionality expands, so does the possibility of security breaches, for two basic reasons: It becomes increasingly more difficult for the development team to eliminate subtle bugs that hackers can search for and exploit; it becomes increasingly more difficult for systems administrators to cover all the bases. With a product as feature-rich and complex as Windows NT Server, it's hard to ensure that you plug all the holes. Network administrators constantly must remain vigilant.

The addition of Internet Information Server (IIS) to Windows NT Server makes this especially true. IIS is an incredibly powerful tool built on top of the Windows NT architecture that makes it easy to establish a presence on the Internet. But, keep in mind that by connecting a network to a TCP/IP network (especially the Internet), you are providing an open door for users (and hackers) to access your system.

Another concern is that more people are using computers and that a larger percentage of these users are becoming more computer savvy. This means that either out of a sense of curiosity or malicious desire to cause harm, users can and often do crash systems and destroy data if the proper security precautions are not put in place.

What does all of this tell you? When it comes to security, a little paranoia is a good thing! If you are paranoid, you are more likely to not only take the proper precautions to protect your network, you also are more likely to remain vigilant in looking for security holes. The key is to balance security with performance and usability. If the security is so tight that users can't get their jobs done, they won't use the system. On the other hand, if you have the world's fastest and easiest network to use, but hackers steal your data and crash your system causing irreparable harm to your business, what have you accomplished?

There are two key concepts you need to understand about security: The first is that ignorance is usually the biggest threat to security. If you are not aware there is a security hole, or are not aware that there are tools you can use to plug a hole, you are in trouble. There are people who are aware of these holes and take great delight in breaking into systems. The second key vigilance. Security is an ongoing process; it doesn't end when you create your last user account or install a firewall. In order to ensure the security of your systems, you must constantly look for and plug holes.

Finally, remember that every network environment is different, and some of the techniques and policies discussed in this book may not be appropriate for your environment.

Before you implement any of the suggestions made in this book, always be sure to back up your system and test changes on a non-production system.

Who Should Use This Book?

Written primarily for the Windows NT Server administrator who needs to have a thorough understanding of the security threats networks face, this book includes sound strategies to help you protect your organization's most important resource: its information. You learn to master the many robust security features that Windows NT Server provides, such as New Technology File System (NFTS), auditing, TCP/IP filtering, and account policies, to name a few. Additionally, you also learn many undocumented or frequently overlooked security holes, and the trips and tricks that enable you to effectively plug those holes.

This book also is written for the managers and business owners who are considering or are using Windows NT Server and want to ensure the security of corporate systems and information.

How to Use This Book

This book is divided into five easy-to-follow parts. The first part of the book provides an introduction to network security problems and issues. For the beginner, Part I serves as an excellent network security primer. For the seasoned network administrator, Part I is an excellent refresher, as well as an in-depth look at the Windows NT architecture. Parts II and III focus on understanding and implementing Windows NT's many native security features. Part IV concentrates on ensuring the security on Windows NT networks connected to the Internet and other network operating systems. The final section, Part V, discusses how you can make Windows NT meet the Department of Defense's C2 security requirements.

Part I: An Overview of Microsoft Windows NT Security

Part I provides a general overview of network security issues and concerns, as well as how Microsoft Windows NT Server combats those problems. Its secure architecture and the many Windows NT Server security tools at your disposal helps you accomplish this.

In Chapter 1, "Understanding the Basics of Security," you are introduced to the basics of network security, such as what security means, who needs it, and how you can plan for it.

In Chapter 2, "An Overview of Microsoft Windows NT Security," you learn about the powerful Windows NT security model and the plethora of security features and tools that Windows NT provides out-of-the box.

Chapter 3, "Windows NT Operating System Architecture," takes you "under the hood" of Windows NT providing detailed coverage of the Windows NT 3.51 architecture, the changes in Windows NT 4.0, and how they relate to the security of your Windows NT network. Understanding the architecture of Windows NT is essential to ensuring the security of your networks.

Part II: Security Implementation on Microsoft Windows NT

Part II covers the many features of the Windows NT security model in detail. You learn many useful tips and tricks relating to Windows NT's security features for domains, file systems, and user accounts. You also learn how network clients can affect Windows NT security.

Chapter 4, "Windows NT Domain Concepts," takes the mystery out of Windows NT's domains. You learn what domains are, why you need them, how they relate to user accounts, and how to manage them efficiently and effectively.

Chapter 5, "Maintaining Security with Domain Trust Relationships," explains the often confusing topic of domains and trust relationships and teaches you how to further refine security on your Windows NT network by using trust relationships between domains.

Chapter 6, "User Account Security and Windows NT," explains the many options you have for securing Windows NT user accounts. It also shows you how to use groups to make administration easier.

Chapter 7, "New Technology File System (NTFS) Security," provides the knowledge you need to understand and implement the ultimate in secure file systems: NTFS.

Chapter 8, "Using Windows NT Security to Protect Domain Resources," shows how you can use many native tools and features that Windows NT Server provides, such as the User Manager for Domains, Event Viewer, and the Registry Editor to secure your Windows NT network.

Chapter 9, "Windows NT Workstation Security," takes a look at some Windows NT Workstation-specific security issues and tips.

Part III: Setting Up an Example Master-Domain Model

Part III is a comprehensive examination of what you need to know to implement Windows NT's Master Domain model. You learn how to plan the domain, prepare the domain controllers, create users and groups, and set up trust relationships.

Carefully planning your master domain is important to successful implementation. Chapter 10, "Planning the Master Domain," helps you understand the requirements and challenges involved.

Chapter 11, "Implementation Steps," tells you how to configure you Windows NT environment for the master domain model, which includes preparing the domain controllers, creating user and group accounts, and configuring resource servers.

Chapter 12, "Setting Up Trust Relationships," walks you through configuring trust relationships between domains.

Part IV: Windows NT Security with BackOffice Products, the Internet, and Other Network Platforms

Internetworking, whether it's the Internet or an extranet, is an incredibly hot topic now, and security is (or should be) of paramount importance to organizations that are internetworking. Part IV explains how to ensure the security of Windows NT networks when connecting to other network operating systems and when using TCP/IP for an intranet, extranet, or when connecting to the Internet.

Chapter 13, "Overview of Security and the Internet," teaches you how to keep your Windows NT networks safe when connecting to the Internet. Topics covered include Internet threats, known security issues, firewalls, proxy servers, and IP filtering.

Chapter 14, "Internet Security and BackOffice," explains how to ensure the security of your Internet-ready BackOffice applications, such as Microsoft Internet Information Server and Microsoft Exchange.

Chapter 15, "Windows NT Integration with NetWare and Other Network Operating Systems," shows you how to connect Windows NT Server to other network operating systems, such as Novell NetWare and Banyan VINES and to ensure the security of your network once connected.

In Chapter 16, "Allowing Macintosh Clients Access to Windows NT Resources," you learn how to connect Apple Macintosh clients to Windows NT Server by installing the Macintosh services and configuring access rights.

Chapter 17, "Integration of Windows NT with a UNIX Environment," explains how to connect Windows NT Server to UNIX networks and covers the related security issues.

Part V: Implementing Department of Defense Security Criteria in a Windows NT Environment

Part V takes you into the realm of ultra-high security for Windows NT—the C2 security criteria. You learn what C2 security means, where it fits into the *Department of Defense's Trusted Computer Systems Evaluation Criteria*, and how you can implement this level of security in your Windows NT network.

Chapter 18, "An Overview of the *Department of Defense Trusted Computer System Evaluation Criteria*," introduces you to the government's standard for network security (developed by the National Computer Security Council, an arm of the U.S. National Security Agency), which defines the criteria for trusted computer products.

Chapter 19, "The Implementation of C2-Level Security with Windows NT," teaches you how to bring your Windows NT network up to the C2 standard.

Conventions Used in This Book

Que Corp. has over a decade of experience writing and developing the most successful computer books available. With that experience, we've learned which special features help readers the most. Look for these special features throughout the book to enhance your learning experience.

Several type and font conventions are used in this book to help make reading it easier:

- *Italic type* is used to emphasize the author's points or to introduce new terms.
- Screen messages, code listings, and command samples appear in `monospace` typeface.
- Anything you are asked to type appears in **boldface**.
- File names are set in ALL CAPS to help them stand out against regular text.

Each chapter begins with a road map, which is a brief list of topics to be covered in that chapter. This allows you to see at a glance what information is included, and it serves as an outline of key topics you'll read about in that chapter.

 TIP Tips present short advice on a quick or often overlooked procedure. These include shortcuts that can save you time.

N O T E A note provides additional information that may help you avoid problems or offers advice that relates to the topic.

CAUTION
Cautions warn you about potential problems that a procedure may cause, unexpected results, and mistakes to avoid.

ON THE WEB

Over the course of this book, you'll find Internet references that point you to World Wide Web addresses or other online resources that that compliment the information in this book. Internet references look like this:

You may access QUE's Web site at the following:

http://www.quecorp.com

▶ **See** these cross-references for more information on a particular topic. **p. xxx**

Sidebar

Longer discussions not integral to the flow of the chapter are set aside as sidebars. Look for these sidebars to find out even more information.

Underlined Hot Keys, or Mnemonics:

Hot keys (keys that enable you quickly to access menus, buttons, and commands) used in this book appear underlined, just as they do on your screen. For example, the F in File menu option is a hot key, or shortcut, for opening the File menu. To access a hot key, simply press and hold the ALT key and press the hot key that corresponds to your choice. For example, to open the Edit menu, press and hold the ALT key and the E key.

Shortcut Key Combinations:

Similar to hot keys, *shortcut key combinations* enable you to substitute keyboard shortcuts for clicking (using your mouse) to navigate through menus for performing a task. For example, if you copied information to the Clipboard and want to paste it into the current document, there are two ways to do it. You could use the mouse to select Edit, Paste or you could press and hold the CTRL key and press the V key to achieve the same result. These keyboard shortcuts are a quick and handy way to save yourself time. In most instances, keyboard shortcuts are indicated in the menu beside the menu selection they perform. Shortcut Key combinations used in this book are represented in the text as CTRL+V.

Menu Commands:

Instructions for selecting menu commands take the following format:

Choose File, Properties.

This means that you should click the File menu option to open it, then click the Properties item in the File menu.

Now that Windows NT has the Windows 95 user interface, the Start button has made its appearance in Windows NT. When you need to select an item from the Start menu, it appears in the text like this:

Open the Start menu and select Settings, Control Panel, Internet.

Other Sources of Information for Network Security

Although this book attempts to serve as a comprehensive guide for Windows NT Server security, any of the following books and Web sites compliment the information in this book nicely.

Internet Firewalls and Network Security, Second Edition, New Riders Publishing, Chris Hare and Karanjit S. Siyan, Ph.D. 1996, ISBN: 1562056328.

Implementing Internet Security, New Riders Publishing, New Riders Development Group, 1995, ISBN: 1562054716.

Internet Security: Professional Reference, New Riders Publishing, Derek Atkins (Editor), Paul Buis, Chris Hare, Robert Kelley, 1996, ISBN: 1562055577.

Network and Internetwork Security: Principles and Practice, Prentice Hall, William Stallings, 1995, ISBN: 0024154830.

Web Sites

National Computer Security Association	**http://www.ncsa.com**
Electronic Privacy Information Center	**http://www.epic.org**
Microsoft	**http://www.microsoft.com**
Netscape	**http://www.netscape.com**
Network Professionals Association	**http://www.npa.org**
Windows NT Magazine	**http://www.winntmag.com**
RSA Data Security	**http://www.rsa.com**
Encryption Policy Resource Page	**http://www.crypto.com**

An Overview of Microsoft Windows NT Security

Understanding the Basics of Security

Explaining the basic meaning of security and what security means in relation to a modern computer network using Windows NT 4.0 Server are the highlights that this chapter offers you. For securing your hardware, included are some common threats and how you can protect your components from them.

Security concepts

Learn about security and its role when planning or maintaining the Microsoft Windows NT Operating System in a network environment. We'll answer the question, "What is Network Security?" and explain what advantages and disadvantages security can have on a network.

Security candidates

The circumstances that require the implementation of security measures are examined. This section discusses the various threats to your network and what harm they can cause.

Areas of protection

The next section focuses on the components of a *Network Operating System (NOS)* that need to be protected. It covers the basics for different types of resources.

Planning security

Basic guidelines are reviewed for planning internal security on a new or existing network. See the different layers of security and what can be done at each level to protect your system from harm.

Fault tolerance

An explanation of the role that fault tolerance takes in the design of a secure network. See some of the ways fault tolerance is incorporated into system components to guarantee network resource availability.

What Is Network Security?

Before you learn about network security, you may want to first define the term *security* in the context of a distributed computing, enterprise-wide environment. Simply put, security is the safeguarding of any program, data, or device from unauthorized use or access.

However, the reality of network security extends far beyond this simple definition to several complex and intricate areas of systems management. The goal of having a secure network is not only to protect the network system components, programs, and data from unauthorized use or access; the goal of a good security plan is to protect the business.

It is understood that a security plan must protect the very data, programs, devices, and network components that comprise the system from any damage, theft, or misuse. It must also ensure the availability of the network services when needed. This task is accomplished using the security tools provided by your network operating system, implementing redundancy into your system design, and by providing the required physical barriers to prevent unauthorized access to system components.

Modern business solutions are becoming more oriented and dependent on distributed computer networks to allow groups of people to work more efficiently together. As the technology grows and becomes more sophisticated, so do the demands for more technically sophisticated methods of protection. In addition, the more elaborate the network system is, the more effort is needed to achieve the desired security result. This normally implies that a more labor-intensive effort is needed to achieve the desired level of security. With proper planning and careful thought at the beginning of your security implementation, you can save both time and money while minimizing the effort needed to provide a high degree of network security and stability.

Along with any implementation of a network security plan comes another side of the issue—restriction of network resource access to the end users of the system. After all, the reason for implementing security on a network is ultimately the goal of keeping your business free from interruption. Allowing the network users to have access to the data and programs they need to perform their jobs without unneeded restriction should be a major objective. The goal is *not* to lock the system down so tight that it restricts productivity, but rather to enable the user's access to any resource for which they are authorized in a quick and efficient manner. At the same time, you must ensure the integrity of network resources in a manner that easily can be controlled, administered, and audited.

CAUTION

You'll find that if you do lock your system down in a very restrictive way, users will find ways of accessing the resources by circumventing your security, usually by sharing passwords or copying data to public areas.

If you're lucky enough to be planning the security design for a new network, you have the opportunity to lay a solid foundation during the design phase and thus avoid many of the pitfalls that a poorly planned network can present. If you are delegated to administering or cleaning up an existing network, read on—you haven't been forgotten.

Who Needs Security?

As our society becomes increasingly dependent on the information systems you develop, the more dependant you become on the safeguards we've developed to protect those systems. Security safeguards protect not only the network system itself, but something far more valuable—the information contained within the network system. The loss of data is much more devastating than the loss of a replaceable network component. Many times the loss of critical data can cause the downfall of a business, or at the very least, can have a substantial impact on user productivity and the bottom line.

Who needs security? Let's put it this way. If you have any information located within a distributed network environment, and that data is needed for the day-to-day operation of your business, you need some degree of network security implemented. It really doesn't matter if the nature of the data is sensitive or not; the data still must be protected to avoid any business losses due to data unavailability, loss, theft, or misuse.

The need for adequate security becomes much greater as the volume and sensitivity of the data increases. It also becomes very important when real time access to critical information is necessary.

Sources of Security Threats

So where do all these threats come from? It depends on what type of security threat you're talking about. For simplicity, you can categorize the types of security threats encountered on a distributed network system into two basic groups:

■ *Human Sources.* Human sources of harm stem from the actions or inactions of people, which then result in modification, loss, theft, or misuse of network data and resources.

■ *Physical Sources.*   Physical sources of harm to a network stem from the loss of a critical network component(s) as to cause the unavailability of data or system resources.

The human sources of harm and what you can do to defend against this type of risk is the primary focus of this handbook. Microsoft Windows NT Server does an excellent job of providing a safe, reliable, network platform on which to place critical data. Nevertheless, to be complete you must also cover the physical aspects of network security. Setting up the perfect security structure within your Windows NT network to protect confidential data doesn't do much good if the data goes down with a server that wasn't backed up. You can rest assured that hackers will be the least of your worries if your data just went to the nearest magnetic pole.

Human Threats to Security

People are the biggest threat to any network system. The common conception is that of a hacker attempting to get into some top-secret corporate or government computer system. This scenario, although real, is not the typical security problem experienced by most businesses. The reality is that the threat is not always from outside the network system, and indeed more often is a result of internal and not external influences.

Internal Risks   In the course of designing a security plan, it is negligent if you do not consider the relationship that exists between the employee and the company. As you all know, problems can arise that cause the employee to become resentful and seek retribution from the employer; this in turn results in the intentional misuse of the system. This is a particularly sensitive situation because the employee may have access to confidential information and other network resources. In other words, an angry employee with a grudge could really cause some damage. Adding to the problem is the fact that detecting intrusions by such individuals can be very difficult if the proper security measures have not been established beforehand.

 T I P   Most network administrators conform to the theory that once a person has given their resignation, it is best to revoke the network access for that user immediately. If the person being dismissed is not aware of the termination, network access should be revoked during or immediately after the termination meeting. And any log-on sessions the person has on the network should be logged off immediately. To many this may seem rather cold, but this not only protects network resources, it also clears the person that's leaving of any responsibility in the event suspicious circumstances occur before their departure. If work still needs to be done by the person that's leaving, modified access can be granted or another person can be assigned to supervise the departing user in the interim.

Internal security risks are not limited to those who want to maliciously harm the system. Take the example of the system administrator who walks away from a console while logged on to the network with administrative privileges. At that point, all the power that has been entrusted to that administrator is freely available to anyone that approaches the console. Although not intentional, a potentially serious situation has occurred none the less. This goes to show that network users are not the only ones that must be responsible for the security of the network.

Unfortunately, internal security risks primarily stem from relaxed or even non-existent security enforcement from within the business organization itself. Many businesses do not practice the implementation of security for several reasons:

1. The company or organization has never had a serious loss of data or interruption of services due to a preventable measure that was not in place.

2. Security for a network involves some amount of administrative effort to design, maintain, and implement. This usually involves some cost to the company.

3. Users are resistant to new security policies that restrict their access and may avoid complying with security standards. Management does not want to have to enforce another policy.

The need for security suddenly becomes a harsh reality the first time a major loss occurs on the system. Have the full support of your business management before implementing any security plan. If you don't, you'll just be wasting your time.

Once the idea of network security is accepted by management, you can start to create a concise security policy that sets the guidelines for both users and administrators. A set of criteria must be developed that defines the resources associated with your network and what access is allowed to each of them. This policy can set both user and administrative standards, because many of the low-level administrative tasks can be delegated to individual users or groups in the Windows NT environment. By the time you finish this book you'll be able to create an effective security policy for a new or existing network.

When the policy is completed, educate the users of the system in the proper use of the network resources and explain to them why the security measures have been put in place. Have the power to enforce the security policy and to have clear standards in place for dealing with those who attempt to intentionally bypass the security measures that are there. Keep in mind that more often the intent of security violators does not stem from any malicious intent but merely from a natural curiosity and the urge to explore the network.

CAUTION

Many companies practice the art of "Security by Obscurity." This rationale has the theory that if something exists on a network but no one is told that it is there, it's safe from harm. Perhaps this may have been true in the early days of computers when users were intimidated by computers and even more by a network system, but not now. The users of these systems are becoming increasingly computer literate, and they love to see what they can find. We've all snooped around a network at some time—well, haven't you?

Because of this, the "it's hidden, it's safe" reasoning no longer applies to the security of the network system's resources. It's much better to supply the adequate rights to a resource than to simply hide it and hope no one stumbles on it.

External Risks   External risks to a system are the ones normally thought of when considering the security design for a network. The threat of external risk can come from several different sources and can take several different forms. The most obvious indication of external threat is the unauthorized access to and subsequent damage or theft of network components. Some less obvious forms of network intrusion include the use of sophisticated equipment to read data directly off the communication lines, or even off the monitors used by the network users. Industrial espionage does exist.

External risks to a network system include but are not limited to:

- The theft of confidential information
- The disclosure of sensitive information to others
- Unauthorized access to network services and resources
- Disruption of normal network services
- The tampering with, modification of, or loss of data
- Software theft or damage
- Hardware theft or damage

Fortunately, several options exist to insulate your network from external risks. These options range from the encryption of transmitted data, to protocol filtering, to the use of firewalls and segmented LANs. All of which can be, and are usually, very effective.

Windows NT Server 4.0 adds some additional security controls to enable customization to both the higher and lower layers of the TCP/IP protocol stack. This enables you to specifically designate which ports are available to inbound network frames at the TPC, UDP, and IP layers.

Physical Threats to Security

When speaking of physical threats, a number of sources must be considered. Each source must be specifically dealt with or you risk the chance of compromising your network's integrity.

- *Equipment Failure.* Equipment failure is one of the most common causes of data loss or unavailability. By designing the proper redundancy systems into the network you can avoid downtime and reduce costs

- *Physical Tampering.* Unauthorized access to network components can lead to physical tampering of the system. A properly secured area for all major network devices (especially mass storage devices) is required to provide adequate protection from this type of intrusion.

- *No Recovery Plan.* In the event of a natural or manmade disaster, a recovery plan must be implemented or you risk substantial business loss. Having a recovery plan may seem a bit extreme, unless you've ever needed one and didn't have it.

As you can see, the human threat to network security has again emerged with the possibility of physical tampering. This single risk can be caused by both internal and external influences. In some respects, it is the simplest type of security to provide, because the control of access to any critical network devices usually means nothing more than keeping them in a securely locked location.

The degree to which you physically secure your network components can range from a locked wiring closet to a secure network installation with full monitoring and alarm functions. The scale to which your installation requires physical security will of course fall somewhere between these two extremes. You must ask yourself what will provide a reasonable amount of protection, what you can afford, and weigh that against the perceived value of your data if it was irretrievably lost. Once you think about it, you might want to buy a bigger lock.

What Should You Protect?

Now that you have explored the reasons for establishing a network security policy, you need to start thinking about which specific areas of the network need protection. We've established that you need to protect two fundamental areas of the network. They are the following:

- The network resources
- The physical components

If you looked at network security as a successive number of barriers, it is easier to visualize the layers of security that surround the core resources on our network system. (See Figure 1.1.)

FIG. 1.1
The layers of network security provide safety to the system.

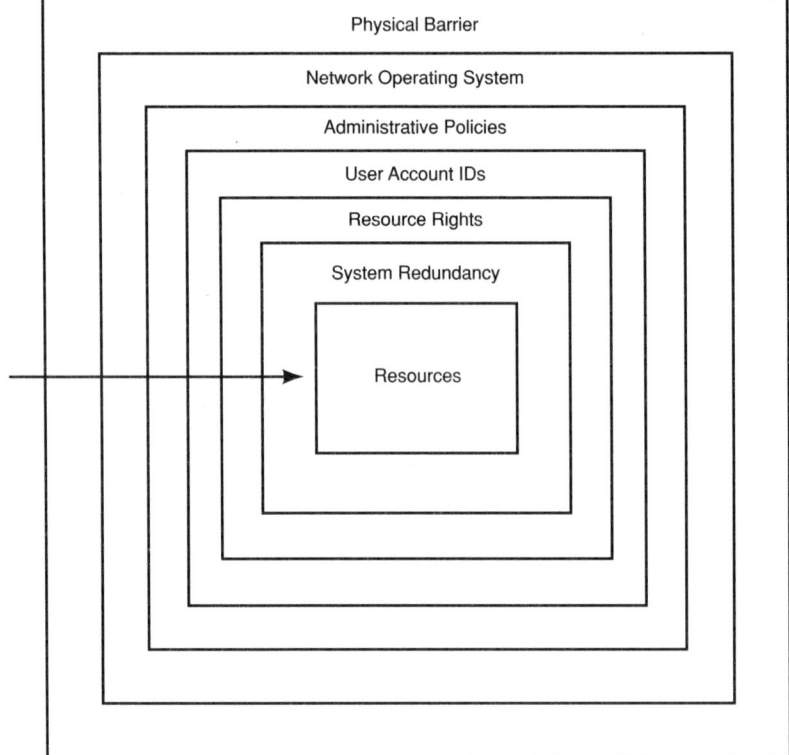

Here are the layers and what each one provides:

- The physical layer of security provides the first barrier against loss.
- Mechanisms designed into the NOS provide the second layer of protection.
- Administrative policies and procedures provide the third barrier.
- User Account IDs provide the fourth means of security assurance.
- Resource rights provide the fifth barrier of protection.
- Redundancy provides the sixth layer of protection to the system.

Let's start with the physical security of the network and examine the common weak points that should be considered when protecting the hardware.

Providing the Physical Layer of Security

Hardware is the heart of any network system. Without the computer hardware, the best software in the world isn't worth a hill of beans. So what do you need to protect your hardware from anyway? Moreover, what specific hardware do you need to protect?

The most common dangers to hardware are environmental in nature. Damage to many devices easily can occur if the device is placed in an adverse environment. For example, let's say you place your 12 servers in a nonair-conditioned room in the middle of the Mojave Desert. Sure, you can be safe and lock the room when you leave. Nevertheless, after about ten minutes, I don't think theft of the equipment will be your biggest problem.

Protect your equipment from environmental hazards such as high heat and humidity or exposure to the elements. This includes other hazards such as electrostatic shock to the equipment, and problems due to dirty AC power being supplied to the components.

Next, protect the system against intrusion by unauthorized persons by maintaining some form of physical barrier between the system and the outside world. As mentioned earlier, the degree to which you maintain this security will vary depending on your circumstances. The specific devices that you choose to protect should include any storage devices. Examples are file servers and drive systems. You should also protect things such as network hubs and any communications devices that supply a user with connectivity to a network resource.

This protection must also extend to the workstations that are utilized for network access by the users of the system. Although not as straightforward as locking up the servers and networking components, protection of the workstations can be accomplished using a variety of methods. The methods of workstation protection can range from a simple hardware inventory of the machines to the use of diskless workstations with boot proms on their network adapters. The specifics of planning the physical security of servers, workstations, and network components are covered in detail a little later in this chapter.

Protection Provided by the Operating System

Microsoft Windows NT Server 4.0 inherently provides the basis for a highly secure network server platform by its very design. The security aspects of networking were one of the major concerns to the developers of the Windows NT product line. The security features built into version 4.0 of Windows NT Server remain at the forefront of distributed networking technology.

▶ **See** "An Overview of Microsoft Windows NT Security," **p. 41**

Because this level of your security wall is a feature of the operating system, it has the added benefit of providing audit capabilities for all server objects owned or controlled by the system. The degree of auditing for certain applications can be controlled; however, the basic auditing features for the system objects remain in force at all times. Logging of system events cannot be stopped. However, the log file containing audit information can be cleared.

This is the first level of protection that starts to focus on the security of the network's resources, instead of the security of the physical devices. From this point on, the design and implementation of network security is done using the tools provided by the operating system.

Using Administrative Policies

Before any account IDs are assigned, administrators can use the tools contained within Windows NT Server 4.0 to configure the amount of access provided to any user of the system. These policies can designate that specific actions are performed at user log-on time. The policies can restrict user access to only certain workstations, impose log-on time restrictions, and limit the amount of server drive space available to the user. The use of *Mandatory User Profiles* with user accounts can even restrict the options available to the user in the windows interface, regardless of where that person logs on. Mandatory user profiles are nothing more than user profiles. The difference is that the administrator of the network can make it mandatory that the user logging on use the profile. If for some reason the profile cannot be accessed during log-on, the user is denied log-on to the system.

This is the second stage of resource protection, but it's the first phase in which design considerations start to play an important role. At this level of the security model, you want to focus on the accessibility of the network administrative utilities such as *Server Manager* and *User Manager for Domains*. The goal here is to limit access only to those authorized to administer the system or some part of it.

The Assignment of Network Accounts

The next level of network security is handled by the user authentication process within the Windows NT security system. No user can access any shared resource without first having an account on the system. Then they must successfully complete the log-on process and provide a password for their specific account before being allowed any access to network resources.

The exception to this rule occurs when a user gains access to the network using the special *guest* account that is built into Windows NT. By default, this account is disabled during the Windows NT Server installation. It is normally left at this default setting and should remain that way under most circumstances.

The most important thing to protect here is the security of the users log-on ID and password. This must be done by educating each user regarding the consequences of divulging their personal account and password information to anyone else. They must understand that the security of the network depends on their participation in the security process. Moreover, by giving log-on information to others, they can be held responsible for any problems that the other person may create while logged in under their name.

Resource Permissions

Share permissions specify which user account IDs can access the resources available over the network. The permissions may be applied to a resource by specifying an individual account as having access, or permissions can be granted by specifying a group in which that specific account ID is a member.

File permissions, on the other hand, are applied directly to the files and directories on an NTFS (*New Technology File System*) formatted drive partition. They have the advantage of preventing access to Windows NT Server files and directories from persons actually using the Windows interface while logged on at the file server. Because direct access to the physical drives is possible when logged on at the server, share points are not needed in order to access data that may reside on the server. Shares can be bypassed and the user can just look at a drive containing sensitive data if allowed to log on at the server.

The solution is to deny any direct log-on to users at the server either by physically locking it up (a good idea) or by disabling the account's capability to log-on locally at the server. If the server must be used directly by network users, NTFS permissions can be used to prevent access to sensitive file information that exists on the server's drives.

Providing the System with Redundancy

A secure network implementation not only provides protection against harm from physical and human sources of danger, it also provides the resiliency needed to survive one of the most common security dangers of all—hardware failure. The most common of these failures is our old favorite, the hard drive crash.

The failure of a critical hardware component in either the server or the networking components of the system easily is prevented by designing redundancy into the system. Redundancy within a distributed network environment is most often evident in the physical design of the network and its server components. For example, you may provide redundancy against a drive crash by mirroring data on multiple mass storage devices. To provide against power loss to a critical piece of equipment, you might install more than one power supply in a device.

These are all modifications to the physical attributes of the system. You also must build redundancy into the logical structure of the network. This means that administrative processes you build into the network system must also support redundancy. An example of this would be the network administrator that manually backs up a server because the backup that was scheduled to run the night before failed. Our redundant system here is the administrative process that says the network administrator has to check the backup logs everyday. And if the logs show that a scheduled backup has failed, the administrator must perform a manual backup immediately. In the case a single system fails, another is always ready to take its place and perform its functions.

The degree to which redundancy resembles fault tolerance may be differentiated by the amount of time it takes to implement the alternate or backup system. For example, data redundancy can be achieved by performing a tape backup of a drive. It also can be achieved by mirroring a drive. What's the difference between the two? Several hours of server down time. While the first option indeed provides data redundancy, it doesn't provide the rapid recovery time that the fault-tolerance method of drive mirroring achieves. Our fault-tolerant method provides both data redundancy and rapid (often instantaneous) recovery times.

Planning Network Security: Two Scenarios

Two general scenarios exist that compel the planning of network security. They are the following:

- A new network installation is being performed.
- The existing security of a network needs modification.

Both scenarios have similar needs, and each layer of network security must be assessed and provided for. The big difference is that the existing network should be well documented and understood before any changes are made to its security.

Planning for a New Installation

A new network installation provides you with the opportunity to design and implement sound security measures before the first user ever logs on. If you use the concept of the security layers from earlier in the chapter, you can develop a checklist of items in each layer that should be protected. Using each checklist, you can then designate specific methods that will allow you to provide a high level of security for each item.

Planning the Physical Security Measures   Create your checklist by identifying the physical components of your system that must be protected. Specifically, you want to list both the server and network devices that will comprise the core of the network hardware. With each network component or device, you can list the nature of the security risk associated with that device. You can determine the measures you need to take to reduce or eliminate the risk to that device. An example is given in Table 1.1. It shows the potential sources of harm associated with network file servers and the method of protection that is effective against them.

Table 1.1   Protecting the Hardware Components

Component	Source of Potential Harm	Protection Method
Network File Servers	Environmental exposure	Provide an environmental component(s) that provides protection from heat, cold, and humidity.
	Poor grade electrical power	Install surge suppression, line conditioning, and UPS (Uninterruptible Power Supply) equipment to clean and filter the incoming power.
	Loss of electrical power	UPS (Uninterruptible Power Supply) equipment should be installed to supply devices with reserve backup power and automatic shutdown services, if needed. Lock unit to restrict access to the power switch.
	Unauthorized Access	Keep the component(s) in a locked room or cabinet.
	Virus introduction	Disable removable media devices or lock component(s) in a room or cabinet.

continues

Table 1.1 Continued

Component	Source of Potential Harm	Protection Method
	Physical Damage	Keep the component(s) in a locked room or cabinet.
	Theft	Maintain an up-to-date inventory with serial numbers for all components. Keep the component(s) in a locked room or cabinet.

You can follow this example for every piece of equipment that stores, transmits, or processes information on your network. If the component is critical to the delivery of information, then that component needs to be physically protected to some degree.

Providing a Secure Operating System   The checklist of items continues with the selection of an NOS. The NOS is the heart of the network and provides the security required to protect your business information. Windows NT Server 4.0 has a rich set of security features integrated into the operating system by design. The security features implemented with the Microsoft Windows NT line of products lend themselves to flexibility without compromising the bottom-line goal of absolute system safety.

Some of the features provided by Windows NT Server are:

- *Discretionary Access Control.*   Controls the access by named users to named objects of the system. *Access Control Lists (ACL)* provide a mechanism by which control of objects may be given to users of the system.

- *Accountability Using Identification and Authentication.*   This requires that a user have an account on the system that is verified using password authentication before the user can gain access to any object or resource on the system.

- *Secure System Architecture.*   This means the system protects itself from the external alteration of any code or data structures in the system. With Windows NT this is apparent in the absolute protection of the operating system's core services from any user application.

- *Object Reuse.*   States that any object used by the system will be purged of all access authorizations that are attached to it prior to its release back into the system for reuse.

- *Audit Ability.*   Windows NT enables you to audit the access to all objects in the system. Auditing can record any of the following events: log-on and log-off activities, file access, object deletion, access violations, and so on.

Another reason to select Microsoft Windows NT Server is because it's easily integrated with other NOS products such as NetWare. Often these systems are already in place and must be used in conjunction with any new installation. Keeping security at a reasonable level can be difficult in a mixed-system environment unless the NOS you use is designed to coexist with legacy systems.

If migrating users from the legacy system to the new system needs to be done, Windows NT also provides the tools that enable you to do this with a minimum of hassle.

Defining the Administrative Security Policy   Before any users are added to the system, the policies that will be used to manage the network must be defined. You also must define the administrative structure of the network in relation to the domain concept used with Windows NT-based LAN systems. Domain, server, user, and resource naming standards also must be developed.

If you are using multiple domains, you need to define any domain trust relationships that will be required to reduce administrative overhead. The concept of domains using trust relationships are covered in detail in Chapter 2, "An Overview of Microsoft Windows NT Security," and Chapter 4, "Windows NT Domain Concepts." At this stage, you want to determine what local and global user groups may be needed in addition to the default user groups provided by Windows NT. These groups will be different for every installation and business.

Additionally, you also need to determine who the members are for each default group that you use. Examples of default user groups in Windows NT are the Administrators group (the system gods) and the Backup Operators group. Each default group allows its members to perform some type of administrative duty that requires a security equivalence beyond that given to a normal user account. During this planning stage, the administrative team that will maintain the system needs to be identified. You must determine which of the Windows NT default groups that you want to utilize and if any custom groups are required. After the administrative responsibilities have been determined for each individual, the administrative user accounts can be associated with the proper groups.

For example, you can plan the security of your network so the users in the Personnel Department have the ability to add and delete employee accounts. You can give personnel in the network support department the right to run tape backups on the server.

Defining the User Policies and Properties   User account policies and properties enable us to specify how the users are allowed to interact with the system. Several aspects of a user account can be configured in Windows NT. Things such as the use of passwords and their minimum length can be specified. Where users can log on (specifically which workstations) and during what hours the user is allowed on the system are also configurable security parameters.

Part
I
Ch
1

Configurable user policies in Windows NT fall into three basic categories, as follows:

■ *Account Policy.*   Account policy permits you to specify options related to user passwords. You can implement a security policy that forces the use of passwords and minimum password length if the password must be changed at regular intervals. The account policy option also enables you to specify account lockout parameters, which prevent repeated log-on attempts by someone trying to guess an account password.

■ *Rights Policy.*   The user rights policy enables you to assign a variety of privileges to a user account or group. Windows NT's default built-in user groups are given rights based on the typical administrative duties that members must perform. For example, the Back up operators group has rights to bypass security and back up the drives on a server. Service accounts have the capability to run a service on the Windows NT platform. In situations where the default Windows NT groups do not supply the proper combination of privileges, custom rights can be assigned to users. Groups with custom privileges can be created and then users can be assigned as members of those groups.

■ *Audit Policy.*   Enables you to specify the level of audit logging-on your system. This provides valuable event log data regarding the various actions of users while on the network system. For example, you can turn on auditing to track user log-on and log-off activities, object and file access, use of object rights, and so on.

Another area that is configurable in Windows NT is the individual properties that each user account will have. Some specific properties include: a list of groups the user is a member of, what hours of the day is the user allowed to log-on to the system, if the user account has an expiration date, or if the user is allowed dial-in permission. Other examples of definable User Properties are:

■ The ability of a user to change his or her password

■ If the account type is Local or Global

■ The designation of a user home directory

■ Assignment of a network log-on script

■ Assignment of a user profile

■ Assignment of a mandatory user profile

■ Assignment of users to default groups

Setting Up Resource Access   In addition to determining our administrative roles, each of the network resources you plan to make available needs to be identified. The method of security that you use for each resource needs to be specified, along with who will be allowed to access the resource.

A resource is typically any service that is provided by the system—an example would be the file services that provide access to the directories on a file server's disk drives. Other examples of resources include printers, modems, and databases. With Windows NT, to make a specific directory or printer available for network access, you share the directory or printer. The shared resource is commonly called a network *share*. Assignment of access to a share can then be done either for a group or for an individual user account.

Define what resources your network servers will host by identifying what resources are needed. Then choose where the resource will be placed and who will be allowed access to the resource.

Here's an example. Say that you know certain users of your system who need access to some common accounting data. This data needs to be restricted so that only members of the accounting department have access. Furthermore, only a few individuals in accounting will be allowed to modify the data; all other users only will be allowed to read the data. Based on these requirements, you can come to the following conclusions:

- A file server must be identified as the host for the accounting data.
- The directory the accounting data will reside in must be shared with permissions allowing access only to accounting personnel.
- A Local User group should be created containing all the users of the accounting department. This group will be given permission to read the accounting data contained in the shared directory.
- A Local User group should be created containing those users of the accounting department that will be allowed to modify the accounting data. Only this group will be given permission to modify the accounting data contained in the shared directory.
- If the server containing the accounting data will be physically accessible, the data must be protected by limiting log-on rights at the server or you must apply *New Technology File System (NTFS)* permissions to the directory that the accounting data resides on.

This logic can extend to all shared resources that will be available on the system. Define the resource, then define the access that will be allowed to it.

Securing an Existing Network

In many ways, securing an existing network is much more difficult than implementing security measures on a new network. One reason is that you must determine the current state of the network. Each resource must be evaluated and the user access permissions that are currently granted must be reviewed. Another reason is that the systems are already in place and being used; the restructuring of any current security must be as transparent as possible to the users of the system. You don't want to impair any users legitimate access to network services because this could in turn affect their ability to do their job. The entire goal of evaluating an existing system is to make it more secure from harm, not to make it more difficult to use.

With that in mind, let's follow the same procedures that you would if you were planning the security of a new network. The difference is that you must first evaluate the current conditions at each layer of our security model. Start with the physical layers and work your way down the model:

- Evaluate the physical security of your network components.
- Verify that the NOS provides adequate security features.
- Review the administrative policies and procedures that are currently in place.
- Check both the user properties and user policies currently in place on the network.
- Examine the resources available on the network and the access privileges given to the users of the resource.
- Ensure that alternate means exist to provide both resource connectivity and administrative support on the network.

After evaluating each layer, formulate a plan to make any changes that may be needed. Then implement the steps one layer at a time to avoid the possibility of creating multiple problems at once should something go wrong. With each step, plan the change, implement the change, and then monitor for any problems that may be a direct result of the change. Once you're satisfied with the results, the next step can be planned and implemented.

The idea is to change one thing at a time. If a problem does occur with the system, you want to be able to quickly determine if the cause of the problem was due to a configuration change that was made. If you were to change several things at the same time, you risk some serious troubleshooting time trying to figure out the source of a problem should one occur. Was the problem due to one of the changes that were made, or due to something else unrelated to the configuration changes? It's easy if you only have to change one configuration parameter back to its original value in order to troubleshoot a problem. Not so easy if you have to change five items back to their original value in order to troubleshoot it.

Planning the Physical Security

The physical security of a network can include many different areas. Each area must be identified and evaluated for its integrity within the system. You have examined the physical security of the individual network components, such as servers and routers. As explained, you must first identify each component and access the risk to it; then, you can protect the equipment by physically securing it and providing the proper environment. Table 1.2 takes a look at the physical remedies to some of the common network threats.

Table 1.2   Guarding the Physical Structure of a Network

Security Threat	Cause of Resource Loss	Physical Solution
Component related loss of any available network resource	Environmental factors such as poor ventilation, high temperatures, or excessive humidity cause damage to sensitive electronic components.	Store all components in areas that comply with the component manufacturer's environmental operating specifications for the device.
	Poor grade of electrical power to site causes component failure.	Install surge suppression, line conditioning, and UPS (Uninterruptible Power Supply) Equipment.
	Loss of electrical power causes important comp-onents to go off-line.	UPS equipment should be installed to supply devices with reserve backup power and automatic shutdown services if needed. Lock the unit up to restrict access to the power switch.
	Physical damage causes the loss of a network resource.	Keep the component(s)in a locked room or cabinet.
	Theft of component(s) causes the loss of a network resource.	Maintain an up-to-date invent-ory with serial numbers for all components. Keep the component(s) in a locked room or cabinet. Keep workstations locked or cabled.

continues

Table 1.2   Continued

Security Threat	Cause of Resource Loss	Physical Solution
	Normal device or equipment failure.	Provide redundant backup systems for any critical components. Have hardware components available to replace failed units. Standardize on equipment with high lifetimes.
	Natural or physical disasters that destroy major parts of your network.	Create a disaster recovery plan that details methods for hardware, software, and data recovery. Implement the off-site storage of data in a secure place.
Unauthorized physical access to network component(s).	Network components are not physically secured.	Lock all components in a secure room or cabinet.
Unauthorized access to network data or resources.	Dual-homed systems allow access from the Internet.	Turn off IP routing and disable the appropriate network card bindings. Implement a firewall system in place of dual homing.
	Use of line sniffing equipment to capture data transmissions over the network.	Protect any transmission lines by making them inaccessible or use fiber optic cabling to prevent packet sniffing by most equipment. Implement the use of encryption on any data transmitted over the wire. Remove the network card if it's not being used.
Damage from computer software viruses.	Infection from network sources.	Instruct users on the use of antivirus software and require its use when executing an unknown program from an e-mail attachment or other network source.
	Infection from removable media such as floppy disks.	Lock, remove, or disable storage devices in the server. Use commercial antivirus software to protect the system. Provide diskless workstations for user access to network resources.

This table gives you an idea of what can be done to prevent any loss of network resources using physical prevention methods. This goes a long way in establishing a baseline of security for your network. However, it's only the beginning of establishing a full security plan. Next, you'll look at another facet of physical security called fault tolerance.

Using Fault Tolerance

The term *fault tolerance* is used to describe the protection of network resources by providing physically redundant system components as a backup in case of a failure occurring to one or more critical network components. Modern hardware configurations are becoming increasingly flexible in providing some type of tolerance out-of-the box. Usually this takes the form of built-in drive redundancy of one type or another.

Drive Media Security

Windows NT 4.0 provides several methods of drive media security, some of which can be implemented at the software level and some that can be implemented at the hardware level. In fact, both methods can be combined in most instances to create a very high level of data security and availability. Let's look at some ways you can protect data on mass storage devices.

Transaction Tracking in Windows NT 4.0   One method of protecting data is the use of transaction tracking logs on an NTFS volume. These log files have information in them that enables the Windows NT operating system to roll back the data contained on the disk drives to the last fully known state in the event of a system failure. Windows NT does this by using the Log File Service to create a file containing all the undo and redo information the system needs to complete a roll back to the last committed transaction. Here you can see the normal process of events that take place during an I/O write operation, as follows:

1. An I/O operation is initiated to save a file to disk.

2. As the I/O operation progresses, the Windows NT system stores information regarding the I/O process and what it's doing in the form of *redo* information in the transaction log. This information is used to repeat the I/O operation or transaction in the event that recovery is needed.

3. At this same time, the system records information on how to *undo* the transaction in the log file. This information is used to roll back any incomplete transaction.

4. The I/O operation is completed successfully and the file update is committed. If the transaction has an error or is incomplete, the system uses the undo information from the log to roll back to the previous state.

For example, let's say your system crashes while it's in the middle of a disk write. The following sequence of events would take place when the system was reinitialized:

1. The system does an analysis pass on the disk drive and determines exactly which disk clusters must be updated. It does this by comparing data on the disk to information kept in the log file.

2. Each transaction that had been logged from the previous checkpoint is then performed over again. The system does this by using the redo information kept in the log file.

3. The next pass is called the undo pass. During this pass, the system backs out any uncommitted transactions using the undo information kept in the log file.

Sector Sparing the Drive Media   As with most other operating systems, Windows NT marks off any bad sectors it finds while formatting a hard disk to prevent data from being written to them. Windows NT also detects write errors due to bad sectors and automatically maps the bad sectors off. Any information being written to the bad sector is rewritten to a good sector on the disk drive.

Drive Mirroring and Duplexing   A highly reliable method of insuring both the integrity and reliability of hard drives is *drive mirroring* and *duplexing*. Mirroring refers to dual hard drives of the same general capacity that are installed in the same server. Information on one drive is mirrored on the other drive. In case of failure on one of the drives, the alternative drive can be used as the only source of information. The drives are continuously synchronized to keep the data on each of them identical.

The next step beyond mirroring drives is the duplexing of drives. This is really the same thing as mirroring, only an added measure of protection is supplied by using a separate controller for each hard drive. This eliminates the common point of weakness, namely the single-drive controller, from taking both mirrored drives down in the event the controller fails.

The advantages to drive mirroring and duplexing include low cost and easy-recovery methods. Most of the time, an improvement in performance is gained from the system's capability to do split-reads on the data. *Split reads* enable data to be returned by the first drive that locates it on its media. The drive that happens to have a drive head positioned closer to the requested data delivers the data first, usually resulting in quicker read speeds. The disadvantage is the fact that you must supply twice the drive space in order to store the same amount of information. However, as hardware prices continue to drop, this will become less of a factor in the decision-making process regarding mirroring.

Drive mirroring and duplexing can be handled at the hardware level with the purchase of most high-end systems. At this level, the mirroring functions are not controlled by the operating system; instead, they are controlled by the hardware. The Windows NT operating system simply sees hardware mirrored or duplexed drives as a single physical drive. This drive can be partitioned as a normal drive without using any of the fault-tolerance options available in the Windows NT disk administration program. The advantage to these systems is the *hot-swappable* nature of the drive media. The systems don't need to be powered down before the drive can be replaced; thus, the term hot-swappable. The system literally never needs to go off-line for the replacement of the failed drive. The downside is of course the cost.

Windows NT 4.0 Server enables us to combine separate physical disks within a system into mirrored (or duplexed) sets via the disk administration program. This does not provide the resiliency of hot-swappable drives because the replacement of the failed drive must occur with the system powered down. However, it does provide integrity of the data and a means to keep the system resources available until downtime can be scheduled.

N O T E   Please note that drive mirroring at the software level is only available on Windows NT Server. It is not an available option on Windows NT Workstation. ▨

Using RAID Systems   *RAID* (*Redundant Array of Inexpensive Disks*) is becoming a standard means of protecting information contained on mass storage devices. All involve the use of multiple disk drives to provide data redundancy and availability. The difference between RAID systems and mirroring or duplexing schemes is the method of providing the data redundancy and the overhead involved.

Technically, RAID includes drive mirroring (as explained in the previous section) in addition to the simple spanning of data across multiple drives. The higher levels of RAID provide an ingenious way of assuring data reliability and availability without the overhead associated with mirroring. They do this by using a checksum algorithm to store parity information on a separate drive with RAID levels 3 and 4 and across all drives at level 5. The checksum information can be used by the system to reconstruct data that has been lost on a failed drive as follows:

There are several different levels of RAID protection that are currently defined and in wide use. They are defined as RAID levels 0-5 as follows:

▨   *RAID level 0.*   This simply means that data is striped across multiple hard drives. This usually results in a performance increase, although it provides no data redundancy in case of drive failure.

- *RAID level 1.*   The true definition of RAID level 1 includes disk mirroring or duplexing with data striping. However, Microsoft has defined level 1 as only the mirroring or duplexing of physical drives.

- *RAID level 2.*   Striping is performed at the bit level across all drives with each consecutive bit being written to the next disk. One disk is provided for data recovery. Note that this method is not typically used with microcomputers.

- *RAID level 3.*   This is the level of RAID that stripes data by the byte across all physical drives. One drive is reserved for checksum data and is used to reconstruct data in case of a drive failure. The drive containing the checksum data is called the *parity drive.*

- *RAID level 4.*   Performs the same way as RAID level 3 does, except data is written across the disks by block and not by the byte. Error correcting data is kept on a parity drive as with level 3.

- *RAID level 5.*   Performs the same way as RAID level 4 with data being written across all drives at the block level. Unlike level 4 where the error correcting data (or parity data) is written to a single drive, level 5 stripes the parity data across all the drives. This provides a performance increase by allowing parity information writes to multiple disks instead of to a single disk that could cause a bottleneck.

How Is Data Recovered with Parity Information?

You might be wondering how checksum or parity information could be used to reconstruct data from a failed drive. It's really a simple concept that can be best explained using the RAID level 3 definition. After learning how level 3 works, you can explain the level 4 and level 5 implementations with more clarity.

The secret to providing data redundancy is the basic checksum algorithm that is used to produce the parity data. So what is parity data? It is the XOR checksum byte data that results when you add the byte values from separate physical drives together. Remember binary addition? Zero plus one is one, zero plus zero is zero, and one plus one is zero.

Let's take an example using a system containing three hard disks. Each hard disk contains information in the form of bytes. You will use a single byte of data from each of the three drives for this example. Table 1.3 shows the binary values contained in each of your three bytes (one byte per drive).

Table 1.3   Byte Value on the Parity Disk

Disk Number	Byte Value
Disk 1 (data disk)	10001101
Disk 2 (data disk)	10101010
Disk 3 (parity disk)	00100111XOR

Now there's a disk 2 failure and it loses the data on the drive. Our byte containing the binary value 10101010 has been lost and must now be reconstructed from the parity information on disk 3. No problem—just add the parity byte value from disk 3 to the value of the byte on disk 1 (as shown in Table 1.4) and the missing data is re-created.

Table 1.4   Reconstructing the Lost Byte

Disk Number	Byte Value
Disk 3 (parity disk)	00100111XOR
Disk 1 (data disk)	10001101
Disk 2 (failed disk)	10101010 (reconstructed byte)

To put this in the perspective of RAID 4, you apply this algorithm on the block level instead of the byte level. RAID 5 uses this block-level algorithm in addition to striping the parity data across all of the drives.

Windows NT uses three of the currently defined RAID levels to provide software-based protection. RAID levels 0, 1, and 5 are configurable from within the Windows NT Server's Disk Administrator utility. Unlike the 100 percent disk space overhead associated with mirroring or duplexing, RAID 5 arrays typically offer a disk-space overhead of 33 percent or less depending on the number of drives participating in the array.

As with mirroring, RAID systems also can be implemented at the hardware level. This provides the capability to use hot-swappable drives to prevent any system downtime. Again, the primary drawback is the cost associated with high-end systems that use this type of hardware.

Network Media Security

Providing fault tolerance with network media gives you an alternative channel of communication in the event a single route or channel is disrupted. Many network topologies are built on the concept of redundant links. Token ring has the inherent capability to loop back between *Multistation Access Units (MSAUs)* in case of a cable break. *Fiber Distributed Data Interface (FDDI)* systems use fiber optics cable and employ dual counter-rotating rings for redundancy.

If possible, use different physical routing paths for redundant links to avoid having the same problem affect both routes. If you're pulling fiber optic cable on a new installation, include one or two extra strands with each pull. This gives you an alternate fiber optics route in case of problems with any of the other strands in the run. This may save the time of pulling replacement strands and reduce the amount of downtime experienced.

Power Supply Backup Systems

The electrical power supplied by most utility companies is not considered of computer grade quality. Often power levels will fluctuate producing both spikes and brownouts that can ruin microcomputer systems and other network equipment. Using the proper surge suppression, line conditioning, or *Uninterruptible Power Supply (UPS)* equipment on your network components easily can solve this problem. Which option you use depends on both the equipment and the level of protection you need. First, let's take a look at the basic differences in the three types of power protection available.

- *Surge Suppression Equipment.* Surge suppression equipment protects network components from electrical spikes that occur on the power line. These spikes can do considerable damage, especially if caused by an electrical storm or lightning strike. Surge suppressors do not clean incoming AC power, nor do they provide a source of power in the event of a brownout of complete power loss. Surge suppression provides less protection compared to the other two alternatives and should be the absolute minimal protection that you provide for your equipment.

- *Line Conditioning Equipment.* One step up from the surge suppressor is the line conditioner. A line conditioner smoothes out the electrical sine wave of the incoming power, thus providing both surge and momentary brownout protection to the equipment. Although it can provide momentary brownout protection, it cannot provide any sustained electrical power if a brownout or blackout occurs.

Part

I

Ch

1

■ *Uninterruptable Power Supply Equipment.* These devices provide surge protection and conditioning of the incoming power. Additionally, they provide an alternative source of power in the event of a sustained brownout or complete blackout of your power system. Any component that is critical to the operation of your network should be protected by some sort of UPS equipment.

Clustering Server Systems

One of the newer methods of fault tolerance involves the use of mirrored systems to provide backup redundancy. Instead of just mirroring a drive or providing backup components within a single system, the system itself is mirrored to an identical platform. This provides the full system with backup protection instead of only a single component. Automatic roll over to an identical platform allows uninterrupted access to system resources in the event any one component takes down the mirrored system.

From Here...

This chapter looked at some of the basic concepts associated with security in general. The concepts examined here can apply equally to most network systems regardless of the type of NOS being used. The following chapters focus on the security features of Windows NT Server:

■ Chapter 2, "An Overview of Microsoft Windows NT Security," examines the Windows NT Server security model. You see how user accounts work and it explains what a domain is.

■ Chapter 3, "Windows NT Operating System Architecture," shows you the internal security features of the Windows NT operating system and how they work. You'll also be exposed to the log-on process and see how objects are used.

■ Chapter 4, "Windows NT Domain Concepts," explores the use of domains in detail. You learn how to create or join an existing domain, and you see how user groups within Windows NT domains work.

CHAPTER 2

An Overview of Microsoft Windows NT Security

This chapter focuses on network security from the Windows NT Server 4.0 perspective. You see how the *New Technology File System (NTFS)* provides an added measure of security for files and directories. The absolute access to file server information via a network share cannot always be guaranteed. NTFS provides you with another method of establishing security against those who can directly access the server. Also, more and more companies are learning the advantages of using the Remote Access Server feature that's built into Windows NT Server. The question of how Windows NT handles remote access security is answered in this section.

Like remote access, Internet access is becoming more and more popular as a resource in itself. Learn some methods of protecting server resources from the security risks that a connection to the Internet inherently presents. Included is an overview of the administrative tools that enable you to configure several aspects of system security. ■

The Windows NT security model

You learn how security works with Microsoft NT Server in a networked environment. The security model you built earlier is broken down into Windows NT related components.

User accounts

The concept of a user account and how it fits in with the Windows NT security scheme. You also see the different elements of a user account that you can configure for security-policy compliance.

Windows NT domains

What a domain is and how it is used within a network to ease administration. You get an example of how domains can be used to simplify the process of granting varying degrees of resource access to user accounts.

Trust relationships

Explains the general concept of domain trust relationships, why they are used, and how they can further ease the network's administrative burden. Trust relationships are classified according to the way groups of computers are configured to trust one another. Define these classifications, called trust models, and learn when they're used.

The Windows NT Security Model

Looking at security from the perspective of Windows NT Server 4.0 is important. In Chapter 1, "Understanding the Basics of Security," you saw the various layers of security that must be provided in order to protect a network system. For your review, here is a list of the layers:

- *Layer 1* The physical layer of security provides the first barrier against loss.
- *Layer 2* Mechanisms designed into the Network Operating System provide the second layer of protection.
- *Layer 3* Administrative policies and procedures provide the third barrier.
- *Layer 4* Logon IDs provide the fourth means of security assurance.
- *Layer 5* Resource privileges provide the fifth barrier of protection.
- *Layer 6* Redundancy provides the sixth layer of protection in the form of physical security to the system.

The following chapters focus on Layers 2 through 5, and for practical purposes form the basis for our Windows NT security model. These layers all can be broken down into other areas in which Windows NT provides some specific measure of protection. To further refine this set of security layers, take each of the layers and see what specific Windows NT security features apply to them as shown in Table 2.1.

Table 2.1 Security Components of Windows NT

Layer Number	Windows NT Security Feature
Layer 2 Mechanisms and features designed into the Network Operating System	*Secure System Architecture* This means the system protects itself from the external alteration of any code or data structures in the system. With Windows NT, this is apparent in the absolute protection of the operating system's core services from any user application.
	Discretionary Access Control Controls the access by named users to named objects of the system. Access Control Lists (ACL) provide a mechanism by which control of objects may be given to users of the system.
	Object Reuse States that any object used by the system will be purged of all access authorizations that are attached to it prior to its release back into the system for reuse.

Layer Number	Windows NT Security Feature
	Audit Ability Windows NT enables you to audit the access to all objects in the system. Auditing can record any of the following events: Log-on and log-off activities, file access, object deletion, access violations, and so on. The auditing feature enables you to monitor all system, application, and security events.
	Accountability Using Identification and Authentication This requires that a user has an account on the system which is verified using password authentication before the user can gain access to any object or resource on the system.
	Encryption Features Automatic encryption of user passwords at the server and over the wire.
	Protocol Filtering The capability to filter TCP, UDP, and IP networking protocols at the port level.
	Backup Software Media backup software is included with Windows NT Server and is compatible with most tape units available.
	Sector Sparing Marks bad areas of disk drives so they will not be used.
	Transaction Tracking Protects against incomplete transactions corrupting the data on a server's hard drive when a power failure takes place.
	Drive Mirroring and RAID Striping Can be done using the operating system software. Drives of unlike types (SCSI and IDE) can be combined into fault tolerant mirrors and arrays.
Layer 3 Administrative	*Domains* Administrative ability to selectively policies and procedures group servers and workstations into logical groups for easier management.
	Account Policy Enables you to specify password restrictions and account lockout parameters.

Part

I

Ch

2

continues

Table 2.1   Continued

Layer Number	Windows NT Security Feature
	Account Properties Enable you specify the system rights that any user account (or group) will be allowed to have.
	Trust Relationships Permit you to establish security links between two or more logical groups of computers (domains).
	User Profiles Permit you to specify the user environment variables for any network user.
	Log-On Scripts Can be used to run applications or set environmental variables when the user logs on to the network.
	Home Directories These are assigned to users and can be used with profiles to customize the user environment.
	Scheduled Backups Used in addition to fault tolerance to ensure the safety of your information.
Layer 4 Windows Log-on IDs	*User ID and Password* All users of the system are required to have a user account and password before they can gain access to any resources.
	User Groups Local and Global Windows NT custom user groups can be created to group users with the same access rights or restrictions.
	Local and Global Accounts Enable you to specify how a user account is allowed to interact with the network.
	Remote Access Security Lets you specify if an individual may use the remote access features of Windows NT to access network resources. Authentication and dial back parameters can also be configured on a per user basis.
Layer 5 Windows Resource privilege access	*Share-Level Access Protection* Permits you to set the parameters that specify the way a network user can access and use any shared network resource.

Layer Number	Windows NT Security Feature
	NTFS Level Protection Gives an added measure of security to further restrict access of both directories and files on NTFS partitions.

The remainder of this chapter covers some of the basic elements of Windows NT security found in Table 2.1. In the following chapters, you'll look at each one of the Windows NT security features in detail to see how they're used. The first of these basic elements that you need to learn about is the Windows NT user account.

Part
I
Ch
2

User Accounts in a Windows NT Environment

One of the basic building blocks of Windows NT security is the *user account* (*UA*). Each user that accesses any Windows NT Server-based resource first must be validated by the system. During the log-on sequence, the user is required to enter a valid name and password before any interactive Windows session is allowed.

User accounts can be *local* to a specific server, or they can be created within the context of a *domain* user account. Nevertheless, just remember that the type of account is determined by the role of the Windows NT Server. The role of the Windows NT server can be that of a *server*, or that of a *domain controller*. A server maintains its own *Security Accounts Database* (*SAM*), while domain controllers share a common SAM with other servers. This means servers contain a local version of the SAM, while *Primary Domain Controllers* (*PDCs*) contain a version of the SAM that is replicated to the *Backup Domain Controllers* (*BDCs*) in the domain. We'll explain more about PDCs, BDCs, and the synchronization of the SAM database in the next section.

Regardless of the type of account, you can set different properties for each of the user accounts you create. These properties determine the way that the user will be allowed to interact with the network system. Chapter 1, "Understanding the Basics of Security," covered some of the properties that can be set on a user account. Here they are again for your review:

- The ability for a user to change his or her password
- Local or Global account type
- The designation of a user home directory
- Assignment of a network log-on script

- Assignment of a user profile
- Assignment of a mandatory user profile
- Assignment of users to default groups

The properties for any user account can be specified at the time the user account is created, and they can be modified at anytime thereafter. User accounts can be created by adding a new account to the SAM database, or by copying the properties of an existing user in the SAM database. User account information from other non-Windows NT systems also may be added using the migration tools provided for Windows NT 4.0.

The security concepts discussed in the remaining sections of this chapter focus on the user accounts in a domain environment. The domain environment offers administration over the resources contained in a group of servers as opposed to the resources on a single computer.

What Is a Windows NT Domain?

A Windows NT domain is nothing more than a group of servers that share a common security accounts database (SAM). Resources on each server can be assigned to users that are part of this common accounts database. This eliminates the need to create a separate user account on every server (or workstation) that contains a usable resource.

For example, let's say you have two separate servers that each have a single printer attached, and you want to allow network access to both printers. In a non-domain environment you would create a user account on the first server and give the user access rights to the printer. Then you create another account on the second server, and give the same user access rights to the printer on that server. This doubles the administrative and user effort that is involved in order for an single individual to access both printers.

- The user name must be entered into a user account database twice instead of just once—once on the first server to *allow* access to its printer, and then again on the second server to allow access to its printer as well.
- Users have to log on to each server in order to gain access to both printers—once on the first server to *gain* access to its printer, and then again on the second server to gain access to its printer.

A domain eliminates the need to create two separate user accounts. Instead, servers use a common SAM database that is shared between them in order to validate the access rights of an individual account. If you had used a domain in our example, the administrator of the network would have had to enter the user account information one time only. Access to both of the printers would have been delegated using the domain's SAM database. Also, any user needing access to both printers would have only been required to log on once. This is the primary reason that domains are used, so that we easily can give access to resources located across multiple servers.

 TIP The use of a domain reduces the administrative effort when *creating* new accounts and assigning access permissions. The other side to this is that it also reduces the administrative effort required when *removing* user accounts. When the user leaves the company, their account only needs to be removed from a single account database instead of from several separate account databases (located on different servers). This alone makes the security of the network easier to maintain and control.

Part

I

Ch

2

With Windows NT 4.0 (and all previous versions of Windows NT) a domain is created when the Windows NT Server software is installed on the first server designated in the domain. Other servers that will become part of the domain are installed after the initial server installation. Additional servers can join the domain during the server installation process (and only during the installation process). The original server that was installed is called the Primary Domain Controller (PDC). It keeps the original copy of the user accounts database. Any servers that join the domain later are called Backup Domain Controllers (BDC); BDCs each keep a non-editable copy of the user accounts database. As a user logs on to the network, the PDC or one of the BDCs will authenticate the user and enable access to the network resources in the domain.

N O T E Either the PDC or BDC can authenticate users when signing on to the domain. The controller that actually authenticates the user is usually the first controller that responds to the log-on request, not necessarily the PDC.

A very important point to note is that once a server has joined a domain, it's a member of that domain for life. Kind of sounds like an old gangster movie, but it's true. The only way for a server to join a different domain is to be completely reinstalled. There is no way to change domain membership. It is also impossible to promote a stand-alone server to that of a PDC or BDC. This is an important point to remember when planning the installation of an Windows NT Server network.

N O T E Later in Chapter 3, "Windows NT Operating System Architecture," you'll see how a *Security ID (SID)* is assigned to a server when it joins a domain (or becomes the PDC in a new domain). This SID is the primary reason why servers are not allowed to change domain memberships. A SID is uniquely assigned to each individual server during its installation and identifies that server as a member of a specific domain. Once assigned, the SID cannot be changed.

When a user account is added to a domain, the change to the user accounts database is made only at the PDC. Copies of the user accounts database located on the PDC are then distributed to the BDCs in a replication process known as synchronization. This guarantees that the user accounts database is safe in the event the PDC crashes. If the PDC does crash, one of the BDCs can be promoted to the role of PDC. Once the BDC has been promoted to PDC, the user accounts database can again be modified (users added and deleted, and so on). You will not be able to modify the SAM if a PDC for the domain is unavailable, although log-on requests will still be performed.

Domain Trust Relationship Security Concepts

The next concept is that of the *trust relationship*. A trust relationship is used when more than one domain is present on a network, and users from one domain need to gain access to the resources on another domain. Often, networks can become very large with resources spread over several domains. When a user needs to have access to a domain's resources, that access can be granted in one of two ways. The two ways that access can be granted are as follows:

- The user can have a user account on the domain containing the resource. Access to the resource is then granted to the account from within the same domain.

- The user can have a user account on a *trusted* domain. Access to the resource is then granted to an account from the trusted domain. The account with the resource is called the *trusting* domain.

The first method of granting access is simple. A user is given access rights to a resource that is located within the same domain as the user account. For example, let's take an imaginary user named Ed (you'll soon see the significance of the name).

Ed needs access to the company's LaserJet printer. The print queue for the LaserJet is shared on a server that is a Backup Domain Controller (BDC) for a domain named ACCOUNT. Therefore, the LaserJet printer is available as a resource on the ACCOUNT domain. Ed's user account is also on the ACCOUNT domain. The administrator of the ACCOUNT domain simply grants Ed's account access to the LaserJet. From then on, when Ed logs on to the ACCOUNT domain he is automatically given access rights to the printer.

Suppose that the company grows, and decides to create a new domain named RESOURCE. The idea behind this is to move all the resources (such as printers) to the new domain where they can be managed by a separate administrator. Now, what if the LaserJet printer is moved to a BDC that's a member of the domain named RESOURCE.

The LaserJet is no longer available on the ACCOUNT domain, so Ed no longer has access to the printer resource. Does Ed need an account on the RESOURCE domain in order to access the LaserJet Printer queue from now on?

No, not if a trust relationship is set up between the two domains. A trust relationship will enable Ed, a member of the ACCOUNT domain, to access the LaserJet printer queue located on the RESOURCE domain. The steps to set up a trust relationship are as follows:

Part

I

Ch

2

1. A *one-way* Windows NT domain trust relationship is established between the ACCOUNT domain and the RESOURCE domain. The ACCOUNT domain is designated as the *trusted* domain (Think of it as the Trust-ED domain; hence, the name Ed). Ed's account is only in the ACCOUNTS domain. The RESOURCE domain is called the *trusting* domain.
2. The administrator of the RESOURCE domain (the trusting domain) grants LaserJet print queue access to Ed's trusted domain account. Ed, who is a member of ACCOUNT domain (the trusted domain) can now send print jobs to the LaserJet queue.

The lesson here is that the trusted domain is the domain that contains the user accounts. The trusting domain contains the resources. If you can just remember that Ed (the users account) is always in the trust*ed* domain, you'll have an easy time understanding trust relationships.

You notice that step one mentions a *one-way* trust relationship. This means that one domain will contain user accounts, and the other domain will contain resources. The domain containing the resources (the trusting domain) will allow users of the account domain (the trusted domain) to access its resources.

What if the resource domain had user accounts and the accounts domain had a shared resource, such as a color printer on one of its servers? Would a user account on the resource (trusting) domain be able to access the color printer on the account (trusted) domain?

No, not unless the resource (trusting) domain user has an account on the account (trusting) domain. This is why it is called a one-way trust relationship; the trust is one way only. Let's use Ed again in an example.

Ed, a member of the ACCOUNT domain, gets a job assignment that moves him to a different department. Because of this, Ed's domain user account is removed from the ACCOUNTS domain and a new account for Ed is created on the RESOURCE domain. While Ed was on the ACCOUNT domain, he had access to the LaserJet printer queue on the RESOURCE domain because of the one way trust relationship that was in place. He had also been given access to a new color printer located on one of the ACCOUNT domain's servers. Ed could print to both printers as needed.

After Ed's account was moved from the ACCOUNT domain to the RESOURCE domain, the administrator of the RESOURCE domain reestablished Ed's ability to use the LaserJet printer simply by assigning his new account access rights to the queue. This was great, but Ed suddenly found that he could no longer access the queue for the color printer over on the ACCOUNT domain. He told the administrator of the RESOURCE domain about his problem. However, because the trust relationship was one way, the administrator could not grant Ed access to a resource on the ACCOUNT domain. So how was Ed going to access the color printer from now on? Two options were available:

1. Create a user account for Ed on the ACCOUNT domain. Use the same user name and password to keep Ed from being prompted for an ID and password when attempting to access the color printer.

2. Create another one-way trust relationship between the RESOURCE domain and the ACCOUNT domain. This time the RESOURCE domain is designated as the trusted domain, and the ACCOUNT domain is designated as the trusting domain.

Using option two would create a *two-way* trust relationship between the ACCOUNT and RESOURCE domain. A two-way trust is nothing more than a one-way trust in both directions. Once the two-way trust was established, the administrator of the ACCOUNT domain could grant Ed's RESOURCE domain account access rights to the color printer.

As you can imagine, setting up trust relationships between several domains could get very complicated if they're not well planned. Many times, trust relationships are implemented because user accounts are scattered over several domains. The establishment of a trust relationship avoids the necessity of having duplicate user accounts across two or more domains.

These trust relationships can be used to reduce administrative overhead if used correctly. They also can be used to customize the administrative areas of responsibility for network supervisors. There is a simple rule you can use most of the time when planning an environment that will contain several domains:

Place the user accounts into a single *account* domain.

That's it. You can place resources in the account domain if desired, but the bulk of the network resources should be placed into *resource* domains. The only accounts within the resource domains are a limited number of administrative accounts. One-way trust relationships are created between the account and resource domains. The account domain becomes the trusted domain (remember Ed?) and the resource domains become the trusting domains. Access to any of the resources across the domains easily can be granted to the users once the trusts have been set up.

This type of domain model is called the *master domain model*. As its name suggests, the master domain model has what could be considered a master domain in it, the one that contains the user accounts. This type of domain model can accommodate as many as 10,000 users. Chapter 4, "Windows NT Domain Concepts," shows some other domain models that can be used with Windows NT Server. Each model has its advantages and disadvantages depending on the size and complexity of your network. The other domain models are:

Part

I

Ch

2

- *The Multiple Master Domain Model* Used with organizations that have more than 10,000 user accounts.
- *The Single Domain Model* For smaller installations.
- *The Complete Trust Domain Model* Used to provide unrestricted user access to all other domains.

Now you should understand how domains can be tied together using trust relationships and what the general reasons are for their implementation. The concept of one-way and two-way trusts has been examined and what access each provides to network users. Now that we've discussed user accounts, domains and trust relationships, let's move on to another kind of security used with Windows NT Server. The application of New Technology File System (NTFS) file and directory permissions in addition to the permissions provided by the sharing of resources is the next subject.

Using NTFS to Secure Data

Resources on a Windows NT Server network are made available to network users by *sharing* the resource. This provides an advantage over the network resource security by allowing share access only to those network users that possess the proper rights to the shared resource. But what if the user accesses the resource directly at the server instead of over the network? Here's another example to illustrate what this means.

Suppose that the administrator for the ACCOUNT domain shares a directory on a server named CORP1. This directory contains the travel itinerary information for the company's salesman. The directory containing the information is on the server's C: drive and is named \travel. To keep it simple, the directory has been shared under the name travel. The network user named Jane has been given read access to the share. When Jane logs on to the network, she is able to connect and map a drive to it. However, Jane only can read the information contained in the shared directory; she is not able to modify anything.

Then one day, Jane's computer is being repaired, so she directly logs on to the CORP1 file server in order to do some work. When Jane opens Explorer, she suddenly finds that she can access the root of the C: drive on the file server and all the subdirectories beneath it. Now instead of having read-only privileges to the C:\travel directory on the server, she suddenly has full rights and can modify or erase any of the data it contains. So how do you prevent such an action from taking place without denying the user log-on access at the server? It's easy—just use NTFS permissions to limit the directory or file access. If read-only NTFS permissions had been applied to the directory, Jane would not have been able to make modifications to the C:\travel directory.

Keep in mind that if you use NTFS permissions and they are more restrictive than the share permissions, the NTFS restrictions will prevail over any share permissions that may be allowed.

For example, if we had shared the \travel directory on the CORP1 server and given the user group Everyone write permission to the directory, any user would be allowed to write to the directory as long as the directory has one of the following criteria:

1. FAT file system
2. NTFS file system, with full control or at least write permissions for the Everyone group. By default, the Everyone group has full control over NTFS based files and directories.

If, however, you then applied read-only NTFS permissions on the C:\travel directory for the Everyone group, users that were previously able to write to the share named "travel" are now limited to read-only access. This is because the NTFS permissions are more restrictive, and the most restrictive security always prevails. The exception to this would be if the user trying to access the share had been given specific NTFS permissions that permitted writing (or full control) to the directory (or share). Even this has an exception, which is when a user has been specifically identified as having no access, either as an individual or as a member of a group.

It may seem a little confusing at first, but it's really a good way to add an additional layer of protection to the files and directories that reside on your servers. One drawback to the use of NTFS permissions is the moderate amount of administrative attention they require. Another drawback is the additional variable this adds when troubleshooting resource access problems. An alternative option to using NTFS is to simply deny users the logon at the server right, or to keep the server(s) containing the information locked and physically inaccessible. In both cases, file and directory access only can be accomplished over the network using the share permissions granted to the various users and groups.

Chapter 7, "New Technology File System (NTFS) Security," examines NTFS permissions and how to apply them. Now let's take a look at another area of network security you must consider if users need remotely to access the network system using Windows NT Server's built-in *Remote Access Server (RAS)* feature.

Security and Remote Network Access

Remote or offsite access to network resources by the users of a Windows NT Server network is most often done using the dial-in capabilities provided by the RAS. This remote form of network access is usually provided to mobile users and requires nothing more than a modem. Typically, connections are made to the network at 14,000bps to 33bps, 600bps using a standard asynchronous modem. However, with the advent of *Integrated Services Digital Network (ISDN)* in many areas of the country, much higher connection rates are now possible. Windows NT Server fully supports the use of ISDN modems for both dial-in and dial-out capability.

Regardless of the connection speed, after the connection has been established, users log on to the network just as if they were connected at the office. After the user has been authenticated, he or she is allowed access to the same network resources he or she would normally be allowed access to just as if he or she were on the network in the office, but a bit slower. The actual authentication process first checks to see if the user calling in has been given RAS dial-in permission. If the user has not been given the proper dial-in access permission, the call is terminated and the remote user is informed that he or she does not possess the permissions required to access the network remotely. On the other hand, if the user has been given dial-in permission, the authentication process continues with the actual domain log-on process.

The administrative capabilities provided with RAS enable you to permit (or deny) dial-in capability on a per user basis. Also, the connection can be configured to use the dial back capability built into RAS to add an additional level of security. The details of RAS configuration are in Chapter 8, "Using Windows NT Security to Protect Domain Resources."

Another means of access to network systems that is becoming more widespread is via a connection of some type to the Internet. This type of network connection presents its own specific set of security problems.

Internet Security Considerations

The Internet has grown dramatically over the last few years with more and more companies deciding to link up with its resources every day. The security threats posed by the Internet are widely known and documented. They can be some of the most devastating of all threats to a network when focused on the sensitive business information contained on most systems. Data contained on network systems can be accessed, stolen, destroyed, misused, or sold by those wanting to harm you or your business. Often the attack is from someone who wants nothing more than to disrupt your business and cause mischief.

Regardless of the risks involved, few businesses will find it possible to carry on commerce without having some presence on the Internet. Many companies find it easy to advertise and sell products using the Internet. Other companies provide support services via the Internet. Whatever the reason, it's clear that the connection to the outside world must inevitably exist, and in turn, methods must be devised that will protect us from those unscrupulous individuals that would harm our livelihoods.

You can do a number of things to help maintain a secure network environment when connected to the Internet. First, you can determine the most secure way of connecting to the Internet by looking at the various security options and protection methods available. Some of these options include the use of a *firewall* to prevent direct Internet access to an internal network LAN *segment*. Providing user access to the Internet using a *proxy* server (such as Microsoft's Catapult Proxy Server) is another commonly used method.

Firewalls and Proxy Servers

Both of these methods protect the internal LAN segment from direct access to the Internet by use of *dual-homed* computers. A dual homed computer has multiple LAN cards that have been installed in a single computer (see Figure 2.1). One network card connects to LAN segment A, usually the internal network segment (referred to as the *clean* side of the network). The other network card is connected to LAN segment B, the external network segment (referred to as the *dirty* side of the network).

FIG. 2.1
Dual home a Windows
NT Server by installing
two network cards.

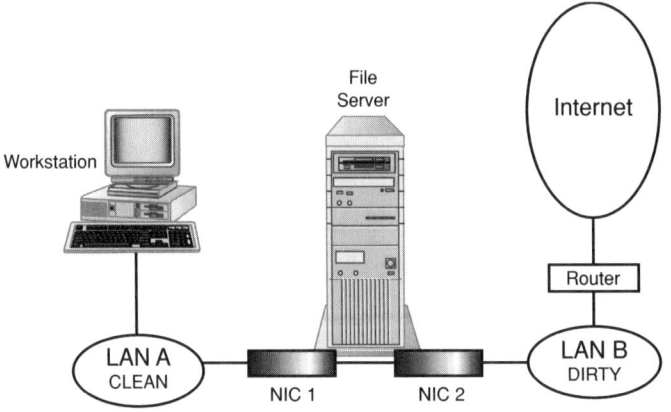

By design, Windows NT 4.0 can act as a router for network traffic between two physically isolated LAN segments using this dual homing capability. By default, the routing function of Windows NT Server is turned off. Traffic from LAN segment A is isolated from LAN segment B and is not allowed to pass from one segment to the other. In other words, traffic from the dirty side of the network cannot pass to the clean side of the network, and vice versa.

Part
I

Ch
2

For example, pretend you have a Windows NT Server named CORP1 that has two network cards installed in it. Network card 1 is connected to LAN segment A, and network card 2 is connected to LAN segment B.

Having the routing function turned off means that computers located LAN segment A (the clean side) can see the dual homed Windows NT Server named CORP1. Computers located on LAN segment B (the dirty side) can see the Windows NT Server named CORP1. Nevertheless, a computer on LAN segment A is not allowed to directly communicate with a computer on LAN segment B through the network cards in server CORP1. This concept is illustrated in Figure 2.2.

FIG. 2.2
Preventing access to the internal LAN from the Internet.

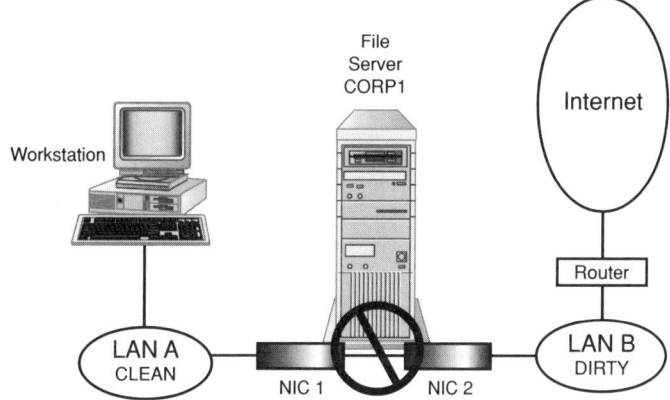

Put simply, a hacker on the Internet has no way of directly accessing a computer on the clean side of your network.

Firewall and Proxy applications use different methods to filter the routing of network packets across two network cards located in a dual homed server. This enables a computer on the internal side of your network to access resources on the Internet without having its own security compromised. For instance, let's use an example where a proxy server has been implemented to provide users with access to the Internet.

Ed, our never-tiring user, is looking up some information for his boss over the Internet. The workstation Ed is working from is not directly connected to the Internet. Instead, the

Internet Browser software on Ed's workstation (Internet Explorer 3.01, for example) is configured to use a proxy server to gain access to the Internet. The proxy server is dual homed—one network card is connected to the same clean LAN segment as Ed's computer. The other network card in the proxy server is connected to the dirty LAN segment that provides Internet access. An example of this is shown in Figure 2.3.

FIG. 2.3
Using a proxy server
as an Internet barrier.

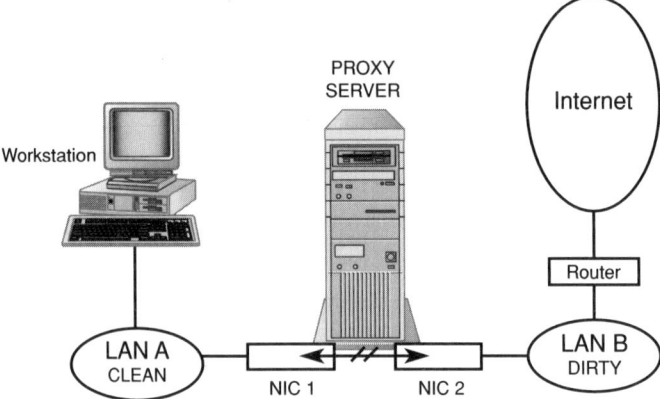

When Ed runs his browser software and issues a command that requires Internet access, the software passes commands over the internal LAN to the proxy server. The proxy server takes the request and forwards it out over its dirty segment's network card to the Internet destination, substituting its own return address for that of Ed's workstation. When the destination computer responds, the response is sent to the proxy server address. The proxy server in turn forwards the reply over its clean segment's network card to Ed's workstation. This provides an effective barrier against direct Internet access while allowing users to safely surf the Web.

Using Nonroutable Protocols

Another way that a network can be protected using some of the built-in features of Windows NT Server is with multiple protocol stacks. A nonroutable protocol such as NetBEUI can be used to enable connectivity between most of the servers and workstations on the network. Those servers or workstations that require Internet connectivity can be allowed to run the routable protocol TCP/IP instead of or in addition to the NetBEUI protocol. That way they can have access to the Internet without being on a physically separate LAN segment and going through a proxy or firewall server. This concept is shown in Figure 2.4.

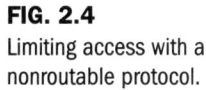

FIG. 2.4

Limiting access with a nonroutable protocol.

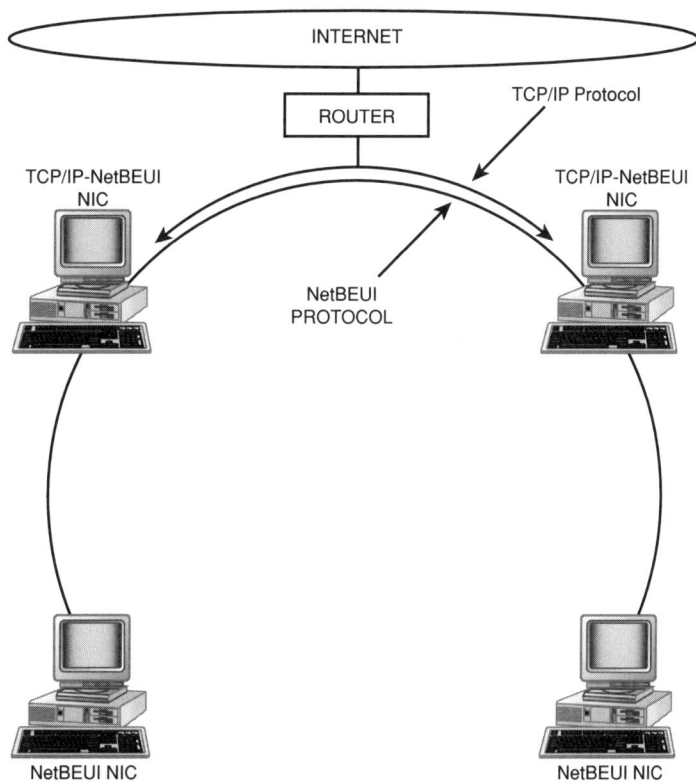

This is all right for smaller installations that have minimum hardware resources. It could be a real nightmare in larger installations when you base your security on your ability to restrict the users from using the TCP/IP protocol stack.

N O T E This brings up an important point to remember when considering the security design of a network: User workstations (specifically PCs) are normally user configurable. This means that the user can reconfigure the workstation with software, protocols, and analyzer software that permit him or her access beyond what he or she normally is entitled. Users may even be able to boot workstations under other operating systems to bypass security.

The only real way to prevent this type of activity is by disabling the floppy drive mechanisms in each user workstation. This can most easily be achieved by removing the workstation's floppy drive and then restricting the user's network access to any directory shares that could contain protocol drivers or other unauthorized software. ▨

Advanced Protocol Filtering

Port level filtering is another method of protection available to you when using Windows NT Server 4.0. This advanced TCP/IP protocol configuration feature is new to Windows NT Server version 4.0. It permits you to configure the availability of the network ports for incoming network requests. Any or all ports used for TCP, IP, or UDP can be disabled via the Windows NT 4.0 Server's network configuration panel. This provides you with an effective means of directly shutting down any communication at the lower to middle levels of the protocol stack.

Chapter 14, "Internet Security and BackOffice," goes into detail on topics related to protecting your network resources from Internet threats. For now, here are some of the administrative tools that are used to configure the security within Windows NT 4.0 Server.

Security Tools Provided with Windows NT

Several different tools are provided with Windows NT Server 4.0 that enable you to configure and monitor the security of your network. The tools can fall into different categories, depending on their function. This section briefly introduces each of the tools that Windows NT 4.0 provides.

Management Tools

The management tools provided with Windows NT Server 4.0 give the network administrator all the functionality that's needed to implement and maintain network security policy. They are the following:

- *User Manager for Domains*   A utility that is used to add and remove user accounts from the Windows NT domain. Also, it is the utility that's used to configure both the User Properties and the User Policy attributes. It is also the User Manager for Domains program that is used to configure trust relationships between domains.

- *Server Manager*   Controls server or workstation participation in the domain. It can be used to promote the status of a server to a PDC, synchronize controllers within a domain, and specify shared resources available on a server. Additionally, Windows NT Services running locally or remotely can be controlled using the Server Manager.

- *Remote Access Server Administration Utility*   Enables you to control and to monitor the remote dial-in availability of your server(s). This tool lets you monitor both local and remote servers running the RAS service.

■ *Registry Editor*   A powerful tool used to modify directly the configuration settings that are contained within the Windows NT Server's registry. The Registry editor can be used to modify both local and remote server registries. Windows NT Server 4.0 has added the capability to control the access permitted to any key(s) located within the registry on a user or group basis.

■ *Windows NT Explorer*   This common interface tool is used to apply both auditing and security policy to the file and directory resources available on the domain. Server directories can be shared with this utility and access permissions assigned. This utility also can be used by resource owners and administrators to apply NTFS permissions. These same functions can be accessed from within the My Computer utility found in Windows NT 4.0.

Part

I

Ch

2

■ *Server Policy Editor*   Enables the network administrator to set policy that affects the way a user can interact with the network using the Windows NT and Windows 95 desktop interface. Policies can be implemented on a group of accounts, on a single user, or as the system default policy for all users. A policy specifies what operating system functions are available to the user.

■ *Windows NT Diagnostics Utility*   Provides detailed information to network administrators about the configuration and status of both local and remote servers on the network. Information concerning the network, system, environment, drives, and server resources can be displayed. This can be a very valuable troubleshooting tool when trying to identify a server or network problems.

■ *License Manager*   Enables you to keep track of the licensing of Microsoft software products. The manager works with the built in auditing capabilities of Windows NT to notify you if software user restrictions or licensing policies have been violated.

Auditing Tools

This set of tools gives the network administrator the capability to monitor the various system parameters associated with the network. The use of these tools enables you to carefully track both user access and system performance.

■ *Event Viewer*   Provides a means of tracking system usage, security violations, system errors, and application information, among many other items. This is the primary tool used to audit the activities on your network.

■ *Performance Monitor*   Enables you to monitor and to record the performance of hundreds of system parameters. This tool can be configured to provide warnings and alarms in case of device malfunction or other system abnormality.

Backup and Tolerance Tools

These utilities control the programs and services that protect your servers from the consequences of power or media loss.

- *Backup Utility*   The built-in backup utility in Windows NT 4.0 can be used with many popular backup devices to ensure the integrity of the information kept on your network.

- *Uninterruptable Power Supply (UPS) Utility*   Enables the operating system to communicate with a UPS using a serial port on the server. This enables the administrator to configure shutdown parameters that are used by the UPS to trigger a graceful and automatic shutdown of the system in case of a complete power failure to the system or the site.

- *Disk Administration Utility*   Permits you to configure the mass storage devices in your servers to be fault tolerant either using mirroring or RAID striping on the software level.

Windows NT Configuration Utilities

The configuration utilities provide you with ways to configure how devices interact with the network or the environment. They are as follows:

- *Network Configuration Utility*   Lets you configure the protocols and services that will be active on a specific Windows NT Server. This utility also permits you to add, configure, or remove *Network Interface Cards (NICs)* and other devices on the server.

- *Dynamic Host Configuration Protocol (DHCP) Manager*   If you use the TCP/IP network protocol you can specify one or more servers to hand out TCP/IP addresses to workstations (called *DHCP clients*). The DHCP Manager enables you to configure TCP/IP protocol parameters that are handed to those clients, including the length of time the client may be allowed to *lease* (or use) the TCP/IP address.

During the course of the book, you'll see how each of these programs and utilities are used to provide system security within the framework of your Windows NT security model. All of the tools mentioned are packaged with the Windows NT Server 4.0 product. They do not require any additional software purchase to make them functional or to turn on additional features. For most installations, these tools are the only ones needed to provide complete control over the security of the network's Windows NT resources.

From Here...

This chapter covers the security aspects directly associated with the Windows NT Server 4.0 operating system. The upcoming chapters take a closer look at each one of these components in detail. Then, you can use what you've learned to set up a working domain model for an imaginary company. Here are some of the subjects that you can look forward to exploring in the upcoming chapters:

Part
I
Ch
2

- Chapter 3, "Windows NT Operating System Architecture," begins the detailed look at the security designed into the Windows NT 4.0 Server operating system. Each of the operating system components is identified, and its role in the system is explained.

- Chapter 4, "Windows NT Domain Concepts," expands on the information presented in this chapter to show you the details of domain creation and management. The tools and utilities that enable you to control various elements of the Windows NT domain environment are examined and explained.

- Chapter 5, "Maintaining Security with Domain Trust Relationships," shows you how domain relationships can be set up to make the administrative tasks much more manageable. Different types of domain models are presented along with the appropriate conditions in which each should be implemented.

- Chapter 10, "Planning the Master Domain," takes you on a practical application of the security methods by using the information you learned in previous chapters. You do this by designing the network security for an imaginary network installation.

CHAPTER 3

Windows NT Operating System Architecture

This chapter "looks under the hood" to see how the Windows NT operating system is protected from system crashes, unauthorized access, and data corruption. This topic is covered to give you a better understanding of how the Windows NT operating system is designed. All of the major components that comprise the operating system are examined, along with how they interact with each other. The architecture of the Windows NT 3.51 operating system is the focus of the first section in the chapter. The architecture changes made in Windows NT 4.0 is the last section's topic in this chapter.

Let's begin with a look at the architecture of Windows NT Server 3.51 and the components that comprise the operating system. ■

Windows NT 3.51 system overview

The major operating system components for NT 3.51 are introduced. See the Kernel and User modes and what each one of these component layers does.

Components of the Windows NT Executive

The components that comprise the Windows NT Executive are identified and each of their functions explained.

Windows NT 4.0 changes

Find out what has been changed in Windows NT 4.0 to improve the operation of the operating system.

Changes to the Windows NT Executive

Windows NT 4.0 brings some major changes to the Windows NT Executive. See what those changes are and how they impact the operating system.

The Win32K Executive

Changes in Windows NT 4.0 Executive include the addition of this new component. It contains some of the components that previously ran in the User mode layer of the operating system.

What happens when you log on

The process of logging on is a series of events.

Windows NT 3.51 Architecture

Windows NT Version 3.51 uses the "modified microkernel" architecture. It consists of two major component layers: The User mode and Kernel mode areas of the operating system (see Figure 3.1). Each of these layers is composed of separate modules that interact with each other. This gives the designers of the operating system the ability to change one portion of the operating system without affecting the other portions of the system.

FIG. 3.1

The Kernel and User mode components of the Windows NT operating system.

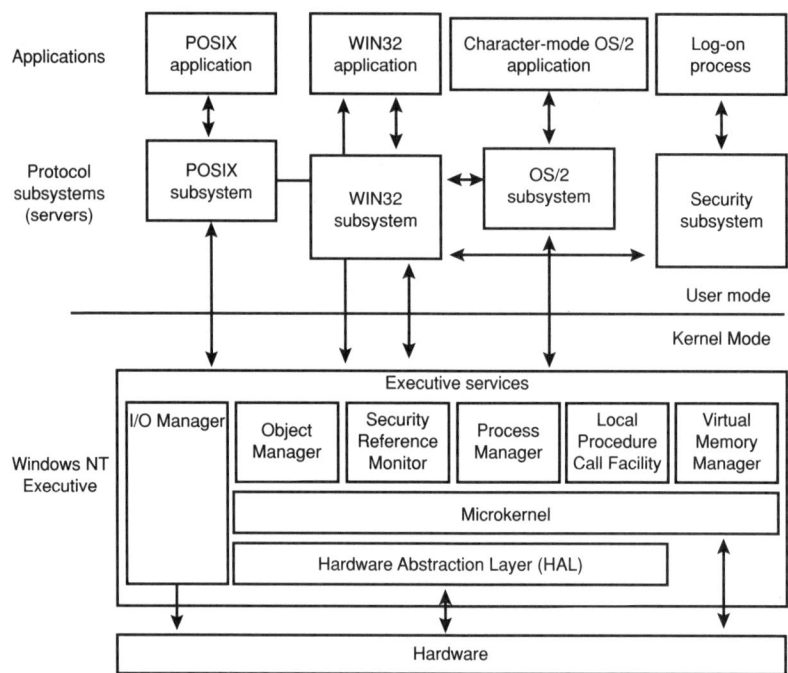

Examining the different components that make up the Kernel mode layer is prudent at this stage. We'll start with the Kernel mode layer because it represents the layer at which core operating system services are located. Low-level tasks such as thread scheduling and multiprocessor synchronization take place at this level of the operating system architecture. Other processes such as virtual memory management take place in the User mode layer, which is located above the Kernel mode layer.

The Kernel Mode Layer

The Kernel mode layer consists of three basic parts. These parts are as follows:

- *Hardware Abstraction Layer (HAL)*   The first part is responsible for interfacing with the computer hardware.

- *Kernel (*or *microkernel)*   The second part provides the basic operating system functions used by the other Kernel mode components.

- *Executive components*   The third part is not actually one component, but rather a set of components. Each of these components implements some type of operating system service, such as the Security Reference Monitor, which implements system security, or the I/O Manager that manages all of the input/output processes that take place within the system. You learn about each one of these components in depth later in this chapter.

Part

I

Ch

3

When all the components are put together they form the Windows NT Executive. In order to put these various operating system layers in focus, you need to understand why the Windows NT architecture is designed the way it is.

Microprocessors, which are the heart of any computer, enable the execution of threads to take place. Threads are run in the context of a process, and each process may run one or more threads. These threads are actually the instructions that tell the computer how to run. These "threads of execution" are allowed to run at different privilege levels within the operating system. Threads that deal with operating system functionality are more important than threads that run for an application. For this reason, threads executing operating-system code are given a higher privilege level than threads executing application code. This prevents an application from inadvertently crashing the operating system. The modules that comprise the Windows NT Executive all run within the Kernel mode because it offers the highest privilege level and the most security for the code that runs on behalf of the Windows NT Executive.

Intel x 86 processors support four privilege levels: These levels are referred to as rings 0 through 3 (see Figure 3.2). Ring 0 is the highest privilege level and is the ring in which all Kernel-mode threads of execution take place. This effectively protects the operating system from any harm that may stem from an application process. All application processes run at ring 3 on Intel processors where they can be prevented from doing any damage to the system.

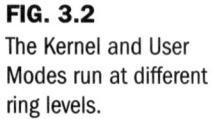

FIG. 3.2
The Kernel and User Modes run at different ring levels.

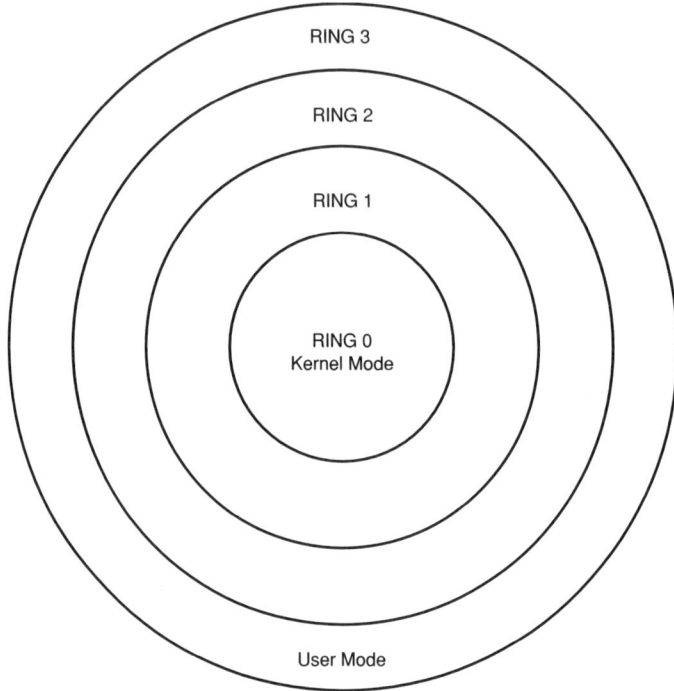

All application programs execute code in a separate and isolated address space to prevent access to code or data belonging to another program. As transfer is passed from one process to another, the operating system alters the processor's page tables, so one process cannot see the other.

Now, let's take a closer look at each one of the Windows NT Executive components in detail.

The Windows NT Executive Components

The Windows NT Executive contains the core operating system modules that control the heart of the system. Each of these modules has its own specific tasks that it performs. Looking at each of these components to see what tasks each one performs, start at the bottom of the Kernel and work your way to the top.

The Hardware Abstraction Layer   One of the important features of Microsoft Windows NT is its capability to be hardware independent. This is accomplished by the *Hardware Abstraction Layer (HAL)* that sits at the very bottom of the Kernel mode layer. This allows a device driver in the Hardware Abstraction Layer to be used on more than one specific hardware platform. Some manufacturers of computer hardware distribute customized versions of the HAL along with their products. These customized versions permit a higher degree of operational capability between the vendor's hardware and the Windows NT operating system. To ensure that your hardware performs well with Windows NT, always apply the manufacturer's hardware abstraction layer patch if one is available.

The Kernel   While exploring the threads of execution, you learned that each process contains at least one thread. Each of these threads is considered a separate unit of activity. It is the job of the Microkernel to schedule each of these units of activity on the next available processor. Scheduling of threads is based on the priority level of the thread. Threads with a higher priority are executed before threads that have a lower priority. They also can preempt a thread with a lower priority.

The Kernel consists of 4KB units of nonpageable system memory; this means the memory used for the Kernel is not paged to disk. The code which runs within the Kernel is not pre-emptive, which means that it cannot be interrupted by another process. Both of these measures ensure the stability of the Kernel module within the operating system.

Part

I

Ch

3

The Object Manager   Operating system resources are represented by abstract data types called *objects*. An object can represent anything from a file directory to a thread process. Each object contains information that identifies the object's description and the methods by which it can be accessed. The Object Manager controls the creation, deletion, and modification of all object types within the Windows NT operating system. Limitations in the form of resource quotas are imposed by the Object Manager on all objects. This prevents the operating system from running low on resources due to objects having control of too many resources. Here are some examples of operating system objects:

- Symbolic link objects
- Port objects
- Thread objects
- File objects
- Directory objects
- Semaphore and event objects

Pointers called "object handles" are given to a process that needs to access an object, which is controlled by the Object Manager. Sometimes referred to as the *global namespace* in Windows NT, the Object Manager has a structure similar to that of a file system. The Object Manager provides status information regarding various objects to the operating system, in addition to performing the cleanup of any unused objects from the system.

The Security Reference Monitor   The Security Reference Monitor is used to control the internal security of the system by governing all access, creation, and deletion of objects within the system. It does this using the access control listing or ACL that is associated with each object. Later in this chapter, we will discuss access control lists in greater detail. Each object contains elements called *access control entries*. Each of these access control entries contains the unique security ID of a user or group. The SID is actually a unique number generated by the operating system that describes each user or group within the Windows NT domain.

The security reference monitor works in conjunction with the User mode security subsystem to allow user access to objects via the log-on process. This is accomplished by creating a *Security Access Token (SAT)* for the user that contains the user's SID and the SID of any groups the user may belong to. After logon, when a user attempts to access an object, the SIDs contained in the SAT are compared to those listed in the object's Access Control List. If a match is found, the user would be allowed the amount of access specified in the *Access Control Entry (ACE)* of the object. This comparison is performed by the security reference monitor every time a user attempts to access an object.

The Process Manager   The process manager handles two types of system objects. The first is the process object, and the second is the thread object. The process object will own both resources and threads in addition to having its own virtual memory space. The thread objects consist of their own kernel stack, environmental block, and set of registers. The Process Manager is responsible for creating and deleting process objects, as well as tracking thread objects. The rules that define the creation or deletion of process objects are not defined by the Process Manager, but are instead defined by one of the user mode subsystems. The Process Manager simply provides a standard set of services that can be used by each subsystem in order to create or use a thread.

The Local Procedure Call Facility   Environmental subsystems within the Windows NT system architecture act as servers to applications running on the system in much the same way as servers do in a client-server network environment. You may be familiar with *Remote Procedure Calls (RPC)* and how they work over a network to provide client/server communication services. *Local Procedure Calls (LPC)* are the equivalent of an RPC, but they are implemented within the context of the single computer's operating system to provide communication between the User mode subsystem and the applications. The local procedure call facility is responsible for maintaining a communications mechanism between the applications and subsystems.

The Virtual Memory Manager   The next component of the Windows NT Executive is the Virtual Memory Manager. It is responsible for mapping virtual addresses in a process's address space to physical pages within the computer's memory system. It allows a thread to access its own memory without infringing on the memory space used by another process. It also makes the physical arrangement of pages within physical memory transparent to the process.

The Virtual Memory Manager also allows the operating system to use more memory than is physically present in the computer. It does this by writing the *Least Recently Used (LRU)* pages of memory to disk if the physical memory in the computer is completely used.

The I/O Manager   Consider the I/O Manager to be the traffic cop for all system input and output operations. It manages all input/output functions for all device drivers within the system. This includes hardware device drivers, network card drivers, and file system drivers. A common interface is provided by the I/O Manager that all device drivers within the operating system can use. Actually, the I/O Manager allows device drivers to work at different levels. This lets high-level I/O drivers pass requests to low-level physical device drivers without needing to know the details of the physical device. For example, a network redirector that is a high-level device driver is able to direct requests to the network without knowing how to control the Ethernet card. This also has the advantage of being able to have several devices active at the same time, with all of them being controlled through a common interface.

One driver talks to another driver using a special data structure called an *I/O Request Packet (IRP)*. The I/O Manager receives the IRPs from one device driver and delivers it to another device driver. This is done using asynchronous I/O so the host application can continue to process while the I/O request is performed. This is in contrast to synchronous I/O that suspends application processing until the I/O request is fulfilled. All I/O requests are processed through the I/O queue by order of priority and not by the order in which the request entered the queue.

A Cache Manager works within the I/O system to improve performance. The use of a cache is normally associated with file system input and output operations, but it applies to any network components under the control of the I/O Manager. Actually, there are three distinctive types of drivers used by the I/O Manager, including hardware device drivers, file system drivers, and network drivers. Starting with hardware device drivers, they are as follows:

■   *The Hardware Device Drivers*   Physical device drivers such as mouse and keyboard drivers are implemented as separate drivers that can each interface with the I/O Manager. This allows you to change device drivers for system hardware as necessary without affecting the operation of any other device or driver.

Part

I

Ch

3

■ *The File System Device Drivers*   The implementation of file system device drivers allows the use of different file systems on the same physical drive. The implementation of the network redirector and the server as file system device drivers allows the I/O Manager to access file directories on other servers in the same manner that it accesses local file directories.

■ *The Network Device Drivers*   Network support is an integral part of the Windows NT operating system and is implemented in the form of network device drivers within the I/O system. Several network device drivers are implemented by the I/O Manager and at different levels. As noted above, the network redirector and server are both implemented as *file system devices*. These file system devices are located in a region of the I/O Manager known as the *Provider Interface*. This is the region where both NetBIOS and Windows Sockets are located. Below this level are the transport protocol drivers, such as TCP/IP, NetBEUI, NWLink, and DLC. A mechanism known as the *Transport Driver Interface* allows the transport protocol drivers to talk to the file system drivers (specifically the network redirector and server drivers). Transport level drivers are written to a specification called *Network Device Interface Specification* version 3.0 (NDIS 3.0). This specification enables information to be exchanged between the actual hardware adapter and the transport protocol driver using a common set of rules. Additionally, it enables a single computer to have multiple network cards installed in it, and multiple transport protocols can be run on each card.

N O T E   In Windows 3.51, the File Allocation Table (FAT) file system, the New Technology File System (NTFS) file system, and the older OS/2 High Performance File System (HPFS) files system were all supported. In Windows 4.0 the supported files systems have been narrowed to FAT and NTFS. ▓

The User Mode Components

The components that make up the user mode layer fall into two categories. The first category contains the user mode components that deal with Windows NT security. The other category contains the environmental subsystems needed to run applications written for a variety of operating systems. Later in the chapter, you examine the security components located in the User Mode layer and see how they interact with the Security Reference Monitor located in the Windows NT Executive. Now let's take a look at the environmental subsystems that are used to run various applications from different operating systems.

The Environmental Subsystems   With Windows NT it is possible to run applications that were written for MS-DOS, OS/2 1.x, and Windows 3.x in addition to 32-bit applications (Win32 apps) written for Windows NT. This flexibility exists because several subsystems have been designed into the operating system which allow non-native Windows NT applications to execute on the Windows NT platform. These subsystems actually emulate the operating systems on which the non-native Windows NT applications run. For example, if you run an OS/2 1.x character-based application under Windows NT, the OS/2 subsystem fools the application into thinking it's actually running on an OS/2 1.x operating system.

These environmental subsystems are allowed to interact with the components located within the Windows NT Executive. They utilize the services of the Executive to provide a specific operating system environment for non-Windows NT applications. The advantage of using multiple subsystems is that if an application causes its subsystem to crash, the crash will not affect the other subsystems or the Windows NT Executive components.

NOTE In Windows 3.51 there is a major exception to this rule. The Win32 subsystem controls the mouse and keyboard input in addition to the screen output for all subsystems. If the Win32 subsystem fails, it affects the other subsystems to the extent that the keyboard, mouse, and screen functions won't work. ▤

Windows NT provides a number of different environmental subsystems in addition to *Virtual DOS Machines (VDM)*. A Virtual DOS Machine is explained shortly. Each of the subsystems, with the exception of the Win32 subsystem, is optional and only is loaded when needed by a client application. Here are the subsystems and VDMs available within the Windows NT operating system:

- OS/2 Subsystem
- POSIX Subsystem
- Win32 Subsystem
- MS-DOS VDM
- Win16 VDMs

The OS/2 Subsystem   OS/2 1.x character-based applications can run under Windows NT using the OS/2 subsystem, but only on Intel x86-based hardware platforms. RISC-based computers do not support the OS/2 subsystem, but OS/2 real-mode applications will run within its MS-DOS environment.

The POSIX Subsystem   POSIX stands for "Portable Operating System Interface for Computing Environments" and is really only a set of standards that are being set by the Institute of Electrical and Electronic Engineers (IEEE). To date, only one of the standards has made it from draft to final form and is only beginning to gain customer acceptance. This standard is called POSIX.1 or IEEE standard 1003.1-1990. It defines C-language API calls between the application and the operating system. Because this only defines API calls, any applications written for POSIX.1 must rely on non-POSIX operating system extensions for services such as security and networking.

The file system needed for POSIX requires support for case-sensitive file names and support for files with multiple names called hard links. NTFS provides these requirements to POSIX applications that need to access the file system. However, POSIX applications may run on any supported file system if the application does not require file system access.

The Win32 Subsystem   The Win32 subsystem is the subsystem responsible for running Win32 applications. In Windows NT 3.51, the Win32 subsystem also controls mouse and keyboard input in addition to screen output. Because this subsystem controls the input/output functions in Windows NT 3.51, all other subsystems must communicate through the Win32 subsystem when interacting with a user (see Figure 3.3).

FIG. 3.3

Components of the Win32 Subsystem in Windows 3.5x.

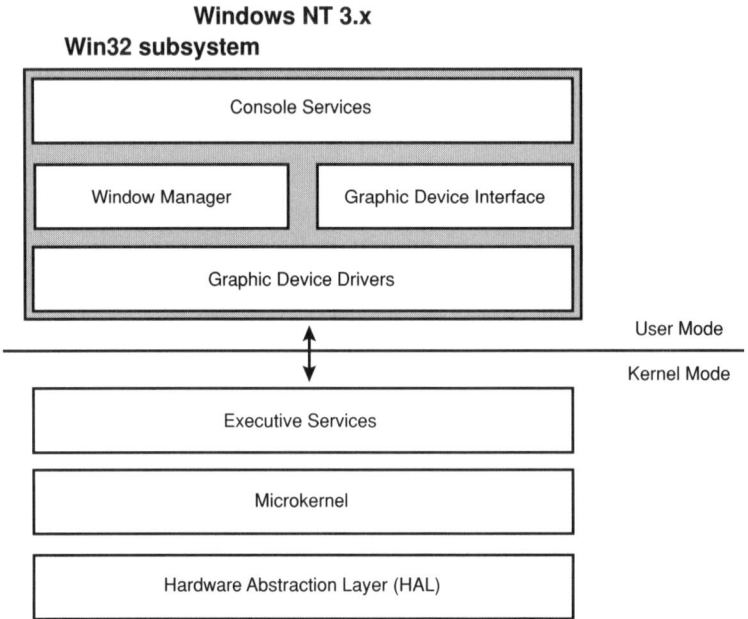

**Windows NT 3.x
Win32 subsystem**

N O T E   Note that Windows NT 3.51 is specified in the previous statement and not Windows NT 4.0. That's because this has been changed in Windows NT 4.0 so that the Win32 Subsystem no longer controls these functions. You learn more about this change later in the chapter during our discussion of "What Architecture Changes are in Windows NT 4.0." ▪

The Win32 subsystem controls input and output using a combination of different services; these services are listed along with a description of their function, as follows:

- *Console Services*   Supplies a combination of services including text window support, shutdown, and hard-error handling functions. It also provides some specialized functions for 32-bit Windows applications such as process creation and deletion.

- *Window Manager*   This service runs as a protected mode process within the Win32 subsystem and is responsible for creating the Windows screen interface. The Windows Manager works with the Graphics Device Interface to relay graphics information to and from applications. Standard user application function requests (such as create a window) are relayed to the GDI by the Windows Manager. In turn, any information concerning changes on the screen that are initiated by the user (such as moving a window) are passed from the Windows Manager to the application.

- *Graphics Device Interface*   This also runs as a protected mode process within the Win32 subsystem. This component is responsible for producing the graphics display on both monitors and printers. The GDI provides a set of standard function calls that are used to interface an application with a specific display device. The GDI relays information that concerns the display characteristics from the application to the device driver. This allows the application to work with any display device (video or printer) without knowing anything about the device. Consider this component to be the translator, taking the information from an application and then translating it into a language that the device drivers can understand.

- *Graphics Device Drivers*   A set of DLLs that contain functions that allow the GDI to access the physical output devices. The most common output devices are monitors and printers. Device drivers take the translated information from the GDI and instruct the physical device to perform some type of action based on the translated information (or instructions). The use of drivers enables very specific device information to be implemented as separate and independent modules that can all hook into a common set of instructions. Some of these drivers are considered to be high-level drivers and others are considered to be low-level drivers. The difference is the low-level drivers actually control hardware operation while high-level device drivers break the GDI calls into smaller pieces that the low-level drivers can understand.

As mentioned earlier, these services are run as a protected process in User mode. For this reason, all other subsystems are considered the clients of the Win32 subsystem in Windows NT 3.5x. All subsystems must utilize Win32 API calls to the Win32 subsystem in order to implement functionality between the application and the user. The bottom line as far as security goes is this: if the Win32 subsystem fails, it affects the entire operating system, because the mouse, keyboard, and screen I/O will be impaired.

The Win32 subsystem also is the component responsible for the operation and control of Virtual DOS Machines (VDM). A VDM enables you to run a Windows 16-bit or MS-DOS based application on a Windows NT machine. Here's a look at the different VDMs and how each one works.

The MS-DOS VDM   Windows NT enables you to run MS-DOS based applications by creating a simulated Intel 486 computer running the MS-DOS operating system. This process is referred to as a Windows NT Virtual DOS Machine or NTVDM. The Windows NT operating system enables you to create multiple NTVDMs at one time on a single machine. When running on an Intel platform, the processor mode called *Virtual-86* is available. This allows the direct execution of a majority of an application's instructions. Only a few I/O instructions must be emulated in order to talk directly to the hardware. Virtual-86 mode is not available on RISC-based computer systems. Instead, the NTVDM handles all 486 instructions including those that need to talk to hardware devices.

Certain environmental characteristics of the MS-DOS operating system must be simulated in order to allow applications to interact with the operating system as they normally would if they were actually running on an MS-DOS based machine. These environmental characteristics are listed as follows:

- *The Intel x 86 Instruction Set*   This is provided by the Instruction Execution Unit.
- *Interrupt Services*   Normally MS-DOS applications rely on the interrupt services provided by the Read-only memory basic input and output services. This is provided by the MS-DOS emulation module within the NTVDM.
- *Interrupt 21 Services*   Interrupt 21 services, normally provided by the MS-DOS operating system, are provided by the MS-DOS emulation module within the NTVDM.
- *Virtual Device Drivers*   Provide the MS-DOS based applications with a virtual set of hardware drivers to simulate those available on an MS-DOS based operating system.

Note that character-based applications only run with a window on Intel-based machines, while DOS-based graphical applications only run on full screens. This is in contrast to a RISC-based system that runs both sessions within a graphical window session.

The Windows 16-Bit VDM   The Windows NT operating system provides a single multi-threaded VDM (sometimes called WOW for Win16 on Win32). Each of the Win16 applications running within the VDM is non-preemptively multitasked. This means that only one 16-bit windows application may run at one time while all other 16-bit windows applications are forced to wait. However, the entire WOW process is preemptively multitasked in relation to other processes running on the system.

The User Mode Security Components The User mode layer of the Windows NT operating system contains several components that work together to form the security subsystem. The security subsystem is comprised of the following components:

- *Log-on processes* These are the user mode processes that are used to authenticate users when they log on to the computer system. The log-on process is used to authenticate both local users and remote users.

- *Local Security Authority* This component is used in conjunction with the log-on process to verify that an individual has a legitimate user account on the system. This account status must be verified before access to the system is permitted. The Local Server Authority is the main component in the user mode portion of the security subsystem. Notice its user mode portion—there is one component of the security subsystem that is not a user mode component—the Security Reference Monitor. We'll explain more about that later in the chapter when we discuss the log-on and authentication process. The Local Security Authority is responsible for all interactive log-on activities and is the component that generates system access tokens *(SATs)*. It also is responsible for the audit control policy and the logging of audit messages generated by the Security Reference Monitor.

- *Security Account Manager (SAM)* This User mode component is responsible for maintaining the user accounts database that is used by the Local Security Authority to validate an individual's account during the log-on process.

These components combined with the Security Reference Monitor form the Windows NT Security Subsystem. This subsystem is not called an environmental subsystem, because it spans both the User mode and the Kernel mode. For this reason, it is called an *integral subsystem*. You learn more about how the Security Subsystem works later in the chapter when you see the log-on process and other object access issues.

Now, let's look at some of the changes that have been made to the operating system's architecture in Windows NT 4.0.

Learning the Architectural Changes in Windows NT 4.0

Windows NT 4.0 system architecture is based on the same architecture used with version 3.5 x, but with some modifications to both the Windows NT Executive and the Win32 subsystem. These modifications were made to improve system performance and still maintain the same degree of system integrity. (See Figure 3.4.)

FIG. 3.4
The Windows NT 4.0
operating system
architecture.

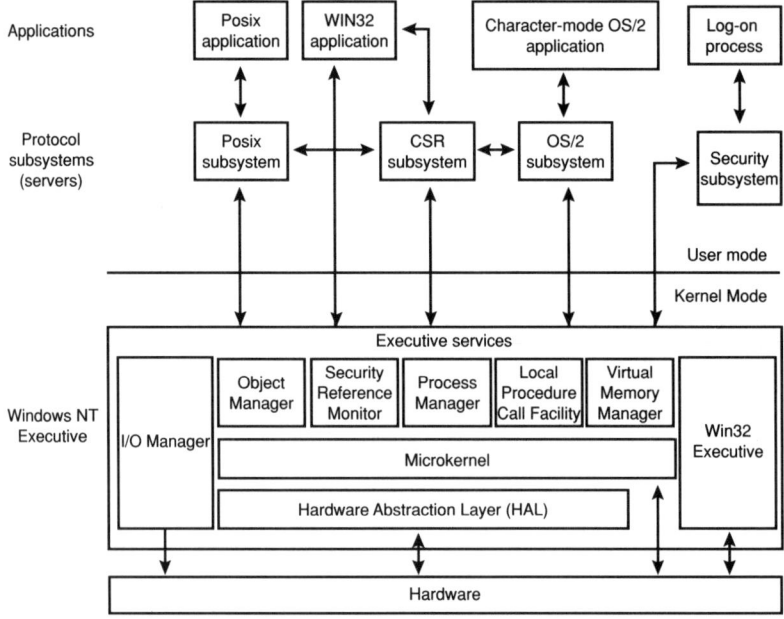

As you learned earlier, the core operating system modules contained within the Kernel mode run at ring 0, the highest and most protected privilege level in the system. It is the kernel components that are ultimately responsible for interfacing with hardware devices. Subsystems in the User mode call upon the Kernel mode components to carry out any function requiring access to a hardware level device. This ensures that an application operating within one of the User mode subsystems (ring 3) cannot crash the system when accessing a hardware device. This protection comes at a price in the form of context switches and ring transitions, which decrease system performance.

A context switch occurs when a Windows application calls an API function in the Win32 subsystem. A ring transition occurs when code in ring 3 calls code in ring 0. This happens because applications must use the Local Procedure Call facility within the Windows NT Executives kernel-mode to communicate with the appropriate subsystem. Also, subsystems call on services in the Windows NT Executive directly. Because the Win32 subsystem contains the *Graphical Device Interface (GDI)*, a number of additional ring transitions occur between the Win32 subsystem and the Windows NT Executive. This adds to the performance loss experienced by the system.

Changes to the Windows NT Executive

In Windows NT 4.0, an additional component named the Win32K Executive has been added to the Kernel mode layer. The Win32K Executive should not be confused with the

Windows NT Executive. The Win32K Executive is actually a new component within the Windows NT Executive. It takes over a majority of the functions performed by the User mode's Win32 subsystem.

As you recall, the Win32 subsystem contained several different components that managed application interaction with the graphical devices in the system (Windows Manager, Graphics Device Interface, and Graphic Device Drivers). This commonly includes graphic output to monitors and printers. Because this interaction was initiated within the User mode layer (in ring 3), ring transitions would take place as calls were passed to the Windows NT Executive (in ring 0) for processing. The Win32K Executive is essentially the new home in the Kernel mode for those components from the Win32 subsystem (as shown in Figure 3.5). This eliminates the ring transitions that would normally take place between the Win32 subsystem and the Windows NT Executive. In turn, the performance of the system is increased.

FIG. 3.5
The modified
Windows NT
Executive in
version 4.0.

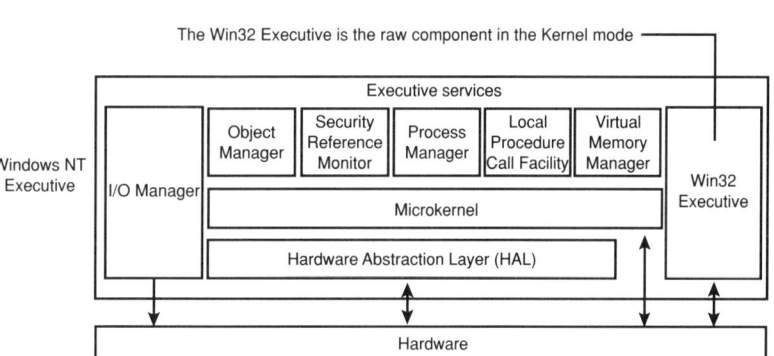

Applications now can make functions call to the Win32K Executive in the Kernel mode instead of going through the Win32 subsystem. This does not completely eliminate the ring transitions that must take place, but it reduces the number. The other improvement to the operating system enables the ring transitions that do take place to be queued and sent in batch form. Instead of performing a transition for every call, the calls are queued up so that a single transition can handle several calls. Again, we have a performance improvement.

The Win32K Executive Components

The Win32K Executive is the new Kernel mode component that essentially took over the graphical input/output services that were provided by the Win32 subsystem. Instead of running as a protected process in the User mode, they now run within the protective confines of the Kernel mode and ring 0 (see Figure 3.6). This also boosts system performance by allowing calls to be made directly from the Win32 Executive to the microkernel and HAL.

FIG. 3.6

The Win32K Executive.

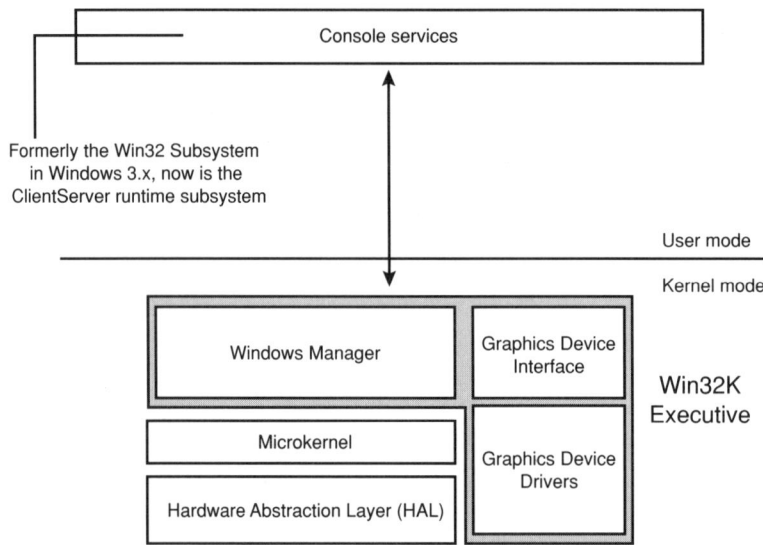

Windows NT 4.0

The Win32K Executive is comprised of several smaller components that each serve a specific function. Here's a list of the different components and the role they play in the operating system environment:

- *Window Manager*   This service is responsible for creating the Windows screen interface. The Windows Manager works with the Graphics Device Interface to relay graphics information to and from applications. Standard user application function requests (such as create a window) are relayed to the GDI by the Windows Manager. Any information concerning changes on the screen that are initiated by the user (such as moving a window) are passed from the Windows Manager to the application.

- *Graphics Device Interface*   This component is responsible for producing the graphics display on both monitors and printers. The GDI provides a set of standard function calls that are used to interface an application with a specific display device. The GDI relays information that concerns the display characteristics from the application to the device driver. This allows the application to work with any display device (video or printer) without knowing anything about the device. Consider this component to be the translator, taking the information from an application and then translating it into a language that the device drivers can understand.

■ *Graphics Device Drivers*   These are a set of DLLs that contain functions that allow the GDI to access the physical output devices. The most common output devices are monitors and printers. Device drivers take the translated information from the GDI and instruct the physical device to perform some type of action based on the translated information (or instructions). The use of drivers allows very specific device information to be implemented as separate and independent modules that can all hook into a common set of instructions. Some of these drivers are considered to be high-level drivers, others are considered to be the low-level drivers. The difference is the low-level drivers actually control hardware operation while high-level device drivers break the GDI calls into smaller pieces that the low-level drivers can understand.

Now that you've seen the individual components that comprise both the User mode and Kernel mode layers of the Windows NT operating system architecture, you can look at the various security processes that use these components.

Windows NT Security System Operation

User mode and Kernel mode layer components perform many of the internal system operations in Windows NT. Let's begin with a quick review of the components that make up the security subsystem. Here's a list of the components and their functions:

■ *Log-on processes*   These are the user mode processes that are used to authenticate users when they log on to the computer system.

■ *Local Security Authority*   This component is used in conjunction with the log-on process to verify that an individual has a legitimate user account on the system. This account status must be verified before access to the system is permitted. The Local Server Authority is the main component in the user mode portion of the security subsystem. The Local Security Authority is responsible for all interactive log-on activities and is the component that generates system access tokens (SATs). It is also responsible for the audit control policy and the logging of audit messages generated by the Security Reference Monitor.

■ *Security Account Manager (SAM)*   Now called the *directory services database*, this User mode component is responsible for maintaining the user accounts database that is used by the Local Security Authority to validate an individual's account during the log-on process.

■ *Security Reference Monitor*   The security reference monitor is used to control the internal security of the system by governing all access, creation, and deletion of objects within the system. It does this using the access control listing or ACL that is associated with each object. Each object contains elements called *Access Control Entries (ACE)*. Each of these access control entries contains the unique security ID of a user or group. The SID is actually a unique number generated by the operating system that describes each user or group within the Windows NT domain.

Before you take a closer look at the log-on process, you'll first want to learn a little bit about security IDs and user accounts. In Windows NT, when a user is created by the system administrator, that user account is assigned a unique security identification number (SID) by the operating system. As long as the user account is active on the system, it will be represented by this unique security ID. If the user is deleted from the system and later re-added to the system, the operating system will assign a completely new security ID to the individual's account. This security ID will not retain any of the security attributes from the users previous account. Any access permissions needed to gain access to system resources will have to be re-applied to the new account.

The Log-On Process

You are familiar with the Windows NT log-on screen and the log-on process. First, you press the Ctrl+Alt+Del keys to open the log-on window. Then, you enter your account ID and password, click the OK button, and like magic you're suddenly logged onto the system. Although this process happens very quickly, many things take place during the log-on sequence.

One of the things that happens is that a security access token is created for the user's session. This security access token contains several pieces of information that are used to gain access to resource objects. The security ID of the user, along with the security IDs of any user groups that the user belongs to, are included in the security access token. Any application or process that runs on behalf of the user will possess a copy of this security access token. If the application or process attempts to access an object on behalf of the user account, the copy of the user's security access token is used to authenticate access to the object.

Each object in the operating system contains a list of access permissions. These access permission lists are compared with the SAT when attempting to access an object. If the permissions list contains the security ID of the user account, or the security ID of any group the user belongs to, access will be permitted based on the permission level designated by the list.

The log-on process begins when a user presses the Ctrl+Alt+Del keys. This sequence of keystrokes is called the secure attention sequence, and it will always display the Windows NT operating system log-on screen. The intention here is to prevent the capture of a user's account name and password by a program that is imitating the Windows NT log-on screen (called a *Trojan Horse* program). This key sequence generates low-level function calls within the Windows NT operating system that can't be duplicated by application programs. However, it is possible to capture the Ctrl+Alt+Del keystrokes under DOS and redirect them. Therefore, it's possible that a DOS-based program running from a MS-DOS boot disk could simulate the Windows NT log-on screen and simply report some type of error while capturing the user's name and password. Again, the best prevention against this scenario is to always maintain tight physical security.

At this time the user must type in his or her account name and password in an interactive process that ultimately grants or denies access to the system. The user name and password gathered by the log-on process is then passed to the Local Security Authority that calls an authentication package.

The authentication package that is used may be custom written if necessary and does not necessarily have to have the authentication package that comes with Windows NT. This enables vendors to write custom packages that enable a user to log on to multiple systems at once, or use some sort of hardware-based device to authenticate users. Examples would be magnetic identification card scanners, voice recognition scanners, or even mechanical key devices.

The authentication package checks the account name and password against the names and passwords listed in the user accounts database. If a match is found the account is validated, the SAM returns the user's SID, and the security IDs of any groups the user belongs to. A log-on session is created by the authentication package. This log-on session along with all the SIDs are then passed back to the Local Security Authority.

At this time the SAT is created by the Local Security Authority. This token contains the SIDs of the user and any groups the user belongs to. In addition to the SIDs themselves, the SAT contains user rights information specific to each SID.

The token is then returned to the log-on process where it is attached to a process created by the Win32 subsystem on behalf of the user. This process, with its attached SAT, is called a *subject* for the user account. At this time the Win32 subsystem starts the desktop for an interactive user session.

If the authentication package cannot verify the user's account in the local accounts database, the information is forwarded to an alternative authentication package if one exists on the network. If the account validation fails, an error message is returned to the user notifying him or her that an incorrect account name or password has been entered. The user may then attempt to log on again.

The User Rights Policy

Normally-limited administrative privileges are assigned to certain users in the system. The capabilities to shutdown the computer or back up its files are considered to be user-rights policy. The difference between user rights and object access is in the way the access is granted. When access is given to an object, the SIDs within the security access token are compared against the entries in the object's access control list (ACL). Rights are assigned when the user activities are not associated with a specific object.

Subjects and Impersonation

As mentioned earlier, a subject is a combination of a process started by the Win32 subsystem combined with the SAT. A subject is usually an application program running on the user's behalf. The application program is said to be running in the security context of the user. The idea here is to restrict the application from having more rights than the user executing it.

Two types of subjects exist within the Windows NT operating system. The first is called the *simple subject* and it represents a process that was given a security context when the user logged on. The other is called a *server subject*, and it represents a process implemented as a protected server. This subject, unlike the simple subject, has other subjects as clients in addition to the user.

When the subject attempts to call a protected subsystem object service, the SAT contained within the subject is used to determine if the subject has sufficient access privileges for the object. At times, a server process may need to access objects on behalf of a client that it normally has no access to. At these times, the server process may take on the security attributes of the client in a process known as *impersonation*. This allows the server process to access the object using the security context of the client.

Objects and Object Types

Earlier in the chapter, we discussed the concept of objects within the Windows NT operating system architecture. As you have learned, all objects represent some process, user, or resource contained within the system. Each of the named objects, as well as some unnamed objects, contain a security descriptor that contains security attribute information for the object. The security descriptor consists of several informational attributes that describe the security access allowed to the object. The information content within the security descriptor is given as follows:

- *Owner security ID*   Indicates the user or group that owns the object.
- *Group security ID*   This descriptor entry is used only by the POSIX subsystem and disregarded by the other Windows NT subsystems.
- *Access Control List*   Lists the users and groups that are allowed access to the object. It also lists users and groups that are specifically denied access to the object.
- *System access control list*   This descriptor entry controls the auditing messages that are generated by the system. It determines which messages will be generated.

Objects are defined as either container or non-container objects. A container object holds other objects; these objects in turn inherit the security attributes of the container object. The security attributes for rights that are applied to an object are specific to the type of object they are being applied to. For example, security attributes for a file object will be different than the security attributes for a print queue.

How the Access Control List (ACL) Works

The *Access Control List* or *ACL* for an object contains information that lists the access and auditing permissions allowed on that object by users and groups. The information listed within the ACL is kept in *Access Control Entries (ACEs)*. Each user or group will have an associated ACE within the ACL. Three types of access control entries exist within the ACL. The first two are called *discretionary* because they either allow (AccessAllowed) or deny (AccessDenied) user access to an object. Access deny (AccessDenied) entries are always listed and processed first. The third *ACE* (*SystemAudit*) is used by the security system for audit purposes, as it keeps a log of security events and generates log security audit messages.

When a user attempts to access an object, the Security Reference Monitor (SRM) checks the SID numbers in the user's SAT against those found in the ACL. After the SRM finds an access control entry (ACE) with a matching SID, it checks to see what type of ACE it is. If the ACE has a discretionary access deny (AccessDenied) value, user access to the resource is denied and no further processing takes place. If the ACE has a value of access allowed (AccessAllowed), then additional processing takes place based on the values present in the *access mask*.

Using Access Masks   Each access allowed (AccessAllowed) ACE for a user or group SID contains a set of access permissions. The access permissions are specific to each type of object and are cumulatively called the ACE's *specific access mask*. Each object may be assigned up to 16 specific access types when it is defined. Access masks that apply to all objects are called the *standard access masks*. They contain sets of access permissions that are used for all objects in addition to any specific access mask definitions. The following list shows the access masks currently used with Windows NT 4.0:

- SYNCHRONIZE   Used to synchronize access, it also allows a process to wait for an object to enter the signaled state.
- WRITE_OWNER   Used to assign write owner.
- WRITE_DAC   Used to grant or deny write access to the discretionary ACL.
- READ_CONTROL   Used to grant or deny read access to the security descriptor and owner.
- DELETE   This is used to grant, deny, or delete access.

In addition to specific and standard access masks, there is also the *generic access mask*. This mask specifies a range of permissions that are all "generic" in nature. They are as follows:

- GENERIC_READ
- GENERIC_EXECUTE

This generic type of access mask can then be mapped to a specific set of access permissions (or specific access mask) by the application creating the object. For example, the mask GENERIC_EXECUTE could be mapped by the application defining the object to one of the object's specific access masks named FILE_RUN. Usually all generic access types are mapped to either a specific of standard access type.

What happens when a user attempts to access an object? Well, another mask is created called the *desired access mask*. This mask is a list of permissions that the user (or application running in the context of the user) can exercise on the object.

Here are the steps that are performed by the Windows NT operating system as it verifies access to a resource by a user or an application running in a user context:

1. The SAT that belongs to the user (or application program running in the security context of the user) is compared to the SIDs for each ACE in the access control list (ACL). If no SIDs from the access token match the SID of the access control entry, the access control entry is skipped.

2. Because access denied entries are listed first, any access denied entry will be processed first. If access is denied to the object, the system checks to see if the desired access mask contained a ReadControl and/or WRITE_DAC request. If it did, the system checks to see if the user is the owner of the object. If the user is the owner of the object, access is granted. If the user is not the owner of the object, access is denied.

3. If access is denied by the AccessDenied ACE, no further processing takes place even if other accesses do exist in both the ACE and the desired access mask. This is because the access denied entry overrules any other access permission. User access will simply be denied to the user.

4. Processing of the ACL continues one ACE at a time until a matching SID is found with either an access allowed (AccessAllowed) or access denied (AccessDenied) entry. If access is allowed by the AccessAllowed ACE, the accesses listed in the desired access mask are compared to the accesses listed in the ACE. If all the desired accesses have not been specified by this ACE, processing continues to the subsequent ACEs to see if they contain the remaining accesses listed in the desired access mask. Access is granted to the user as soon as all the accesses in the desired access mask match those in found in one or more ACEs.

5. Access will be implicitly denied if the contents of the desired mask and ACE(s) do not completely match by the end of the ACL.

The Role of Windows NT Registry

An important part of the Microsoft Windows NT operating system from a security standpoint is the Windows NT registry. You may already be familiar with the Windows NT registry if you've worked with Windows NT for any period. The registry contains all of the configuration information that was originally stored in a multitude of initialization files (*.ini) back in the Windows 3.x days. Windows NT and Windows 95 have done away with the initialization files and replaced it with a registry. The registry contains keys that hold various values that are required for the proper system configuration and operation. Each key can also contain sub-keys that in turn can contain data or other sub-keys.

All of these registry keys are contained in one of five registry *subtrees*. Each of these subtrees contains their own key structure that is specific to that subtree. How does this tie-in with security on a Windows NT system? All of the security information for the local machine is contained within one of these subtrees. Moreover, if the Windows NT Server happens to be a domain controller, all the security information for the entire Windows NT domain also is contained within the registry's subtree key structure. That's right, the entire directory services database (formerly SAM database) for a domain is contained within the registry of a Windows NT PDC or BDC.

The registry subtree named HKEY_LOCAL_MACHINE contains the directory services database and other security information. These specific registry keys and subkeys are called *hives* because they represent a discreet set of related keys and subkeys. Unlike other keys, these keys are not dynamically created but are a permanent part of the operating system. Each of the hives is associated with one or more sets of standard files, in which various key information is stored.

The HKEY_LOCAL_MACHINE subtree contains several keys that maintain the security information for our system. The keys that specifically need to be mentioned are as follows:

- HKEY_LOCAL_MACHINE\SAM   This key contains the directory services database (formerly the SAM) for user and group accounts. If the machine is a domain controller, the domain's directory services database is contained in this key. The associated standard files for this key are: Sam, Sam.log, Sam.sav

- HKEY_LOCAL_MACHINE\Security   This key is used by the Windows NT security subsystem and contains local security policy information. The associated standard files for this key are: Security, Security.log, and Security.sav.

The HKEY_LOCAL_MACHINE\SAM key contains all user and group security information for the local computer and for the domain, if the machine is a domain controller. This key is automatically mapped and replicated to the key named HKEY_LOCAL_MACHINE\Security\SAM.

CAUTION

Never attempt to modify the HKEY_LOCAL_MACHINE\SAM key or any of its subkeys using the Windows NT registry editor utility program. All the information contained within the registry is stored in binary format and can't be edited manually. Any changes that need to be made to user or group security, or NTFS permissions, should be done via the appropriate administrative utility such as User Manager for Domains.

It is also important that the registry information be backed up on a regular basis, especially if frequent changes to the directory services database occur. This easily can be done using the Windows NT Backup utility provided with the operating system. Also, maintain more than one domain controller on a single domain so that a copy of the directory services database always is available on an alternate machine.

From Here...

Now that you've finished learning about the Windows NT operating system architecture, you can move on to examine setting up domains and trust relationships.

- Chapter 4, "Windows NT Domain Concepts," takes you through the hows and whys of setting up a Windows NT domain. You see the many ways that a domain can make the administrative tasks less troublesome.

- Chapter 5, "Maintaining Security with Domain Trust Relationships," builds on the information you learned in Chapter 4 to include the concept of trust relationships. You learn why, when, and how they're created along with some common domain models that use various trusts.

- Chapter 6, "User Account Security and Windows NT," focuses on the details of creating and maintaining user and group accounts. We'll explain the different types of built-in Windows NT accounts and when you should use them.

Part
I

Ch
3

Security Implementation on Microsoft Windows NT

CHAPTER 4

Windows NT Domain Concepts

Introducing you to how the Windows NT Domain is used with group servers and resources is the gist of Chapter 2, "An Overview of Microsoft Windows NT Security." This chapter expands on that information and shows how domains are created and managed within the Windows NT environment. It begins with a look at the basic components that make up a domain, such as controllers and workstations. The advantages of using domains as opposed to individual server-based accounts is discussed. After that, we'll look at some of the details associated with domains, such as how they're created and how user accounts work within them. ■

Domain principles

This section gives an overview of what a domain is and how it works. You see the different components that make up a domain and introduce the Windows NT Directory Services.

Domain advantages

The reasons for using a domain and the advantages that a domain environment provides.

Domain creation

Examine some of the planning issues that need to be considered when implementing a domain environment. Issues such as server size and placement are some of the topics discussed.

User accounts in a domain

The creation of a domain user account and the various properties that can be assigned to it. The configurable options that enable administrators to specify how the user accounts can interact with the system also are examined.

How groups work

Groups allow you to allocate administrative duties in addition to allowing access to network resources. See some of the built-in user groups and learn how to determine a user's ability to administer the system.

Understanding Domains

Domains are used in a Windows NT environment to divide computers into logical groups. These groups then can be managed to provide access to resources based on a user's domain membership. We briefly described what a Windows NT domain was in Chapter 2, "An Overview of Microsoft Windows NT Security." Let's take a closer look at the domain concept within a group of networked computers.

First, don't confuse a Windows NT domain with a UNIX domain. They imply two different meanings (for now anyway, more about this later in the chapter). The UNIX domain is simply a method of naming computers that operate over a TCP/IP intranetwork. Primarily used with the directory service called *Domain Name Services (DNS)*, the grouping of UNIX hosts (or other TCP/IP based hosts) under a "domain name" allows them to be easily looked up and identified by friendly computer names rather than IP addresses.

On the other hand, a Windows NT domain is a group of servers running the Windows NT Server operating system that all share a common user accounts database and a common security policy. A domain also can contain other computers that are not running Windows NT Server, such as Windows NT Workstation and Microsoft's OS/2 LAN Manager machines. These machines participate in a domain by allowing user access to their local resources based on the user's domain account.

Administrators easily can grant access to resources across several servers based on a user's domain membership. It doesn't matter if the user is working on another Windows NT Server or an MS-DOS based workstation. The access privileges granted to the user for any domain resource are tied directly to that user's domain account. Any time a user wants to access a domain resource, such as a file directory or printer, they must be validated as an authorized user of the resource. This is all part of the function that the *Windows NT Server Directory Service* provides. The service provides an easy way to manage both user accounts and resource access. Windows NT Server Directory Services provide the following functions:

- *Single logon to file, print, and network applications*   Instead of having to log on to separate servers in order to gain access to their resources, the Directory Service provides a convenient single logon for users. Users do not have to supply a separate log-on ID and password to access the resources on a different server.

- *Centralized Administration*   The Windows NT Server Directory Services provide a way to manage the network's user database and resources from a central location. This flexibility extends to allow management of the network from several different locations if desired.

■ *Secure Accounts Database*   Information contained within the user accounts database is secured through replication to other servers within the Windows NT domain. This provides an online backup of all account and security information for any user or resource in the domain.

The domain is the basic building block on which the Windows NT Server Directory Services are based. The security accounts database (*SAM*) account information for all objects within a domain is contained in special registry key files called *hives*. These hives are located on special Windows NT Servers called *domain controllers*. Two types of domain controllers are used in the Windows NT environment. They are:

Primary Domain Controller or *PDC*   There is only one PDC per domain, and it contains a master copy of the registry hive file that holds the security information for the entire domain.

Backup Domain Controller or *BDC*   Several BDCs can be present in the domain—at least one is highly recommended, even for the smallest networks. The BDC contains a copy of the master hive files and can authenticate users when they log on to the domain. It also provides a working copy of the SAM in the event that the PDC server experiences failure. This copy can be used to authenticate users when they log on to the domain.

Part
II

Ch

4

Although the BDC authenticates users, it does not allow the modification of the domain's account database and resource information. Any changes made to the accounts database must be done to the hive files located on the PDC. When an administrator runs the "User Manager for Domains" utility to add a new account, the account database on the PDC is opened, regardless of where the utility is being run. For example, if the Windows NT Server name CORP1 was the ADMIN domain's PDC, and the server name CORP2 was the BDC, an administrator that is logged on at the CORP2 server running the "User Manager for Domains" utility actually makes modifications to the hive files on the CORP1 server. Although copies of the hive files exist on CORP2, those files are never modified, just updated. This is because they are read-only copies of the master hive files located on CORP1.

If the PDC is not available, the accounts database cannot be modified. For example, right before the administrator sat down at the CORP2 server (the BDC) to add a new user, the CORP1 server (the PDC) went offline. The administrator still would be able to run the "User Manager for Domains" utility but would receive a message notifying him or her that the PCD was unavailable and that changes to the database can't be completed at this time.

Is the administration of the domain impossible until the PCD comes back online? Not at all; the accounts database can be modified if one of the BDCs is promoted to the role of PDC. This easily is done using the "Server Manager" utility from any Windows NT server in the domain. This allows the read-only copy of the database (or hive files) to become the master database for the domain. This account database can then be modified just as the database on the original PDC was.

> **CAUTION**
>
> Promotion of a BDC to a PCD can be accomplished while the original PDC is offline, although any changes to the accounts database on the PDC that were not replicated to the BDC before going offline will be lost. If maintenance is planned on the PCD, the demotion of the PDC and subsequent promotion of a selected BDC can be done while both machines are online. The accounts database always is replicated immediately before the change of controller status; thus, no changes are lost to the accounts database.

The Windows NT Workstation also can be a member of a domain, and although they do use the accounts database, they do not share any network log-on authentication duties. Windows NT Workstations contain their own local security accounts database that is independent of other machines, and they do not need to participate in the Windows NT domain environment if access to domain resources is not needed. However, they can join a Windows NT domain if desired. This enables additional functionality between the Workstation and the Windows NT domain, such as the following:

- The Workstation gains the capability to recognize domain accounts in addition to local accounts. This means that a person having a domain account can log on to the Workstation as well as to any local Workstation accounts.

- The domain user remotely can access the Workstation resources. This is because rights to files and other resources on the Workstation can be granted to domain accounts instead of only to local user accounts.

- Administration of the Workstation's resources can be administered by a member of the domain administrator's group. This allows a central point of control for Windows NT Workstation management and domain management.

Another type of computer that can participate in a Windows NT domain is the OS/2 LAN Manager Server. In fact, these older legacy systems can co-exist in a Windows NT domain and act as BDCs. However, they cannot assume the role of PDC within the domain environment. This role is left exclusively for Windows NT Servers to fill.

Windows for Workgroups, Windows 95, and MS-DOS machines can participate as the equivalent of workgroup members. This allows them to be listed by network browsers under the same domain name that the users log on to. For example, you log on to the ADMIN domain from your Windows 95 workstation. Your network administrators have set up all WFW, Win 95, and MS-DOS workstations to show up as members of the domain where the user logs on. They've done this by designating the domain name (ADMIN in this case) in the workstation's "workgroup" network configuration parameter. This way, when other users browse the network using Network Neighborhood or another utility, your workstation appears to be in the ADMIN domain. The computers on your network easily can be organized by using this method.

As you'll see in the following chapter, domains can participate in *trust relationships* with other domains. This allows the resources of one domain to be used easily by the members of another domain. The combination of the Windows NT domain and trust environments provides excellent manageability of network resources. Because of this, you'll have a chance to look at some of the reasons for using a domain.

Why Use a Domain?

Domains provide several advantages over individual server-based authentication where users log on to a single server to gain access to its resources. In a single-server setting, if the user wants access to a network resource from his or her workstation that's controlled by a network server, he or she first needs to log on to the server by providing an account ID and password. The user's account and password are authenticated by the server. The user is then allowed access to the requested resource based on the user's assigned privileges on that server. If the user then wants access to other resources controlled by a second server, the user must log on or attach to that second server. This may be adequate for small networks with few users, but it can be an administrative nightmare in organizations with a large number of users and more sophisticated network needs.

Part
II

Ch

4

For larger network environments, a single-user database that can authenticate users and allow them to access resources on multiple servers is needed. This eliminates the need for multiple user accounts for any one individual on the network. A single user account can be created that will allow a person access to resources located on any server within the domain, provided he or she has the proper permissions to the resource.

Another reason for using a domain is because it provides a central point of administration for all user accounts and resources. As noted, a domain permits a single user account to be created, thus eliminating the user's need to log on or attach to an individual server. This works both ways, because it also eliminates the additional administrative burden of creating and maintaining multiple user accounts on separate servers. User accounts only need to be created one time within the network environment. Any resource permissions the individual needs are then granted to the domain user account from a central administrative utility. The administrative utilities can be executed from any Windows NT Server within the domain as long as the PDC is operational.

The security of the user database is a major concern to all system administrators (at least it should be). Even if you have a limited number of users, having to re-create your accounts database from scratch is a scary thought to most of us. To prevent the loss of the accounts database on single servers, frequent backups would need to be made to ensure the security of the account information. If a failure of the drive media occurred that affected the accounts database files, the account files usually would have to be restored to the system once the media problem was fixed. Any changes that took place after the last backup of the accounts database would be lost because they would not be restored. Again, this could be a potential nightmare in a larger organization with hundreds of accounts, not to mention the wasted time and lost productivity due to the unavailability of network resources.

Domains fix this problem by providing a means of immediate online backup for the Security Accounts Database (SAM). As explained earlier, this is accomplished using servers that share a common accounts database. One server is designated as the Primary Domain Controller (PDC) and physically contains the *master* copy of the SAM database. Other servers participate as Backup Domain Controllers (BDC) and they each contain a copy of the SAM database. Each BDC server's copy is updated from the PDC's master copy at frequent intervals. This ensures the integrity of the SAM database in the event the PDC fails or is taken offline. It also gives users the ability to authenticate on the network and to gain access to resources without being dependent on any one server for logging on.

Creating Domains

Now that you have an idea of how domains are used, you need to learn how they are created. Actually, the act of creating a domain is a simple procedure that takes place during the Windows NT server installation procedure. When a Windows NT Server is installed, you're presented with the option of joining a current domain or creating a new domain. If you join an existing domain, the server becomes a Backup Domain Controller (BDC). If you decide to create a new domain, the server becomes the PCD. All that's needed to create a new domain is a unique name for the domain and a password (that you create) for the domain administrators account. It is an easy process; however, the creation of the domain does take a little planning if you want to avoid problems.

It's simple—just throw a few servers together. Set one up as the PDC, set two more up as BDCs. Fire them all up, add some accounts, and let the users go for it, right?

You actually could do this and get away with it under most circumstances. But I'm guessing that most of you would rather have some level of comfort knowing the servers had been scaled and placed properly. In reality, both scaling and location must be taken into serious consideration before implementing any domain that services a large number of users.

One of the items that should be considered when scaling the servers is the number of domain controllers that will be required. If the number of controllers in the domain is too low, each of the controllers could be kept so busy that the user accounts may have difficulty authenticating on the network. To estimate the number of domain controllers that should be placed in a domain, consider the following issues:

- How many user accounts is the domain expected to support?
- What will the hardware configuration of the domain controllers be?

Currently, 40,000 accounts are supported within a single Windows NT domain. Therefore, you might be thinking that a single domain would handle 40,000 user accounts. Well, not exactly. You see, an account in a Windows NT domain can refer to a user account, but it also refers to computer and group accounts.

Computer accounts represent a machine on the network, such as a Windows NT Workstation that is a member of the domain. When a Windows NT Server or Workstation joins an existing domain, it is given a *Security ID (SID)* just as users are given when they are added to the accounts database. Note that WFW, Windows 95, and MS-DOS workstations may be listed as members of the domain in Server Manager, but they are not given accounts on the domain.

Part

II

Ch

4

The built-in groups within Windows NT (such as the Domain Admins group) and any custom groups you create are also given SID numbers. Thus, they also constitute a domain account. We'll discuss some of the details regarding user accounts and groups a little later in the chapter.

Therefore, the total number of users, Windows NT computers, and user groups comprise the sum of the domain accounts. For all practical purposes, around 25,000 actual user accounts can be managed on a single domain. Any more users than that require that the user accounts be split between two domains. Windows NT provides a means of splitting accounts across two or more domains by using a Multiple Master Domain Model. More details about domains and domain models are given in Chapter 5, "Maintaining Security with Domain Trust Relationships."

A big consideration related to the number of accounts on the domain has to do with the maximum size of the SAM file. As you recall, the SAM file is a binary registry file located on the domain controller(s). The greater the number of accounts, the larger the SAM file. A SAM file larger than 40MB may take several minutes to load into memory. This problem is compounded if the hardware platform is a slower machine with inadequate memory or slow processor speed.

Table 4.1 shows you how much file space is used in the SAM file for each type of account.

Table 4.1   Space Used by Account Objects in the SAM File

Account Type	Space Used
User Account	1.0K
Global Group Account	512 bytes for the group plus 12 bytes for each group member
Local Group Account	512 bytes for the group plus 36 bytes for each group member
Computer Account	.5K

If you're creating a new domain, it's possible to estimate the size of the SAM file by multiplying the number of accounts by their associated size. Once you have an idea of the size of the SAM file, you can scale the hardware used for the domain controllers. Let's put this in perspective by using another table. Table 4.2 lists some recommendations that help you evaluate your domain controller's hardware requirements—these recommendations are based on the size of the SAM file. Remember to take into consideration the growth potential for user and computer accounts in your organization before estimating the size of your SAM file.

Table 4.2   Domain Controller Hardware Recommendations

User Accounts	Computer Accounts	Group Accounts	SAM Size	CPU	Memory
2,000	2,000	30	3.12	486/33	32MB
5,000	10,000	100	10.4	486/66	32MB
7,500	7,500	100	11.3	Pentium, MIPS, Alpha AXP	32MB
10,000	10,000	150	15.6	Pentium, MIPS, Alpha AXP	48MB
25,000	25,000	200	38.3	Pentium, MIPS, Alpha AXP	96MB
40,000	0	0	40	Pentium, MIPS, Alpha AXP	128MB

Other factors also must be taken into consideration when planning the domain. We just examined the hardware requirements for the controllers based on the size of the SAM file. This helps you determine the horsepower you need for a specific controller, but it doesn't address some of the other issues, such as server availability.

Networks often span local offices and extend across town or across the nation using high-speed connections such as T1 lines. Windows NT domains may contain servers and work-stations that are physically separated from one another over these WAN lines. Although these lines are fast, they still are relatively low-speed connections compared to Ethernet's 10MB/sec or Token Ring 16MB/sec line speeds. For this reason, it is desirable to place domain controllers on the same local (high-speed) network as the user workstations. Users logging on to the domain do not have to be authenticated over a low speed WAN link if a domain controller is present on their local network. This reduces traffic on WAN links, saving precious bandwidth.

Typically, the PDC will be placed on an area of the network that is in the same location as the network administrator. Remember, when the accounts database is modified, it is modi-fied on the PDC. If the PDC is in Los Angeles and the network administrator is in New York, connection to the PDC over the WAN link must be accomplished before the accounts database can be modified. Locating the PDC on the same high-speed network wire as the system administrator's workstation eliminates administration of the domain over a slower WAN link and again helps reduce bandwidth usage across the wire.

N O T E Some traffic is generated by the domain controllers as they communicate with each other. This traffic takes place when the PDC synchronizes with the other BDCs on the network. The synchronization takes place in order to maintain backup copies of the security accounts database on BDCs.

Some other points to consider when planning the placement of BDCs are given as follows:

- Speed of the WAN link
- The reliability of the WAN link
- User location and authentication requirements
- The number of users at a single location
- The availability of local resources

As you'll soon discover, several different domain models exist. *Trust relationships* are used to establish relationships between domains. The way that the Trust relationships are set up determines the domain model being used. For example, a single domain that does not have any trust relationships with other domains is called a *Single Domain Model*. A group of individual domains that all trust one another is called a *Complete Trust Domain Model*. This deserves mentioning, because the type of domain model you choose to implement also will affect the physical placement of Backup Domain Controllers. Chapter 5, "Main-taining Security with Domain Trust Relationships" gives you a detailed view of the differ-ent domain models and how each of them is used.

Part

II

Ch

4

Now that you've learned about what you need to consider when creating a domain, here's another question: How do you move servers from one domain to another?

Changing Domain Memberships

You've installed a Windows NT Server in the company's ADMIN domain as a Backup Domain Controller (BDC) and things are going along fine. Then one day you decide that you don't really need this Windows NT Server in the ADMIN domain after all. You've got two other BDCs in the ADMIN domain already that provide security for the domain's account database, and you really want to create another domain for the network administrators. No problem—just change the name of the domain that the server belongs to and promote the server to a PCD, right? Just split the domain.

Yes, it does appear that you can do it. Changing the domain name is possible. So is promoting the server to a PCD. Everything appears to work just fine until you decide to set up a Trust relationship between the split domains, or between the split domains and a third domain. For some reason it just doesn't work. Why? Both domains have matching SID numbers.

As mentioned earlier in the chapter, domains are created during the installation of the first Windows NT Server in the domain. The server installation creates the new domain and it creates a unique SID number for the new domain. This SID number is constructed from time, date, and domain information and is statistically unique to the point that it should never be duplicated or re-created. This domain SID number then is used to prefix the SID numbers given to all BDCs, user accounts, and groups within the domain. The SID number identifies the holder of the SID as a member of a specific domain.

This brings up an important point. Servers participating within a domain environment are identified by their domain's unique SID number and not by the name of the domain they belong to. The reason the Trust relationship failed in our example was that the servers knew they both belonged to the same domain. They knew it because they both shared a common SID number prefix. Because a domain cannot have a Trust set up "within" itself, the Trust failed.

So how do you change the domain membership of a Windows NT server? You don't. You must reinstall the server software and either create a new domain, or join an existing domain. That's all, folks; don't even try to find a workaround for this one. You are wasting your time. This is the reason that domain planning is so important. If you plan the domain structure right the first time, you'll save yourself the trouble of reinstalling your Windows NT server a second time.

Now that you have an idea of how and why domains are used, you're ready to expand on this and look at how user accounts work within the domain environment.

How User Accounts and Domains Work

Before a domain user is allowed to access any domain-based network resource, he or she first must perform a valid logon. The domain log-on sequence requires the user to provide both an account name and password. If logging on to a Windows NT Server or Workstation, the user interface will not open until the user has been successfully authenticated. After the user has been validated as a domain member, he or she can be given access to the resources located in the domain. The user will be challenged for an account name and password if attempting to access a secure domain resource from a Windows 95, WFW, or MS-DOS workstation over the network.

As you learned in Chapter 3, "Windows NT Operating System Architecture," access to the domain's resources is controlled by matching the SID number in the user account's *access token* with a SID number located in the object's *Access Control List (ACL)*. By objects, we mean file shares, print queues, and other domain resources. When a match is found, the access *mask* in the ACL's *access control entry (ACE)* is used to define the exact rights a user has to the object. In addition to allowing object access, user accounts enable the administrators of the domain to set system policy regarding user rights. The system policy affects the way a user can interact with the network system.

Part
II

Ch
4

Creating a User Account in a Domain

Domain level accounts for network users are created using the "User Manager for Domains" administrative utility. This is one of several built-in administrative utilities that are provided with the Windows NT Server product. This particular utility enables you to create, modify, and delete the user accounts for a domain. The utility also enables you to specify basic user information in addition to security restrictions on the account. Let's look at some of the configuration parameters for a domain user account. Figure 4.1 shows you the New User dialog box for entering the individual's account information.

This main dialog box enables you to specify the following information:

- *Username*   The user's unique account name, such as JohnD, Jdoe, or JohnDoe. The username can contain up to 20 uppercase or lowercase characters except for the following: " / \ [ ] : ; | = , + * ? < >.
- *Full name*   The full name of the individual owning the account.

■ *Description*   This can be any descriptive text that you want (such as the person's job title).

■ *Password*   The confidential password associated with the user's account can be up to 14 characters long and is case sensitive. To enter or change a password, you must type the exact same set of characters in both Password and Confirm Password boxes.

■ *User Must Change Password at Next Logon*   Just as it implies, the user will be forced to change the password that he or she was originally assigned before being allowed access to the system. If you set a maximum password age (you'll see how shortly), this value automatically turns on when the password has expired.

■ *User Cannot Change Password*   This prevents a user from changing his or her password. This is most often used when several people use a single log-on account. For example, this setting can be used for the domain's *guest* account (if it has been enabled).

■ *Password Never Expires*   This is useful when configuring user accounts that are used with applications that run as Windows NT services. Sometimes they are called the *service* account. Actually, this allows an application service to run in the security context of a designated user account. This setting overrides any "Maximum Password Age" setting that may have been set. It also overrides the "User Must Change Password at Next Logon" setting.

■ *Account Disabled*   This setting prevents the use of an account. This is often used with template accounts that are used to create new accounts. The built-in Administrator account cannot be disabled with this setting.

■ *Account Locked Out*   This box only is selected if the user account is currently locked out. Clearing it enables the user account. This box is used only to clear the lock out status and cannot be used to set the lock out status.

FIG. 4.1
Provide the basic account information in the New User dialog box.

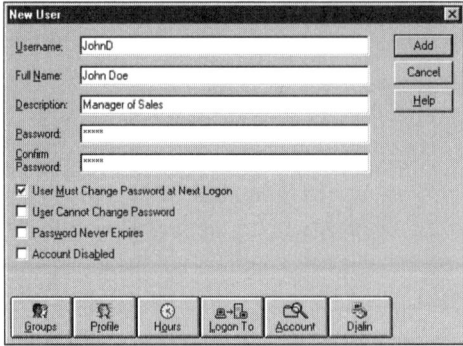

The New User dialog box also contains buttons along the bottom that enable you to configure other features of the user account. The first button along the bottom is the Groups button. Clicking it opens the Group Memberships dialog box shown in Figure 4.2.

FIG. 4.2
Use the Group Memberships dialog box to add the user to local and global groups.

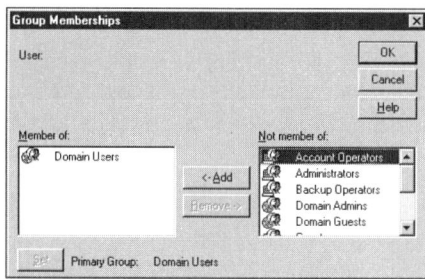

This enables you to add or remove the user from any of the built-in or custom *user groups* that exist within the domain. We explain more about user groups a little later in this chapter.

When the Profile button is selected, it lets you assign a user profile path, log-on script name, or home directory path to the user account. The User Environment Profile dialog box shown in Figure 4.3 appears.

Part

Ch

FIG. 4.3
Specify user profiles, log-on scripts, and home directory paths by selecting the Profile button.

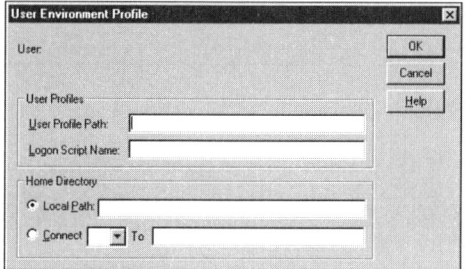

The options you can specify in this dialog box directly can effect the way the user is allowed to interact with the system. The following options can be specified:

- *User Profile Path*   You can configure the network so users can log on anywhere and have the same Windows desktop with their individual settings and preferences. This is done by creating and then assigning a profile to the account. This feature also can be used to assign a mandatory user profile. Mandatory profiles are usually implemented to restrict the user's access to certain desktop components or activities. For instance, a mandatory profile could be configured that does not contain the Settings group on the Windows desktop. This way you could prevent users from modifying any of the workstation's configuration settings. The mandatory profile must be available or the user is not allowed to log on.

- ▪ *Logon Script Name*   This box is used to assign a log-on script to a user. If a log-on script is assigned to a user, it runs each time the user logs on to the domain. The script file can be an executable program, or a batch file with a .bat or .cmd extension. Log-on scripts usually contain commands that set the user environment or start some type of application. Directory replication is used in conjunction with log-on scripts to ensure the log-on script is available on all domain controllers that could authenticate the account. The script file is replicated across all controllers in the domain to the server's log-on script path (usually \WINNT\SYSTEM32\REPL\ IMPORT\SCRIPTS).

- ▪ *Home Directory*   When a home directory is specified for a user account, any File Open and Save As dialog boxes will default to this location for any application that does not have a working directory defined. The location of the home directory can be on the user's local workstation or on a network drive share. A single home directory can be assigned to multiple accounts. If a home directory is not specified, Windows 4.0 Server and Workstation clients will automatically have a default home directory set to the local computer's hard drive. The default directory is set to the root directory on new installations of Windows 4.0, so set it to the \USER\DEFAULT directory on computers that have been installed using an upgraded version of Windows 4.0.

- ▪ *Local Path*   Enables you to specify the path to the home directory as being on the user's local workstation.

- ▪ *Connect To*   Lets you specify a network share as the home directory and permits you to designate the drive letter the system uses to connect to this share.

Other options also may appear in this dialog box depending on the other network services that are installed.

Clicking the H<u>o</u>urs button opens up the Logon Hours dialog box (shown in Figure 4.4) that enables you to specify the times when a user is allowed to access domain resources on the system. The system defaults to allowing access all the time. Although this can prevent a user from accessing a domain resource, it will not affect a user's ability to use a workstation.

The calendar displays the seven days of the week in one-hour increments. A box that is filled indicates the user is allowed access during that time period. After highlighting one or more of the one-hour increments, the Disallow button can be used to clear the highlighted time period. The cleared boxes indicate that a user is not allowed to connect to domain resources during that time. Highlighting cleared boxes and clicking the Allow button re-enables the user logon during that time period.

FIG. 4.4

Specify times that users are allowed access to domain resources.

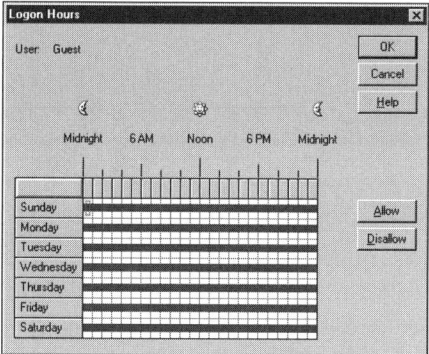

If a user is connected and does not log off before he or she runs out of time on the system, two things can be configured to happen: The user can be forcibly disconnected from the system, or the user can be allowed to remain connected to any current resources but not allowed to connect to any additional resources. The "Forcibly disconnect remote users from server when logon hours expire" setting within the Account Policy dialog box determines how the expired account is handled.

The next button along the bottom of the New User dialog box is the Logon To button. Click it to open the Logon Workstations dialog box shown in Figure 4.5. This dialog box lets you restrict where the user is allowed to log on. The default is to allow the user to log on to any workstation. To restrict the workstations available to the user for domain resource access, mark the button "User May Log On To These Workstations," and then specify the computer names of the workstations the user will be allowed to log on from.

FIG. 4.5

Specify where the user will be allowed to log on.

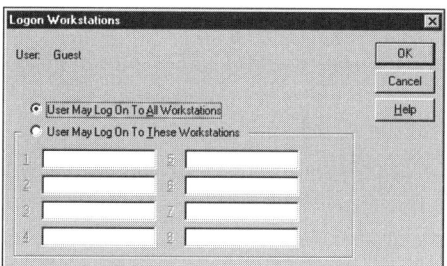

The Account button is the next user configurable option available in the New User dialog box. The Account Information dialog box (shown in Figure 4.6) is used to specify an expiration date for the account. The default is no expiration date.

Part

II

Ch

4

FIG. 4.6

Specify the Account type and expiration date.

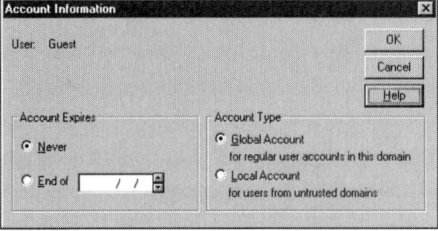

In addition to an expiration date, this dialog box is used to specify the account type for this user. User accounts are either global or local accounts with most accounts being global accounts. A global account designates common user accounts within the user's home domain (or where the user's account resides). Local accounts are given to users from other non-trusted domains so those users can gain access to the domain resources.

The Dialin button in the New User dialog box is new to Windows NT 4.0. It appears if the Remote Access Service has been installed on the server. It offers the domain administrators an easy way of granting dialup permission to users when their accounts are created. This saves time because the administrator no longer has to run the Remote Access Administration program in order to give users RAS permission. It also comes in handy during normal user management duties. The Dialin Information dialog box shown in Figure 4.7 lets you configure both the dialin permission and the call back feature.

FIG. 4.7

Users now can be given RAS permission using User Manager for Domains.

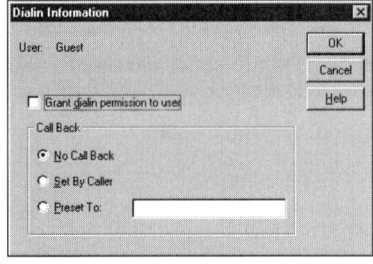

Using the call back feature to specify the return of calls to a known telephone number can heighten RAS security. For example, say your company wants to let employees call in from home, but they also are concerned about unauthorized users obtaining an authorized RAS user's account name and password. To ensure that the person calling in is actually the person who's been given RAS permissions, you can configure the call back feature to complete the RAS connection when a user calls in. The user calls in to the RAS server and is authenticated as a valid user with RAS permission. The system will then disconnect the user and hang up the modem line. It immediately calls back to the phone number designated in the "Preset To:" box of the user's Dialin Information dialog box.

This call back feature also works well for customer support organizations that use RAS to administer remotely customer computers over long distance phone lines. Setting the call back feature on the customer's RAS server allows the support organization to establish a RAS session without incurring the long distance charges. When a problem is reported at a remote site, support calls the customer. The customer's RAS server verifies that the support account is calling using the standard Windows NT authentication methods. Then the customer's RAS server hangs up and calls the support organization back to establish the session. Any long distance charges incurred by the support organization (for the original call) are limited due to the short duration of the call (usually fewer than 30 seconds).

If the Set by Caller option button is marked, the user calling into the RAS server will be authenticated. Then the RAS server l prompts the caller to provide a phone number that can be used for call back. After the number has been entered, the RAS server disconnects and calls the user back at that number.

User Rights versus Permissions

Part

II

Ch

4

After a user has an account on the Windows NT domain, he or she is given access to certain resources on the domain. These resources are really objects that the system controls user access to by using *permissions*. Permission granted to a user on a specific object allows the user to perform some type of action on the object. This could be a file read operation or a write operation to a printer queue.

The other type of security used with Windows NT is called the *User Rights Policy*. User rights are different than user permissions, because they specify the actions a user may perform on the system. For example, if a user is given the "Back up files and directories" right, the Windows NT Backup program executing in the security context of the user will have read permission on all the files in the domain. The backup rights will enable the user to backup all the files, regardless of the permissions that user has been granted to any files or shares.

The User Rights Policy dialog box shown in Figure 4.8 is accessed from the User Manager for Domains Policies menu.

FIG. 4.8
User Rights override permissions on objects.

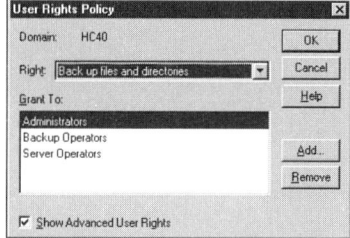

The most common user rights are listed with a description as follows:

- *Access this computer from network*   This right allows a user to connect to the computer over the network. When this right is specified in a domain environment, it permits the user to connect to all domain controllers within the domain. If this right is specified at the workstation level, it only applies to connections to the workstation and not to any other computers.

- *Add workstations to domain*   This right allows users to add workstations to the domain. When a workstation is added to a domain it can recognize the domain's user and global group accounts. This right is given to the Domain Administrators and Account Operators groups and cannot be revoked from them.

- *Back up files and directories*   When a user is given this right, he or she is allowed to supercede any share or NTFS permissions while performing backup operations. If this right is granted on a domain level, it gives that user backup rights on all domain controllers within the domain. If granted at the workstation level, it applies only to the workstation on which the right was granted.

- *Change the system time*   This right allows a user to change the system clock (or internal clock) on the computer. If this right is given at the domain level, it permits that user to set the time on all controllers within the domain. If set at the workstation level, it applies to the workstation only.

- *Load and unload device drivers*   Permits the user to dynamically load and unload device drivers. If the user is given this right at the domain level, it applies to all controllers within the domain. If this right is applied at the workstation level, it applies to the local machine only.

- *Log on locally*   This gives the user rights to log on to the server or workstation locally in addition to over the network. If this setting were applied at the domain level, the user would be allowed to log on to any domain controller. If applied at the workstation level, the user would be allowed local log on to that workstation only.

- *Manage auditing and security log*   If a user is given this right, he or she can manage the auditing of files, directories, and other objects by using the Security tab in the Properties dialog box of the object. This does give the user the ability to use the Audit feature on the Policies menu for configuring security events to be audited. Only Administrators have that ability. When this right is applied in a domain environment, it allows management on all controllers in the domain. When applied at the work-station level, it permits management at the workstation only.

- *Restore files and directories*   Gives the user the ability to restore files and directories to the computer and supersedes any share or NTFS permissions that may be in place. When applied at the domain level, it allows the restoration of files to all domain controllers. If applied at the workstation level, it allows the restoration of files to the local workstation only.

- *Shut down the system*   Allows the user to shut down the server or workstation. This right allows users to shut down any controller when applied at the domain level. It allows the user shutdown rights to the local computer when applied at the workstation level.

- *Take ownership of files or other objects*   Allows a user to take ownership of a file, directory, or other Windows NT objects. If applied at the domain level, users can take ownership of any object located on any domain controller. If applied at the workstation level, the user may take ownership of objects on the local computer only.

- *Bypass traverse checking*   This is an *advanced* user right that doesn't appear unless the "Show Advanced User Rights" check box is marked. With bypass traverse checking enabled, an individual's ability to access a file or directory object is based on the permissions listed for that specific directory. Any higher-level directory permissions has no effect on the user's ability to access the current directory. With bypass traverse checking disabled, the permissions of the higher level directories have a direct effect on what the user can do in the current directory. For example, John is given full permission to the server's "c:\documents" directory but has been denied access at the root directory "c:\". With bypass traverse checking enabled, John can have complete control of the "c:\documents" directory. With bypass traverse checking disabled, the system would see that John is denied access at the root directory for "c:\documents." Because he is denied access at the higher-level directory, he also is denied access to the lower-level directory. Bypass traverse checking is *enabled* for the group "Everyone" by default. When applied at the domain level, it affects the user's right on all controllers. If applied at the workstation level, it applies to the local workstation only.

- *Log on as a service*   This is an advanced user right that allows a user to be registered with the system as a service. This right typically is given to accounts that are used by some application service that must log on during system startup. If the right is applied at the domain level, it allows the account to log on as a service on any controller in the domain. If applied at the workstation level, it restricts the right to the local workstation.

Part
II

Ch
4

Several other advanced user rights also can be configured; however, they are usually reserved for programmers that are writing Windows NT applications and not normally applied to system users.

Creating User Groups

This section looks at the concept of the user groups and how they're used to simplify the domain administration task. You learn about two types of groups that are used within the Windows NT domain environment. The first type of group, the *Local* group, can contain user accounts from the local domain and user accounts from any *trusted* domains. They also can contain other groups called *Global* groups. Global groups only contain local domain user accounts, but they can traverse domains that have trust relationships in place. You can take a closer look at the difference between Local and Global groups a little later in the chapter. For now, let's find out exactly what a user group is.

What Is a User Group?   A *group* is a collection of individual user accounts that each inherits the permissions or rights given to that group. This makes the task of assigning user privileges much easier by allowing permissions for an object to be assigned to many users at once. The idea is to assign permissions for an object (file share, printer queue, and so on) to the group, then add users to the group. Groups also are utilized in Windows NT to delegate administrative control of the system to specific user accounts.

Several built-in groups exist within Windows NT that provide their members with some type of control over the system (or its users). Before you learn the specific types of built-in user groups, you need to examine the difference between Local Groups and Global Groups.

Local Groups versus Global Groups   A Global group only contains user accounts, it does not contain other group accounts. Moreover, the Global group only contains local user accounts from the domain in which the Global group was created. Global groups can be given access permissions to specific objects such as file, directories, shares, and print queues. But that's not the way they were intended to be used.

Now you might be thinking, "If they're not used to grant permissions or rights to users, what are they used for?" They're used to place users into Local groups.

Here's how it works. User accounts go into Global groups, Global groups go into Local groups. Table 4.3 outlines how it works.

Table 4.3 Local and Global Group Usage

Account Type	Needs Access To	Use this Group
Local domain User Account	Domain controllers, member servers, and domain workstations from the local or trusting domain(s)	Global group
Local domain User Account or a trusted domain User Account	Local domain controllers	Local group
Global groups from the local domain or from trusted domains	Local domain controllers	Local group

You'll understand it better after we've completed our discussion on trust relationships. For now just be aware that Global groups can traverse domains when a trust relationship is in place. Local groups cannot traverse domains, but they can contain Global groups from a *trusted* domain. It will all make sense soon.

Built-in User Groups Several built-in user groups exist within the Windows NT operating system. Each group is granted specific rights and capabilities that permit its members to perform certain administrative functions on the system. For example, members of the Print Operators group can start and stop the sharing of printers. This makes it easy to assign various administrative privileges to users by simply adding them to the appropriate user group. In fact, that's the only way to give users the ability to perform most administrative functions. Although you can assign specific rights (such as change the system time) to individual accounts with the User Policy, administrative abilities (such as creating and managing user accounts) are delegated by assigning the user to one of the built-in administrative accounts.

Most of the built-in user groups are local groups. This means they can have users and global groups from trusted domains as members, as well as users and global groups from the local domain. There are three built-in groups that are global groups:

- Domain Admins
- Domain Users
- Domain Guest

Members of these groups can be allowed to perform operations within a trusting domain. This is accomplished by placing the global group (that the user is a member of) in the appropriate local built-in administrative group on the trusting domain. For example, you could have all the members of the Domain Users group perform account management in a trusting domain. Adding the Domain Users group from the trusted domain to the Account Operators group on the trusting domain would do this. Once again, this will become easier to understand once the concept of trust relationships has been covered. For now, let's look at the various local built-in groups and see what type of administrative control each gives to its members. Table 4.4 shows you the local built-in groups that exist for controllers, member servers, and workstations.

Table 4.4 Local Built-In User Group Description

Group Name	Group Location	Description
Administrators	Domain Controllers, Member Servers, and Workstations	Allows members full administrative control of the computer and domain controllers and is the only group automatically granted every built-in right and capability. The Domain Admins global group is a member of this group by default; however, it may be removed.
Backup Operators	Domain Controllers, Member Servers, and Workstations	The members of this group can back up and restore files on domain controllers regardless of any applied permissions on the files or directories. They also are given the right to log on locally at the servers and shut them down.
Server Operators	Domain Controllers, Member Servers, and Workstations	Server operators manage the resources available on the domain. They can create, manage, and delete both printer and network shares. They also can format the server's hard drives, backup and restore files, lock and unlock the server, change the system time, log on locally, and shut down the server.
Account Operators	Domain Controllers, Member Servers, and Workstations	Permits its members to run User Manager for Domains and create, modify, and delete most user accounts and groups. They cannot modify or delete the Domain Admins group, the other Operator groups, Administrator's group, or members of these

Group Name	Group Location	Description
		groups. They can log on locally and shut down the server. They also can add computers to the domain using Server Manager.
Print Operators	Domain Controllers, Member Servers, and Workstations	The members of this group can create, delete, and manage printer shares on the domain controllers. They can log on locally and shut down the server.
Users	Domain Controllers	Allows users to log on locally to workstations but not servers. The Domain User group is a member of this group, but it may be removed.
Guests	Domain Controllers	Grants limited "one time" access to infrequent users of the system. It permits guests limited access to workstations, but gives no server access rights to the individual. The Guest global group is a member of this local group by default, but it may be removed.
Replicator	Domain Controllers	Supports directory replication functions and should only contain the service account used in conjunction with the Replicator service. This group should not contain any other user accounts.

Part
II

Ch
4

The system also creates other *special* groups that are not listed in User Manager for Domains but are sometimes listed when assigning permissions. The membership in these groups is set by the system and is not configurable. Therefore, they do not appear in the User Manager for Domains utility. The special groups are as follows:

- *Everyone* This group contains all local and remote (Interactive and Network) users on the system. By default this group is given access to the network. They can be given to network resources such as network and printer shares.
- *Interactive* Anyone logged on to the computer locally.
- *Network* Anyone logged on to the computer over the network.
- *System* The operating system.
- *Creator Owner* Used to assign or transfer permissions to the creators of a file, directory, or print job.

The three built-in global groups that exist on all domain controllers are the following:

- *Domain Admins* By default, this group is a member of the local administrator's group on the domain, and it also is a member of the local administrator's group on both servers and workstations. The built-in Administrator user account is a member of the Domain Admins group by default. This membership enables the individual logged on under the Administrator user account to administer all controllers in the domain, as well as all other Windows NT Servers and Workstations in the domain. Adding a user account to the Domain Admins group permits that account to perform full administrative functions within the domain or on the member workstation or server. Administration of a trusting domain can be accomplished by adding the Domain Admins global group from the trusted domain to the Administrator's group of the trusting domain. Administrators are the only users who can modify this group. This group cannot be deleted.

- *Domain Users* All new accounts that are added to a domain become members of the global Domain Users group. Initially, the only account in this group is the Administrator user account. The Domain Users group is a member of the local Users group for the domain and for any Windows NT Workstations or member servers. This enables new users normal access to the resources available on the domains, workstations, or member's servers. Only Administrators and Account Operators can modify this group. This group cannot be deleted.

- *Domain Guests* This group initially contains the built-in Guest user account and belongs to the domain Guest local group. It allows restricted access to the resources contained in the domain. Place individuals in this group that only need limited access to the domain's resources. The Administrators and Account Operators can modify this group. This group cannot be deleted.

From Here...

This chapter shows you how domains create manageable groups of computers with a common security accounts database. In the following chapters, you see how domains can be linked using trust relationships. The information presented in the next few chapters also helps clarify any questions you may have regarding the operation of local and global user groups.

Here are some of the topics covered in upcoming chapters:

■ Chapter 5, "Maintaining Security with Domain Trust Relationships," explains the trust relationship. This alliance between separate domains enables the centralized administration of user accounts and resources on multiple domains.

■ Chapter 6, "User Account Security and Windows NT," takes a closer look at the authentication process and how it works across trusted and non-trusted domains. This chapter also looks at the Windows NT registry parameters associated with user accounts.

■ Chapter 11, "Implementation Steps," studies the setup of a Master Domain Model that was planned in Chapter 10, "Planning the Master Domain." You see how the domain structure is set up in a sample installation.

■ Chapter 12, "Setting Up Trust Relationships," further expands on the example from Chapter 11 by setting up the various trust relationships needed to satisfy your installation requirements.

Part

II

Ch

4

Maintaining Security with Domain Trust Relationships

This chapter answers some questions you may have about trust relationships and their purpose. We start by giving you an idea of what a trust relationship is and why it's used. The different types of domains that you can set up are shown as well as the types of domains present on your network, which are a determining factor when you decide which of the trust models you want to implement. The trust models offer benefits that help the administrators control the resources available on the network.

Let's begin by taking a look at the concept of a trust relationship between domains. Actually, trust relationships can involve many domains and be complicated. You start with the function of a basic trust relationship between two domains, then you move to more complicated trust setups between multiple domains. ■

What Is a Trust Relationship?

In small organizations that have a relatively simple network, a single Windows NT domain usually works well. The administrative responsibilities for different areas of the network easily can be distributed by implementing the built-in user groups that Windows NT Server provides. However, larger organizations with multiple departments may not be suited to having a single domain hosting all the resources of the network. Trust relationships enable the administration of network user accounts from a central location by one group, while at the same time providing a means of localized management for the resources available on the network by different groups. Simply put, trust relationships link two or more domains together for the purpose of using a common security accounts database.

This means you can give administrative duties for maintaining the accounts database to one group in its own domain, say the company's administration department in an *account domain*. And you can give individual department managers control of their local resources, such as directory and printer shares, in their own separate *resource domains*. For example, the documentation department can control access to the printers they use, and the accounting department can control access to the accounting files. The concept of account domains and resource domains is discussed in more detail later in this chapter.

From a security standpoint, this makes sense, because it limits the number of user accounts on the system to one account for each individual. When a person joins the organization, only one network account has to be created and configured, and when a person leaves the organization only one account needs to be removed from the system. At the same time trust relationships enable you to distribute easily the administrative control and ownership of resources between the individual departments. The administrator of the department's resources can allow a member of the central account database (a network user account) access to the resources contained within his or her respective domains as he or she sees fit. This gives you more diversity in the way your network and its resources can be administered. The flexibility of Windows NT trust relationships makes it possible to set up tiers of administrative responsibility that can be organized in a way that suits your specific needs.

Trusted and *trusting* are two terms used frequently during this discussion of domains. Each term refers to the domain's role in the trust relationship. To help you better understand these terms, we'll bring back Ed, an old friend from Chapter 2, "An Overview of Microsoft Windows NT Security." He's the user that you'll work with in the trust relationship examples. Although it may seem silly at first, you'll see how Ed can keep the two terms *trusted* and *trusting* from being confused with one another. Before you look at the terms *trusted* and *trusting*, you first should get an idea of how trust relationships are most often used.

Account Domains versus Resource Domains

As mentioned earlier, trust relationships are most often set up to allow one central user-account database to exist. Although many domains can exist on the network, each of which has its own account database, only a single-account database will exist that contains account information for users of the network. This central-account database is then used by administrators in other domains to grant permissions to resources by way of the trust relationships that have been set up.

The use of one domain as the *accounts* domain with other domains being used as *resource* domains is the most common way that trust relationships are used. The domain that contains the SAM database with the network's user accounts in it is the accounts domain, while other domains containing the resources for individual departments are called *resource domains* (see Figure 5.1). Resource domains have network resources that are made available to users of the network. A couple examples of shared resources would be printers and directory shares.

FIG. 5.1
Setting up one domain as the user-accounts domain.

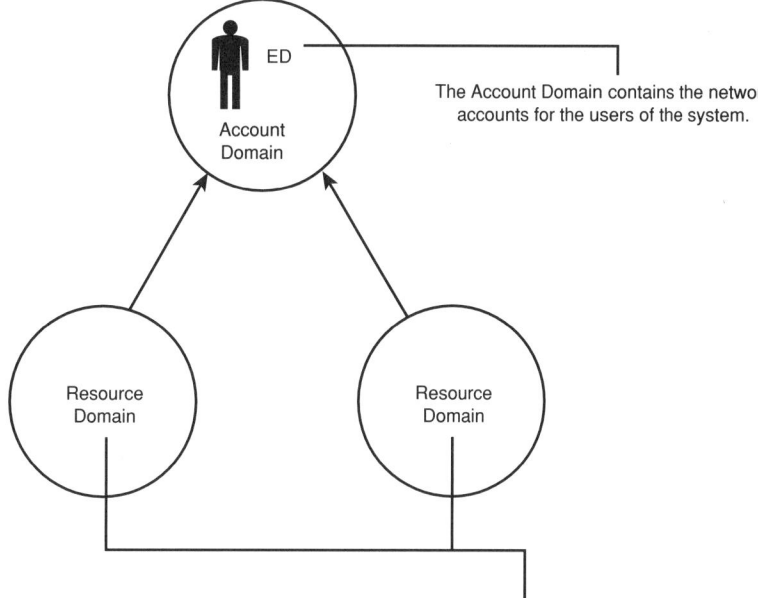

ED

Account Domain

The Account Domain contains the network accounts for the users of the system.

Resource Domain

Resource Domain

The Resource Domains contain file and print resources controlled by individual departments.

Part

II

Ch

5

You can see in the illustration that the arrows between the account and resource domains point to the account domain. This is typically the way that domain trust relationships are diagrammed to show the direction of the trust. The domain that the arrows point to is always the *trusted* domain, while the domains on the other end of the arrows are the *trust-ing* domains. The account and resource domains are shown again in Figure 5.2, but now they are shown in the context of a trusted and trusting domain.

FIG. 5.2

Looking at the trust relationship in terms of trusted and trusting domains.

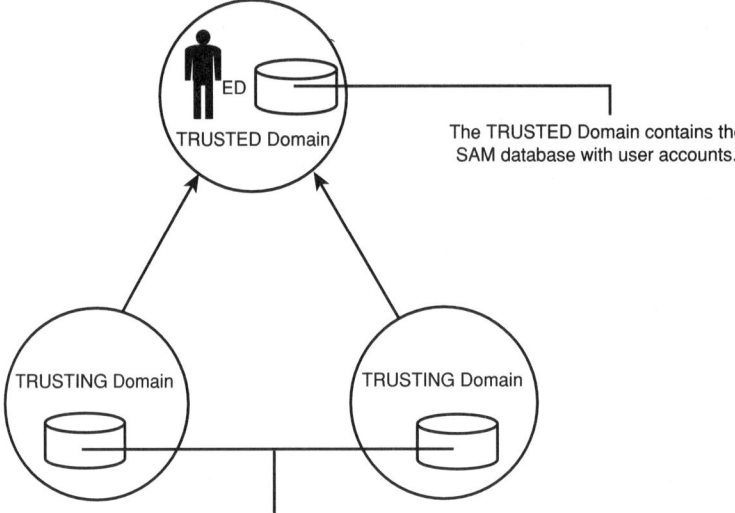

The TRUSTED Domain contains the SAM database with user accounts.

The TRUSTING Domains each have their own SAM database, but no user accounts are added to them.

The naming syntax is easier to remember if you think of the trusted domain as the domain with our user Ed in it, or the trust-Ed (trusted) domain. This really can help you keep the meaning of the two terms straight when discussing trust relationships.

 Here's a tip to remember when working with complex trust relationships: Plan the trust relation-ships between multiple domains by drawing them using circles and arrows. The arrows always point to the trusting domain. It's much easier to understand the flow of security between domains if you use the circle and arrow approach, as shown here, to illustrate the trust relationships. If you ever take any of Microsoft's Certified Professional exams for Windows NT Server, you'll find several questions that pertain to domains and trust relationships. Using that piece of paper they give you before the test to diagram the questions will save you time, and it just might help you get the correct solution to the question. It really works.

Knowing what a trust relationship is used for, you may wonder how this security link between two domains actually works. How are users that belong to one domain allowed access to the resources on a completely different domain—one on which they have no individual account?

The administrative answer to that question is given in Chapter 4, "Windows NT Domain Concepts" when user groups are outlined. The technical answer to that question is given later in this chapter. For now, let's take a look at the administrative functions that trust relationships provide.

In Chapter 4, "Windows NT Domain Concepts," you see that in addition to user accounts, domains also contain local and global group accounts. A table explaining the different ways groups are used and showing how groups make more sense with trust relationships is there. Hopefully, this is where that promise is made good, and the group concept starts making more sense if it's not clear already. The table in Chapter 4 is shown again for your reference as Table 5.1.

Table 5.1   Local and Global Group Usage

Account Type	Needs Access to	Use this group
Local domain User Account	Domain controllers, member servers, and domain workstations from the local or trusting domain(s).	Global group
Local domain User Account or a trusted domain User Account	Local domain controllers	Local group
Global groups from the local domain or from trusted domains	Local domain controllers	Local group

Part

Ch

5

You want to focus on domain users that need access to resources in a trusting domain. The table says that you have a local domain user account that needs to have access to the following:

- *Domain Controllers*   The user needs access to the resources located on the domain controllers in the same domain that the user's account is in. And the user needs access to resources on controllers located in trusting domains. The trusting domain contains its own SAM database that does not contain a local account for the user.

- *Member Servers*   The user needs access to a resource located on a member server in the user's own domain, or on a member server located on a trusting domain. The member server has its own local SAM database that does not contain an account for the user.

■ *Domain Workstations*   The user needs access to a resource located on a Windows NT Workstation in the user's own domain or on a Windows NT Workstation located in a trusting domain. The Windows NT Workstation has its own local SAM database that does not contain an account for the user.

Notice that the table refers to the user accounts as *local domain user accounts*. This identifies a user account in its home domain, or in the same domain that the account was created in. This should not be confused with the type of user account that has been *assigned* to an individual.

In Chapter 4, "Windows NT Domain Concepts," the section "Creating a User Account in a Domain" covers the account settings that can be specified for each user. The option of specifying the user as having either a *global* or *local* account is available both during and after the account setup. The global account can be used to give a user access to both local domain resources and resources on trusting domains. The only purpose of the local user account is to allow you to create accounts for users that already have log-on accounts in *untrusted* domains. This is done so they can access the resources available on your domain. The local accounts cannot be used for logging on within the domain in which they are created. For example, if you create a user account named LocalUser in the ADMIN domain and then try to log on to the ADMIN domain using the new account, it fails. You receive a message saying that the user name can't be found.

A local user account can be added to both local and global groups. However, it will permit the remote domain user access to only those resources within the local domain. If the local account happens to be placed into a global group, the user will not have any transitory access to resources on the other trusting domain that the global group has been given access to.

The default account type is set to global when the user account is created. There are two reasons global accounts are created instead of local accounts, and they are as follows:

■ So the user can log on to the domain. Local user accounts cannot log on directly to the domain in which they were created.

■ To let users access resources located in other trusting domains.

To understand how access across trusting domains works, you go through an example of setting up a trust relationship. Then you can use the trust relationship by giving user accounts in the accounts domain access to resources in the resources domain.

Set up this example using two domains. One of the domains will be your account domain called ADMIN. The other domain will be your resource domain called SHARES. The SHARES domain won't contain any user accounts except for the built-in ones.

The SHARES domain will have directory shares located on assorted servers within the domain that our user Ed will need access to.

Before you can give Ed any sort of access to the resources located on the SHARES domain, you first need to set up a trust relationship between it and the ADMIN domain. If you don't set up a trust, the only way that Ed will be able to access the resources located on the SHARES domain is if he is given a duplicate account name and password on that domain. Because that is what you are attempting to avoid, set up the trust relationship.

Establishing Trust Relationships

Establishing the trust between ADMIN and SHARES is a simple procedure accomplished by using the User Manager for Domains utility. Before you actually set up the trust relationship, let's draw the trust relationship using circles and arrows to show the direction of trust (see Figure 5.3).

FIG. 5.3

The trust relationship between ADMIN and SHARES.

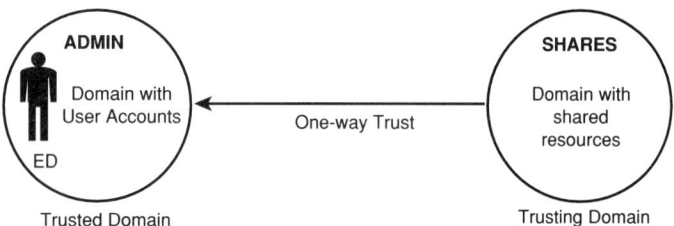

Your circle and arrow drawing helps you identify the ADMIN domain as the trusted domain and the SHARES domain as the trusting domain. Now that we've determined which one of the domains is the trusted domain and which one is the trusting domain, you easily can go ahead and set up the trust relationship.

To begin, an Administrator in the ADMIN domain (your trusted domain) must run the User Manager for Domain Utility and specify the name of the trusting domain and create a password. The Administrator of the SHARES domain (your trusting domain) will run the User Manager for Domains utility and will specify the name of the trusted domain. Then the password created by the Administrator of the ADMIN domain will be used by the Administrator of the SHARES domain to complete the setup of the trust relationship. Having the administrator of the trusting domain supply a password provides an effective way to prevent unauthorized trust relationships from being put into place.

Let's go through the steps required to set up a trust relationship between the ADMIN and SHARES domains. We'll start with the steps taken by the administrator of the ADMIN domain. Follow the steps listed here to set up a trust relationship:

Part

II

Ch

5

N O T E   Substitute the name of your trusted domain for the name ADMIN and the name of
your trusting domain for the name SHARES in the following examples. ▪

1. Log on to one of the ADMIN domain controllers as Administrator, or as a user that
   is a member of the Administrators group.

2. Run the User Manager for Domains utility located in the Administrative tools group.

3. From the Policies menu choose Trust Relationships. This opens the Trust
   Relationships dialog box. Make sure that the name of the domain that's given at the
   top of the dialog box is ADMIN (i.e., the name of your trusted domain). If it's not
   ADMIN you're focused on the wrong domain. Change the focus of User Manager
   for Domains to the trusted domain by using the Select domain option on the User
   menu.

4. Two boxes appear in the Trust Relationships dialog box. Click the Add button next
   to the Trusting Domains: box to reveal the Add Trusting Domain dialog box.

5. Next to Trusting Domain, type in the name **SHARES**.

6. In the Initial Password box, type in the password of your choice (example: password). Retype the password in the box labeled Confirm Password and click the OK
   button. The completed Trusting Domains dialog box is shown in Figure 5.4.

FIG. 5.4

Enter information for
the trusting domain.

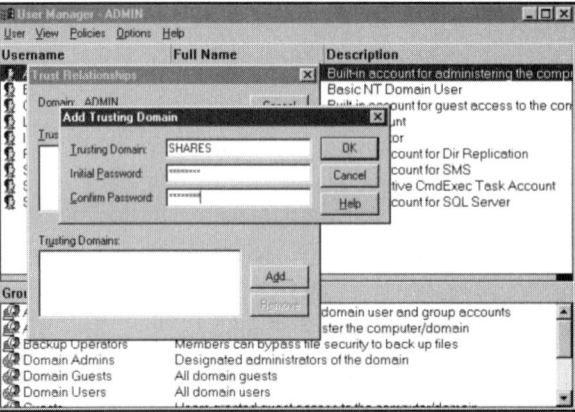

7. The name SHARES now should appear in the Trusting Domains: box as shown in
   Figure 5.5. Click the Close button to close the Trust Relationships dialog box. You
   can close the User Manager for Domains utility.

8. Give the administrator of the SHARES domain the password you specified in Step 6.

FIG. 5.5

The completed Trust dialog box on the trusted domain.

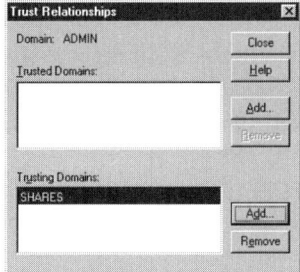

Before the trust relationship is completed, the administrator of the ADMIN domain must give the password (the one he or she specified during his or her portion of the setup) to the administrator of the SHARES domain. Then the administrator of the SHARES domain performs the following steps:

1. Log on to one of the SHARES domain controllers as Administrator, or as a user that is a member of the Administrators group.

2. Run the User Manager for Domains utility located in the Administrative tools group.

3. From the Policies menu choose Trust Relationships. This opens the Trust Relationships dialog box. Make sure that the name of the domain that's given at the top of the dialog box is SHARES (i.e., the name of your trusting domain). If it's not SHARES, you're on the wrong domain. Change the focus of User Manager for Domains to the trusted domain by using the Select domain option on the User menu.

4. Two boxes appear in the Trust Relationships dialog box. Click the Add button next to the Trusted Domains box. The Add Trusted Domain dialog box appears.

5. Type in the name **ADMIN** in the Domain box.

6. Type in the password provided by the administrator of the ADMIN domain (Step 6 in the ADMIN setup instructions.) The completed dialog box is shown in Figure 5.6. Click OK to continue.

FIG. 5.6

Supply the password given by the ADMIN domain administrator.

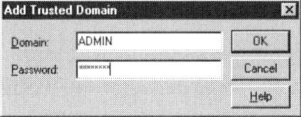

A dialog box may appear telling you that the trust relationship could not be verified at this time. This can occur when you (or your computer) have any type of open connections to the trusted domain controller. This is normal. Click the OK button to continue. Otherwise, you should see a message such as the one in Figure 5.7 telling you that the trust relationship has been verified.

FIG. 5.7
The trust setup
is completed
successfully.

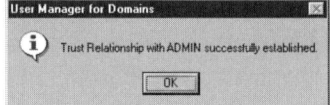

7. The name ADMIN now appears in the <u>T</u>rusted Domains box as shown in Figure 5.8. Click the Close button to close the Trust Relationships dialog box and return to the User Manager for Domains program.

FIG. 5.8
The ADMIN domain will
be listed as a trusted
domain.

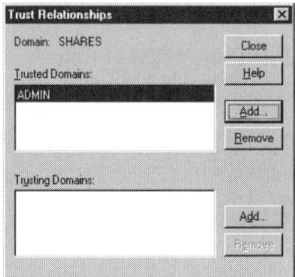

8. You now can exit the User Manager for Domains program.

The type of trust that you have just set up is called a *one-way trust* relationship. It's called a one-way trust because the users from the ADMIN domain are able to access the resources on the SHARES domain, but any users that might exist on the SHARES domain cannot access the resources available on the ADMIN domain.

The One-Way Trust Relationship

As the name implies, this trust relationship works in one direction. Users in domain A have access to the resources on domain B, but users on domain B do not have access to resources on domain A unless they have a duplicate account on domain A.

Use the trust relationship you set up between the ADMIN and SHARES domains as an example. This means a user that specifies the ADMIN domain in the log-on dialog box can be permitted access to SHARES domain's resources. They can do this *without* having a duplicate account name and password on the SHARES domain. However, any user that specifies the SHARES domain in the log-on dialog box must have a valid user account name and password (or be able to supply them) on the ADMIN domain to be permitted access to any of ADMIN's resources.

The reason we set up the trust relationship was so that we could give our network user Ed access to the resources on the SHARES domain without having duplicate accounts for him. Now that we have the trust relationship in place, we can give our network user Ed access to the resources on the SHARES domain.

Using Groups in a Trusting Domain   There are two ways to give Ed access to resources located within the SHARES domain using the trust relationship we set up. The first method grants resource access on the SHARES domain to Ed as an individual. The second method grants resource access on the SHARES domain to Ed based on his group membership(s).

Although it is possible, the first method is not preferred because it involves micro-management of user accounts. It's much easier if users are placed into the appropriate global groups and if these groups are placed in the appropriate local groups. This way, users are granted resource access by placing them in the proper groups, not by granting the individual access. This is evident in the way the Add Users and Groups dialog box presents itself when you're assigning access permissions to a resource. By default, only the groups are listed within the dialog box's Names window. To assign access to a specific individual, you first must select the Show Users button.

Before the user account is created, global groups usually have been predefined and placed in the proper local groups that provide the appropriate resource access. Users easily can be given the appropriate permissions to any trusted domain resource at the time their user accounts are created simply by adding them to proper global group(s). User accounts don't need to be manually given permission to resources on the trusting domain, or the local domain for that matter. It is a much more efficient way of managing users and resources.

Let's use an example with our network user Ed and the trust relationship between the ADMIN and SHARES domains. You set up your trust relationship with ADMIN as the *account* domain because the user accounts for Ed's company are contained within its SAM database. Our other domain, SHARES, doesn't have any user accounts because it's only a *resource* domain. But it does have shared file directories that network users such as Ed need access to. The SHARES domain has a file server that is used to store common document templates used by Ed's research department. These templates are stored in a directory on the server named FILE_SERVER1 under the resource share name of TEMPLATES. In order to give Ed and the other members of his department access to the share, several things are done.

First, a custom global group is created on the ADMIN domain that contains the user accounts that belong to the members of Ed's department. This global group is called "Research Team" and is created by the administrator of the ADMIN domain using the User Manager for Domains utility. The following procedure is used to create the custom global group:

1. Select the New Global Group option from the User menu to open the New Global Group dialog box.
2. Enter the name Research Team in the Group Name field.
3. A brief description of the group should be entered in the Description field.
4. Each of the research group member's names listed in the Not Members windows is added to the Members windows by highlighting the names and clicking the Add button. The completed dialog box is shown in Figure 5.9.
5. Click the OK button to save the custom group.

FIG. 5.9

Adding users to a custom global group.

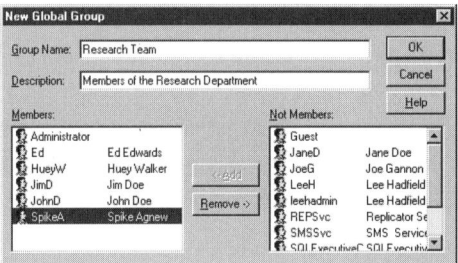

When the TEMPLATES share was created on FILE_SERVER1, a local group also was created on the SHARES domain. This local group, called Templates Group was created with the sole purpose of providing access to the TEMPLATES share. To better understand this, we'll go through the steps needed to create the Templates Group local group. Then we'll go through the steps of creating the actual TEMPLATES share and assigning share permissions to it.

The Administrator of the SHARES domain uses the User Manager for Domains utility to create the local group and assign the ADMIN global groups membership in it. The steps listed here are used to create the Templates Group local group in the SHARES domain, as follows:

1. Select the New Local Group option from the Users drop-down menu. This opens the New Local Group dialog box.
2. Enter Templates Group in the Group Name field.
3. Enter a brief description of the group in the Description field.

4. Select the Add button. This opens the Add Users and Groups dialog box.

5. Change the List Names From drop-down list from the default selection of SHARES to ADMIN. Dropping the list down and selecting ADMIN does this. The ADMIN selection is listed because of the trust relationship you put in place. The names and groups listed within the Names window now reflect the users and global groups from the ADMIN domain instead of the SHARES domain (see Figure 5.10).

FIG. 5.10

Selecting the ADMIN global groups.

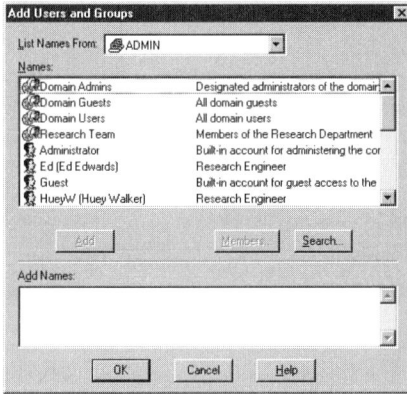

6. Highlight the global group named Research Team and click the Add button. This places the ADMINS\Research Team entry in the Add Names window as shown in Figure 5.11.

FIG. 5.11

Assign membership to the ADMIN global group.

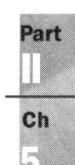

Part
II
Ch
5

7. Click the OK button to add the Research Team global group to the names listed in the Members window of the Local Group Properties dialog box (see Figure 5.12). Click OK again to complete the creation of the local group.

FIG. 5.12

The completed
custom local group
with members.

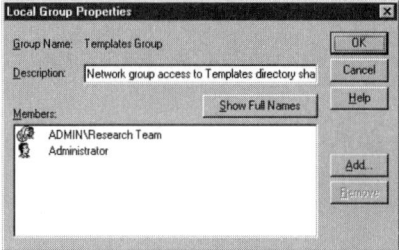

After the groups are created, the next task is to create the TEMPLATES share and assign
the access permissions to it. This is done at the FILE_SERVER1 machine using the Windows NT Explorer. It also could have been done using Server Manager or the My Computer file manager window. To create and assign access to the TEMPLATES share, follow
these steps:

1. Open Windows NT Explorer and highlight the file directory that will be shared as
   the Templates share (such as d:\docs\templates). Then right-click to open the drop-
   down option menu for the directory.

2. Click the Properties option to open up the Properties dialog box for the directory.
   Select the Sharing tab.

3. On the Sharing page, select the option button next to Shared As.

4. Change the Share Name to TEMPLATES and add a brief comment to the Comment
   field.

5. Click the Permissions button to open the Access Through Share Permissions dialog
   box. By default the Everyone group is given Full Control. This effectively lets
   anyone with a user account on the network access the template share and perform
   any operation they want. You don't care if any users on the network use the templates, but you don't want anyone but the members of the research department to
   be able to modify the templates. For this reason, you change the Everyone Group's
   access to that of read-only by selecting READ from the Type of Access drop-down
   list.

6. The local Templates group is given Full Control to the share by clicking the Add
   button to open the Add Users and Groups dialog box.

7. SHARES, the default domain choice, already should be displayed in the List Names
   From drop-down list. If it is not, click the List Names From drop-down list to display
   the SHARES domain groups. Highlight the "Templates Group" local group.

8. Click the Add button to add the Templates Group entry to the Add Names window.

9. Select Full Control from the Type of Access drop-down list and then click the OK button. This adds the Templates Group local group entry in the Access Through Share Permissions dialog box as shown in Figure 5.13.

FIG. 5.13
Full control access
is granted to the
Templates Group,
which is a local group.

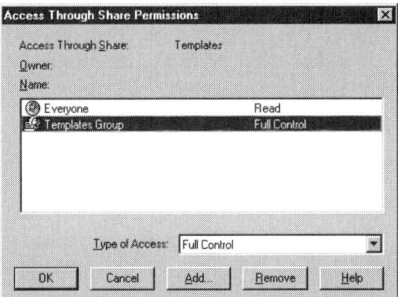

Now Ed and the other members of the Research department can access the template file directory located on the SHARES domain without having a user account on the SHARES domain. The advantage to this arrangement becomes more apparent as the size of the company (and its network system) grows. Why? Because it reduces the administrative overhead required to maintain the security of the system.

Using this method, the access privileges for any resource can be predefined with local groups. Those local groups also are predefined with any global group memberships that may be required to give users from trusted domains the access to local domain resources. The big advantage to this is that share permissions can be set once and then left alone.

The resource permissions for any shares on the domain do not need to be modified when users are added and deleted from the system. When a new account is added to the network, it simply is assigned membership in the appropriate global groups. The group memberships give the user account access to any resources it may need access to. If the user needs his or her permissions for an area of the network expanded or restricted, just add or delete him or her from the appropriate groups. When a user is removed from the network, he or she automatically is removed from any groups he or she may have been a member of. No further management is needed to close out that user's account and keep the system secure.

The Two-Way Trust Relationship

A two-way trust relationship between domains actually means that a one way trust relationship has been set up in both directions. This usually is done because both domains contain user accounts that need access to resources on the other domain. Or, as you'll see shortly, a two-way trust is used when implementing the *Multiple Master* domain model to split a large user accounts database.

Setting up a two-way trust relationship is simple. Follow the procedures for setting up a one-way trust between domains, first on domain A. Then perform the same setup on domain B. If you wanted to set up a two-way trust between the domains ADMIN and SHARES, you could just go ahead and perform the same steps, except you would reverse the domain names. You would start the setup of the trust on the SHARES domain, because it would be the trusted domain. The administrator of the SHARES domain would then need to provide the password to the administrator of the ADMIN domain so he or she could complete the trust setup on his or her side.

You also may have noticed that you're setting up the trusted domain's side of the relationship before you set up the trusting side. This is the preferred method, because the trusting domain can have its access password verified immediately by the trusted domain. If we set up the trusting domain first, the trusting domain isn't able to validate the trust setup with the trusted domain. Validation will not occur until the trusted domain has been given the trusting domain's name and access password. Then instead of getting an immediate confirmation of the trust setup, you'll have to monitor the event log to see if the trust relationship setup was successful.

Controller Interaction

Up to this point you have been dealing with administrative functions related to creating domain and trust relationships that ultimately simplify the management of user security. Some of you must be interested in what's happening between the security systems of the two domains, or "under the hood" so to speak. In this section you see some of the interactions that take place between domain controllers when validating the authenticity of a user or account on a trusted domain. This also exposes the network activity created by this process, and the interactions that take place between domain controllers. This interaction is minimal, but it ultimately consumes a certain amount of your network bandwidth.

Those are the administrative activities that take place before a trust relationship is capable of providing access to resources in a trusting domain. What you need to know now is the system process that takes place when a trust relationship is established between two domains. We also want to look at the communication that takes place between the domains when the trust is established. In order to do this, we are going to be using a tool (available with Windows NT 4.0 Server and System Management Server) to monitor the traffic between domains during the trust setup. This enables you to see how the domain controllers talk to each other when you initiate the trust relationship.

We don't want to get too far off track, but you should know some security issues related to the use of the Network Monitor.

Security Issues with Network Monitor

The Network Monitor is a powerful tool that can be used to capture network packets and interpret them without any special equipment. It simply utilizes any compatible network card that can be placed into the *promiscuous* mode to provide detailed packet information. This is a security issue for networks, because it can be used to gather sensitive or confidential information directly off the wire.

Fortunately, the version of Network Monitor included with Windows NT 4.0 Server only captures packets that are directed to the local adapter on the server (in addition to network broadcast packets). This prevents any user logged on at the server (with the readily available Windows NT 4.0 Server version of the Network Monitor installed) from monitoring all the network traffic that's generated on the wire. The version of Network Monitor that ships with *Systems Management Server (SMS)* is the only version that permits the monitoring of the entire network and connection to remote adapters.

CAUTION

The version of Network Monitor that ships with Systems Management Server is much more powerful than the Windows NT Server version. This is because it enables the monitoring of all network traffic, not just broadcast traffic or packets directed to the local machine's adapter. For this reason, you should restrict the installation of the SMS version of Network Monitor and its subsequent use to authorized individuals only.

Part

II

Ch

5

Both versions provide the capability to monitor the network for other instances of Network Monitor (see Figure 5.14). This feature reports if any other copies of Network Monitor have been installed on your network, if they are running, and if they are currently capturing data. Other information provided lets you know the name of the machine on which any copies are installed or running, and the name of the user account running the Network Monitor. It also provides the *MAC (Media Access Control)* layer address of the network card, and the version of Network Monitor installed or running on that machine. This permits you to monitor the network actively for users running the Network Monitor.

N O T E Many companies have strict rules that forbid the use of the Network Monitor by the network system users. Their networks are continuously monitored for unauthorized instances of Network Monitor. Any violation of the policy is considered to be a serious security threat.

FIG. 5.14
Information on other
instances of Network
Monitor.

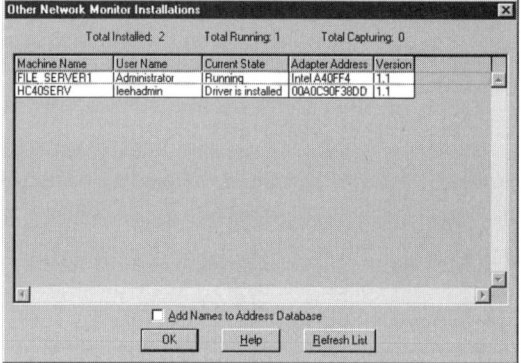

You will be using some information gathered by Network Monitor during the setup of the
ADMIN/SHARES trust relationship. Some of the packets collected at that time will be
used to illustrate the communication that takes place between the domain controllers.
Now let's go on to look at what happens when you initiate a trust relationship between two
domains.

What Happens During a Trust Setup

Several things take place when a trust relationship is established between two domains.
In order to implement the trust, an *interdomain trust account* is created in the directory
database of the trusted domain. This account is created when the administrator of the
trusted domain defines the trusting domain using the administrative application User
Manager for Domains.

Earlier in the chapter you set up a trust relationship between the ADMIN and SHARES
domains; the interdomain trust account actually was being set up when you performed
the trusted domain (ADMIN) portion of the setup. When the trusted side of the relationship was set up, you provided the name of the domain that would be the trusting domain.
You also provided a password. The subsequent account that was created is nothing
more than a standard global user account that has the USER_INTERDOMAIN_TRUST_
ACCOUNT bit in its control field set. As you'll see, this bit identifies the account as an
account used for trust relationships only. The account is not visible in the User Manager
for Domains listing of accounts and cannot be modified. Each of the domain controllers in
the ADMIN domain contains the interdomain trust account object in their SAM database.
The password you created during the trust setup is contained within this object and is
used when establishing a session with the trusting domain.

You may view the interdomain trust account for the ADMIN/SHARES domain trust relationship by opening the Windows NT registry editor on the ADMIN *Primary Domain Controller (PDC)*. The account is located within the following HKEY_LOCAL_MACHINE subtree on the *trusted domain* controller's registry:

\SAM\SAM\Domains\Accounts\Users\Names

The account key for our interdomain trust account from the ADMIN/SHARES example is shown in Figure 5.15.

FIG. 5.15
The SAM contains a registry entry for the interdomain trust account.

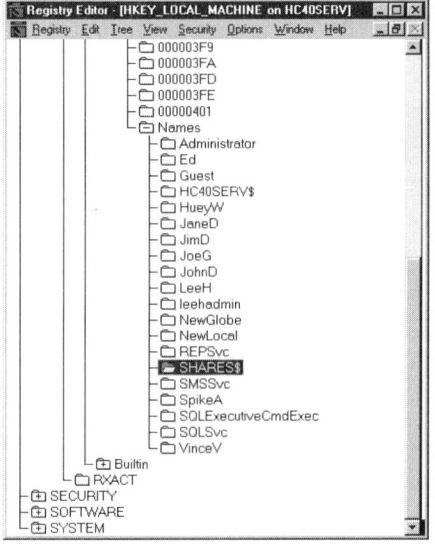

The interdomain trust accounts name will appear as the trusting domain's name (SHARES in this example) with a dollar sign ($) tagged on the end. The name of the account created in our example is SHARE$.

In addition to the interdomain trust account that's created on the trusted domain, the *Local Security Authority (LSA)* of the trusting domain creates a *trusted-domain object* and a *secret object*. The trusted-domain domain object represents the trust and contains the name of the trusted domain and its domain *Security ID (SID)*. The secret object contains the password used when establishing a session with the trusted domain. Each of the domain controllers in the trusting domain contains the trusted-domain object and the secret object in their SAM. The location of the LSA secret object that contains the password can be viewed with the Windows NT registry editor. Focus the registry editor on the HKEY_LOCAL_MACHINE subtree on any trusting domain controller and look in the following:

Security\Policy\Secrets

Part
II

Ch
5

Here you'll find an object named G$$TrustedDomainName that contains the password used to establish the session with the trusted domain. Figure 5.16 shows the registry entry that was created during our setup of the ADMIN/SHARES trust relationship.

FIG. 5.16

The password used to connect the trusting domain with the trusted domain is located in the G$$ADMIN object.

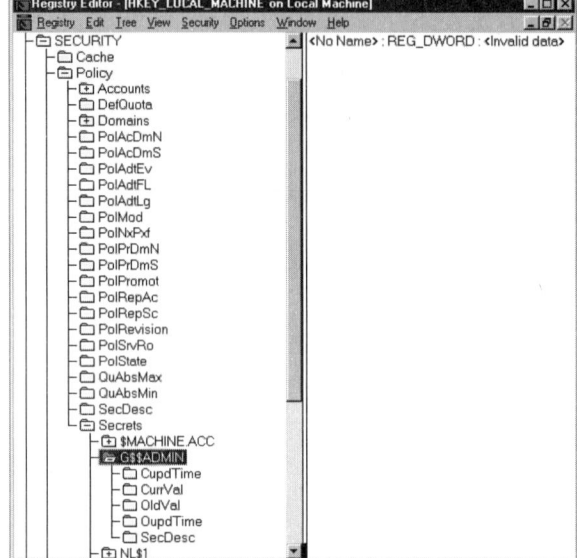

Viewing the SAM and SECURITY Subkey Information

Although you are able to see the registry entry, you are not able to see any of the data contained within the object. This is because the security information contained within these hives (SAM and SECURITY) are binary in nature and cannot be edited directly or viewed. In fact, if you're following along on a Windows NT 4.0 machine you may have noticed that the registry subkeys SAM and SECURITY are grayed out in the registry editor. Because they are grayed out, you won't be able to list the subtrees and keys contained within them unless you modify the permission applied to them. Adding permissions is similar to assigning share permissions, except it's done using the registry editor. Follow these steps to give yourself permissions to view the subtrees and keys within the SAM and Security subtrees:

1. Log on the Windows NT Server as a member of the Administrators group.

2. Locate the registry editor program in *Systemroot*\system32 called regedt32.exe and run it.

3. Open the subtree named HKEY_LOCAL_MACHINE on Local Machine.

4. Highlight the subkey entry named SAM.

5. Choose Permissions from the Security menu to open the Registry Key Permissions dialog box.

6. Click the Add button to open the Add Users and Groups dialog box.

7. At this point, you can assign access permissions to domain groups or users. Select a group, or select an individual account by clicking the Show Users button. After the account has been highlighted, click the Add button to add it to the Add Names window.

8. In the Type of Access drop-down list, choose Full Control. Then click the OK button to return to the Registry Key Permissions dialog box. The account you selected should be listed along with its access privilege level in the Name window.

9. Mark the box next to Replace Permissions on Existing Subkeys and click the OK button to apply the permissions and exit back to the registry editor screen.

After the access permissions have been modified, you will be able to view the keys and subkeys contained within the SAM subkey. Follow the same procedure to modify the permissions on the SECURITY subkey.

Use caution; these entries may not be capable of being modified, but they can be deleted. Doing so will corrupt the integrity of your SAM database!

After the LSA trusted-domain and secret objects are created on the trusting domain, the domain controller on the trusting domain attempts to create a session with the domain controller on the trusted domain. It does this by attempting a normal session logon using the name of the interdomain trust account (SHARES$ in this example). You can take a look at the events that take place during this time by using the Network Monitor to examine the network packets sent between the trusted and trusting domain controllers. During the setup of the trust relationship between the ADMIN and SHARES domains, you ran the Network Monitor to capture the network traffic that crossed between the PDCs of two domains. As we cover the trust initialization process we'll look at some of relevant network traffic that was captured during the ADMIN/SHARES trust setup.

Part
II

Ch
5

Establishing the Trust's Communications Link

To illustrate how the trust relationship communications link is completed, use the example trust setup from earlier in the chapter. In that trust setup, you first completed the setup of the trusted domain (ADMIN) side. You then completed the setup on the trusting domain (SHARES) side. The activities discussed here are the system processes that occur once the administrator of the trusting (SHARES) domain specifies the trusted (ADMIN) domain's name and password and clicks the OK button to initiate the trust.

N O T E The following example contains steps that are specific to networks running both the TCP/IP protocol and the WINS naming service. If your network is running another protocol, the events related to the TCP/IP protocol that are covered don't apply. However, the general sequence of the other events and actions related to the trust establishment remain the same.

Taking into consideration that the trusted (ADMIN) domain's side of the trust already has been set up, the following actions are initiated by the trusting (SHARES) domain's PDC named FILE_SERVER1. In the packet captures that you will see, the PCD of the ADMIN domain is named HC40SERV.

The process begins with the PDC (FILE_SERVER1) on the trusting (SHARES) domain sending out a request to WINS for the IP address of the trusted (ADMIN) domain's PDC (HC40SERV), as shown in Figure 5.17.

FIG. 5.17

A query request for the IP address of the trusted domain controller is sent to WINS.

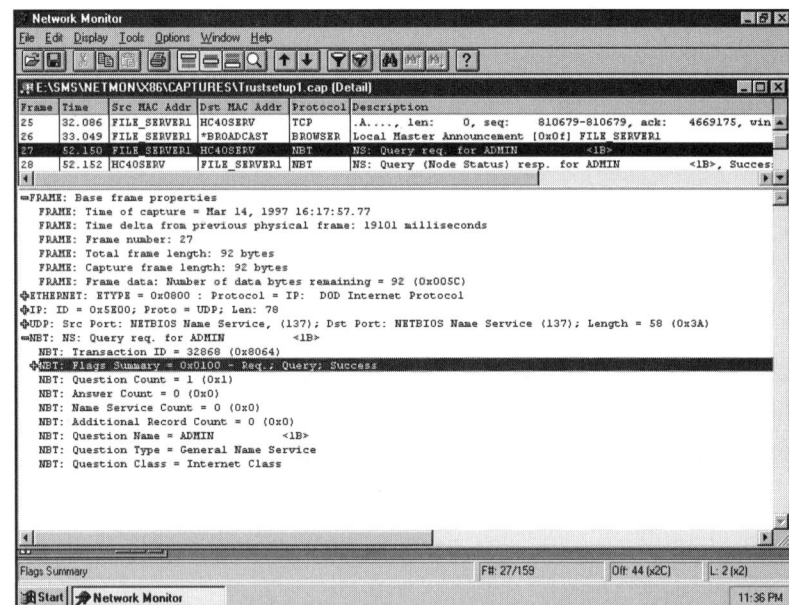

The request is answered by the WINS server, and the IP address (128.2.1.10) of the trusted (ADMIN) domain's PDC (HC40SERV) is sent back to the trusting (SHARES) domain's PDC (FILE_SERVER1), as shown in Figure 5.18.

Next, the trusted (SHARES) domain PDC (FILE_SERVER1) queries the IP address it just received using a NETLOGON\GETDC mailslot to get the NetBIOS computer name of the trusted (ADMIN) domain's PDC (HC40SERV). The response is shown in Figure 5.19.

FIG. 5.18

The IP query result is sent back to FILE_SERVER1.

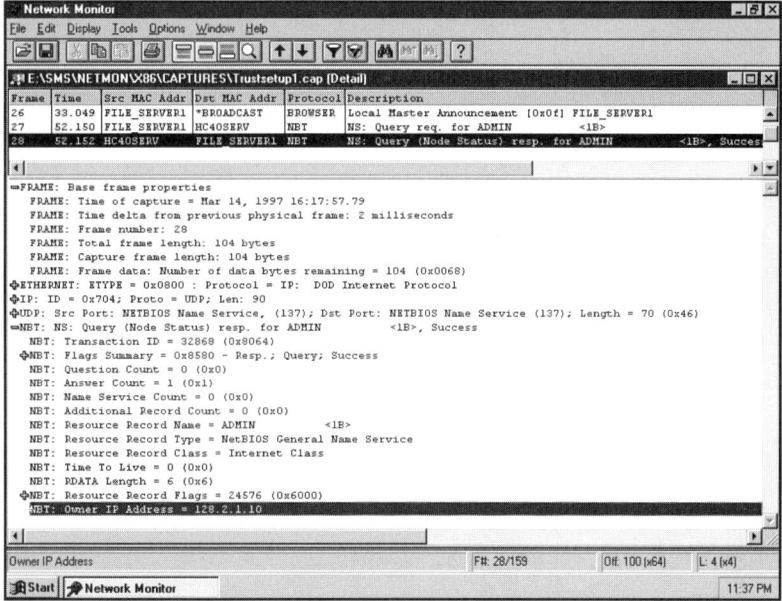

FIG. 5.19

The query for the NetBIOS machine name of the trusted domain's PDC.

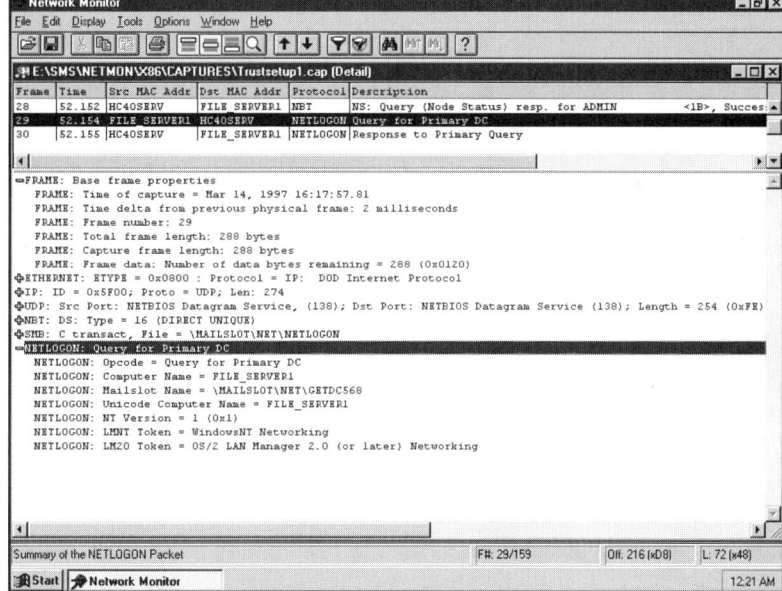

Figure 5.20 shows the next series of events that take place. The first three packets listed establish a TCP session with the PDC (HC40SERV) of the trusted (ADMIN) domain. The next two packets establish a NetBIOS session with the PDC of the trusted domain, and the next three packets negotiate the SMB protocol with the PDC of the trusted domain. The last SMB packet (number 41) listed in Figure 5.21 is of particular interest and is shown in the detail pane of the packet listing.

FIG. 5.20

The TCP and NetBIOS sessions are established, and the SMB protocol is negotiated.

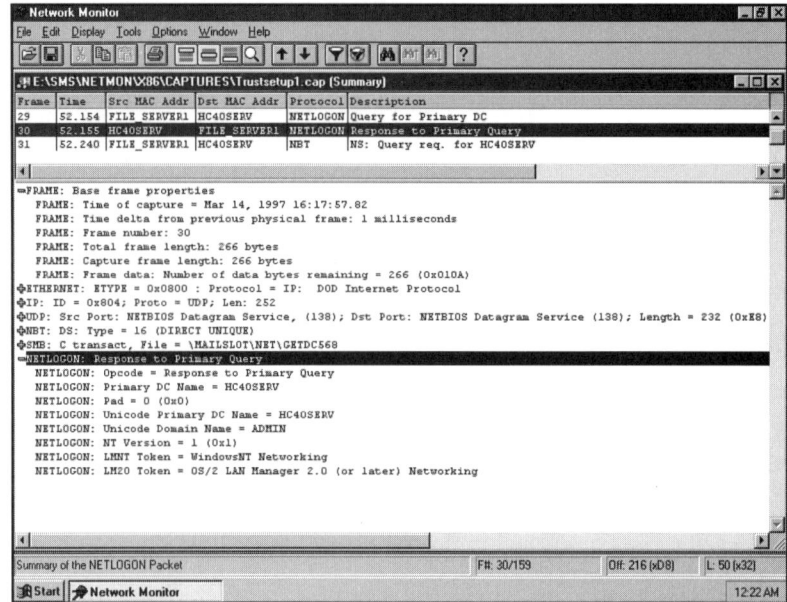

This is the response that informs the trusting domain that a trust has been set up and needs to be established.

Because the USER_INTERDOMAIN_TRUST_ACCOUNT bit in the interdomain trust account's control field was set, the log-on attempt requested by packet number 40 will fail with the error "0xC0000198" Status_Nologon_Interdomain_Trust_Account. This error occurs because the special interdomain trust account cannot be used for a normal session logon. When this error is returned to the domain controller of the trusting domain, the system is aware that a trust account exists within the trusted domain and that a trust relationship must be established.

After this error is returned, the TCP session is terminated. Figure 5.22 shows you frames 42–73 that were captured after the error message was returned. Frame numbers 42–44 show the TCP session being terminated.

FIG. 5.21
Packets captured
after the log-on error
are returned to
FILE_SERVER1.

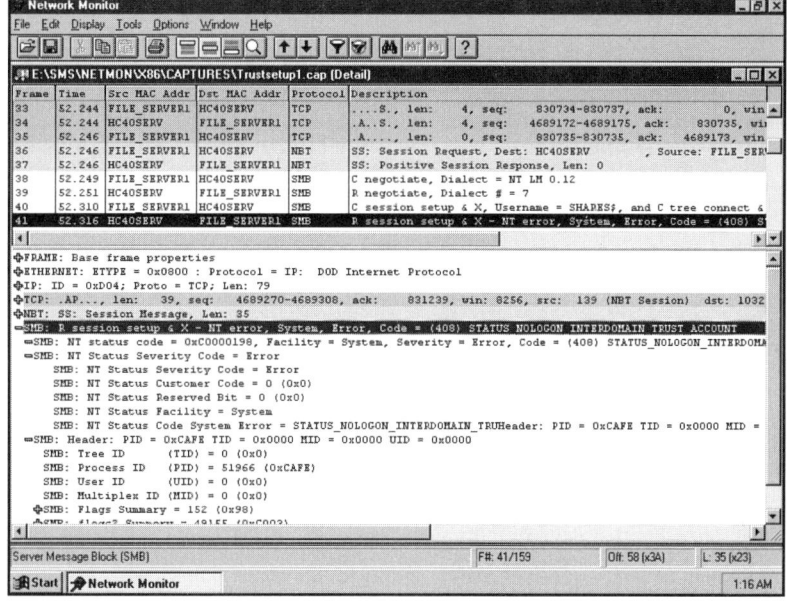

FIG. 5.22
Frames 42-73
of our capture.

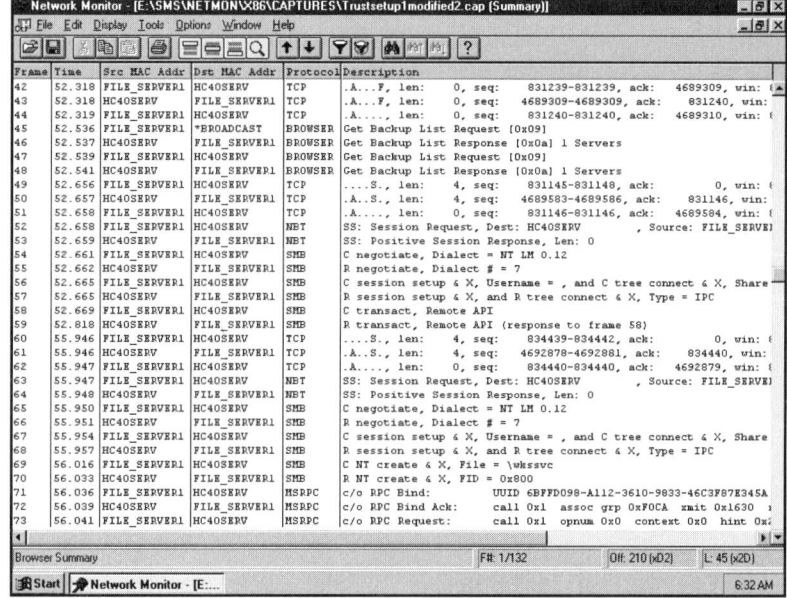

Part

II

Ch

5

The following events take place after the TCP session has been terminated. See Figure 5.23 and Figure 5.24 for the capture display of the frame numbers related to these events. The events are as follows:

■ The PDC of the trusting domain (FILE_SERVER1) requests a list of backup browser servers in the trusted domain (frames 45–48).

■ The trusting domain PDC then establishes a TCP and NetBIOS session with a backup *browser* in the trusted domain. This is shown in frames 49–53.

■ Next, the SMB protocol is negotiated and an IPC$ connection to the PDC (HC40SERV) of the trusted domain is established as shown in frames 54–57.

■ Frame 58 shows the trusting domain's PDC (FILE_SERVER1) remoting the NetrWkstaGetInfo API over RPC to acquire the computer and domain name of the server. Frame 59 shows the response to frame 58.

FIG. 5.23

Frames 74-105 of our capture.

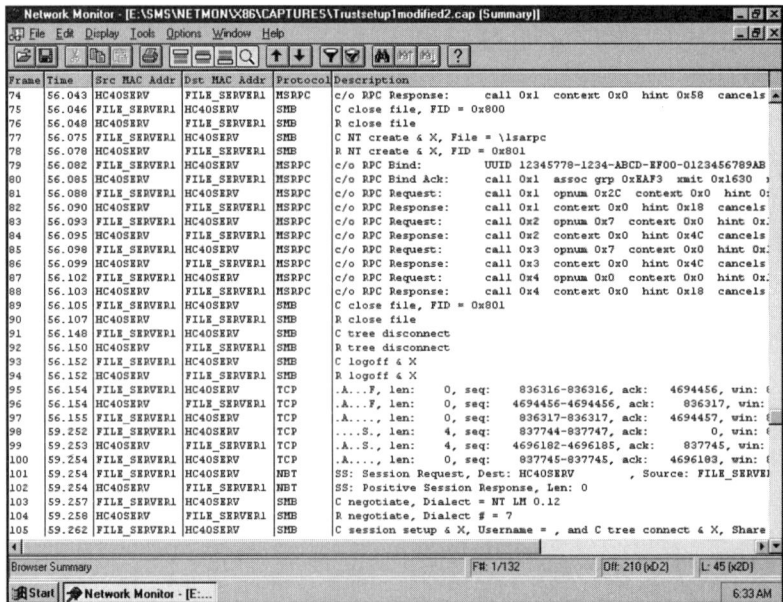

A null session with the trusted domain controller is then established that uses *remote-procedure call (RPC)* transactions to call remote APIs. This process of calling remote APIs completes the actions needed to establish the trust relationship between the two domains. The following actions are performed:

■ The PDC of the trusting domain (FILE_SERVER1) then establishes a TCP session with the PDC of the trusted domain (HC40SERV), as shown by frames 60–62. This is followed by the establishment of a NetBIOS session between the two controllers as shown by frames 63 and 64.

■ Next the SMB protocol is negotiated and an IPC$ connection is made to the trusted domain controller (HC40SERV) using a null user account as shown in frames 65–68.

■ Frames 69–72 show the trusting domain controller (FILE_SERVER1) establishing a named pipe session with the HC40SERV server. Frames 73 and 74 show FILE_SERVER1 remoting a NetrWkstaGetInfo API over RPC to acquire the computer and domain name of the server. Frames 75 and 76 show the named pipe session being closed.

■ Another named pipe session is opened between the trusting PDC (FILE_SERVER1) and the trusted PDC (HC40SERV) as shown in frames 77–80.

■ In the next series of frames (81–88) four remote API calls using RPC are sent to the Local Security Authority of the trusted domain PDC (HC40SERV). The named pipe session is closed in frames 89 and 90. Frames 91–94 show the IPC$ connection being broken, followed by the end of the TCP session in frames 95–97.

■ Frames 98–115 show another TCP/NetBIOS/Named pipes session being established that passes three more API calls using RPC to the Local Security Authority on the trusted domain's PDC (HC40SERV).

■ A WINS query to domain <1C> in frame 116 for trusted domain controllers is returned by HC40SERV in frame 117.

■ The trusting domain PDC (FILE_SERVER1) then queries the network for a log-on server in the trusted domain (ADMIN) by broadcasting a SAM LOGON request from the client on the local subnet (as shown in frame 118). The trusting domain PDC (FILE_SERVER1) also delivers the SAM LOGON request from client (see frame 119) directly to any controllers that answered the WINS query to domain <1C> query (frame 116). This log-on request is directed to the mailslot \MAILSLOT\NET\NTLOGON at the target domain controller.

■ Frame 120 shows you the SAM response to SAM LOGON request that indicates a successful logon. At this time the trusting domain PDC (FILE_SERVER1) closes the LSA object (frames 121–122), breaks the IPC$ connection (frames 123–126), the SMB Logoff command is executed (frames 127 and 128), and the TCP IP session is broken (frames 129–131). See Figure 5.24.

Part

II

Ch

5

FIG. 5.24
Frames 106–131
of our capture.

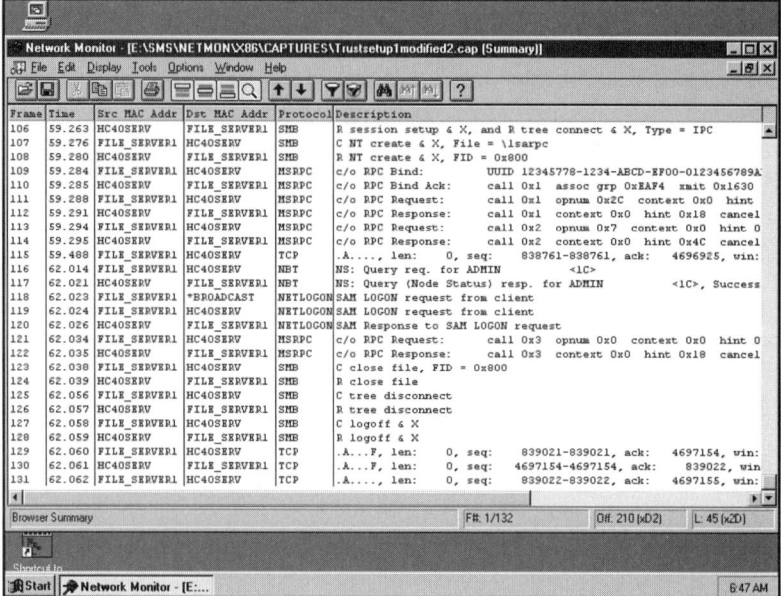

At this time the trust relationship has been established between the two domains. The process took approximately 3.1 seconds and consisted of 131 frames. The network traffic generated was just over 17K.

Once the trust has been established, the trusting domain's PDC changes the password for the trusted-domain object. This also is part of the periodic maintenance that is performed on these trust accounts. The PDC in the trusting domain changes the password for the LSA secret object every seven days. It then notifies the PDC of the trusted domain and requests a password change for the domain trust account located in its directory database to match that of the new LSA secret object password.

N O T E   Note that the password change *only* is initiated by the trusting domain's PDC and never by a trusted domain controller. ▪

The password is changed within the directory database of the trusted domain's PDC. The trust account and LSA secret objects that exist in each of the domains are then distributed to the BDC using the normal synchronization of the SAM and LSA databases. The following lists the events that take place:

■ BDCs in the trusted domain receive updated trust account object information when their directory-database is updated via normal domain synchronization.

■ BDCs in the trusting domain receive updated LSA secret object information when their LSA database is updated via normal domain synchronization.

Because the BDCs in each domain contain up-to-date trust object information, a secure channel session can be established between any controller in the two domains. This secure channel is required for the trust relationship to function correctly.

In Chapter 6, "User Account Security and Windows NT," you take the same type of in-depth look at user authentication to see what processes occur and what network traffic is generated during the account authentication process. Now you need to get back to the administrative aspect of domain trust relationships by looking at the domain models that are used on Windows NT networks.

The Common Domain Models

A domain model represents how the Windows NT domains on your network participate (or don't participate) in trust relationships with each other. There are four domain models that can be implemented using Windows NT trust relationships between domains. Actually, three models implement trust relationships between domains, and one represents a self-contained domain that doesn't participate in any trust relationships at all. The type of domain model you implement is determined by several factors, including the following:

■ The number of users that will have accounts on the network—a large number of user accounts may require the use of more that one account domain.

■ The way resources on the network will be managed—domain models enable you to establish specific resource domains that are not confined by geographical location. This enables the management of any resource independently from any other resource.

■ How the user accounts are distributed—domain models are most often implemented to gather all user accounts within *account* domains. These domains also may have resources associated with them, but their primary purpose is the consolidation of user accounts into a central domain.

■ The organizational structure of the company also can be reflected in the way resource domains are created and named.

■ They enable you to configure your network using the "one user is one account" philosophy. In fact, defining multiple accounts with the same name and password for a single user on the network can cause administrative inconsistencies when assigning permissions to the user. This is because each account is issued a different SID number.

Let's look at each one of these domain models and see how they are used. Begin with a domain model that really isn't a model at all, just a single domain.

Single Domain Model

The concept of a single domain model is simple—just place all user accounts and resources within the same Windows NT domain. Users log on to the same domain that contains the resources (file shares, printers, and so on) that they need to access. Figure 5.25 shows you what a single domain looks like with all the user accounts and resources consolidated into one logical group.

FIG. 5.25

In the Single Domain Model, all user accounts and resources are contained within the same domain.

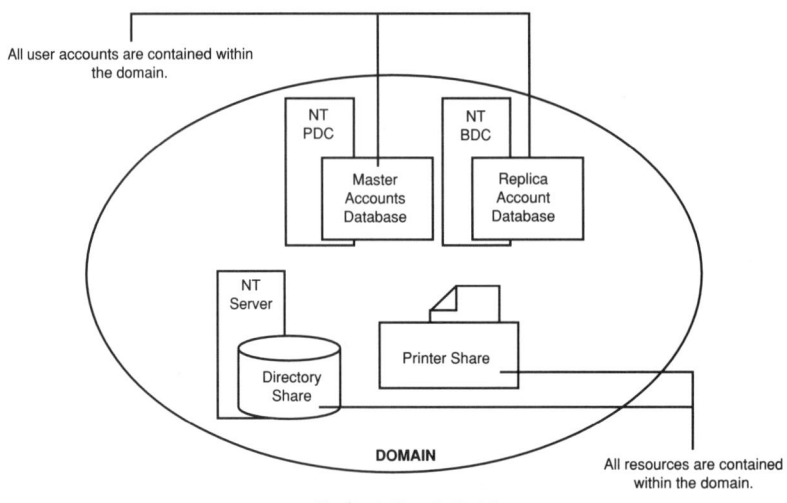

The Single Domain Model

The advantage to a single domain model is having only one user account database to manage. Users only have to log on once to access any resource in the domain they have been permitted to use. Managers with the appropriate access are able to control any resource in the domain regardless of its geographic location. Additionally, the network administrators are not burdened with the additional management of trust relationships.

Some disadvantages are that it doesn't perform well if the number of users and groups defined in the domain exceeds the limitations of the domain controller's hardware. Large numbers of servers on the domain also may slow down network browsing. Another disadvantage of a single domain model is that it does not permit the individual group management of domain resources. Management for both users and resources is centralized.

Also note that the single domain model should not be used on Windows NT networks with more that 40,000 accounts; this doesn't mean 40,000 user accounts, it's the combined total of all user, group, and machine accounts within a domain. It usually equals about 26,000 user accounts per domain.

▶ **See** Chapter 4, "Creating Domains," **p. 96**

Now take a look at a domain model that uses trust relationships so that a single accounts database can provide users with access to resources across multiple domains.

Master Domain Model

Earlier in this chapter we discussed the concept of account domains versus resource domains. The Master Domain Model takes advantage of account and resource domain concepts to provide a single user account database that can be used to access resources on other domains. Figure 5.26 shows the Master Domain Model and the relationship between the account and resource domains.

FIG. 5.26
This figure illustrates the relationship between the account and resource domains within a Master Domain Model.

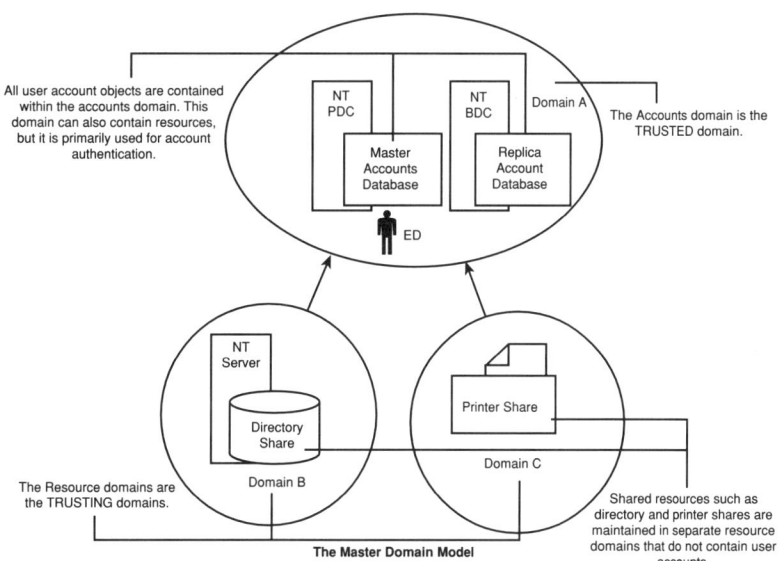

Part

II

Ch

5

You'll notice that trust relationships have been established between the resource domains and the account domain. The account domain takes the role of the Trusted domain while the resource domains assume the role of trusting domains. All user accounts are maintained on the trusted domain while a majority of the resources can be maintained on the trusting domain. The advantages to using a Multiple Master Domain Model are the following:

- The ability to provide a single user logon for resource access to resources across multiple domains.
- Centralized Management of the user accounts in the account domain.
- The ability to designate independent management for each of the resource domains.

The user accounts contained on the trusted account domain can be given access to resources in the trusting resource domain directly, or by the user accounts membership in a global group. Figure 5.27 shows how a user account in the trusted domain can be placed into a global group. The global group is then placed into a local group on the resource domain. The local group in turn is given the appropriate permissions to access the target resource on the resource domain.

FIG. 5.27

Users into global groups, global groups into local groups.

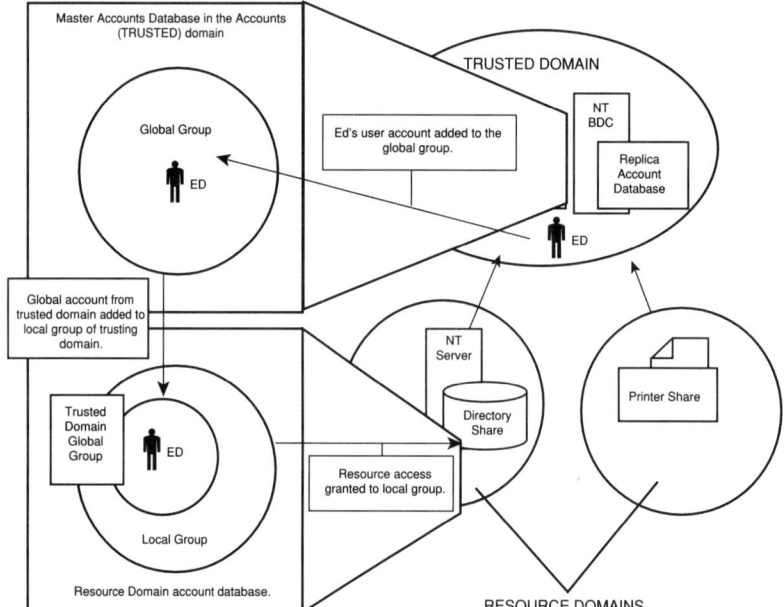

The Master domain model also enables you to assign administrative control for the trusting resource domain to global groups or global user accounts from the trusted domain. For example, earlier you set up a trust relationship between the ADMIN and SHARES domain. This was a one-way trust relationship with the ADMIN domain assuming the role of the trusted account domain.

Suppose you want to assign administrative privileges for the SHARES domain to several network users. You want the group of users able to fully administer the resource (SHARES) domain, but you don't want them to have any administrative capabilities on the accounts (ADMIN) domain. To accomplish this, you first create a custom global group on the ADMIN domain. Then, you add the individual user accounts that need administrative access to the resource domain to the new custom global group. Finally, you add the global group you created in the ADMIN domain to the Administrators local group on the SHARES domain.

Here are the steps to configure an administrative group for the SHARES domain. You begin by creating the custom global group on the ADMIN domain and adding user accounts to it, as follows:

1. Log in under an administrative account on the ADMIN domain and start the User Manager for Domains program.
2. Choose New Global group from the User menu to open the New Global Group dialog box.
3. In the Group Name box type in a descriptive name for the group. We'll use the name "SHARES Admins" for our global group name.
4. Type in a brief description of the group's purpose in the Description box.
5. Highlight the names of one or more user accounts in the Not Members window and click the Add button to move the names to the Members window (see Figure 5.28). Click the OK button to return to the User Manager for Domains main window when you're finished adding names.

Part
II

Ch

5

FIG. 5.28
Creating the global user account for administrators of the SHARES domain.

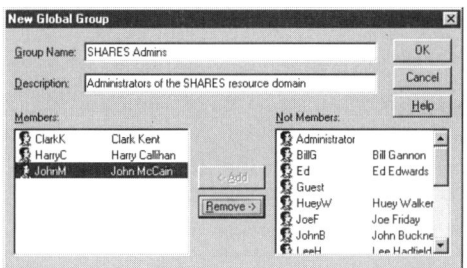

You now should see the new global group name "SHARES Admins" listed in the Groups area of the User Manager for Domains screen. The next step is to simply place the global group you just created into the local Administrators group on the SHARES domain. Here's how:

1. Log on using the Administrator account on the SHARES domain. (No other accounts besides the GUEST should be in the domain.)

2. Highlight and double-click the local group named Administrators located in the Groups area of the User Manager for Domains window. This opens the Local Group Properties dialog box.

3. Click the Add button to open the Add User and Groups dialog box.

4. Choose ADMIN from the List Names From drop-down list (see Figure 5.29). This places the names of the global groups and global users from the ADMIN domain into the Names window.

FIG. 5.29

List global users and groups from the ADMIN domain.

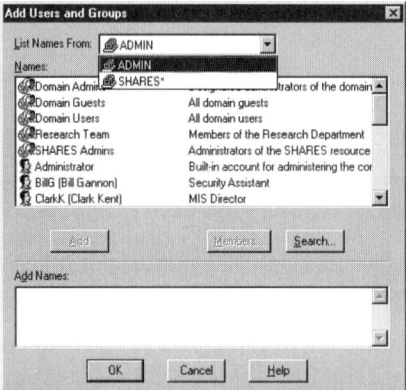

5. Highlight the global group SHARES Admins in the Names window and click the Add button. This places the SHARES Admins global group into the Add Names window as shown in Figure 5.30.

6. Click the OK button to close the Add User and Groups dialog box and return to the Local Group Properties dialog box. You should notice that the ADMIN\SHARES Admins group now is listed in the Members windows (see Figure 5.31).

7. Click the OK button to close the Local Group Properties dialog box.

FIG. 5.30
Add the
ADMIN\SHARES
Admin global group
to the Add Names
window.

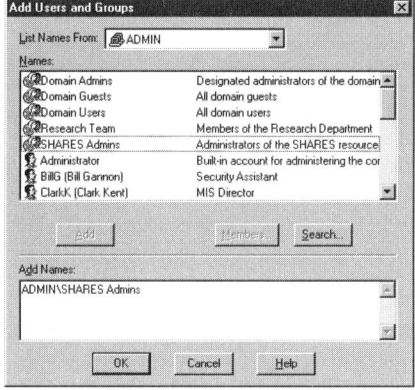

FIG. 5.31
ADMIN\SHARES
Admins now is listed
in the Local Adminis-
trators group.

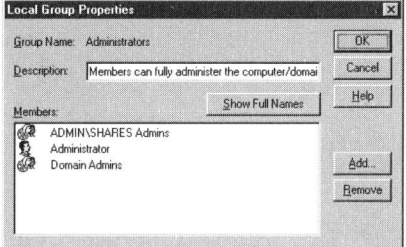

That's the last time you will need to log on to the SHARES domain to perform any administrative duties. From now on, anyone that is a member of the ADMIN domain's global
group named SHARES Admins will be able to administer fully the SHARES domain. They
are able to create any additional local groups that may be needed on the ADMIN domain.
Members of this group are able to define resources and local groups on the SHARES
domain, and they are able to assign access privileges to the domain's resources.

While the members of the SHARES Admins group enjoy full administrative rights on the
SHARES domain, they have no administrative control whatsoever in the ADMIN domain.
They are not allowed to perform any administrative task in the ADMIN domain without
being given additional rights. Exactly who joins the SHARES Admins global group is kept
in the complete control of the Trusted (ADMIN) domain administrators. They can add or
delete users of the SHARES Admins global group at any time.

Part

II

Ch

5

Multiple Master Domain Model

As you just saw, the Master Domain Model enables you to have a single repository for user accounts while being able to maintain individual control over resources. So what if you work for a large organization that has too many user accounts for one single accounts domain? You can implement a Multiple Master Domain Model.

This model provides the same benefits as a Master Domain Model. One user, one account still can be realized, along with the independent management of resource domains. However, because you have an account limitation of 40,000 accounts (approx. 26,000 user accounts) per domain, more than one account domain must exist to accommodate all the accounts.

Let's try an example using a company with 50,000 users. Half of the users are placed into the first account domain—we'll call it ADMIN1. The other half of the users are placed into the second account domain, we'll call this one ADMIN2. This is most easily done by taking users with last names starting with letters from the first half of the alphabet (A–M) and placing them in the first account domain (ADMIN1). Then take users with last names that start with letters from the last half of the alphabet (N–Z) and place them into the second domain.

To create a Multiple Master Domain model, you set up a two-way trust relationship between the two account domains (ADMIN1 and ADMIN2). You then set up standard one-way trust relationships between both the account domains and each resource domain present on the network. This is shown in Figure 5.32.

The advantages to a Multiple Master Domain Model are as follows:

- It scales to any size user environment.
- It allows one user, one account.
- Resources can be managed independently by separate groups.
- Centralized management of accounts is possible.

The disadvantages of implementing a Multiple Master Domain Model are the following:

- Local and Global groups may have to be defined multiple times.
- User accounts are not contained within a single domain.
- Several trust relationships have to be managed.

Just as with the Master Domain Model, user accounts are placed in global groups on the account domains, and the global groups then can be moved into the local groups in the resource domains. You may have to define a custom global group in both account domains if users from both domains need access to a specific domain resource.

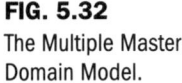

FIG. 5.32

The Multiple Master Domain Model.

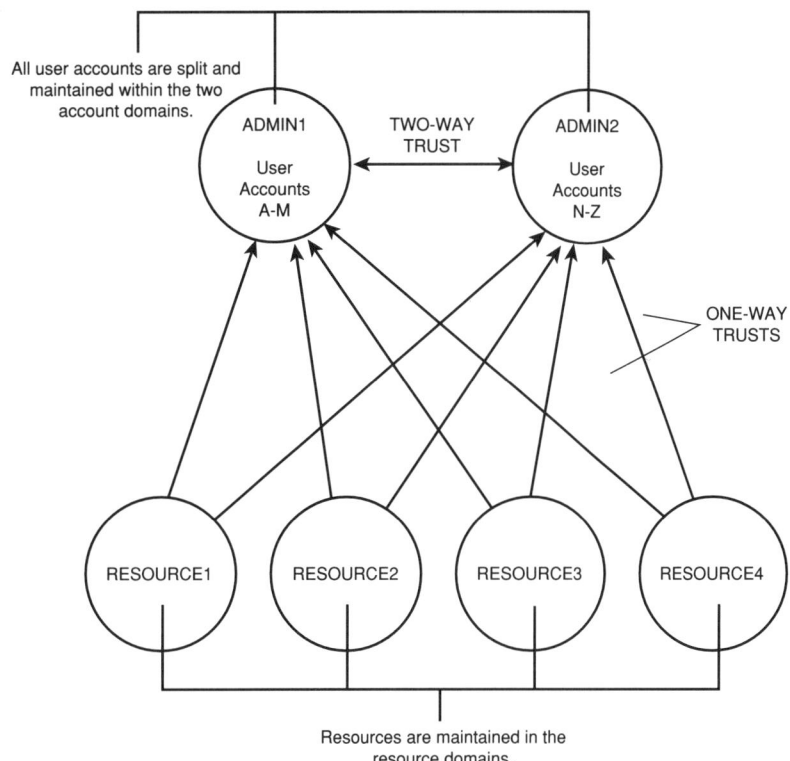

All user accounts are split and maintained within the two account domains.

Resources are maintained in the resource domains.

For example, you have defined a local group called DOCUSERS on the RESOURCE1 domain that has access to the DOCUMENTS share in that domain. You have users in each of your account domains (ADMIN1 and ADMIN2) that need to have access to the DOCUMENTS share. In order to give users in each account domain access, a custom global group is created in each of the account domains. Users that need access to the DOCUMENTS share on the RESOURCE1 domain are placed into their respective account domain's global group. Then both of the global groups are given membership in the Local Group named DOCUSERS in the RESOURCE1 domain.

The number of trust relationships that must be put in place for any one Multiple Master Domain model will vary depending on the number of account domains and the number of resource domains. The general formula for determining the number of trust relationships in a Multiple Master Domain Model is A*(A-1)+(R*A) where A equals the number of account domains, and R equals the number of resource domains. You can take the Multiple Master Domain Model shown in Figure 5.32 and use the formula to calculate the number of trusts needed. In that example, you had 2 account domains and 4 resource domains, so the formula is 2*(2-1)+(4*2). That is 2*1+8 or 2+8 or 10.

If you look at Figure 5.32, you can count the number of trust relationships to see if the formula works. First, you have a two-way trust setup between the account domains. That accounts for two of the trust relationships—one trust relationship each way. Then each of the four resource domains has two one-way trusts, one to domain ADMIN1 and one to ADMIN2. Four domains at two trusts each account for the other eight trusts, for a grand total of ten trusts. The formula works. If you don't like the math approach, you can just draw out the Multiple Master Domain Model using circles and arrows. Then just count the number of arrows.

The next domain model you want to look at decentralizes the management of the network and creates the greatest number of trust relationships.

Complete Trust Domain Model

From a security standpoint, the Complete Trust Domain Model offers a less centralized approach to administering user accounts and resources on a network. With the Complete Trust Domain Model, all domains trust all other domains. No single domain or domains have control over the network. Each domain contains its own user accounts and resources. Resources in any domain can be accessed via the trust relationships that are in place.

The advantages to the Complete Trust Domain Model include the following:

- Management can be distributed if no central MIS group is available.
- Users and the resources they use are most often grouped together.
- Resources and user accounts can be administered in each domain independently of other domains.
- It also fits networks with an unlimited number of users.

The disadvantages of the Complete Trust Domain Model are as follows:

- No central control of the network's user accounts or resources.
- A certain amount of cooperation must exist between domain managers to prevent inappropriate permissions from being given to users or groups.
- The number of trust relationships can become unmanageable.

The biggest problem with the Complete Trust Domain Model is the number of trust relationships that must be established and maintained (see Figure 5.33). A simple network with four domains participating in a Complete Trust Domain Model will have twelve trust relationships set up. If you had five domains participating, you'd need twenty trust relationships, which is more than most administrators would like to worry about.

FIG. 5.33
Each domain requires
a two-way trust with
every other domain.

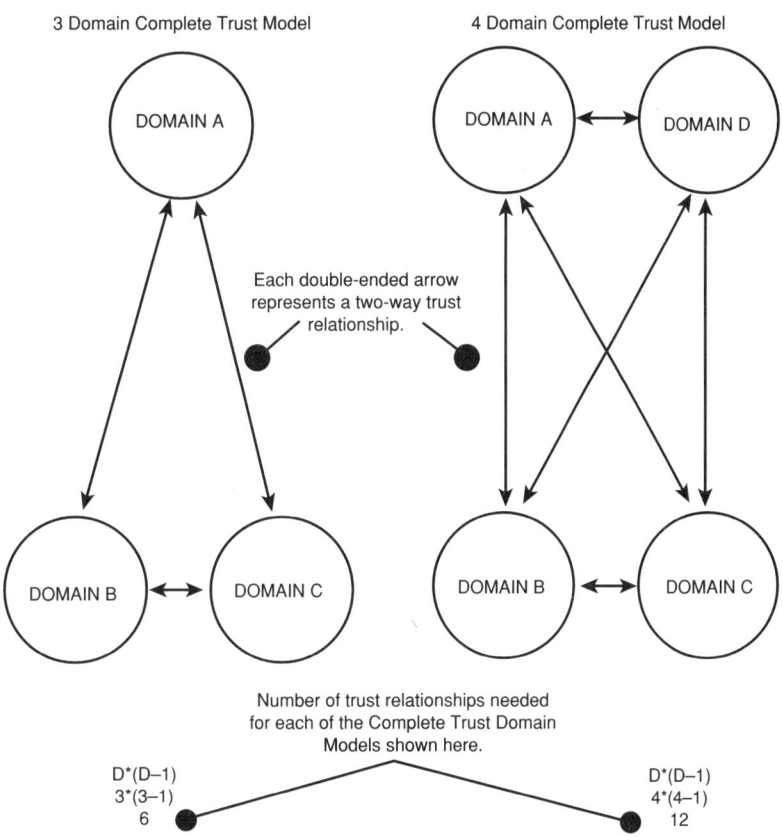

3 Domain Complete Trust Model

4 Domain Complete Trust Model

Each double-ended arrow
represents a two-way trust
relationship.

Number of trust relationships needed
for each of the Complete Trust Domain
Models shown here.

$$D^*(D-1)$$
$$3^*(3-1)$$
6

$$D^*(D-1)$$
$$4^*(4-1)$$
12

Also, the use of a complete trust includes more individuals in the network management process. This is acceptable if all of the administrative personnel are trained and know how to manage a Windows NT network. It's not good if they have little knowledge of Windows NT system administration.

The Non-Transitive Nature of Trusts   As you've seen, trust relationships can be implemented in several different ways. Any of the trust models described here can be implemented on different levels depending on the needs of your organization. Often trust will be implemented where Domain A trusts Domain B, and Domain B then trusts Domain C. This does not imply any sort of trust relationship at all between Domain A and Domain C as shown in Figure 5.34.

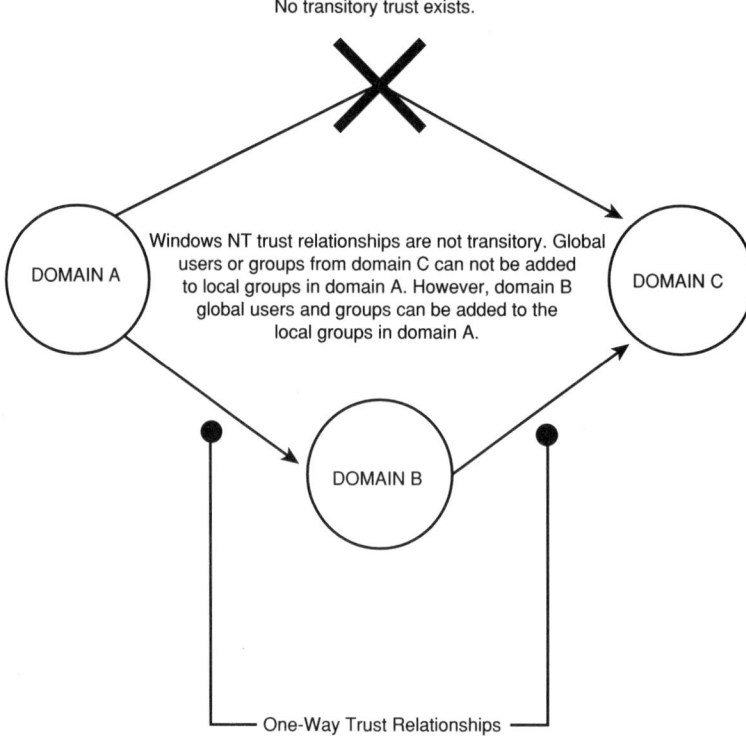

FIG. 5.34
Windows NT trusts
are non-transitory.

No transitory trust exists.

DOMAIN A

Windows NT trust relationships are not transitory. Global
users or groups from domain C can not be added
to local groups in domain A. However, domain B
global users and groups can be added to the
local groups in domain A.

DOMAIN C

DOMAIN B

One-Way Trust Relationships

In the next section, you learn some of the common problems you can experience when implementing trust relationships.

Troubleshooting Trust Relationships

Trust relationships are simple to configure and require no maintenance. They can be created and removed on-the-fly without taking servers off-line or disrupting network services. Most of the time, when a trust relationship fails, a mistyped password at the trusting side of the domain is the cause. Connection problems could prevent the set up of a trust relationship, but only until the connection is reestablished. If you still experience problems setting up a trust after the password has been verified, try using the Network Monitor and the information provided earlier in the chapter to resolve the problem. You'll be able to tell if the correct actions are taking place between the domain controllers.

From Here...

This concludes the overview of domain trust relationships and how they can be used to manage effectively the security of your network. In the upcoming chapters you see the user account object in detail and how user authentication actually takes place. Later we cover another type of resource security—NTFS permissions. Here's a glance at where to go from here.

- Chapter 6, "User Account Security and Windows NT," looks at the user authentication process and pass-through security. You also learn some of the registry items that relate to user accounts.

- Chapter 7, "New Technology File System (NTFS) Security," examines the added layer of security that NTFS provides. You find out why the NTFS file system is used and how to configure it.

- Chapter 8, "Using Windows NT Security to Protect Domain Resources," looks at the administrative tools available to you when managing the security of a Windows NT domain. You learn how to secure file and printer resources in addition to the registry.

Part

II

Ch

5

CHAPTER 6

User Account Security and Windows NT

User accounts are mechanisms that enable a person to be validated as a system's user for logging on. They also are used to grant or deny access to the system's resources, such as directory shares or print queues. This chapter looks at the user account and its properties, including the SID number. You see how the user is authenticated on the system during logon. After that, you examine how resource access by a user account is validated by the Windows NT system. You see some common problems associated with user accounts and how they can be resolved.

Let's begin by reviewing the Windows NT user account and how it is used by Windows NT Server to provide access to the system and its resources. ■

User accounts

Review the user account and how it provides access to network based resources.

User authentication

User level security is defined and the basics of user log-on authentication are examined.

Log-on authentication and validation

Take a detailed look at the authentication or user validation process that occurs when a user logs on to the network.

Accessing the resources

Examine the processes that take place when a user attempts to access a network resource using remote logon.

Account troubleshooting

See some of the problems that are experienced with user accounts and the log-on process.

Examining the Windows NT User Account

The Windows NT operating system uses the user account to identify users who are allowed access to the network resources. Before any user can access a resource controlled by a Windows NT server, they first must be authenticated as a valid user of the system or domain. This is accomplished using an account validation process that includes the user supplying a name and password. The system references the name and password to security information contained within its *Security Accounts Database (SAM)* and either grants or denies logon. If the logon is denied, the graphical user interface on the Windows NT Server or Workstation is not started, and the user has no way of accessing system resources. If logon is denied from a Windows 95 or WFW workstation, the user interface starts and is fully operational. However, the user doesn't have access to any of the network's domain resources controlled by Windows NT security.

The information regarding user, group, and machine accounts is regularly replicated between the domain's *Primary Domain Controller (PDC)* and any *Backup Domain Controller (BDC)* that may be on the network. This permits the user account validation to be performed by the PDC or any of the BDCs in the domain. Once validation takes place, a user can access the domain's resources based on the permissions granted to his or her account on each of the resources.

Shared versus User Level Security

The type of security just described is called *user level security* and features a single-user logon (at least it should when set up correctly). After the name and password have been successfully entered, the user can access any resource he or she is given permission to without having to enter either the name or password in again.

This is in contrast to *share level security* where different passwords can be placed on each individual share, necessitating that users remember several passwords. Share level security is most often used on peer-to-peer networks such as a Windows for Workgroups 3.1 or Windows 95. It allows a user to share a resource such as a file directory from their workstation by assigning a read-only or full-access password to it. Each different share can have different passwords, which makes resource access sometimes difficult for users who are required to remember multiple passwords. The advantage to share level security is that it requires little configuration. The disadvantage is that it's not very secure, because a common password is used universally to access a resource. It also does not allow any custom variations on access to a resource. It usually does not permit any type of auditing.

Conversely, Windows NT user level security offers a much finer degree of access control over resources. It permits network administrators to audit the use of any network resource by the users of the system. It also enables the user to supply a name and password only once to gain access to multiple resources (if the user has been given permissions to the resource, that is).

User level security is based on user account information contained within the SAM database. This includes a unique name that identifies the individual account, which also contains an account-specific password. Associating a password with the name provides security against unauthorized system access. Other information contained within the SAM includes the names of any groups the account is a member of. Log-on information, such as the user's home directory and log-on script path also is in the SAM along with a list of restrictions pertinent to the account.

The User Account Types

The user account may be defined as a *global* account (the default) or a *local* account. Global accounts enable the user to log on interactively to the system and perform some type of action. The local account cannot be used to log on interactively. Instead it is used to allow user accounts of non-trusting domains to access resources in the local account domain, and at the same time to restrict the user from being able to log on to the local account domain in an interactive log-on session. In addition to permitting only remote logon, local accounts cannot participate in domain trust relationships like global accounts can.

The Built-In User Accounts When Windows NT Server or Workstation is installed, two built-in user accounts are automatically created. The first account is the *Administrator* user account, and the other is the *Guest* account. If the server is being installed as a PDC, the accounts created are domain accounts and are members of the domain's SAM database. If installing a stand-alone or workstation, the accounts will be members of the local machine's SAM database.

The Administrator Account The Administrator account is used after a Windows NT Server or Workstation originally is installed to manage the system. It is the only account that initially exists and is able to log on and perform any management function on a new PDC, stand-alone, or Windows NT workstation (unless the workstation has joined an existing domain during installation). It automatically is included in the Administrator's local group. This account cannot be deleted, nor can it be removed, disabled, or removed from the Administrator's local group. After you've logged on as the Administrator, you can

Part

II

Ch

6

create other user accounts that are members of the Administrator's local group, but you can't create another Administrator account. The other group members will have all the rights the Administrator account has and will be able to perform the same management duties. The difference is that they can be removed from the Administrator's local group; the Administrator's account cannot be removed.

 For an increased measure of security, the Administrator account can be renamed to obscure its importance by not having the name available.

The Administrator's account has automatic rights to perform administrative tasks on any domain controller, workstation, or member server that resides in a domain or trusting domain. When installing a PDC, stand-alone or workstation, the Windows NT setup program prompts for the administrator password to be initially used with the account. The password supplied is used to log on under the administrator account on the new PDC, stand-alone, or workstation the first time after installation. The password can be changed anytime after installation.

You will be prompted for an administrator account name and password when installing a BDC, member server, or Windows NT Workstation as a domain member. The administrator account information that you supply can be the name and password of any member of the Administrator's local group; you do not have to specify the actual Administrator account and password.

 Create at least one other account that is a member of the Administrator's local group and use it to perform management duties. Reserve the actual Administrator account for emergency situations. When auditing is enabled, you can more easily monitor the administrative activity on your network by identifying the specific users that perform administrative tasks.

The Guest Account   This account is provided so individuals that do not have accounts on the system can gain access to non-sensitive network resources. An individual user on the system that has a disabled user account also can gain access to the same non-sensitive resources using the guest account. We say non-sensitive resources, but actually the guest account is like any other account. It can be given access to any resource either directly or by its group membership. In fact, the guest account can be given membership in the administrator groups. Because the guest account does not require a password, you should be careful if this account is enabled. By default, this account initially is disabled on Windows NT Servers and Workstations, but it can be enabled at anytime. The Guest account is a member of the Domain Guests global group, and the Domain Guests global group is a member of the Guest local group.

N O T E   This is a good example of the "users into global groups, global groups into local groups" concept discussed in Chapter 5, "Maintaining Security with Domain Trust Relationships" in the section "Master Domain Model."

The Guest account can be used in two ways when accessing the system. A *local guest logon* is used when an individual logs on locally to a Windows NT Workstation or member Server using the Logon Information dialog box. This allows a guest user to work interactively on the workstation or member server. The right to log on locally is not given to the guest account on Windows NT domain controllers. This prevents guest users from logging on locally to a PDC or BDC and starting an interactive Windows session.

The other type of guest logon is the *network guest logon*. This is an account that is used by a domain account or a local computer account that is logged in under an interactive session. The account that is logged on interactively can use the guest account (if it is enabled) to connect to another computer that uses the guest account. The guest account at the destination computer must be enabled with no password in order for the connection to succeed. The destination computer can be any of the following:

- A Windows NT Server Domain Controller
- A Windows NT Server that is a domain member
- A Windows NT Workstation that participates in either a workgroup or a domain
- A LAN Manager version 2.x client computer

After the connection has been established, the user using the network guest logon will have all the rights, permissions, and group memberships that the guest account has been granted on the destination computer. This is an important point to remember as you look at some of the algorithm flow charts of that presented later in this chapter.

You can disable either the local or network guest log-on feature (or both) by using the User Manager for Domains utility. If you want a user to be able to log on locally to a server or workstation under the guest account but do not want network guest access enabled, use the following steps:

1. Open the User Manager for Domains utility and double-click the user account with a Username of Guest. This opens the User Properties dialog box.
2. Check to see if the Account Disabled check box is marked. If it is marked, clear the box by clicking it. Click the OK button when finished to return to the User Manager Domain-name window.

Part
II

Ch
6

3. Select Underlinedirect Rights from the Policies drop-down menu to open the User Rights Policy dialog box. "Access this computer from the network" should be the default selection that appears in the Right: box. If it is not, select it from the drop-down list.

By default, the Administrator account and the built-in group Everyone have the "Access this computer from the network" right. You may have noticed that the Everyone group is not in the User Manager for Domain's Groups listing. It is a hidden, built-in group used by the system and cannot be modified. By default, it contains *all* user accounts, including the Guest account. Before access can be restricted to network guest logons, you need to remove the Guest account from having the "Access this computer from the network" right. Because this right has been granted for the group Everyone, the Guest account automatically is granted the same rights to access the computer from the network. First, you have to revoke the Everyone's group access rights. Now, in order to allow users of the network access to the system, you have to replace the Everyone group with the local Users Group. Follow these steps:

4. Highlight the Everyone entry in the Grant To: portion of the User Rights Policy dialog box and click the Remove button.

5. Click the Add button to open the Add Users and Groups dialog box. Make sure the local domain is listed in the List Name From box. If it isn't, choose the local domain from the drop-down list.

6. Scroll down the Name window and highlight the local Users group entry with the description "Ordinary users" and click the Add button. The Users local group Domain-name\Users now appears in the Add Names: dialog box.

7. Click the OK button to return to the User Rights Policy dialog box. You should see the entry "Users" listed in the Grant To: window. Click the OK button to return to the User Manager for Domains main window.

Now when an account attempts to access a resource using the network guest logon, they get the message listed in Figure 6.1.

FIG. 6.1

The network guest access now is denied.

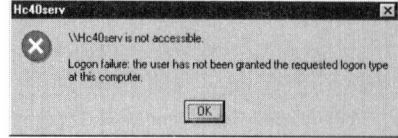

If you want to allow the network guest logon but not the local guest logon, use the following steps:

1. Open the User Manager for Domains utility and double-click the user account with a User name of Guest. This opens the User Properties dialog box.

2. Check to see if the Account Disabled check box is marked. If it is marked, clear the box by clicking it. Click the OK button when finished to return to the User Manager Domain-name window.

3. Select User Rights from the Policies drop-down menu to open the User Rights Policy dialog box.

4. The "Access this computer from the network" Right: box should be listed. If it isn't, select it from the drop-down list. In the Grant To: window either the Everyone group, the local or global Guest groups, or the Guest account must be listed.

If any one of the preceding is not listed, either the Everyone group or the local Guest group needs to be added to the Grant To: window. Do this using the Add button, and choose the appropriate group from the Add Users and Groups dialog box. Selecting the Everyone group allows all user accounts access to the computer over the network. Don't choose this if you have limited network access for some users or groups.

5. Choose "Log on locally" from the Right: drop-down menu. The names of the local Guest account, the local Guest group or the global Guest groups should not be listed in the Grant To: window. If any of them are listed, remove them by using the Remove button. When finished, click the OK button to return to the User Manager for Domain main window.

By default, only the administrative accounts have the right to log on locally to a Windows NT Server, and the Everyone group is given access from the network rights. The only thing you need to do to allow network guest logon while restricting local guest logon is to enable the Guest account. (By default the guest account on a Windows NT domain is disabled and should remain that way to maintain a high degree of security.)

After reviewing some of the account basics, you now can take a closer look at how the operating system performs authentication and access validation against the user account. Let's start with a look at the data structure of Security Identifier, which is used to identify uniquely each user account.

Part

II

Ch

6

How the Security ID (SID) Is Constructed

Each user, group, and machine account is associated with a unique *Security Identification number (SID)*. This SID is generated when a user or group account is created and uniquely identifies that account for as long as the account exists on the system. The system uses this statistically unique number to regulate the user's access to any resources that may be available. Theoretically, a SID number should never be re-used with another account. A SID number is created using a hashing algorithm based on three 32-bit numbers that are derived from the following:

- The name of the computer
- The current system time on the computer
- The current thread's (used to create the SID) user-mode execution time

You can view the format of a SID number by opening the Windows NT Registry editor. When a user logs on to a Windows NT Server or Workstation, a user profile is created for the account. This profile contains desktop information and settings specific to the individual and is stored in the form of a *hive file* on the system. The registry contains the locations of these hive files and lists them by the individual account's SID number. To view the list of SID numbers for user profiles on a Windows NT Server, open the key as shown:

> HKEY_LOCAL_MACHINE\SOFTWARE\Microsoft\Windows NT\CurrentVersion\ProfileList

In Figure 6.2, you see the profiles that have been created on the FILE_SERVER1 server that you used in earlier examples.

FIG. 6.2

Profile information is listed by the account's unique SID number in the registry.

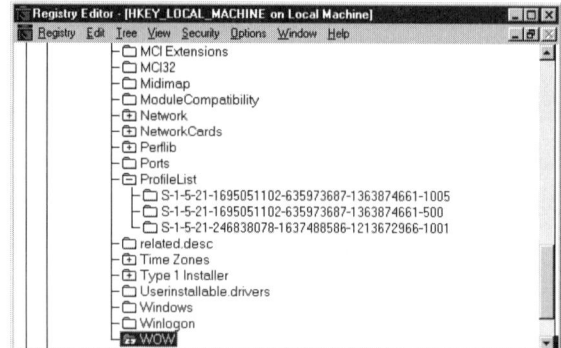

The figure in this example contains three numbers. Two that are similar, and one that has a different sequence of numbers in the middle. The reason for the difference is that the odd SID number actually belongs to a user account from the trusted domain ADMIN. Because the ADMIN domain created this SID, it contains identifiers within the SID that identify the account as an ADMIN SID.

Figure 6.3 shows the key:

    HKEY_LOCAL_MACHINE\SYSTEM\CurrentControlSet\Control\hivelist

This key gives the location of the system's hive files, and it also lists the location of user profile information by SID number. The SID number shown in Figure 6.3 is broken down into its different data structures.

FIG. 6.3

The SID number's components.

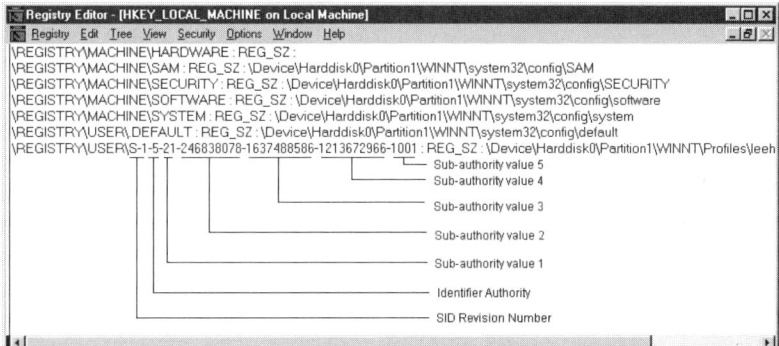

The individual and group SIDs are listed within special data structures called *Security Descriptors (SD)*. The Security Descriptors are used to list the individual and group accounts that are given access permissions to an *object*. The access rights given to a user are actually assigned to the user's SID number.

If you delete a user account and then re-create it with exactly the same account name and password, the account will not have automatic access to the resources the original account did. This is because the SID numbers will be different. Any Security Descriptors that contained the original account's SID number will not have the new account's SID number. Therefore, access to shared resources by the new account is not possible until the new account is specifically granted access rights by adding its SID (either by individual inclusion or group membership) to the objects Security Descriptor. In other words, you'll have to give them access to the resources again.

Part

II

Ch

6

Before you learn how a user is given remote resource access, you will see the log-on and authentication process that takes place. This process must be completed successfully before any access to network, workstation, or server resources is ever permitted.

How Log-On Validation Works

Logging on to the computer or a domain is required before the *Graphical User Interface (GUI)* starts on the Windows NT Server or Workstation. The user supplies a name and password that is validated against an account database. If the account is authenticated successfully, the GUI user interface starts and the user is allowed further access to the computer or network. The database that the log-on name and password are validated against depends on several factors.

For instance, if the user is attempting to log on to a Windows NT Server, the account name and password are compared to the domain's account database. If the server is a member of a trusting domain, the user also is given the option of authenticating against the trusted domain's account database.

A user logging on at a Windows NT Workstation that is not a member of a domain has his or her user account name and password validated against the Workstation's local accounts database. However, if the Windows NT Workstation is a member of a domain, the user has the option of logging in to the local workstation's account database, which is the domain account database that the workstation is a member of, or any domain account database that belongs to a domain that is trusted by the workstation's parent domain.

This means that a user at a Windows NT Workstation that is a domain member can log on using the same name and password to both the local accounts database and the domain's account database. If logging on to the local accounts database, the local security authority uses the log-on information and compares it with account information local to the machine. If logging on to the domain, the local security authority forwards the log-on request to a domain controller for validation.

You should remember that the two accounts are not the same account. They may have the same name and password, but the SID number that is assigned to the accounts are both different from each other. This can lead to confusion when users attempt to access network resources thinking they have logged on correctly when they really haven't. Giving access permission to ADMIN\JoeF may not allow the local Workstation account WORKSTATION\JoeF the same access rights to a network resource. Therefore, if JoeF logs on to his local workstation instead of the domain, he may not be able to access the same resources.

The Authentication Process

User authentication is performed in Windows NT using the MSV1_0 Authentication package that is called by the LsaLogonUser API. This is the default authentication package that ships with Windows NT, and it uses the SAM database as the container for all account security information. The MSV1_0 Authentication package also supports *pass-through authentication* using the Netlogon Service. Pass-through authentication means the Netlogon Service passes the log-on information to other computers for validation by their MSV1_0 Authentication packages. The authentication package at the remote computer then compares the log-on information it receives against the account information contained in its own local or domain user account database.

The MSV1_0 Authentication package actually is split into two parts, and each performs a specific function when validating user accounts. We'll call them Part A and Part B for simplicity. Part A accepts the actual user log-on information and always executes on the physical computer the user is logging on to. Part B is the part of the authentication package that compares the log-on information to the SAM database information. Part B does not necessarily have to execute on the same physical computer the user is logging on to. When a user is logging on to a workstation that is not a member of a domain, the authentication package references the local account database. In this case, Part A of the MSV1_0 Authentication package simply passes the log-on information it gathered from the user to Part B of the package. Part B then compares the log-on information it receives to the account information contained in the SAM database of the local machine.

The scenario is different when the user is not logging on to a local account database. For example, a user logging in on a Windows NT Workstation as a member of a domain can choose to log on to the domain instead of logging on to the local computer's account database. When Part A of the authentication package accepts log-on information, it recognizes the domain logon is requested. Because the database it needs to authenticate with is on a remote machine, it does not pass the log-on information to Part B of the authentication package on the local computer. Instead, the MSV1_0 Authentication package uses the Netlogon Service to pass log-on information to one of the target domain's controllers. Part B of the MSV1_0 Authentication package running on the responding domain controller accepts the information and processes it against the domain's account database.

How Passwords Are Used

Each user account has two passwords that are stored with the other user account information in the SAM database. The first is the LAN Manager compatible password and the second is the Windows NT password. Both of the passwords are doubly encrypted and stored within the SAM database. The first encryption is called a *one-way function (OWF)* version of the clear text password. It is the non-decryptable version of the password. The second encryption is a decryptable version that exists to confuse any would-be hackers. It can be decrypted by anyone having access to the double-encrypted password, the user's *Relative ID (RID)*, and the correct algorithm.

You might be asking why two passwords are kept instead of a single Windows NT password. The answer simply is because the first password enables backwards compatibility with the older LAN Manager 2.x server password convention. This convention specifies that the password be non-case sensitive, no more than 14 characters (14 bytes) long, and use the *Original Equipment Manufacturer (OEM)* character set. All characters are converted to uppercase before encryption, so the non-case sensitive requirement is satisfied.

This password, referred to as the LAN Manager OWF or ESTD version, is derived by encrypting a constant with the clear test password using the National Institute of Standards and Technology (NIST) Data Encryption Standard (DES) encryption. The LAN Manager OWF password is 16-bytes in length and is derived from the 14-byte clear text password. The first eight bytes of the encrypted password are calculated using the first seven bytes of the clear text password. The last eight bytes of the encrypted password are calculated from the last seven bytes of the clear text password.

The second user password stored in the SAM database is the Windows NT password or the Windows NT OWF password. This password uses the Unicode character set instead of the OEM character set. This password is case sensitive and can be up to 128 characters in length. The encrypted version of the password is computed using the popular and well known RSA Public-Key Cipher. This algorithm (developed in the late 1970's by Ron Rivest, Adi Shamir, and Leonard Adleman) is used to encrypt and decrypt keys. It also is used to generate and to verify digital signatures. Windows NT uses the RSA MD-4 encryption algorithm, which computes a 16-byte digest of a variable length string to clear text password bytes.

Interactive, Service, and Network Logons

The MSV1_0 Authentication package receives log-on information from the LsaLogonUser API. The LsaLogonUser supports interactive, service, and network logons by passing the following information to the authentication package:

- The name of the domain that contains the user account.
- The name of the user account.
- Some function of the user password.

The user password is represented differently depending on the type of logon being performed (interactive, service, or network).

Interactive and service logons occur on the same machine that is running Part A of the MSV1_0 Authentication package. The authentication package receives a clear text password from the LsaLogonUser and converts the password into the LAN Manager and Windows NT OWF versions of the password. From here, the password is passed on to the Netlogon Service if the domain name is different than the server's domain name. If the domain name is the same, the password is passed to Part B of the MSV1_0 Authentication package. The OWF versions of the password then are compared to the OWF versions of the password that reside in the SAM database to see if they match.

When a network logon occurs, the client is sent a 16-byte challenge called a *nonce*. The response to this challenge will be different for LAN Manager and Windows NT clients. Here are the events that take place during a network logon:

- LAN Manager clients compute a 24-byte challenge response by encrypting the combination of the 16-byte nonce and the 16-byte LAN Manager OWF password. The "LAN Manager Challenge Response" then is sent to the Windows NT server.

- A Windows NT client computes the same 24-byte "LAN Manager Challenge Response" that the LAN Manager client computes. Additionally, it computes its own 24-byte "Windows NT Challenge Response" by encrypting the combination of the 16-byte nonce and the 16-byte Windows NT OWF password. Both challenge responses then are sent to the Windows NT server.

The Netlogon Service passes the challenge responses along with the following information to the Windows NT server's LsaLogonUser API:

- The domain name
- The user name
- The original challenge
- The LAN Manager challenge response
- The Windows NT challenge response

Part
II

Ch
6

This information is passed to Part A of the Windows NT server's MSV1_0 Authentication package. Part A then passes the information unchanged to Part B of the Windows NT server's MSV1_0 Authentication package. Here, Part B compares the OWF password that was passed on to the OWF password located in the SAM database. An appropriate challenge response is computed and compared to the challenge response that originally was passed on.

How the Netlogon Service Is Used

The Netlogon Service enables pass-through authentication to occur between the client computers and the Windows NT servers. It performs three basic functions, as follows:

- Selects the domain that the authentication request will be sent to.
- Selects the controller within the domain that the authentication request will be sent to.
- Acts as the mechanism that passes the authentication request through to the selected server.

The Netlogon service handles authentication requests in three steps:

1. The discovery process that is used to select a controller in the target domain that will be used for authentication.
2. The next step establishes a secure channel between the computer passing the request and the controller that is selected. This is done to ensure that both of the connections are exactly who they say they are.
3. The third step actually passes the log-on information to the authenticating server.

What Happens During the Discovery Process?   The discovery process happens under several different circumstances. Discovery takes place in order to find a domain controller that can be used to authenticate the user logon. This happens when a user attempts to log on to a specific domain from a Windows NT Workstation or a Windows NT Server that's not a domain controller. Before the user can be authenticated by the domain's SAM database, a controller containing the database first must be found. After the controller is located, its information is cached and is used for subsequent calls to the SAM database.

Discovery also takes place during the startup of a Windows NT Workstation that's a member of a domain. The workstation sends out a discovery request to find the domain controllers when it starts up. The controllers respond to the discovery query, which then is cached by the workstation and is used for subsequent calls to the domain's SAM database. When a user logs on to the workstation, the cached information is by the Netlogon Service to direct the authentication request off to one of the domain controllers.

The discovery process also takes place during the startup of a domain controller to find the names of any trusted domain controllers. Domain controllers know about the other controllers in their own domain because of the information contained within their SAM database. However, they are not aware of the controllers available in any domains that are set up via a trust relationship. When a domain query is sent to the trusted domain, any available controllers in the trusted domain then respond. The information on these controllers is cached and is used for subsequent calls to the trusted domain's SAM database. An example of the discovery process can be seen in Figure 6.4.

FIG. 6.4

The discovery process on a trusting domain controller.

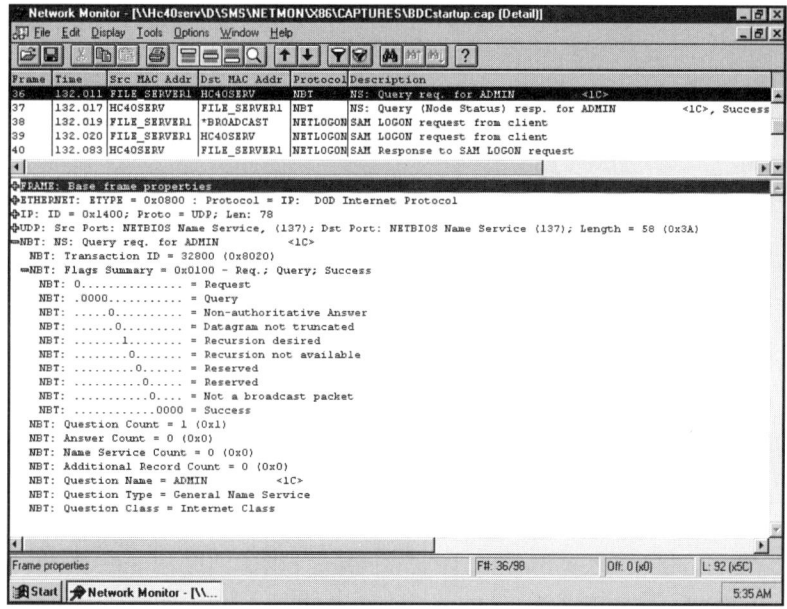

This example uses the Network Monitor utility to capture network traffic during the startup of the controller named FILE_SERVER1 within the trusting domain named SHARES. The trusted domain name is ADMIN, which has one PDC named HC40SERV. The first packet shown contains the discovery request sent by FILE_SERVER1, and the second packet is the response from the trusted domain controller HC40SERV. The other three packets initiate the Interdomain trust account logon sequence.

▶ **See** "Establishing the Trust's Communications Link." **p. 137**

If a response to the trusting domain controller's query is not received, another series of queries is sent every 15 minutes until a controller is located on the trusted domain. If a valid request is issued for a resource on the trusted domain and a domain controller has not yet been located, another request is sent out immediately.

Setting Up a Secure Communications Link If the discovery process was successful, a secure communications channel is set up between the Netlogon Service of the Workstation and the Netlogon Service on the trusted domain. This channel is needed to pass authentication requests to the authentication package located at the domain controller. This secure link is established using standard user level security and some special user accounts. One of these accounts, the Interdomain trust account, is discussed in Chapter 5, "Maintaining Security with Domain Trust Relationships." It enables the Windows NT server computer to perform pass-through authentication to a controller on a trusted domain. Other special accounts are the following:

Part

II

Ch

6

- *Workstation Trust Account*   This account works like the Interdomain trust account, except it allows authentication requests to be sent to the domain controllers in the domain the workstation is a member of.

- *Server Trust Account*   This account enables the server to get backup copies of the master domain database from the domain controller.

The setup of the secure channel can be seen in the last three packet entries in Figure 6.4. Similar to the discovery process, if the secure link cannot be established immediately, the connection is re-attempted every 15 minutes or whenever a pass-through authentication request is received. The Windows NT Workstation or Server caches the last ten users' log-on credentials for use in the event a secure link can't be established to a domain controller. This allows the user to log on in case the domain controllers all are down or network connectivity from the log-on machine to the controllers is interrupted.

Why Pass-Through Authentication Is Used   Pass-through authentication is used when the user's account cannot be authenticated at the local machine. This happens when a user logs on interactively to a Windows NT Workstation or Windows NT Server (not a domain controller) that is a domain member. It also occurs during a *remote logon* when a user is logged on to one domain and requests the resources on another domain.

It is possible to be logged on in several different ways to a Windows NT environment. Each log-on scenario is handled differently, depending on where the user is logging on from. Here are some of the different log-on scenarios:

- *Logon to a Windows NT Workstation that is not a domain member*   Log-on information supplied in the Logon Information dialog box is compared against the workstation's local accounts database. The From box in the Logon Information dialog box only lists the local machine name.

- *Logon to a Windows NT Workstation that is a domain member*   The From box in the Logon Information dialog box lists the local machine name and the domain name the workstation is a member of. If the user chooses the local workstation name in the From box, their log-on information is authenticated by the local SAM database. If the user chooses the domain name instead, the Netlogon service forwards the request to a domain controller where the log-on information is authenticated against the domain's SAM database.

- *Logging on to a trusted domain from a member Windows NT workstation or server*   This causes the Netlogon Service to pass the authentication request to a domain controller in the trusted domain. The account is checked against the domain's SAM database for a match. If the account can't be authenticated, and the Guest account is enabled in the trusted domain controller, the user is logged on to the trusted domain as a guest.

Differences Between Interactive and Remote Logon

The interactive logon is just that, an interactive user log-on session at the computer. Conversely, a remote logon is not an interactive session at the computer. It is a logon that is attempted when a user wants to access resources on domains and computers other than the one they are interactively logged on to. For example, a user is logged on to a workstation and he or she attempts to connect to a share in another domain using the "`net use x: //servername/sharename`" command.

How an Interactive Logon Works   When you successfully log on to a workstation or server, you initiate an interactive log-on session. The user supplies his or her account name and password in the Logon Information dialog box. This information is used to authenticate the account and start the Windows graphical user interface (GUI). Users logging on to a Windows NT Workstation or a noncontroller Windows NT Server that is a member of a domain can choose to log on locally by selecting the workstation name in the Login Information dialog box. Or they can select to log on to the domain by selecting the domain name in the Login Information dialog box. Logging on locally attempts to authenticate the user's account by checking the SAM database of the local machine. Selecting the domain name in the Logon Information dialog box attempts to authenticate the user's account against the domain's SAM database at a domain controller using pass-through authentication.

If the Workstation is not a member of a domain, the domain option isn't available in the Logon Information dialog box. The only option for the user is to log on and to be authenticated against the local SAM database of the workstation. If a user is logging on to a domain controller, the option to log on to the local machine is not available. The user only is allowed to log on to the domain the server is a controller in. However, if any trust relationships have been set up between the controller's domain and another domain, the user is able to select the names of any *trusted* domains in the Logon Information dialog box. The Netlogon Service then forwards the user account information to a domain controller in the trusted domain for log-on authentication against its SAM database.

Part

II

Ch

6

Gaining Resource Access Using Remote Logon   The remote logon process is used when a user interactively logged on to one computer needs access to resources on another computer. An example of this is when you use Explorer or File Manager to map a drive to a network server's share.

How the log-on process actually functions depends on how the user is logged on and what the user is logged on to. The flow charts in Figure 6.5 through Figure 6.10 give you an example of the remote log-on process that takes place when a simple `net use:` command is issued at the command line from a Windows NT Server.

FIG. 6.5
The remote log-on
process, chart 1 of 6.

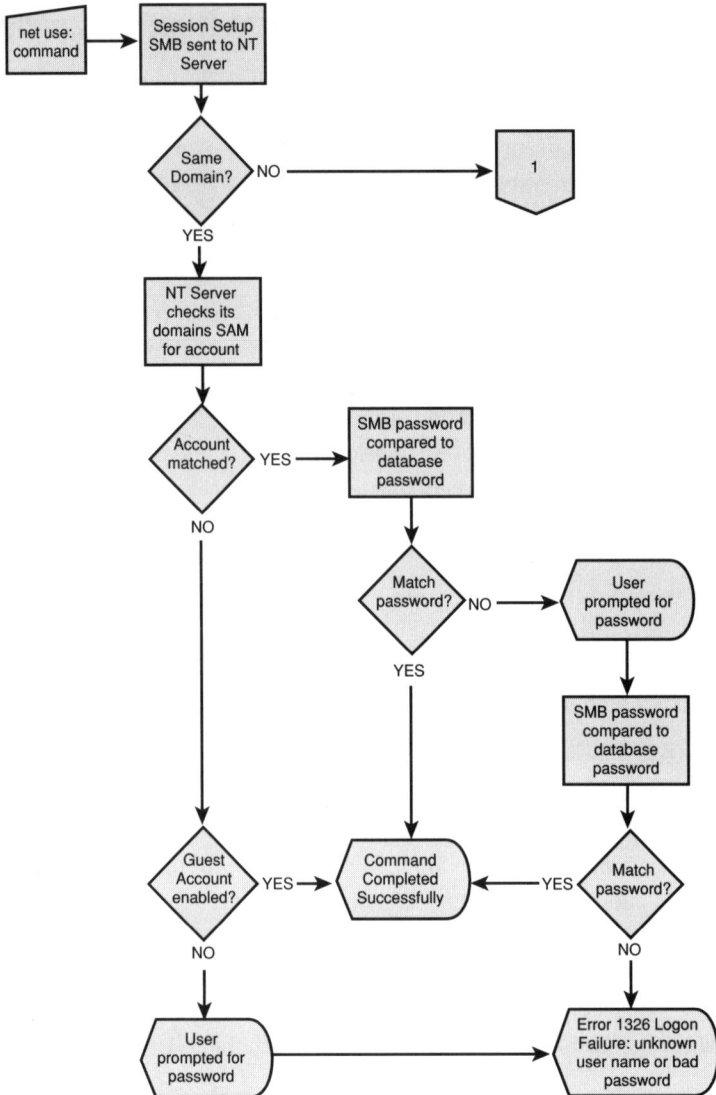

FIG. 6.6
Chart 2 of 6.

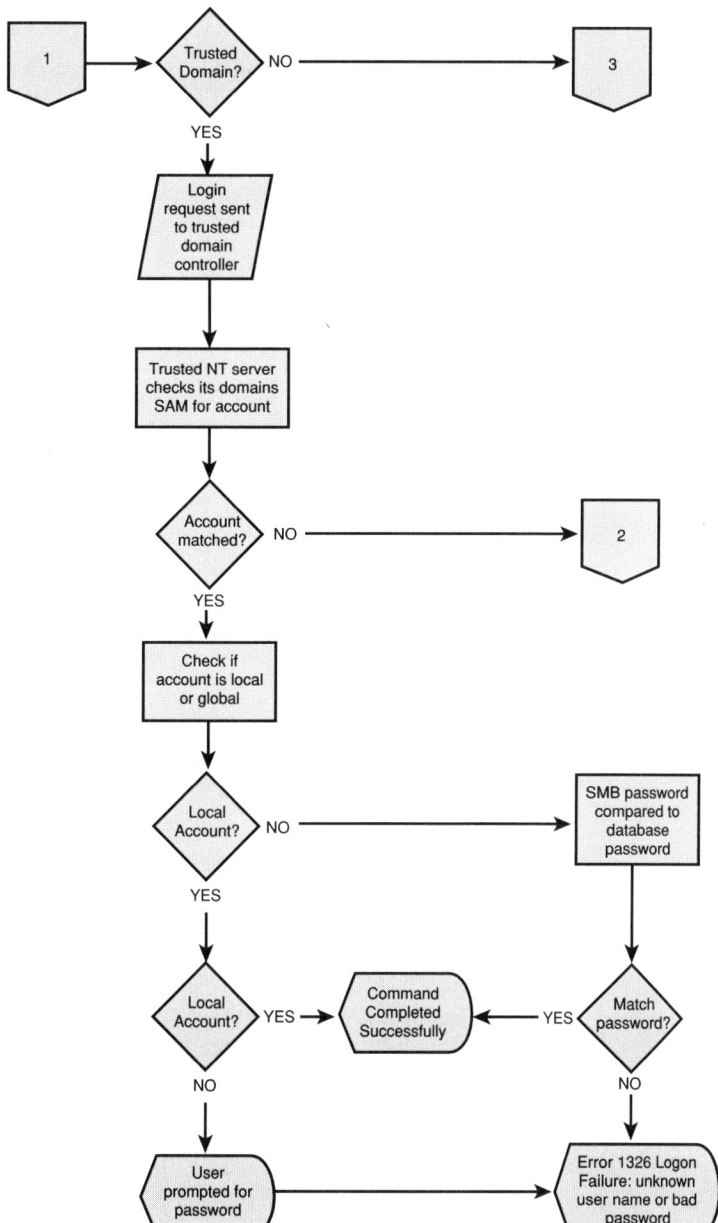

FIG. 6.7
Chart 3 of 6.

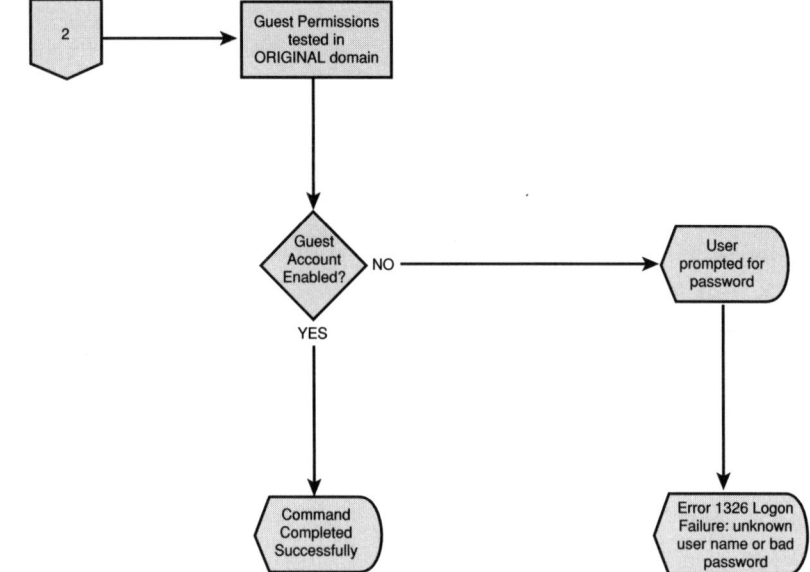

FIG. 6.8
Chart 4 of 6.

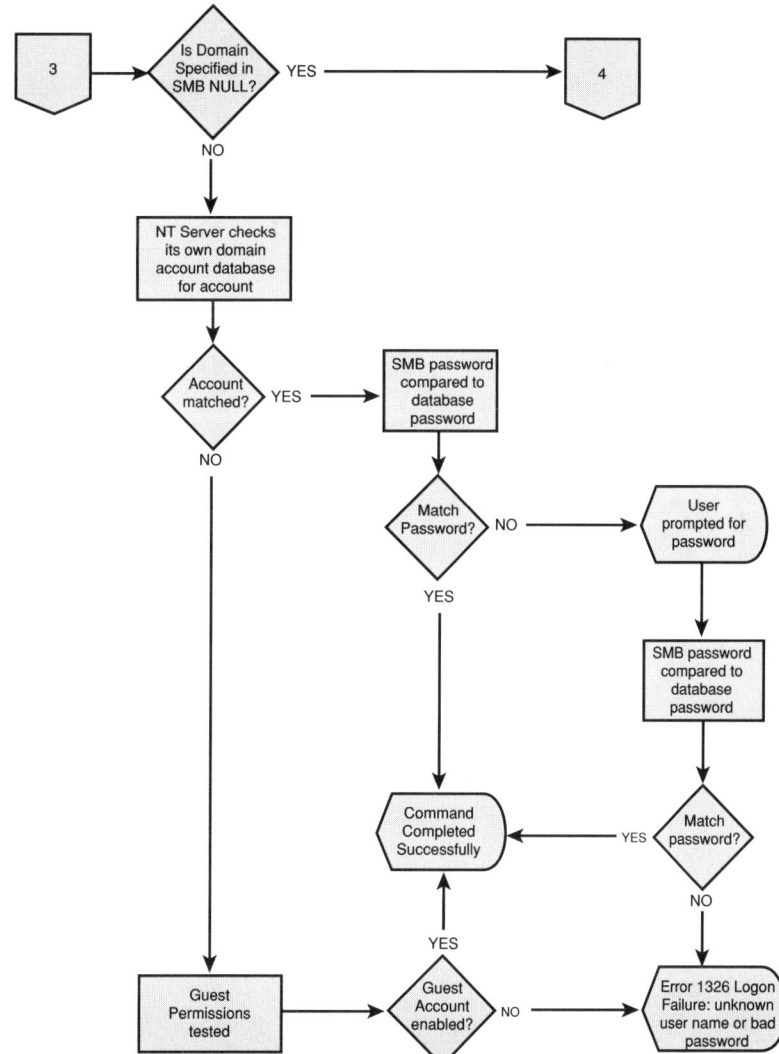

FIG. 6.9
Chart 5 of 6.

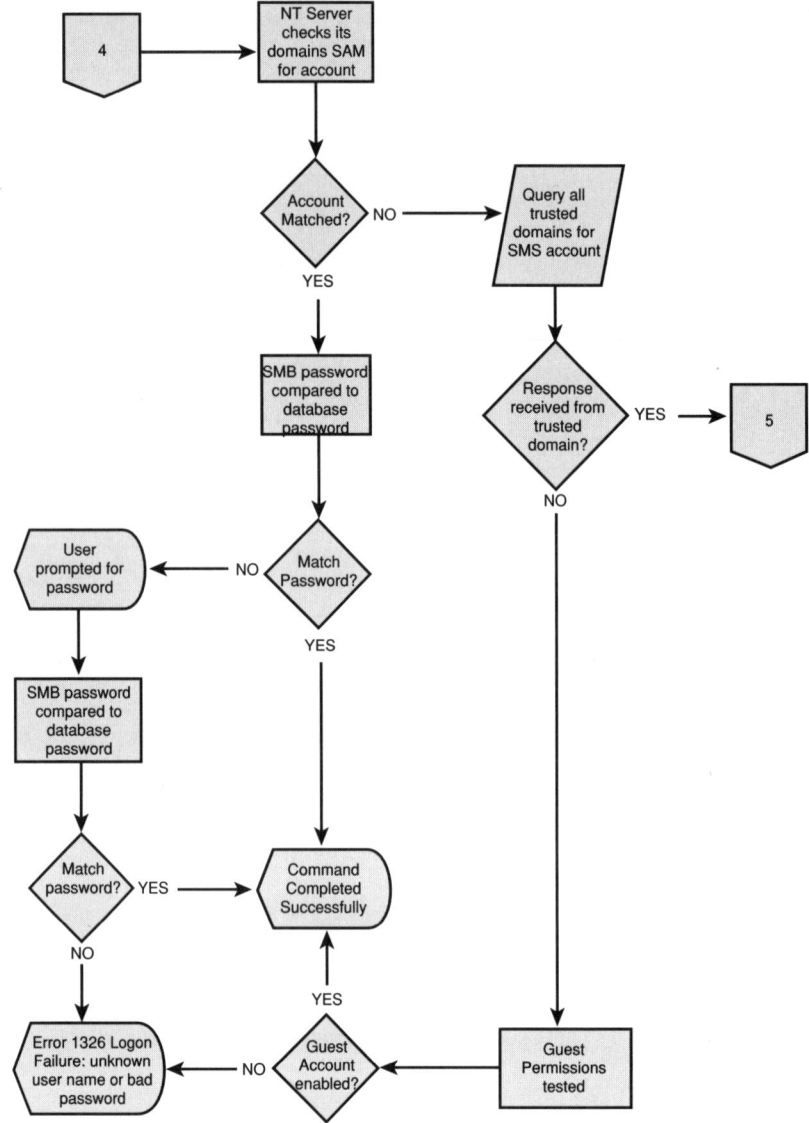

FIG. 6.10
Chart 6 of 6.

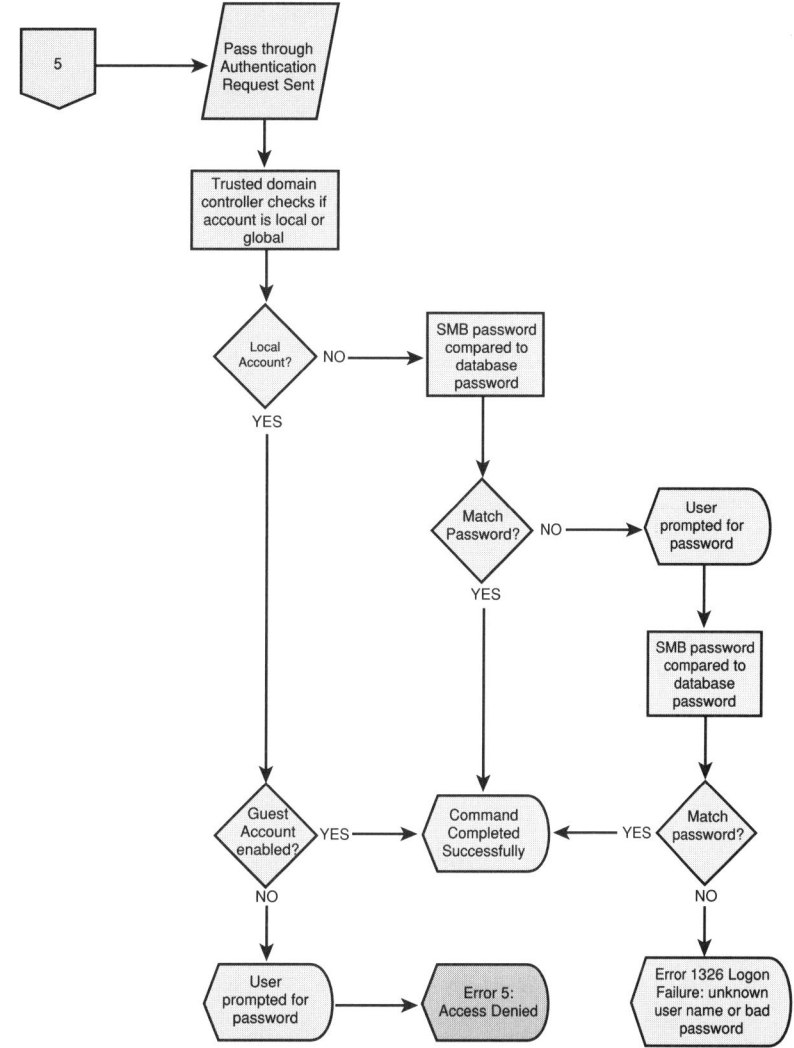

These flow charts illustrate the different ways a user can access a remote resource. Notice how often the guest account comes into play. Turning on the guest account does have some underlying ramifications that certainly can pose a security threat unless the guest privileges are monitored closely.

The charts make reference to the *Server-Message-Block* or *SMB*. This is a structure within a network packet that is used as the vehicle for client redirector requests and the corresponding server responses. The different parts of an SMB (see Figure 6.11) consist of the following:

■ *The header*   This portion consists of environmental and parameter fields.

■ *The command(s)*   Specifies the request that the redirector wants the remote station to perform.

■ *The optional data area*   This part of the SMB can contain up to 64K of data that is directed to the remote station.

FIG. 6.11
The different parts of the SMB.

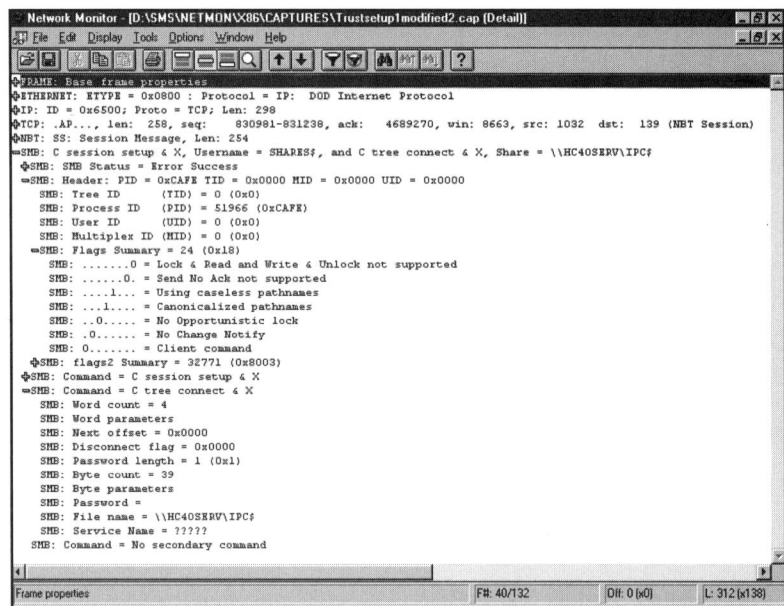

The process of creating the user's access token and *user identifier (UID)* for a client accessing a remote resource is shown in the following steps:

1. A security access token (token 1) is created during the initiation of the interactive user log-on session. The token is assigned to the initial user process.

2. The user attempts access to a remote resource (performs a `net use:` command as shown in the preceding flow charts) on another server (server B).

3. Server B authenticates the user account and creates another access token (token 2) for the user.

4. Server B stores token 2 in a local table.

5. Server B creates a UID for the user and maps the UID to token 2 in its local table.

6. The UID is sent back to the client redirector.

7. The client redirector inserts the UID into any SMBs that are subsequently sent to Server B.

Any other requests for resources on server B will include the UID that was created during the initial resource connection.

▶ **See** "The Logon Process," **p. 80**

Concluding this chapter is a look at some common problems that can occur with user account logons in a domain environment.

Common Problems with User Accounts

Most of the problems that occur when a user attempts to log on and is denied access are because of duplicate accounts with mixed passwords. For example, John has an account on domain A with the account named "John" and the password "go." At the same time, John has a user account named "John" with a password of "stop" on domain B. When John is logged on to domain A and attempts to view or access resources on domain B, his access is denied.

The remedy to this situation is simple. Either match the passwords on each of John's accounts, or set up a trust relationship between domain A and domain B to eliminate one of John's accounts. Using the one user, one log-on account concept that's used with domain trust relationships is the easiest way to eliminate such access problems. In this example with John, you also could match the two passwords to eliminate the access problem he has.

Another problem can occur when the BDCs in a domain are not synchronized fully with the master account database at the PDC. This can cause users to experience log-on problems until synchronization within the domain has taken place.

For example, say you change John's password on his domain. This change is made to the master account database on the PDC. Before the password change to the account database has been replicated to the BDCs, John attempts to log on with his new password. The first controller to respond is a BDC that has not had the password change updated within its copy of the account database. John's logon fails until the BDC's account database is up-to-date. This situation easily can be remedied by performing a full domain synchronization using the Server Manager administrative program.

Several of the changes that are made to the account database require the full synchronization of the domain controllers. These can be changes initiated in User Manager for Domain or in the Server Manager and can include the following:

- The creation of a new user or group account
- Changing a user's password
- Modifying the domain's user policy
- Modifying group memberships
- Changing the log-on script path or location of a user's home directory
- Changing the user's valid log-on times
- Modification of the account type or expiration date
- Changing the machines that the user is allowed to log on from
- The creation of a new workstation or server account in the domain

Usually, the synchronization process is handled by the Netlogon Service and occurs before any log-on problems are experienced. However, if you suspect a problem due to synchronization, go ahead and perform a full domain synchronization using the Server Manager program.

From Here...

This chapter covers the specific properties of Windows NT user accounts and the process involved when a user account attempts to be authenticated in a Windows NT environment. For further reference on topics discussed in this chapter, see the following:

- Chapter 7, "New Technology File System (NTFS) Security," examines protection that can be added directly to the files and directories that exist on NTFS partitions.
- Chapter 8, "Using Windows NT Security to Protect Domain Resources," looks at the tools that Windows NT provides the network administrators. Also shows you how to use these tools to provide network security.
- Chapter 9, "Windows NT Workstation Security," examines the security issues surrounding the participation of a Windows NT workstation in a domain environment.

New Technology File System (NTFS) Security

Using the NTFS file system to create the primary barrier of protection against unauthorized access to files and directories is the subject of this chapter. With Windows NT 4.0 the two file systems that can be used are the standard *FAT (File Allocation Table)* file system or the NTFS file system. Each of these file systems works differently, and only NTFS offers the capability to add security directly to files and directories. This chapter focuses on the security aspects of NTFS and not the mechanics or performance issues that exist between it and the FAT file system. You see how to protect data by adding access permissions to drive resources, and you learn how share permissions are complimented by NTFS permissions. ■

NTFS overview

Gives you a quick overview of the NTFS file system and what makes it different than the FAT file system.

NTFS advantages

Explore the features of NTFS that can enhance the security of the server's file and directory resources.

Using NTFS

You can use this to set up permissions on files and directories.

NTFS and Share level permissions

Share level security works with NTFS security to provide a secure network environment that is easy to administer.

NTFS auditing

NTFS auditing provides you with a way to track disk resource access and use.

What Is NTFS?

The Windows NT operating system enables you to format hard drive volume using the NTFS file system instead of the commonly used FAT file system. Formatting a hard drive with NTFS enables security to be implemented on the file and directory level, in addition to any share permissions that might be present. NTFS is a file system developed by Microsoft specifically for the Windows NT operating system. It alone provides the capability to secure files and directories located on Windows NT Workstations and Servers. When used in conjunction with share level security, it provides yet another way to enhance the security of the file and directory resources that are available on the network.

Why Use the NTFS File System?

Share permission can't protect files and directories from being accessed locally by a user during an interactive log-on session. Share level security only controls network (or over the wire) access to resources. If a user has been given rights to log on locally they can access the root directories on the computer's hard drive. These users don't need to rely on share permissions to acquire access to file or directory information. This is why it is important to take advantage of NTFS security on any media that contains information that is either sensitive or critical to the operation of your business.

N O T E   Previous versions of Windows NT also enabled *HPFS (High Performance File System)* volumes to be read. Windows NT 4.0 only recognizes the FAT and NTFS file systems. Older HPFS volumes that reside on Windows NT 3.X machines first must be converted to NTFS using the convert.exe utility before upgrading to Windows NT 4.0. ■

NTFS also gives you the capability to audit the success or failure of file and directory access by any individual or group. The success-failure auditing of files and directories can be enabled for specific events or for all events. Events include the following:

- Read
- Write
- Execute
- Delete
- Change Permission
- Take Ownership

Besides giving the added security of tracking how files and directories are used, auditing also can give you an idea of what files and directories are accessed the most, so you can plan server load balancing.

The FAT file system, although better suited to certain types of operations, does not allow for auditing or any local access control limitations on its files and directories. Clearly from a security standpoint, NTFS is the preferred file system.

Share Permissions versus NTFS Permissions

Share permissions give you a way of specifying which users or groups have access to a directory that has been shared as a network resource. They do not limit a local user's ability to access and manipulate files on the workstation or server as shown in Figure 7.1.

FIG. 7.1
Security without the use of NTFS.

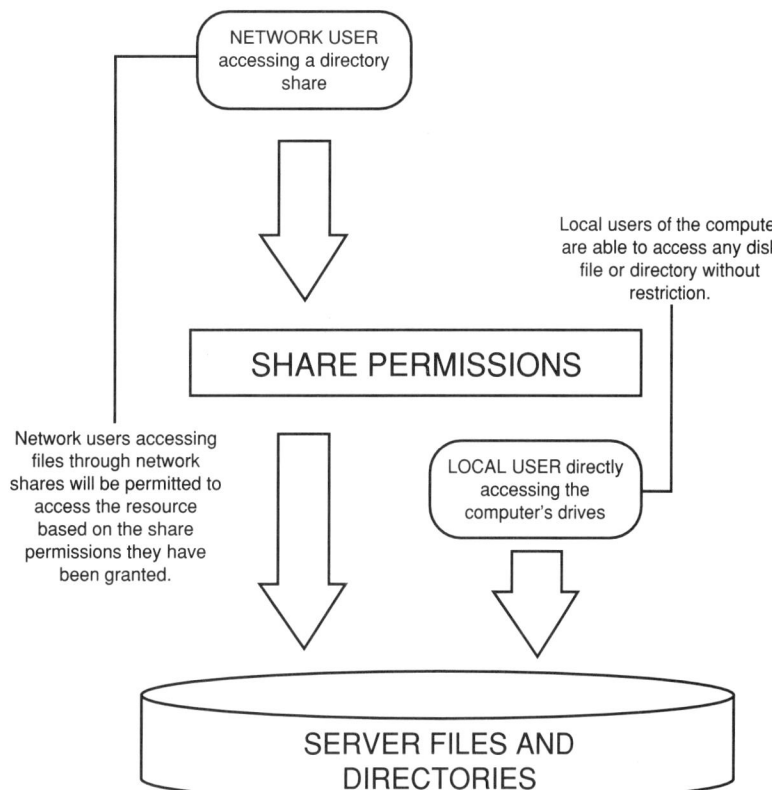

On the other hand, NTFS permissions limit a local user's ability to access and manipulate files or directories. Figure 7.2 shows you how NTFS permissions still apply to users that are accessing files or directories from a network share.

Part
II

Ch
7

FIG. 7.2
Security with NTFS permissions.

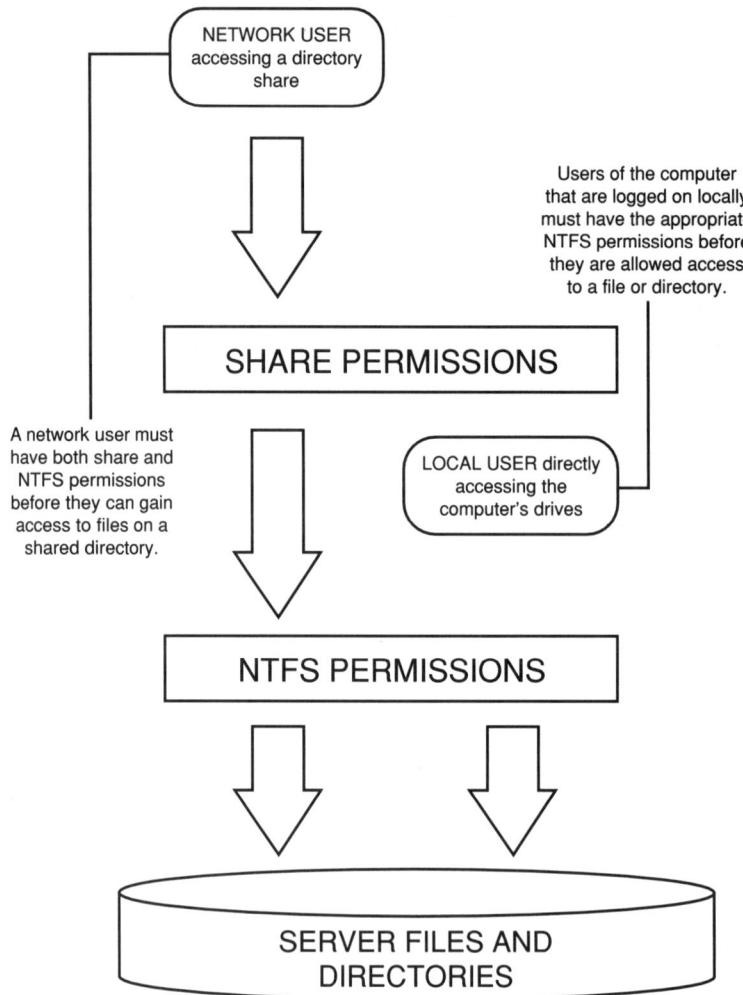

When both types of security are used, NFTS permissions applied to a directory or file override share permissions.

How to Implement NTFS Security

Before you can use NTFS to secure the files and directories located on a hard disk, the disk's partition must be formatted with the NTFS file system. The option of formatting a partition with NTFS is given during the initial setup of Windows NT Workstation or Server. After the Windows NT installation, the formatting of any new drive partition with NTFS can be done from the Disk Administrator utility or from the command line. If the partition is currently formatted with the FAT file system, the convert.exe command line utility can be used to change the file system to NTFS without losing any information. Once converted, the files and directories can have NTFS permissions applied to them just as any other NTFS volume.

Creating an NTFS Volume

There are several ways a disk partition can be formatted with the NTFS file system. The first way is during installation of the Windows NT operating system. During the setup procedure, you are given the opportunity of creating partitions and formatting them with the FAT or NTFS file system. If you are installing on a drive that already has been formatted with the FAT file system, the setup program gives you the opportunity to convert the drive to NTFS as shown in Figure 7.3.

FIG. 7.3
The setup program enables you to convert an existing FAT partition to NTFS during installation.

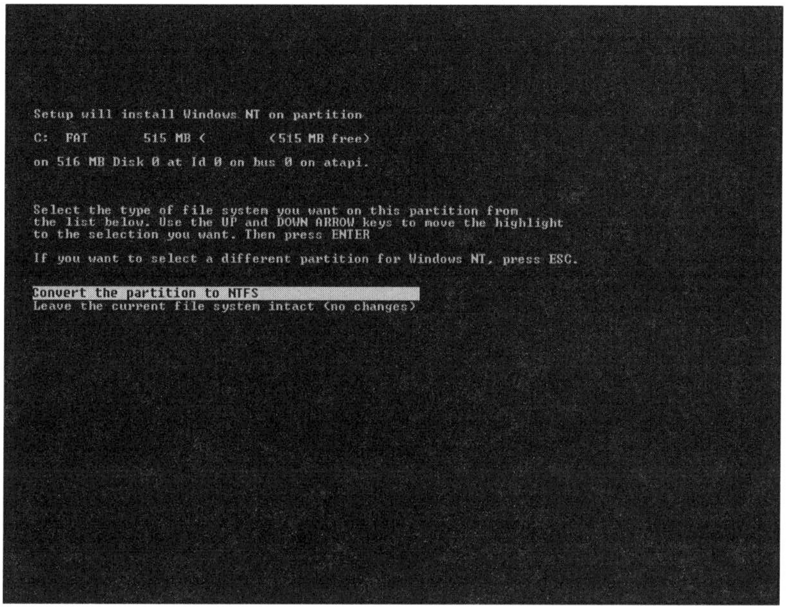

```
Setup will install Windows NT on partition

    C:  FAT        515 MB <        (515 MB free)
    on 516 MB Disk 0 at Id 0 on bus 0 on atapi.


    Select the type of file system you want on this partition from
    the list below. Use the UP and DOWN ARROW keys to move the highlight
    to the selection you want. Then press ENTER

    If you want to select a different partition for Windows NT, press ESC.

    Convert the partition to NTFS
    Leave the current file system intact (no changes)
```

If you select the conversion option during setup, a warning screen appears informing you of the incompatibility of NTFS with non-Windows NT operating systems (see Figure 7.4). This is just letting you know that the NTFS partition is not operational under any other operating systems in the event you are running a dual-boot system. In other words, if you format the partition with NTFS and start up under Windows 95, you will not be able to see the NTFS formatted partition (without an NTFS-reader utility program, that is).

Part
II

Ch
7

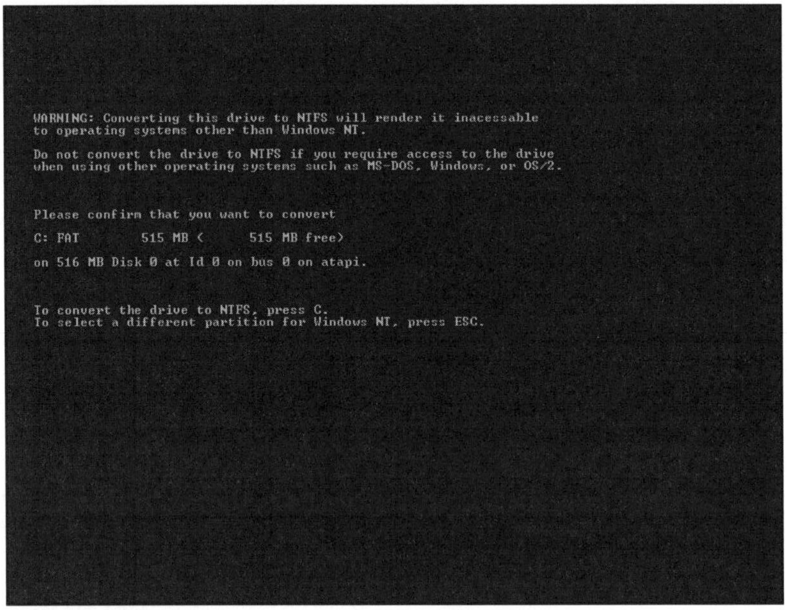

FIG. 7.4

Other operating systems in a dual boot configuration cannot recognize the NTFS partition.

```
WARNING: Converting this drive to NTFS will render it inaccessable
to operating systems other than Windows NT.

Do not convert the drive to NTFS if you require access to the drive
when using other operating systems such as MS-DOS, Windows, or OS/2.


Please confirm that you want to convert

C: FAT          515 MB (      515 MB free)

on 516 MB Disk 0 at Id 0 on bus 0 on atapi.


To convert the drive to NTFS, press C.
To select a different partition for Windows NT, press ESC.
```

When additional drives are added to the computer, the new drives can be partitioned and formatted with NTFS using the graphical Disk Administrator utility. Existing partitions also can be formatted with NTFS from the command line using the format.exe utility. Although the Disk Administrator utility can be used to partition and format a new hard drive, it cannot be used to convert an existing FAT partition to an NTFS partition. This must be done using the convert.exe utility from the command line.

Using the Disk Administrator utility to partition and format a drive with NTFS under Windows NT 4.0 is a simple procedure—just follow these steps:

1. Log on to the server or workstation under an account that has administrative privileges and start the Disk Administrator utility.

2. From the View menu select Disk Configuration.

3. Highlight the new unpartitioned drive space (Free Space) and click the right mouse button to open the drop-down menu. Select the Create option from the menu (see Figure 7.5) to open the Create Primary Partition dialog box.

4. Designate how much of the new drive will be committed to this partition by entering the appropriate size in megabytes (MB) in the Create partition of size box. Click the OK button after entering the partition size.

5. The new drive space is now identified in Disk Administrator as a drive that is not formatted. Right-click the unformatted drive space to open the drop-down menu. Select Commit Changes Now from the menu.

FIG. 7.5

Create the partition for the NTFS volume.

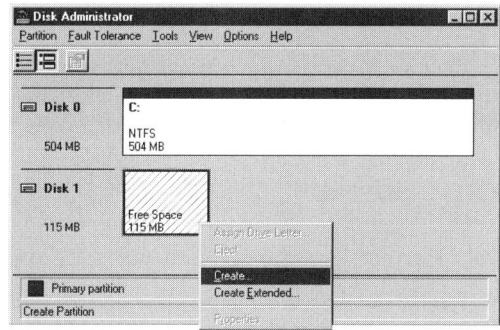

6. The Confirm dialog box appears asking you to confirm the changes you've made to your disk configuration. Click Yes to save the changes. This is followed by a dialog box informing you that the disk configuration was updated successfully and that you should create another Emergency Repair Disk using the rdisk.exe utility. Click the OK button to continue.

7. Right-click the newly partitioned drive space to open the drop-down menu. From the menu select the Format option to open the Format drive:\ dialog box (where *drive* is the drive letter of the newly partitioned space).

8. Select NTFS from the File System drop-down list (see Figure 7.6) and click the Start button. The Format drive:\ warning dialog box appears reminding you that any current information contained on the drive will be lost. Click the OK button to start the format procedure. A bar at the bottom of the dialog box will indicate the progress of the format, followed by the Format Complete message.

FIG. 7.6

Select the NTFS file system from the Format dialog box.

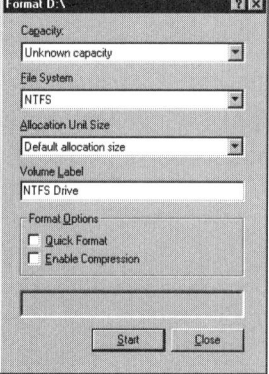

Part

II

Ch

7

9. Click the OK button to close the message box, then click the Close button to close the Format drive:\ dialog box.

A partitioned disk area also can be formatted with the NTFS file system using the format.exe utility from the command line. The format command line utility is most often used when you want to specify a disk allocation size unit larger than the 4K limit imposed by Disk Manager. To format a partition with NTFS from the command line, use the basic syntax:

```
FORMAT drive: [/FS:file-system]
```

Where `drive` is the letter designation of the partition and `file-system` is equal to NTFS. For example, if you're formatting a new partition with NTFS that has a drive letter designation of D:, the command line syntax would be:

```
FORMAT d: /FS:ntfs
```

After you complete formatting the partition with NTFS, you can implement both security and auditing on the volume using Windows NT Explorer or one of the other utilities.

Converting from FAT to NTFS

If you are adding a FAT drive to the system and want to implement NTFS security on its contents, you first must convert the file system to NTFS. Once the drive is physically installed in the computer, use the `convert.exe` command line utility to convert the FAT file system to NTFS.

For example, you have just installed a drive from an older server into a Windows NT 4.0 Server. The drive was originally formatted with the FAT file system and contains information that you want to keep. You also want to implement NTFS security on the contents of this drive. The drive was added to the system and assigned the drive letter designation "D." The drive properties for the FAT drive does not show a Security tab (see Figure 7.7). Security permissions for any files or directories on the drive only can be implemented on the share level using the Sharing tab.

To implement NTFS security on the FAT drive (your D: drive), you use the convert utility from the command line with the following syntax:

```
CONVERT d: /FS:ntfs
```

The conversion utility displays informational text indicating the progress and completion of the conversion process as shown in Figure 7.8.

FIG. 7.7

You can't set NTFS security on a FAT partition.

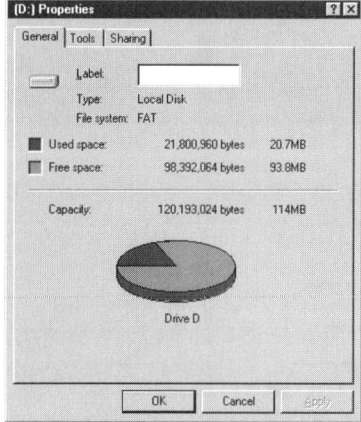

FIG. 7.8

Converting a FAT drive to NTFS from the command line.

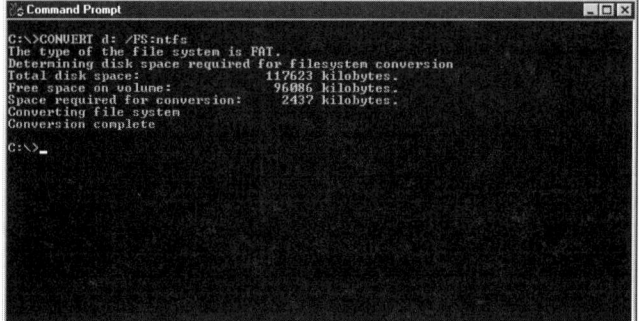

The conversion process causes the loss of a small percentage of usable drive space (2–3 percent) that is subsequently used within the structure of the NTFS file system. After the conversion process is complete, you can apply NTFS permission on the drive or any of its files and directories. If you look at the properties page for the drive after the conversion process is complete, you can see that a Security tab now is available in the Properties dialog box (see Figure 7.9). The Security tab enables you to assign permissions to the file, directory, or drive. It also enables you to implement auditing or take ownership of the selected item. Now that you've explored the installation of an NTFS volume, look at how NTFS is used.

Part

II

Ch

7

FIG. 7.9
The Security tab is available now for implementing NTFS security.

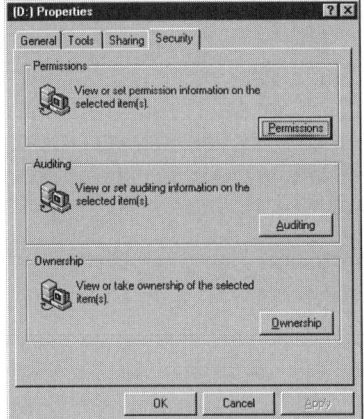

How NTFS Security Is Applied

You may apply NTFS security to limit user access to any drive, directory, or file located on the NTFS volume. Additionally, you can audit the success or failure of access to any directory or file by any individual or group on the system. Applying either security or auditing easily can be done using the Windows NT Explorer or My Computer file manager utilities. In the following examples you see how to apply both security and auditing on selected files and directories. Let's begin with a look at the application of NTFS permissions at the file level.

Setting File Access Permissions

Setting the NTFS permissions at the file level allows the owner of the file to control any access to the file. It also enables the owner of the file to designate other accounts that can regulate access to the file by changing the access permissions. The owner of the file can authorize individuals (or groups) with the following access permissions:

- *No Access*   Inhibits all access to the file by the specified individual or group. This type of access overrides all other types of access a user may have to the file as an individual or member of a group.

- *Read (RX)*   Enable read access or execute access to the file only. It does not permit modification or writing to the file.

- *Change (RWXD)*   Permits the file to be read, modified, or deleted.

- *Full Control (All)*   Permits the file to be read, modified, and deleted. It also permits accounts to take ownership of the file and set permissions.

■ *Special Access*   Selecting this option enable any or all types of access to be applied to the file. This includes read, write, execute, delete, change permission, and take ownership.

The permissions on a file are cumulative. This means that a user having membership in a group with read privileges to the file also could belong to a group that has full access to the file. The user would have the greater of the access permissions—full access in this case. The exception to this is the No Access attribute. This overrides any other access privilege that a user may have been granted, either individually or as a member of a group.

One of the rules that applies to NTFS permissions says that in order to change the permissions on a file you must be the owner of the file. That's not exactly true; by default the group Everyone is given Full Control access privileges to all new files (unless the file has inherited a specific set of permissions from its parent directory). When the group Everyone has Full Control access, any user can set permissions or take ownership of the file.

However, if the file's *parent directory* has specific NTFS permissions applied to it that limits user access to the file, the file automatically inherits the access attributes from its parent directory. That does not include the owner attribute, which will always designate the creator of the file. The only time the owner attribute of the file does not reflect the original file creator is when the creator grants ownership access to another user. Then, that user actively must assume ownership by using the Take Ownership option.

In the following example let's use Windows NT Explorer to assign permissions to a document file located on an NTFS volume. This particular document (named DAVE LETTER.DOC) was created by the user named David and was saved in a common document directory. This document directory has the Full Control access permissions given to the Everyone group, and when David saved his document, it automatically inherited the permissions of its parent directory. The system automatically assigned Full Control permissions to the file for the Everyone group. Dave doesn't want his document modified, so he applies read-only access permissions to the file using the following procedure:

1. Using the Windows NT Explorer or My Computer file management utility, locate the file and right-click it to open the drop-down menu.
2. Select <u>P</u>roperties from the menu to open the properties dialog box for the file.
3. Select the Security tab and click the <u>P</u>ermission button to open the File Permissions dialog box.
4. To change the access permission for the group Everyone to read-only, select Read from the <u>T</u>ype of Access drop-down list. You'll see that the permissions listed for the group Everyone in the <u>N</u>ame window have changed from Full Control (All) to Read (RX).

Part

II

Ch

7

At this point, if David clicked the OK button he wouldn't be able to modify the file. Because he gave the group Everyone (of which he is a member) read-only permission, when he modifies the file and attempts to save it, he gets the error shown in Figure 7.10. To modify the file, he must give himself the Change permission.

FIG. 7.10

Read-only access
prevents the file from
being modified and
written to disk.

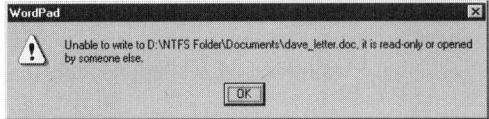

5. Click the Add button to open the Add Users and Groups dialog box.

6. Select the domain of the owner (David in this example) from the List Names From drop-down list.

7. Click the Show Users button, so the individual account names appear with the group names in the Names window.

8. Select the appropriate user account from the names listed in the Names window (David in your example) and click the Add button. This adds the account name (David) to the Add Names window.

9. Select Change or Full Control from the Type of Access drop-down list and then click the OK button. In this example this adds David's name and permission levels to the File Permissions dialog box as shown in Figure 7.11.

FIG. 7.11

Adding change
permissions for the
owner of the file.

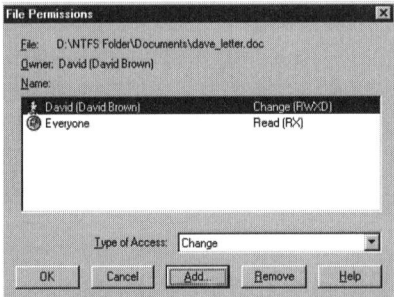

10. Click the OK button twice—once to close the File Permissions dialog box, and again to close the file name Properties box.

At this time any other users on the system will be able to read the document file, but they will not be able to modify it and save it back to disk. The only person able to change the file in this example is David. Any other user gets the error shown in Figure 7.10 when they try to modify the file. However, because the Everyone group has been given full control of the directory, another user could load the read-only document and then save it under a different name.

Now that David has protected his document by assigning read-only permissions to it, he doesn't have to worry about anyone modifying it. What he does have to worry about is someone deleting the file! The read-only permissions he applied to the document file protect it against modification but don't protect the file from deletion. Anyone could delete the file because the Everyone group has Full Control of the documents directory. The Full Control permission (which includes delete permission) at the directory level enables the users of the system to delete any file in the directory regardless of the specific permissions applied to the file itself.

Assigning Directory Permissions

Instead of users assigning individual access permissions to files located within a common directory, users are most often assigned their own personal directory. This gives the user a greater degree of flexibility when assigning access permissions to the files within their directory. Moreover, the implementation of NTFS security at the user directory level can prevent files from being deleted by other users.

The access permissions that can be applied to directories are similar to the permissions that can be applied to individual files. The access level defined within the first set of parentheses following the name indicates the access attributes that apply at the directory level. The second set of parentheses contains the access attributes that apply at the corresponding file level. You'll notice that the List and Add permissions do not have a corresponding file level access attribute.

- *No Access (None) (None)* Inhibits all access to the directory for the specified individual or group. This type of access overrides all other types of access a user may have to the directory as an individual or member of a group.
- *List (RX) (Not Specified)* Permits users to list the files within the immediate directory and any of its subdirectories. Users cannot open, modify, take ownership, change access permissions, or delete files created within the subdirectory. They can change to subdirectories of the current directory.
- *Read (RX) (RX)* Gives the specified user or group permission to list and open files and subdirectories. Change focus from the current directory to subdirectories. Files can be executed if they are application files.
- *Add (WX) (Not Specified)* Applying this access permission to a directory enables the specified individual or group to add files to the directory, but they cannot view the contents of the directory.

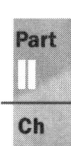

Part
II

Ch
7

- *Add & Read (RWX) (RX)*   This permission enables users to view file and directory names in addition to opening files and viewing their data. Users also can execute a file if it is an application file. Files and subdirectories also can be added to the current directory when this permission is specified for an individual or group.

- *Change (RWXD) (RWXD)*   Lets the individual or group specified list, read, modify, and delete files and their contents. Users also can add subdirectories to the current directory and change into any of the current directory's subdirectories.

- *Full Control (All) (All)*   Gives the specified user or individual full control over the directory and its contents. They can list the contents, change to subdirectories, view data files, run application files, add files, add subdirectories, delete files, delete directories, change file permissions, change directory permissions, take ownership of files, and take ownership of directories.

- *Special Directory Access*   Enables you to create a set of custom directory access permissions.

- *Special File Access*   Enables you to create a set of custom file access permissions.

As with file permissions, the directory permissions given to a user or group are cumulative. This means that a user having membership in a group with read privileges to a directory also could belong to a group that has full access to the directory. The user would have the greater of the group access permissions—full access in this case. The exception to this is again the No Access attribute. This overrides any other access privilege that a user may have been granted, either individually or as a member of a group.

The same rule that applies to NTFS file permissions on individual files also applies to NTFS directory permissions. That rule says in order to change the permissions on a directory, you must be the owner of the directory. The directory always inherits the permissions that were applied to its parent directory. However, when the group Everyone has Full Control access, any user can set permissions or take ownership of the directory.

If the *parent directory* has specific NTFS permissions applied to it that limits user access to the directory, the subdirectory automatically inherits the access attributes from its parent directory. That does not include the owner attribute, which always designates the creator of the directory. The only time the owner attribute of the file does not reflect the original directory creator is when the creator granted ownership access to another user. That user must actively assume ownership by using the Take Ownership option.

In the previous example, you saw how NTFS permissions applied to individual files still could not prevent other users from deleting the files. Applying directory access permissions instead of individual file access permissions can solve this problem. The user could have created a personal directory, applied the proper directory permissions to it, and then created his or her file within the new directory. The procedure is outlined as follows:

1. Using Windows NT Explorer or the My Computer file management utility, locate the common document directory that you want to create a personal directory in and open it.

2. Select New from the File menu and then click Folder. A new folder icon appears enabling you to provide a name for the new folder. Supply a name (David's Folder for example) and press the Enter key.

3. Right-click the new folder to open the drop-down menu. Select Properties to open the directory name Folder Properties dialog box and then select the Security tab.

4. Click the Permissions button to open the Directory Permissions dialog box.

5. Set the permissions for the group Everyone by selecting Read from the Type of Access drop-down list. This changes the permissions for the group to Read (RX) (RX).

6. Click the Add button to open the Add Users and Groups dialog box.

7. Click the Show Users button, highlight the name of the account owner (David in this example) in the Names window, and click the Add button.

8. Select Change from the Type of Access drop-down list and then click the OK button.

9. Mark the box next to Replace Permissions on Existing Files (see Figure 7.12) and click the OK button.

FIG. 7.12

The completed
Directory Permissions
dialog box.

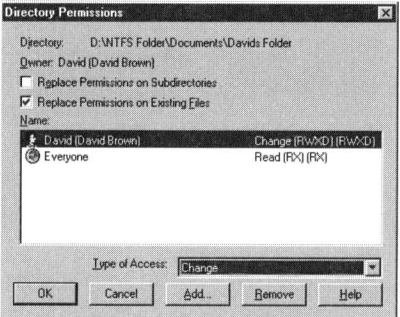

Now that the directory has been created and permissions applied to it, the user can create a document within the directory without worrying that it will be deleted or modified. Using our example once again, you can see that after David creates a document file in this new directory, the permissions on that file are set to read-only for the Everyone group (see Figure 7.13). The Change permission is automatically assigned to the directory owner.

Part

II

Ch

7

FIG. 7.13

File permissions inherited from the directory.

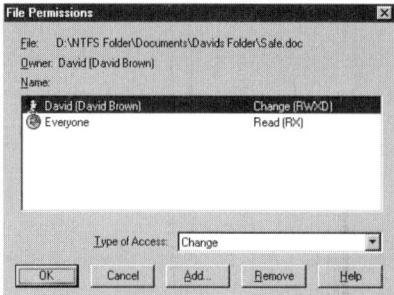

You'll notice that the access rights for the file shown in Figure 7.11 and Figure 7.13 look the same. It appears that the group Everyone has read-only access, and the owner has Change permission on each of the files.

Although both files appear to have the same security, they don't. The file located in the common document directory shown in Figure 7.11 can be deleted by the group Everyone. This means anyone can delete the file if they want. The file located in the private user subdirectory cannot be deleted by the group Everyone. It only can be deleted by the owner, and only then because the owner granted himself Change permission for the host directory. Any users on the system that do attempt to delete the file located in the private directory will receive an Access is denied error.

Using Special Directory and File Access Permissions   Two special categories of permissions are defined by Special Directory Access and Special File Access. Each of the categories enables you to specify some or all of the access permission available in any combination you want. When you select Special Directory Access (from the Type of Access drop-down list *only* in the Directory Permissions dialog box), the dialog box shown in Figure 7.14 appears.

FIG. 7.14

Fine tune directory permissions with the Special Directory Access dialog box.

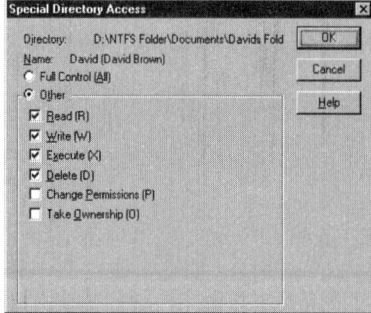

Special Directory Access breaks permissions down into the individual or single permissions that can be assigned to a user or group. For example, when you assign Change (RWXD) permission to a directory you are actually assigning read (R), write (W), execute (X), and delete (D) permission. If you only wanted to assign read (R) and delete (X) to a directory, you could do it here. The entire list of permissions that can be assigned on a directory level is shown in Figure 7.14.

Special File Access is similar to Special Directory Access. It allows you to assign specific permissions that will be applied to the files contained within that specific directory structure (see Figure 7.15). The Special File Access dialog box also permits you to select the option Access Not Specified. This option prevents the files placed in the directory from inheriting the access permissions placed on an individual or group from its host directory.

FIG. 7.15

Individual file permissions can be specified in the Special File Access dialog box.

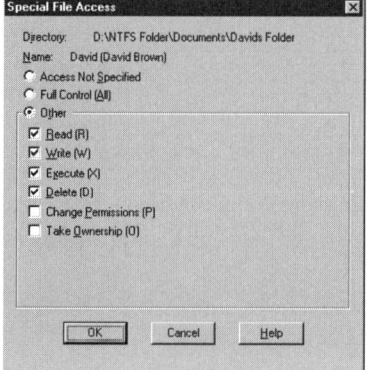

To illustrate this, let's take the previous example where you gave the Everyone group Read (RX) access to the directory named Dave's Folder. As you saw in the example, applying the Read permission for the group (Everyone) at the directory level caused all files within the directory to assume the Read (RX) access permission for the group.

Rather than giving the Everyone group Read (RX) permission as you did in this example, give them Special File Access with the Access Not Specified option selected instead by following these steps:

1. Select the folder and open its Folder Properties dialog box. Choose the Security tab and click the Permissions button to open the Directory Permissions dialog box.

2. Highlight the Everyone group and select Special File Access from the Type of Access drop-down list. This opens the Special File Access dialog box.

Part

II

Ch

7

3. Mark the option button next to Access Not Specified and click the OK button. The Everyone's group access permissions now reflected in the Directory Permissions dialog box now reflects List access for the directory and (Not Specified) for the inherited file access attribute for the Everyone group (see Figure 7.16).

FIG. 7.16

Special File Permissions applied to the Everyone group.

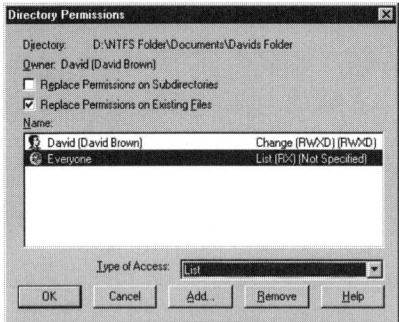

4. Mark the box next to Replace Permissions on Existing Files and click the OK button. Click the OK button again to exit the folder properties dialog box.

If you look at the Security properties for one of the files located within the directory, you see that the Everyone group is no longer listed as having any access (see Figure 7.17) to the file.

FIG. 7.17

Access Not Specified removed the Everyone group from the File Permissions.

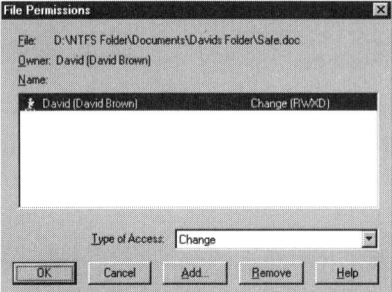

Now system users are able to list the files within the directory, but they aren't able to perform any other actions on the files. They won't be able to read, modify, copy, move, or delete the file, only list it.

Moving Files versus Copying Files   When a file is moved from one directory to another directory, the NTFS permissions that have been applied to the file move with it. This is not true when a file is copied. Copying makes a copy of the file in another directory, and the copy inherits the access privileges in place at the destination directory. Think of it this way—when a file is moved, it packs up everything (including its access permissions) and moves to the new directory. When a file is copied, it copies its permissions *from* the destination directory (its new home).

As you can see, applying NTFS permissions to files can give you complete control over the accessibility of any file or directory on the Windows NT system. Now let's take a look at how NTFS permissions can ease the administrative burden of maintaining share permissions.

Combining NTFS and Share Permissions

Combining NTFS permissions with share permissions can provide the network users with an easy way to self-maintain security on their own private directories located on common network shares. As you learned earlier in the chapter, NTFS permissions override any share permissions that may be in place. You can use this as a tool when you set up network shares. Let's take a look at the example shown in Figure 7.18.

FIG. 7.18
Combine share level with NTFS permissions easily to set up secure network shares.

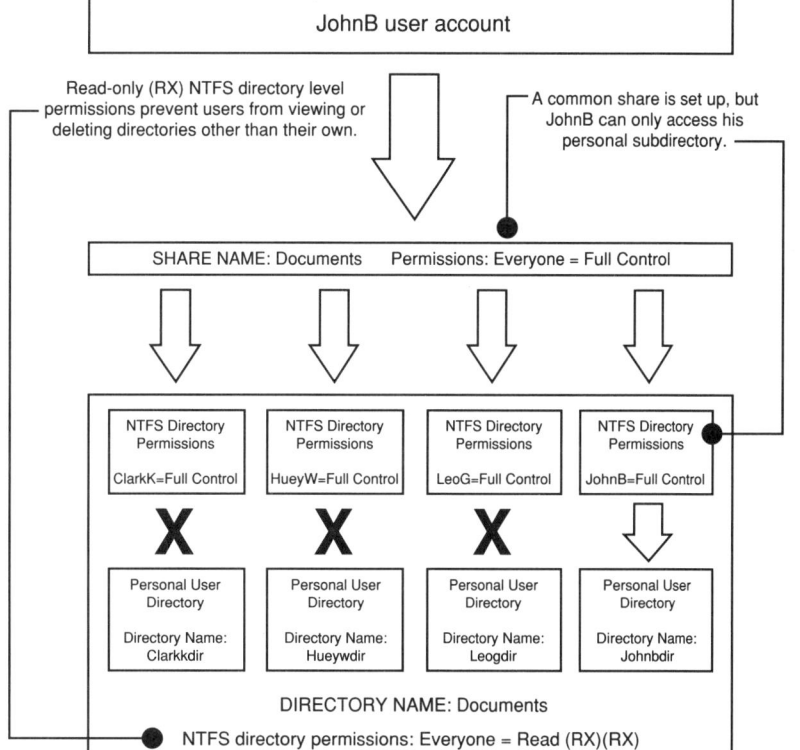

Part

II

Ch

7

Here you have a common network share named Documents. The share-level privilege is set to Full Control for the Everyone group (the default permission when a share is created). The NTFS-level permissions applied to the Documents *directory* restrict users from accessing any subdirectory located in the directory either locally or over the network, unless they have explicit permission. The individual user directories are created and given to each user. Administrative personnel simply assign the individual user Full Access permissions to their personal directory. This allows the individual user to control freely the contents of their directory without being able to access another user's directory.

If a user wants to assign another user access permissions to their personal directory, they are free to do so without having to involve the network administrator. Because the user has Full Control access over their personal directory, they can simply change the NTFS permissions on the personal directory to suit their needs.

You can vary the combination of NFTS permissions to meet your specific requirements and customize your security. If you secure your disk resources using NFTS, you have protected the data from both local and remote access. Share level permissions only protect the items when accessed over the wire. If used correctly, NTFS permissions can provide the security while the share provides the access. Any item should be totally secure using the default permissions of Full Control for the Everyone group that are applied when a share is created. Just as long as the NTFS permissions are present, they override any access gained via the share.

 When you're applying NTFS permissions, note that you must give a user the *Delete* permission if you want the user to be able to create a directory. This may seem strange, but try removing a user's Delete permission from their personal directory and then have the user try to create a new directory folder. They should get an error attempting to rename "New Folder." You can see the audit trail for the delete process when directory auditing is turned on.

Now let's look at one of the other features that NTFS provides: the capability to audit user access to disk resources.

Using NTFS Auditing

If you want to know who is accessing disk resources, you can turn on the auditing of files and directories. You enable auditing on disk resources by first setting the audit policy in the User Manager for Domains utility. Then you must specify what files or directories will be audited, and what individual or group access will be audited. This is done using the Auditing dialog box located in the file or directory properties dialog box.

The previous example (see Figure 7.18) shows the application of NTFS permissions and a directory structure that includes a common shared directory. Within this common directory, several private user directories were created and assigned to users. Each user has access to his or her own subdirectory or folder, but can't access anyone else's directory.

This example takes for granted that the local Administrators group has retained Full Control access permission on each of the directories shown in Figure 7.18. If the Administrator of the system does not have these permissions, they will not be able to apply the auditing attributes to the user directories or files.

Begin by turning on the system's audit policy. This causes the system to create audit messages in the Event Viewer's Security Log, but only after you tell the system what and who to audit. This is done in the subject directory's properties dialog box.

To turn on the system audit policy for file access, follow these steps:

1. Log on to the Windows NT Server with administrative rights and run the User Manager for Domains utility.
2. Select Audit from the Policies menu. This opens the Audit Policy dialog box.
3. Mark the option button next to Audit These Events.
4. Mark both the Success and Failure boxes next to File and Object Access, then click the OK button.

For this example, audit the access to the common Documents directory that contains the individual user directories. You can audit the group Everyone—this will then show you access to the directory by any user on the system.

5. Open the properties dialog box for the common directory (the Documents directory in our example) and click the Auditing button. This opens the Directory Auditing dialog box.
6. Click the Add button to open the Add Users and Groups dialog box and highlight the Everyone (All Users) entry listed in the Names window. Then click the Add button.
7. Click the OK button to return to the Directory Auditing dialog box (see Figure 7.19).
8. Mark the box next to Replace Auditing on Subdirectories, and make sure the box next to Replace Auditing on Existing Files also is marked.
9. Select the permission you want to audit by marking each of the Success or Failure boxes that apply. For this example, mark them all. When you're finished, click the OK button.

Part

II

Ch

7

FIG. 7.19
Select the events to
audit by marking the
appropriate Success
or Failure check boxes.

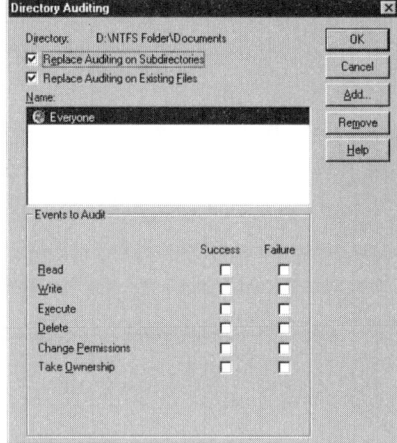

10. Click <u>Y</u>es in the confirmation dialog box to apply the audit attributes to the directories and files. Click OK to exit the *directory* Properties dialog box.

Now that auditing has been turned on, you can see the results of any user access to the directory in the Event Viewer's Security Log (for example, the Event Log).

You set up accounts for several users in the example, and each was given a user subdirectory that they were allowed access to within the common shared directory. When a user opens the shared directory that contains all the separate user directories, the actions are recorded in the Event Log. Because you turned the success/failure auditing on, all attributes and any action taken by the user is reflected in the Event Log. Let's use another example to illustrate the event log and what information it gives.

The user named Huey Walker (account ID HueyW) has just logged on the system and has opened the shared Documents directory. He's able to list all four of the user directories including his own. When he opens his own user directory (Hueywdir) the Event Log records the events shown in Figure 7.20.

FIG. 7.20
The event log entries
for the successful
object access that
takes place when
a user has the
appropriate access
permissions.

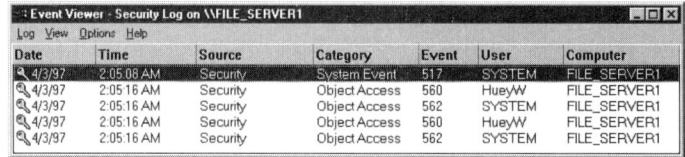

N O T E   Discount the first entry with the event code of 517 in the previous figure and the
following figures. It is a record of the security log file initialization by the system and
happens when the log file is cleared. To make the logs in the example easier to read, they have
been cleared before each event that is shown. ■

Now if the user HueyW attempts to open the directory named Leogdir that belongs to the
user LeoG, the Event log records the failed attempt with the Event Log entries shown in
Figure 7.21.

FIG. 7.21

The padlock icon in
the Event Log entry
notes a failed access
attempt.

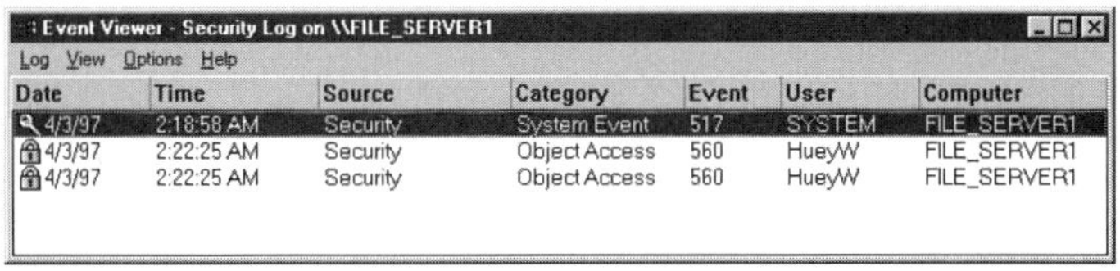

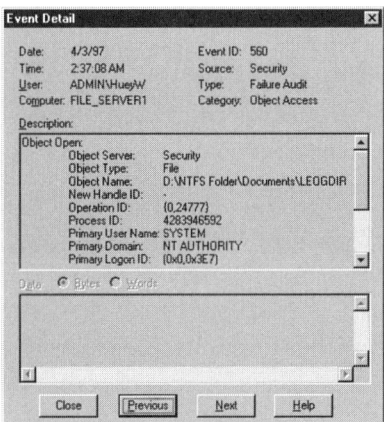

At this time our user Huey receives an Access is denied message with a Retry or Cancel
option. If Huey selects the Retry option, the Access denied message re-appears and the
Event Log records the same two entries again. If Huey selects the Cancel option, nothing
further is recorded in the Event Log.

You can look at the information contained within the failure entries that were recorded in
the Event Log to view specific information on the failed attempt. The failed attempt by the
user HueyW to access the Leogdir directory is shown in Figures 7.22 and 7.23.

FIG. 7.22

Detailed information
on the failed access
attempt is located in
the Event Log entry.

FIG. 7.23

This part of the event detail lists the client's user name that initiated the failed access attempt.

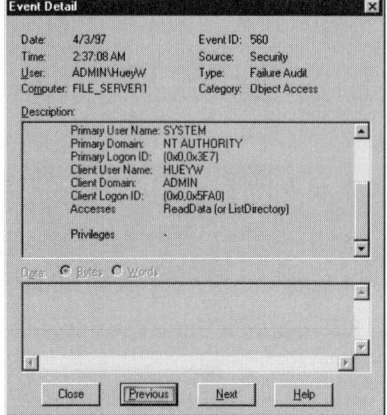

The information contained within the Event Log entry gives specific information about the failed access attempt, as follows:

- *Date* The date the event occurred.

- *Time* The time the event occurred.

- *User* This tells you what the primary ID is of the user who initiated the action, if impersonation is not taking place. If impersonation is taking place, the client ID is given. Both the primary and client ID's are recorded where applicable.

- *Computer* Specifies the name of the computer where the event took place.

- *Event ID* This is a numeric code that represents the specific event type. The event ID in your example is 560. The friendly meaning of the code is usually listed in the very first line of the event Description.

- *Source* Specifies the Windows NT component responsible for generating the event in the log. Our example specifies Security, which means that Windows NT security auditing is responsible for generating the message.

- *Type* Indicates whether the access attempt was a success or a failure. A success is represented in the Event Log entry with a key icon, while a failure is represented by a padlock icon.

- *Category* This entry corresponds to one of the event types that can be audited. These types correspond to the success/failure policy that was enabled using the User Manager for Domains.

This information allows you to spot unauthorized access attempts and gives you detailed information about who is accessing what. As you'll see in Chapter 8, "Using Windows NT Security to Protect Domain Resources," the audit policy enables you to track many more items besides file and object access.

From Here...

This chapter focuses on NTFS permissions and how they can be used to supply security to the disk resources located on Windows NT Server. The next chapter studies some of the administrative utilities available to you when maintaining Windows NT security. Here's a look at what's coming up:

- Chapter 8, "Using Windows NT Security to Protect Domain Resources," explores the tools provided by Windows NT that are used to manage the system.

- Chapter 9, "Windows NT Workstation Security," looks at the differences in security used on a Windows NT Workstation and used on a Windows NT Server.

- Chapter 10, "Planning the Master Domain," covers the security planning used in subsequent chapters when a sample installation is shown.

Part

II

Ch

7

Using Windows NT Security to Protect Domain Resources

Explaining what Windows NT Domains are, how to set them up, and how to best implement them in conjunction with other domains through the use of trusts encompasses many of the other chapters in this book. In this chapter you see how to use a variety of Windows NT tools as well as user profiles and restrictions to keep your domain's resources secure. ■

Using Windows NT management tools

Learn about the management tools available in Windows NT Server, including User Manager for Domains, Server Manager, and Event Viewer.

Providing access to file resources

How to assign NTFS permissions, as well as some strategies for ensuring that access is granted in a secure manner.

Controlling printer resources

The best ways to make sure that access to printing resources is limited to the people you want to have printing access.

Registry security with Windows NT 4.0

As everyone who has worked with Windows NT is aware, the registry is the heart and soul of the operating system. This section talks about how best to maintain registry security.

Using other methods of controlling user access

You know the tools, so now learn about some of the other techniques for controlling access to domains, including log-on restrictions, disk quotas, and user profiles. Also, you can find out how to troubleshoot user profile problems.

Using Windows NT Management Tools

Windows NT ships with a number of management tools that help you administer your Windows NT domain. User Manager for Domains helps you create user accounts and configure when, where, and how they log on to the domain. You can configure their desktop environment so they get the same desktop environment wherever they log on from. If you are working in a particularly strict environment, you even can configure their log on so they can't change their desktop.

Server Manager enables you to manage the servers in your domain. You can synchronize your domain controllers, promote Backup Domain Controllers, configure shares and permissions, identify logged-on users and what files they have open, configure replication, and configure where system alerts are sent.

The Windows NT Event Viewer is used to keep an eye on what's going on with the system. Any System, Application, or Security events that occur on the system are logged and can be viewed with the Event Viewer. You even can view the logs of other machines on your network.

The Windows NT User Manager for Domains

The Windows NT User Manager for Domains is your primary tool for securing the user accounts on your network. From the User Manager for Domains you can create new users (you walk through this in Chapter 4, "Windows NT Domain Concepts."), modify existing users, restrict the times that users can log on, and from which workstations; and assign user home directories and mandatory user profiles. It also is from within User Manager for Domains that you can configure your auditing policies. Auditing is one of the most powerful features of the User Manager for Domains and should be used to its fullest possible advantage. To identify security issues with your servers and domains, you are introduced to auditing and to using the Windows NT Event Viewer. Figure 8.1 shows the User Manager for Domains application.

Using the Server Manager

Now that you know how to handle users, you can use the tool to manage your servers. The Windows NT Server Manager is the tool you use to handle all of the server-level management for your domain. This includes managing server properties, server shares, installed services, which server is the *Primary Domain Controller (PDC)*, and which servers are the *Backup Domain Controllers (BDC)* for the domain. You also can synchronize the accounts database on all the domain controllers in the domain.

FIG. 8.1

User Manager for Domains is a powerful weapon in your security arsenal. Be sure to take full advantage of all the features it offers.

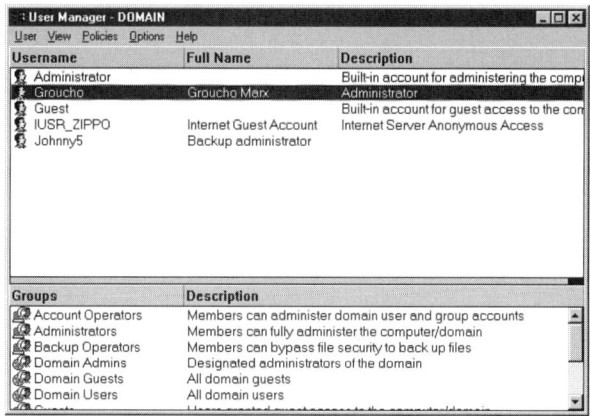

N O T E   If you want to use Server Manager to manage your domain, you must be a member of the Administrators, Domain Admins, or Server Operators group. If your user account doesn't have that capability, consider creating an account specifically for managing the domain. A good rule of thumb is not to use the administrator account unless absolutely necessary.

The first use for the Windows NT Server Manager is the capability to synchronize all the domain controllers in your domain. Why would you want to synchronize all the domain controllers in your domain? Let's briefly recap the domain architecture. The PDC is the domain controller that maintains the centralized user account database. This database is periodically replicated to the BDCs. All changes are made on the PDC database, while the BDC's database is updated only by the PDC replication. To help reduce the load on the PDC, BDCs also provide user authentication for the domain. Now, if your company just fired 70 people, and you wanted to be sure no one got onto the network to wreak havoc, you would delete or disable all those user accounts. Microsoft strongly recommends disabling accounts, because after an account is deleted, it cannot be re-created.

From a security perspective, unused accounts in a domain can be considered a security problem. The best idea is to disable the account, make sure any information, permissions, or other information unique to that user is duplicated and accessible from an existing user account, and then delete the account. These changes would take place on the PDC. Until the database is replicated to all the BDCs, one of those users still could authenticate to the domain by accessing a BDC for the authentication. To ensure that your changes are replicated immediately, open the Windows NT Server Manager application. See Figure 8.2.

FIG. 8.2

Note that the backup
server Beppo is grayed
out. This means that
the server is not
available to be
managed.

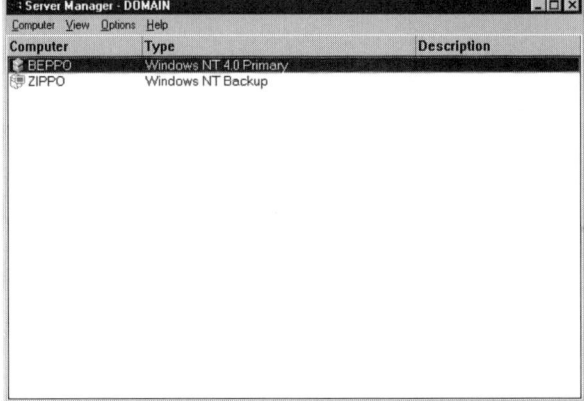

Highlight the PDC, and from the Computer pull down menu, select Synchronize Entire
Domain. See Figure 8.3 for an example.

FIG. 8.3

You are not told
when the synchroni-
zation is complete.
You need to refer to
the event log to tell
when the synchroni-
zation is done.

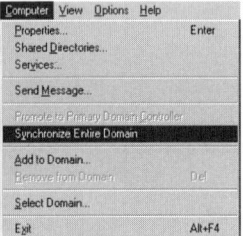

The system then tells you the synchronization may take a few minutes, and asks you to
confirm your choice. Choose Yes, and you get a message that the BDCs have been asked
to synchronize. To verify that synchronization is complete, check the Event Viewer on the
PDC and any BDCs for lines indicating either synchronization is complete, or there is a
problem. Time for synchronization varies depending on the size of the domain database
and the number of BDCs.

Now take a look at what you can control on your server from the Windows NT Server
Manager application.

1. With the Windows NT Server Manager application open to the main window, (this
   window displays the name of the domain across the top bar) double-click the server
   you want to manage. See Figure 8.4.

2. Select the Users button at the bottom of the window. See Figure 8.5. From here, you
   can see which users are on the system, how long they've been on, and how long
   they've been idle. You also can see what resources are shared by users. From this
   screen you can disconnect any or all the users just by highlighting the user and
   clicking Disconnect—Disconnect All disconnects all the users.

FIG. 8.4
This screen shows you a snapshot of the system's activities, including Sessions, Open Files, File Locks, and Open Named Pipes.

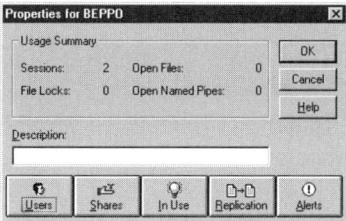

FIG. 8.5
One thing to keep in mind when using this function: If you disconnect a user, they can reconnect to the resource unless you disable their account or change the resource permissions. You also can pause or stop the Server service on the server to prevent logons.

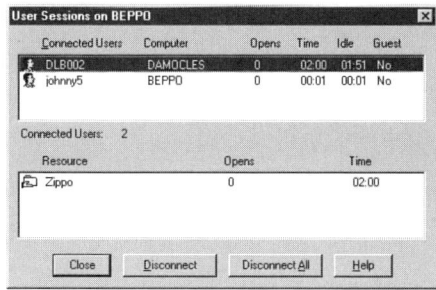

3. Close this window by clicking Close. Let's open Shares next by clicking Shares. This is where you would disconnect users from a specific resource. See Figure 8.6.

FIG. 8.6
From this window you can disconnect users from a specific resource, instead of from the entire server.

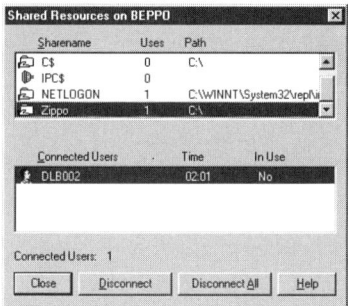

4. Disconnecting users from a resource is similar to the way you disconnected users from the server in the last section. Highlight the resource from which you want to remove users. Highlight a user and click Disconnect to remove them from the resource. Clicking Disconnect All disconnects all the attached users from that resource.

5. Next let's look at the use of alerts from Windows NT Server Manager. Select Alerts from the main screen. This opens the Alerts window. See Figure 8.7. From here you can create a list of computers (entered by Windows NT Computer Name) which will receive administrative alerts. To those of you familiar with SNMP, this is similar to the way you redirect traps.

FIG. 8.7
You can configure all the servers in your domain to send their administrative alerts to a single (or multiple) console(s). This enables you to keep track of problems on servers without checking each one individually.

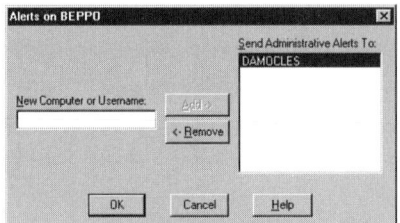

6. Close the Alerts window by clicking Close. Close the Server Properties window by clicking OK.

7. To manage shares on a server through Server Manager, select Computer, Shared Directories. This opens the Shared Directories dialog box. See Figure 8.8. From this dialog box you can create shares, stop sharing an existing share, and modify the properties of the share. These work in the same manner as the share properties in Windows NT Explorer, so I won't discuss this in depth.

FIG. 8.8
Remember, as soon as you create a share, you have made that information potentially available to anyone on your network. Be sure to restrict permissions as much as possible while allowing users the proper access.

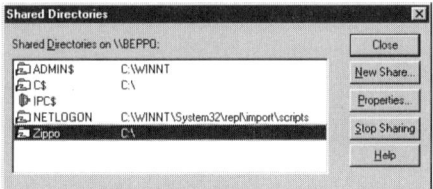

There are a couple other functions of Windows NT Server Manager which need to be mentioned at this point. Windows NT Server Manager is the place where domain trust relationships are managed. This topic is covered in depth in Chapter 5 "Maintaining Security with Domain Trust Relationships" and Chapter 12, "Setting Up Trust Relationships."

This application also allows you to replicate directories from one server to another. While this is a useful service in some instances, it isn't discussed in-depth here. A final useful feature is the capability to send a message to all the users on a server in the domain from your desk. See Figure 8.9.

FIG. 8.9
It is always a good idea to let users know if you will be doing maintenance on a server. Few things make an end user as angry as losing three hours of work because the network administrator didn't tell anyone the server was being shut down.

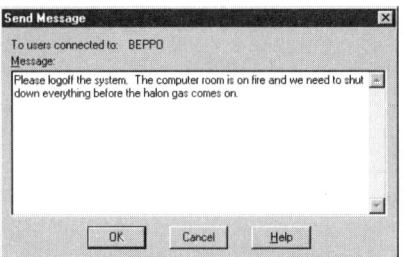

Spotting Security Problems with Event Viewer

The Event Viewer is potentially the most important of the applications in this chapter, if you suspect you have a security problem. By using the auditing capabilities of Windows NT in conjunction with the Event Viewer, there is little that you can't monitor within Windows NT. If you recall, I mentioned earlier in the chapter that auditing needs to be activated in the User Manager for Domains application. Here's a look at exactly how you do that before we discuss how this is useful to you from a security perspective. The steps for activating auditing are as follows:

1. Log on as a user with administrator capabilities.
2. Run the User Manager for Domains from the Administrative Tools group.

N O T E If you do a lot of user ID maintenance, you may want to create a shortcut on your desktop for this application. This will save you some mouse dragging every time you need to change a user ID.

3. Select Policies, Audit. This opens the dialog box in Figure 8.10.
4. Select the events you need to monitor. Refer to Table 8.1 for a list of auditable events.

FIG. 8.10

Before you enable auditing, decide what you need to see. Enabling too many items fills your logs quickly and causes you to lose important events in the noise of the unneeded events.

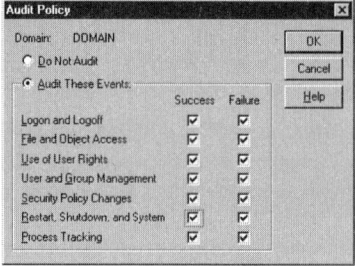

Table 8.1   Functions that Can Be Set to Be Audited in User Manager

Event	Audits the Following
Logon and Logoff	Logons and network connections.
File and Object Access	Access to files or directories. Also audits the sending of print jobs.
Use of User Rights	Any use of user rights other than logons/logoffs.
User and Group Management	Any changes to accounts or groups, including create, change, delete, as well as password changes.
Security Policy Changes	Any changes to audit, trust relationship, or user rights policies. This one is important—if you see events here and you weren't the one making the changes, find out who was.
Restart, Shutdown, and System	Any shutdown/restarts of the system. Also any changes that would affect system security.
Process Tracking	Tracks processes started by applications, as well as some other application processes and the closing of an application.

N O T E   Auditing of file and folder requires an NTFS partition. It doesn't work on a FAT drive. You also need to be a member of the Administrators group, or have equivalent access. ▓

5. If you want to try to get a feel for what types of events these generate, try enabling them all and keeping a close eye on the log for a week or so. Then use the data to decide which alerts you really need to see.

Great, now you know how to turn on auditing. But do you know what good it does you? Let's use a real-life example for this one. An administrator I know had a machine on the Internet. One morning, he tried to perform an administrative task and it didn't work.

He tracked down the error and discovered there had been a break-in. His server had been hacked. More research showed someone logged on at 3:00 A.M.—an odd time for someone to be working on the system. Further research led him to a high school in the deep South, one which apparently had a student or two who fancied themselves Ace Hackers. The point is, if the hacker hadn't messed up their Trojan Horse, the administrator might never have known what happened, or worse, found out after they destroyed his production server.

If that had been your Windows NT 4.0 Server, how would you have known there was a problem? You know you are a security-conscious Systems Administrator (You're reading this book, aren't you?), so you have log-on auditing enabled. When you checked your logs in the morning, you would have noticed the failed log-on attempts, as well as the fact that a user logged on at 3:00 A.M. You immediately would have disabled that account, changed passwords where needed, scanned the server for viruses, and restored the system from a clean backup, eliminating any chance that something unpleasant was on your system. How do you use Event Viewer for this? Here's how:

1. Log on as a user with administrator capabilities.

2. Run the Event Viewer from the Administrative Tools group. This opens the application shown in Figure 8.11.

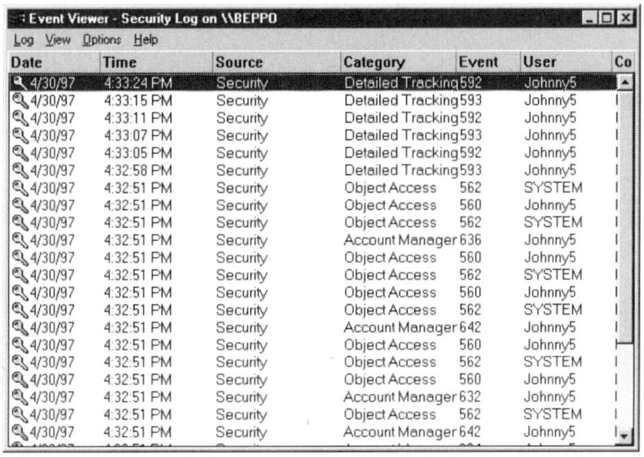

FIG. 8.11

You also can use this to view System and Application events.

3. From the Log pull-down menu, select Security.

4. You now see the list of Security events. By double-clicking any event you can get a detailed description of the event. See Figure 8.12.

That is the Event Viewer and what it can do for you. You are strongly advised to use it to its fullest advantage, as it can be your first indication that someone is either trying or has succeeded in compromising your system.

FIG. 8.12
While some of the detailed descriptions are useful, some are obscure. Working with the application regularly gives you an idea of what should and shouldn't be happening on your system.

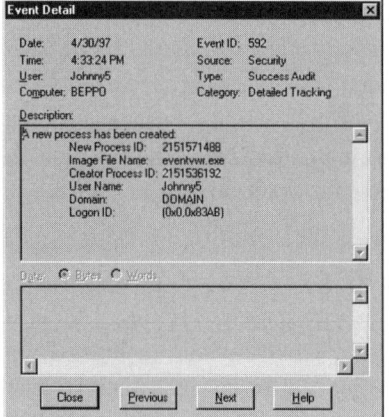

Controlling Printer Resources

Using the built-in features of Windows NT printing, you can control who has access and what that access is for any printer in the domain. My favorite question about printers and security is, "What do my printers have to do with security?" An excellent question such as this deserves an answer.

Let's say that your users all have Full Control over all the printers. One enterprising, soon-to-be ex-employee gets the great idea that if he watches the printers, he can place any of the "interesting" files on hold, and then print them all after hours. The typical user, seeing that the job didn't print, resubmits. The LAN Administrator, having much better things to do than monitor what jobs are on hold in the queue, doesn't know what the employee has done. Meanwhile, the soon-to-be ex-employee is reading the details of the upcoming IPO, which the CEO's secretary had to send to the printer twice because the first job never printed.

Now that you know why, how do you control access to your printers? Before you start, keep in mind that permissions must be set on each printer. There is no global way to set permissions. Also, to change permissions on a printer, you must be the owner of the printer or have Full Control permission to the printer.

The four levels of permission are:

- *No Access*   Can't print.
- *Print*   To the selected printer.
- *Manage Documents*   Permission to manage all documents for only that printer.
- *Full Control*   You can do anything with that printer, including granting rights to other users. Use this permission sparingly.

OK, now that you know what permissions can be assigned to your printers, here is how you can actually set them. Remember, printer permissions can be assigned to users or groups. Groups usually are easier to manage from an administrative perspective and can give you more granularity if printer access is something you really want to control in your environment. Follow these steps:

1. To change printer settings, open the printer's Properties, and click the Security tab. See Figure 8.13. Next, click the Permissions button.

FIG. 8.13

Remember, when a printer is created, all network users can print to it by default. If you have an expensive color printer that you don't want people to print to, remember to change the default permissions.

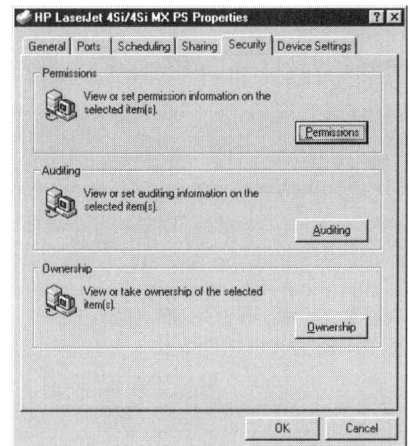

2. Figure 8.14 shows the Printer Permissions dialog box. You can add, delete, or change permissions for any user or group on the system from this window.

FIG. 8.14

When changing permissions for printers, it is important that you don't inadvertently remove your Full Control capabilities, especially if you have them by virtue of being in a group. Once Full Control has been removed from your account, you can't put it back from that account.

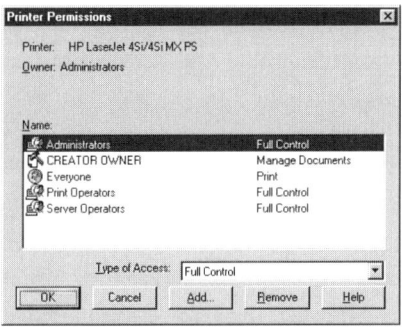

Another capability you have within the properties of a printer is the capability to turn on auditing. One place that auditing is very useful is if you are charging departments for use of a high-end printer. Auditing enables you to look at who printed what and gives you the capability to bill a department for the number of pages it printed.

N O T E   Remember, if you want to audit printer events, you must enable File and Object auditing in User Manager for Domains. ▓

Registry Security with Windows NT 4.0

You need to be familiar with the importance of the Registry with Windows NT. Learning about how to make sure the Registry is secure is the next step. You do this by taking a look at three different methods of maintaining Registry security. The first method to discuss is our old friend auditing. If you suspect someone is tampering with the Registry, or you are concerned that your Registry may be vulnerable, enable auditing. To enable auditing of the Registry, you need to perform the following steps:

1. Log on as a user with administrator capabilities.
2. Run the User Manager for Domains from the Administrative Tools group and enable auditing as discussed earlier in the chapter.
3. Load REGEDT32.EXE. See Figure 8.15.

FIG. 8.15

It is always a good idea to back up your Registry before making *any* changes.

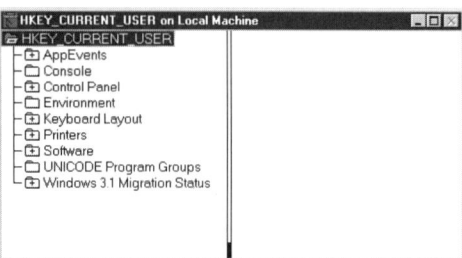

4. From the pull-down menu, select Security, and click Audit. From here you can select the Registry events you want to audit. See Figure 8.16. You can audit at various levels of granularity, from a key to a hive. You also can restrict auditing to a certain level of the Registry, and not audit the sublevels.

FIG. 8.16
If you audit the Registry, select only the events necessary. This limits the number of unneeded events in Event Viewer and makes it easier to focus on the critical events.

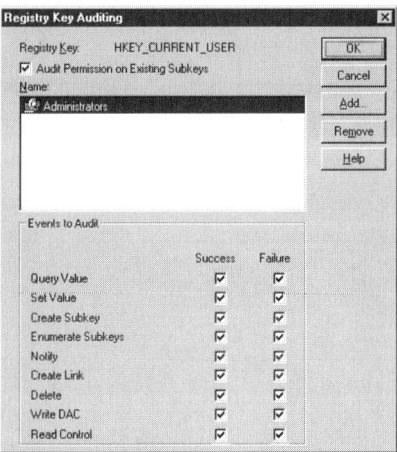

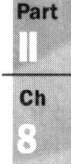

5. After the auditing is enabled, monitor Event Viewer as discussed earlier for any suspicious events.

A couple of other points on auditing the Registry: You must have Administrator rights on the system you are trying to audit. Also, because the Registry is not a distributed database, but exists uniquely on every machine, you need to set up auditing on each machine you want to keep an eye on. This holds true for setting permissions as well.

The second method to consider when securing the Registry is the capability to grant specific levels of access to specific users and groups.

N O T E It is important to point out that unless you are very familiar with the Registry, setting or changing permissions on pieces of the Registry is dangerous. You might inadvertently disable your machine by accidentally removing a permission the system needs to operate. Also, you might potentially open a hole that you weren't aware of and enable a hacker to grab your password list, corrupt your Registry, or in an extreme case, lock you out of your own system.

Permissions can be set on sections of the Registry with the following steps:

1. Load REGEDT32.EXE. Refer to Figure 8.15.
2. From the pull-down menu, select security, and click Permissions. This opens the Registry Key Permission dialog box, as shown in Figure 8.17.

FIG. 8.17
It is important to
back up the Registry
before making any
changes. Be sure
your Emergency Repair
Disk is up-to-date.

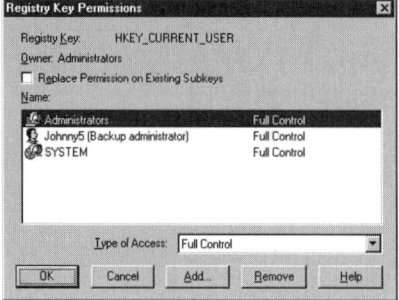

3. Permissions are set much the way NTFS permissions are set in Windows NT Explorer. With the Registry, you can set permissions to **Read**, **Full Control**, or **Special Access**, which allow you to pick the permissions you want to assign with a finer granularity to that user.

 If it is absolutely necessary to change permissions on a key, it is a good idea to audit that key for event failures. That way, if you accidentally changed a permission that the system needs, you will see it in Event Viewer.

The third method of Registry security to consider is the general steps to make sure it is protected. First, limit the users who have access to the Registry. There is such a thing as having too many administrators. Limit them as much as possible. Another thing you can do is remove the Registry Editor application from all the machines except the management stations. Make all your changes from that workstation.

If you use all the tools and techniques discussed, you should have no problems keeping people out of your Registry.

N O T E There is a potential problem with Registry entries when upgrading from Windows NT 3.51 to Windows NT 4.0 that should be mentioned while talking about Registry security. When you upgrade to Windows NT 4.0, you lose entries under the following registry key:

HKEY_LOCAL_MACHINE\SYSTEM\CurrentControlSet\Control\ServiceGroupOrder*List of items*.

This key is overwritten during the upgrade to Windows NT 4.0. Microsoft's recommended fix is to reinstall the affected application(s) or driver(s). Reinstalling re-creates the necessary registry keys. Microsoft is aware of this and promises to update users as soon as more information is available.

For more information, check Microsoft's Web page at **http://www.microsoft.com/kb/articles/ q163/4/13.htm.** If you have access to the Microsoft KnowledgeBase, check article Q163413, last updated on March 28, 1997.

Using Other Windows NT Tools and Features to Control User Access

In addition to the preceding utilities, there are other features and tools that can be used to control how a user accesses and interacts with the system. It is important from a security perspective to discuss each of these features. They include the use of *Mandatory User Profiles* as well as account configuration options, such as setting *user home directories*, controlling the machines from which users can log on and controlling when users can log on.

How Mandatory User Profiles Work

One of the tools that can really let you control your environment is *profiles*. Profiles are files that contain all the settings defining the desktop environment for a user. There are a number of different types of profiles, but in a security-conscious environment, the one that is the most useful is the Mandatory User Profile.

A Mandatory User Profile is a server-based profile, which is assigned to an end user by the administrator using the User Manager for Domains application. See Figure 8.18 to see where this is done.

FIG. 8.18
When using Manda-
tory User Profiles, it is
important to
remember that the
profile contains
hardware settings
such as video
configuration. Setting
the display to 800×
600 SVGA will likely
annoy the person with
the 14" VGA monitor.

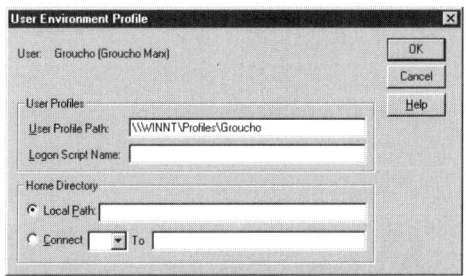

The feature that separates a Mandatory User Profile from the other types of profiles is the fact that it is read-only. Any changes to the system's environment that a user makes during a session are reset as soon as they log on again. This includes background colors, display attributes, screen layout—everything. This is because Mandatory User Profiles usually are assigned to groups of users and are used to present a consistent environment, both for support and for security reasons.

N O T E   A couple of important pieces of information: Mandatory User Profiles always end with
a .MAN extension. That is what differentiates them from a standard profile. Another
important fact is that if a Mandatory User Profile isn't available at logon, that user is denied
access to the domain. ▪

To create a Mandatory User Profile, just follow these steps:

1. Log on as a user with administrator capabilities. When creating a Mandatory User
   Profile, it is a good idea to create an account specifically for that purpose. This can
   save time if you need to go back later and do more profiles or fix an old one.

2. Configure the Windows NT environment of the machine you are working on to be
   exactly the way you want the user profile to look. Be sure to set all the user defined
   properties you need to set.

3. Start User Profile Editor (Figure 8.19). You need to grant access to the user(s) or
   group(s)that will be using the profile. You also need to go through each of the items
   and finish configuring the environment. This is where you can really restrict what a
   user can and cannot do.

FIG. 8.19

The User Profile Editor
is used to configure
who can use a profile,
as well as a number
of useful application
settings.

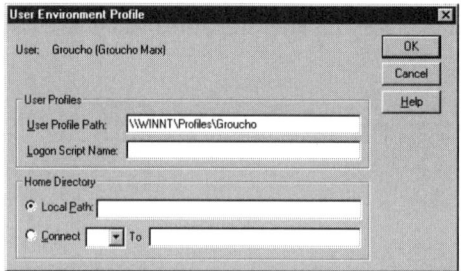

4. Now that your configuration is done, you need to save it. As with any Windows
   application, you need to do a File, Save As. Because this is a Mandatory User
   Profile, you need to select Mandatory Profile as the file type. You need to provide
   the .MAN extension and the proper path for the file as well.

5. Now that you have saved the .MAN file, you need to assign it to a user. Run User
   Manager for Domains (refer to Figure 8.1) and click Profile at the bottom. This
   opens the dialog box in Figure 8.20.

FIG. 8.20
When assigning the Mandatory User Profile, be sure to specify its Universal Naming Convention (UNC) path so that it can be loaded across the network.

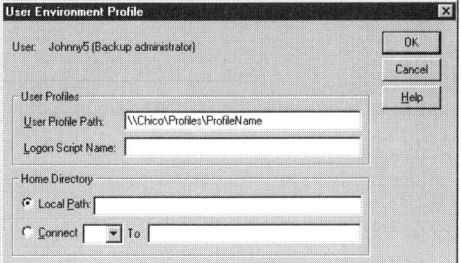

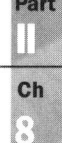

4. Select OK, and then exit User Manager for Domains. The next time the user logs on he or she should load the Mandatory User Profile you just created.

N O T E User Profiles are available for both Windows 95 and Windows NT clients. These profiles are not interchangeable. Each Operating System needs its own profiles created, due to the different architectures.

Troubleshooting User Profile Problems

In general, the biggest issues you will see when you use mandatory profiles are the differences in video hardware. If you are assigning mandatory profiles to groups of users, make sure that the machines they will be connecting from share common display capabilities. If Amy logs in on Laura's machine with its 640×480 VGA display, and her profile is set to 800×600, it will be difficult to find things on the screen. If you are modifying a profile for a single user, be sure to do it from a machine with a comparable configuration.

If your problem is not with the display hardware but is appearing elsewhere in the configuration, try the following steps:

1. Try logging on from another machine with a similar hardware configuration. If a problem persists, it's the profile. If it disappears, it is probably a problem with a specific machine.

2. Assign the profile to be modified to the Profile configuration account by using User Manager for Domains. Then log on as your Profile configuration account and modify the Windows NT environment to correct the problem. Save your changes and log on again as the user who was having the problem.

3. Re-create the profile from scratch, and assign it to the user. If this doesn't work, be sure you are creating your profiles correctly.

Assigning Home Directories to Users

A home directory is a place to store a user's data, be it files or executable programs. In a secure environment, each user is generally restricted to his or her home directory for personal file storage. Shared directories are then set up for the storage of files that need to be shared. In less secure environments, one home directory can be set up for multiple users. This might be used in a case where a team or department wants to share files in a single area.

N O T E   A user's home directory becomes the default directory for all `File Open` and `Save As` commands, unless an application has been configured to default somewhere else. ▤

The question often asked is, "Why do we even need home directories?" After all, most desktop PC's are shipping with a one gigabyte or larger hard drive. Why use network storage? There are a couple of compelling reasons. One reason is for capacity planning. If you use file server storage for personal documents, it is much easier to add four gigabytes of storage to the server than it is to add new hard drives to 20 workstations. It's much more cost effective as well. Another more security-related reason for using home directories and storing personal files on the server is that servers get backed up. If you are an administrator of a network or a server, you recognize the value of a reliable backup that gets tested once a month. Your end users probably do not. How many of your users back up their workstations? In many large offices, the number can be counted on one hand. If the data is on the server, it's on the tape, and maybe even offsite. This is a much more secure, reliable way of storing data.

Security plays a part for another reason as well. It requires a password and permissions to log on to the server and to access a user's files. In most instances, to access files on a user's hard drive you just need to wait for a bathroom break or lunch. If the user isn't conscientious about locking their machine, you can generally access any file on their hard drive.

One other point, however—if the user is nice enough to leave their machine logged on to the network when they go to lunch, the walk-up user has access anyway. If there is one thing to really drive home to your users, it is not to leave their PC's unlocked. Power on passwords, screen saver passwords, and in some cases encryption are the words of the day.

OK, we've talked about the good a user home directory can do for you. Here is how you set one up—just follow these steps:

1. Log on as a user with administrator capabilities.

2. Run the User Manager for Domains from the Administrative Tools group.

3. Select the appropriate *Username* and double-click it. This opens the user properties screen. If you are creating a new user, Select Ụser, then New Ụser.

4. At the bottom of the dialog box, select Pṛofile.

5. This opens the User Environment Profile dialog box. See Figure 8.21.

FIG. 8.21

Remember, if you set the user home directory in this window, User Manager for Domains automatically creates the directory and assigns the appropriate permissions.

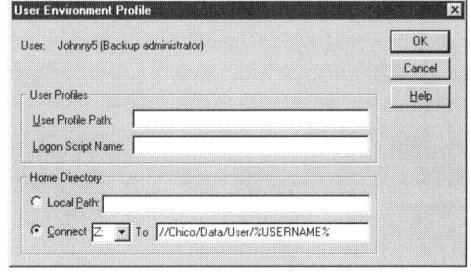

6. At the bottom of the dialog box you can either set the user home directory to a local path or connect it to a network drive on the server. If you are using the network drive (recommended) you must use the Universal Naming Convention (UNC) address. If you are unfamiliar with UNC, path names, it has the following format:

\\machine name\share\directory\home directory\

N O T E If you are using the user's account name as the directory name, you can substitute **%USERNAME%** in the place of *home directory*. This simplifies things considerably if you are creating a large number of users. It also provides an easy directory naming convention.

7. When you are done, select OK and when the user logs on to the network again, he or she will have a User Home Directory.

Restricting Drive Space Use

The first thing to keep in mind when discussing limiting drive space usage is that the ability to do so is not included in Windows NT. That means that if you want to limit the amount of drive space a user is able to fill on your server, you must look to third-party applications to accomplish it. A list of some third-party applications that allow you to do this are included at the end of this chapter.

Now that you know what you need to limit drive usage, a more important question still remains. Why do you need to worry about restricting drive usage, and more importantly still, what does this have to do with Windows NT security?

Drive usage, if left unchecked, can have some serious ramifications. Possible scenarios: Scenario 1 is when a hacker breaks into your server using the account the college co-op used last summer. (Of course this would never happen, because you're going to read all about setting account expiration dates later in the chapter.) What can he or she do? If the account is configured correctly, which it will be because you've read this book, then the important files are secure, the registry is inaccessible, and access to the user account database is locked up tight.

However, you still have a problem. What happens when the hacker decides that the co-op's home directory would make a great place to park 800 megabytes of child pornography? Now you have two problems. First, you, as the administrator of the server, could potentially be looking at legal problems for the existence of child pornography on your server. Second, if you only had 800 megabytes of free space in the first place, your server is now less than usable. Depending on what drive was filled, this could impact anything from the Windows NT page file, to users being unable to store any new files, to print jobs being unable to queue. This generally is considered a bad thing.

Scenario 2 is a little less of an issue from a legal standpoint, but can be just as serious from a usability standpoint. Let's say that Phil, the Manager of the Sales Department, is going on a business trip. Phil decides that it is too inconvenient to carry his laptop on the plane, so he is planning on checking it as baggage. As an aside, *never do this!* And fire anyone in your company who does. (OK, that's probably extreme, but give it some thought anyway.) Because Phil knows there may be a problem with checking his laptop as luggage, he decides he will play it safe and back up his machine. Unfortunately for his network administrator, rather than backing up to tape or removable media, backing up from Phil's perspective means copy C:*.* to *X:* (where X is your favorite network drive.)

Naturally, Phil knows enough to get the flags right and get all the subdirectories. Now there is an additional gigabyte of account files, employee reviews, sales presentations, and cool network games sitting on the server. All the issues mentioned, such as print spooling not working, lack of swap file space, and all the other calamities are now affecting your server, and you haven't even been attacked.

The bottom line is, unless you really trust your security and your users, you might want to give some serious thought to adding one of the following applications to your security arsenal:

Quota Manager for Windows NT

New Technology Partners
40 South River Road, BLDG 44
Bedford, New Hampshire 03110

Phone(800) 226-2755 or (603) 622-4400

Fax (603) 641-6934

http://199.107.233.3/software/ntp/

Quota Server for Windows NT

Northern Technologies

http://www.cleveland.co.uk/quotaserver/mainpage.html

Miss Marple

Adlon Datenverarbeltung

Josef StrobelStrasse 38

Ravensburg, Germany 88-213

Phone: (49) (751) 760729

Fax: (49) (751) 760788

This list is in no way an endorsement of any of the products listed. The author has used Quota Manager in a limited implementation, and it worked as advertised, but the application was not tested in any severe circumstances. Evaluation versions of these products are available and you are encouraged to try it in a lab environment before you place it on a production server. As with any application, be sure to do your research before putting any applications into your production environment.

Setting Workstation Log-On Restrictions

If you are trying to secure your Windows NT domain, one of the more powerful features of Windows NT log-on security is the capability to limit the workstations from which a particular user can log on to the network. "This looks like a great feature on paper, but what good does it do in real life?" is a question often asked.

Here's another example. Let's say that Jeanne is a LAN Administrator that you just hired to help with LAN support. She constantly is interacting with your users and is frequently at their desks working on their systems. And as a good Network Manager, you give all your administrators two accounts: One with general user permissions, which allows them to access shares, printers, read their mail, and so on, and one with administrator rights, which is used for doing server maintenance, setting up users, and any other tasks that might require the additional rights.

Unfortunately, Jeanne came from an environment that was significantly more lax than yours, and she is used to logging on as an administrator whenever she needs system access. To make matters worse, Jeanne is notorious for leaving herself logged on at the user's machine when she is finished with the problem. A big security issue ensues.

With the ability to control the machines, Jeanne can use her administrator user ID and prevent this from becoming an issue. It may be inconvenient for Jeanne in the short term, but until she breaks her old habits, you don't have to worry about an irate user deleting the CEO's schedule because he or she found his or her machine suddenly could access anything on the server.

Another instance where this feature is useful is in a very restrictive environment, where you may want users only logging on from specific machines. This could be part of a standard security policy or it could be specifically implemented to ensure workers remain in their own cubicles while working. Another valuable use for this feature is to limit your exposure in the event that a user ID and password are discovered by someone outside the company. Even if a hacker gets a user ID and password, they also must have the capability to access the specific machine that user ID is tied to. This increases your security by an order of magnitude. To set a workstation log-on restriction, follow these steps:

1. Log on as a user with administrator capabilities.

2. Run the User Manager for Domains from the Administrative Tools group.

3. Select the appropriate *Username* and double-click it. This opens the user properties screen.

4. At the bottom of the dialog box, select Logon To.

5. This opens the Logon Workstations dialog box. See Figure 8.22.

FIG. 8.22
Remember, while setting the allowed workstations, you must identify them by Windows NT computer name.

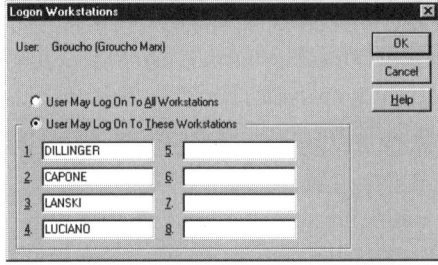

6. Select the User may log on to These Workstations option button. Fill in the Windows NT computer names for the allowed machines. You can enter up to eight machines.

7. When finished, select OK and your changes will be made the next time the user tries to log on.

How to Set Log-On Time Restrictions

You know how to limit what workstations a user can log on from. Now you need to know how to limit what time your users can log on.

From within User Manager for Domains, you have the capability to restrict when a specific user account can log on to the Windows NT domain. (You learn how to do this later in this section.) This can be useful for several reasons. First, for the obvious security reasons. If you want to be sure users only are able to log on to the domain during business hours, you can restrict users to 9:00 A.M. to 5:00 P.M., Monday through Friday.

If users need access during off hours, they would have to contact an administrator and explain why they need the access. This is a secure environment. Unfortunately, it isn't extremely useful in a lot of environments. In today's fast paced, mobile computing environment, users are frequently in before 5:00 a.m., in the office until 8:00 p.m., or dialed in after an out-of-town business meeting to check their e-mail. In the average environment, what good is this feature? Let me give you another example.

Suppose you have five servers in your domain, one for each of your departments. Combined disk space between the servers is 18 GB. Every night, because you are dedicated to maintaining data integrity, you run a full backup of all your servers using several DLT tape drives. Assume it takes four hours to back up all your data. To be thorough, you want to be sure you get all the data and don't have to skip any open files, so you schedule your backup to run from 12:30 a.m. until 4:30 a.m. You're safe, right?

Oops, Phil in accounting left his PC logged on, and he has the mail database open. The backup skipped mail. The next night Jean leaves the president's scheduling application open. It gets skipped. Continue this trend and if the server crashes or a disk fails, there is no telling what files are skipped that night. I hope it wasn't the president's schedule. He'll be a little upset when all his appointments for the next six months aren't on a recent tape.

Now you have a couple of choices. You can make it a policy that everyone turns off their machines before they leave. Great idea, but people just never seem to remember—they get caught in a meeting, they're off site for the afternoon and can't get back, they just forget, and so on. You know how that happens.

You could always be sure that you are the last one to leave, and walk around the office making sure all the machines are turned off. If that's the plan, I hope you have a small office. The suggestion I would make is to use the Logon Time Restrictions in Windows NT. Make sure none of your users can log on during the 12:30 a.m. to 4:30 a.m. backup window. Follow these steps to set these restrictions:

1. Log on as a user with administrator capabilities.
2. Run the User Manager for Domains from the Administrative Tools group.
3. Select the appropriate *Username* and double-click it. This opens the user properties screen. If you are creating a new user, Select User, then New User.

4. At the bottom of the dialog box, select H̲ours.

5. This opens the Logon Hours dialog box. See Figure 8.23.

FIG. 8.23
Remember, the blue section shows the hours when logon is allowed; the blank sections show the hours when it is disallowed.

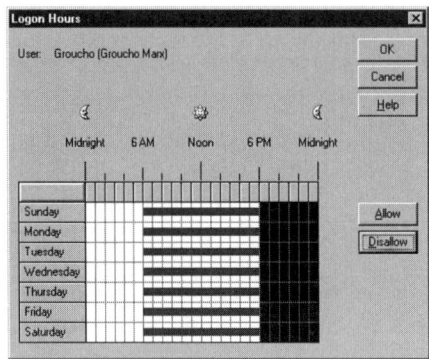

6. Highlight the section of hours you want to restrict. Click D̲isallow to prevent the users from logging on during these times.

N O T E   You can select times during any day of the week, in one hour increments. To re-enable a time, select the time or block of times, and click Allow. ▪

7. When finished, click OK and the next time your user(s) tries to log on during the restricted time, they will be unable to. If they are logged on during these hours, they will be disconnected.

An additional thing to remember: If you edit the Account Policies within User Manager for Domains, you can determine what happens to a user when the log-on hours end. If you select the Forcibly Disconnect Remote Users From Server When Logon Hours Expire option, users are warned before the log-on hours expire and are disconnected. If you don't select this option, then no new connections can be made to the server, but existing user connections can continue. A message will be sent every 10 minutes that logon is not allowed at this time. You should select the Forcibly Disconnect option in all but the most exceptional instances, such as batch jobs, and so on. You set the policy for a reason—backups, security, whatever. Be sure to enforce it.

How to Set User Account Expiration Dates

Another handy feature of User Manager for Domains is the capability to set expiration dates on user accounts. This feature is not used a lot, and with most user accounts, is not useful. In high-security environments, it might be a good idea to expire accounts every 90 days to be sure that all your users are constantly re-authorized for system access. This is a fairly large amount of overhead for any but the most security conscious environments, because the overhead is significant. A more common use for this feature is demonstrated in the case of a temporary or co-op employee.

Jane is a college co-op at Wayne's Army Surplus Distributors Inc., and she will be working in the Accounting Department for the summer. Susan, the manager of the department, submits a request to get Jane a user account, so she can use network resources such as printers, file storage, and shared directories. Jane gets her account, works the summer, and leaves for college in the fall.

Susan, being a busy manager, forgets to send a delete form to the LAN Administrators. She remembers several months later, but decides that because the LAN Administrators were invited to Jane's going away party, they must have deleted the account. Wrong. Now there is a hole in the domain. When Jane mentions her work at Wayne's to a guru buddy of hers, he dials into the company and tries her account. It works, and now he has access to the company's accounting files. If an account expiration date had been set when Jane was hired, this issue would not exist. The account would have expired on her departure date, and unless it was re-enabled, it would remain useless. Security hole plugged. Now that you have an idea when to use this feature, here's how:

1. Log on as a user with administrator capabilities.
2. Run the User Manager for Domains from the Administrative Tools group.
3. Select the appropriate Username and double-click it. This opens the User Properties screen. If you are creating a new user, Select User, then New User.
4. At the bottom of the dialog box, select Account.
5. This opens the Account Information dialog box. See Figure 8.24.

FIG. 8.24
If there is doubt as to when a temporary employee departs, add a month. If the account isn't deleted when they depart, it still expires eventually, closing your security hole.

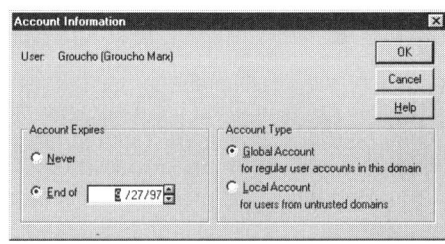

6. Fill in the date you want the account to expire.
7. Click OK and when the date you select arrives, the account will expire and will be disabled. To re-enable an account, change the expiration date and check the user properties to be sure the account is enabled.

From Here...

This chapter discusses many of the utilities and strategies for securing domain resources in a Windows NT environment—User Manager for Domains, for creating and configuring user accounts; and Server Manager, which enables you to manage servers, including promoting Backup Domain Controllers, synchronizing domains, and managing trust relationships. We've also discussed assigning NTFS permissions, securing the Windows NT registry, and using User Profiles to manage domain security. If you understand the concepts covered and apply a little security common sense, you should be able to implement any level of security necessary to keep your network secure.

The following chapters provide more information on securing your Windows NT environment:

- Chapter 4, "Windows NT Domain Concepts," gives you an in-depth look at how domains work.

- Chapter 5, "Maintaining Security with Domain Trust Relationships," looks at how to properly implement domain trust relationships without compromising the security of your Windows NT network.

- Part III, "Setting Up an Example Master-Domain Model," contains three chapters that walk you through actually setting up a Master Domain network. This section contains Chapter 10, "Planning the Master Domain," Chapter 11, "Implementation Steps," and Chapter 12, "Setting Up Trust Relationships."

CHAPTER 9

Windows NT Workstation Security

Taking a closer look at security from the standpoint of Windows NT Workstation is the focus of this chapter. In many ways, Windows NT Server and Windows NT Workstation are very similar, but one of the things that sets them apart is the way security is implemented. Windows NT Workstation has its own security accounts database and acts as its own security authority, even if it's a member of a domain. ■

Workstation versus domain security

This examines the difference between workstation and domain security. See when each type of security is used and how the two interact in a network environment.

Joining a domain

Learn how to add a workstation to a domain and what advantages this gives the user of the workstation. This process involves the network administrator granting the workstation a machine account on the domain. You see how this is done from the workstation and how it can be done using the Server Manager adminstrative utility.

Workstation resource security

Become familiar with the security of resources located on the Windows NT Workstation. Each Windows NT Workstation can share its resources, such as disk drive directories or attached printers with a limited number of network clients. You learn how the same methods of security that are used with Windows NT Server can be implemented when sharing work-station resources.

Workstation and Domain User Security

A Microsoft NT Workstation is very similar to Windows NT Server in some ways. They look the same because they use the same Windows 95 graphical user interface (GUI), and they both share the same kernel architecture. Both of them work with a user account database to authenticate users, and both of them can share resources over the network. Despite these similarities, Windows NT Workstation is a different product with a different purpose than Windows NT Server.

The primary system-design goal of Windows NT Workstation was to provide a working platform for a locally logged-on user that would provide maximum responsiveness. Windows NT Server, on the other hand, has a primary purpose of providing network file access; therefore, it has been optimized for network performance and not user responsiveness. Because of this basic difference in purpose, Windows NT Workstation does not participate in a domain as a Primary or Backup Domain Controller, and it will never be used to authenticate domain user log-on requests.

Instead, the Windows NT Workstation contains its own user accounts database that can be used to authenticate users. Note that it can use this because the Windows NT Workstation also can be a member of a Windows NT domain. Being a member of a domain allows the local user to log on to the workstation's account database, or it lets them log on to the domain's account database. When a user logs on to the domain the workstation forwards authentication requests to a domain controller for verification instead of verifying the account locally.

You might be asking why it makes a difference where you get authenticated—just as long as you get logged on, right?

Well, it depends on the type of resources you want to access. First, let's define resources as being *domain resources* or *workstation resources* as follows:

- **■** *Domain resources* These resources are located on servers that participate in a domain environment. Access to these resources is granted on the basis of a user's *domain* account. In order to access a resource of this type, the user must have an account in the domain (or a trusted domain) and the appropriate access permissions.

- **■** *Workstation resources* These are resources such as printers and directories on the local Windows NT Workstation. Permission is granted to these local resources using account information from the workstation's own account database.

If you log on to a Windows NT Workstation using an account from the workstation's local account database, then you won't be able to access any domain resources unless you have the following prerequisites:

1. Have a duplicate account ID and password in the domain containing the resource.

2. The duplicate domain account must have been given the appropriate access permission to the resource.

However, if the Windows NT Workstation has joined a domain, both the local workstation resources and the resources of the domain both can be easily accessed by giving the user a single domain log-on account. This is because an *implied* trust relationship is set up when a Windows NT Workstation joins a domain. After a workstation has joined a domain, the workstation logon is much like a logon to a trusted domain from a server. The user has the option of logging on to the workstation using an account from the workstation's local account database or logging on using an account from the domain's user account database.

When the workstation is a member of a domain, access to the workstation's resources can be granted to domain accounts in addition to local user accounts. You can think of it as kind of a minitrust relationship between the workstation and the domain of which it is a member. The domain is the *trusted* member of the party and contains user accounts that can be used to access the workstation's resources. The workstation acts as the *trusting* party in the relationship. As a member of a domain, the workstation permits the assignment of access privileges to domain accounts for access to its resources.

Part
II

Ch
9

How a Windows NT Workstation Joins a Domain

The Windows NT Workstation can join a Windows NT domain during installation or anytime thereafter. In fact, the workstation can even change domain memberships as long as a computer account is created in the target domain for the workstation. The computer account is used much like a user account on the domain, except it represents the workstation and not an individual user. This allows the implied trust relationship to be set up between the domain and the workstation. This in turn allows the workstation to pass log-on requests to a domain controller.

The computer account can be created before the workstation joins the domain, or the account can be created as the workstation joins the domain. Before the workstation actually joins the domain, the domain administrator can add the name of the workstation to the domain using the Server Manager administrative utility. If the workstation account is created as the workstation joins the domain, a domain administrator account ID and password must be provided during the process (at the workstation).

Creating a Computer Account for the Windows NT Workstation

The administrator of the home domain that the workstation will be joining can add the workstation's computer name to the domain before the workstation setup procedure is initiated. This allows the individual setting up the Windows NT Workstation to add it to the domain without having to supply the domain administrator ID or password.

The administrator of the home domain creates the computer account using the Server Manager administrative utility. After the computer account has been created, the Windows NT Workstation can join the domain, and users at the workstation can log on using a domain account. The reason for using a domain account at the workstation is the account's capability to permit access to resources at the workstation in the home domain and to resources in domains that trust the workstation's home domain.

For example, pretend you have an Accounts Domain named ADMIN that contains the user accounts for all the network users. The ADMIN domain contains several resource shares and has a trusting resource domain (named SHARES) that also contains several resource shares. Users logging on with a domain account ID and password from the ADMIN (home) domain can access resources on the workstation in the ADMIN domain, and they can access the resources in the SHARES domain. If the Windows NT Workstation was not a member of the ADMIN domain, users logging on at the workstation would have to log on using an account from the workstations account database. They could not log on using a domain account and password from the ADMIN domain.

If they wanted to access a resource on the workstation, it wouldn't be any problem as long as the user has the appropriate access permissions. If the user wanted to access one of the resources on the ADMIN domain, they would have to have a user account on the ADMIN domain that was created with exactly the same account ID and password.

If the user wanted to access a resource share on the SHARES domain, the same rule would apply. They would have to have a user account on the SHARES domain that used exactly the same user account ID and password. As you learned earlier, resource domains such as the SHARES domain in this example typically do not contain user accounts. This would prevent a user logging on to the workstation with a local account from accessing any resources on the SHARES domain, regardless of any security that was applied to its resource shares.

The Windows NT Workstation in the following example will be added to the domain named ADMIN. To add a Windows NT Workstation computer account to a domain, follow these steps:

1. Log on to the ADMIN domain with Administrator privilege and start the Server Manager utility.

2. Select <u>A</u>dd to Domain from the <u>C</u>omputer menu option. This opens the Add Computer To Domain dialog box shown in Figure 9.1.

FIG. 9.1

Adding a computer account to the domain allows the Windows NT Workstation to use the domain's accounts database.

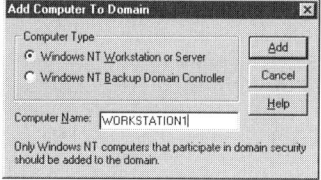

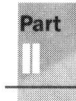
3. Mark the option button next to the Windows NT <u>W</u>orkstation or Server option under Computer Type.

4. Type in the Windows NT Workstation's computer name in the box next to Computer <u>N</u>ame.

5. Click the <u>A</u>dd button to add the computer account. Click the close button when you're finished.

The Windows NT Workstation's computer name now is listed in the Server Manager with other members of the domain.

How to Join a Domain During the Workstation Setup

During the Windows NT Workstation installation process, you are presented with a dialog box that enables you to specify whether the workstation will participate in a Domain or a Workgroup. Participation in a domain enables users to log on to the workstation using their domain account ID and password. The default selection at this stage of the setup procedure designates that the workstation will participate in a Workgroup and not a Domain. The difference is that a workstation which is a member of a Workgroup only uses its local database to authenticate user logons. The Workgroup name simply identifies the workstation as a member of a group of computers that will have a common master browser. The workstations that are members of a workgroup all will be grouped under the same workgroup name in browser lists.

Joining a domain by adding the computer account to it during the setup requires that the domain administrator be available to supply her or his account ID and password. This is not required if the administrator of the domain already has created a computer account for the Windows NT Workstation in the domain using Server Manager. The Windows NT Workstation setup prompts you to choose whether the workstation will be participating in a domain's workgroup. To join a domain, mark the option button next to the domain option and supply the domain's name of which the workstation will become a member. If the computer account has not been created, mark the option that enables you to create a computer account in the domain, then get the domain administrator. If the computer account already has been created, the option to create a computer account should be cleared.

If you opted to create the computer account, you are presented with a dialog box that requests a domain administrative account ID and password. This is when the domain administrator must be available to supply the information. If the ID and password are not specified correctly, the workstation will fail to connect to the domain controller and the computer account will not be added. Hence the attempt to join the domain fails. A correct administrative ID and password enables the workstation to join the domain, and the computer account automatically will be created. The workstation's name is then listed in Server Manager as a Windows NT Workstation.

The Logon Information dialog box on the Windows NT Workstation now presents a Domain drop-down list. The Domain drop-down list is not present when the workstation is designated as a member of a workgroup. However, a user logging on at this workstation can choose to log on via a local workstation account by selecting the name of the workstation from the Domain drop-down list. Alternatively, a user may select the name of the workstation's parent domain from the Domain drop-down list and log on using a domain account.

Workstation Security in a Domain Environment

As mentioned, the Windows NT Workstation contains its own local user accounts database. This database is totally independent of any other machine or domain. It contains its own built-in users and groups, such as the administrator account and the Administrator's group. This allows the owner of the workstation to retain complete control of the workstation and any resources that may be associated with it. The workstation owner simply logs on under the local administrator account to perform administrative tasks on the workstation. Or, the owner can create a personal user account that belongs to the workstation administrator's group. This would allow the user to perform administrative tasks with his or her personal account ID.

If a Windows NT Workstation is set up as a member of a workgroup, it does not permit users to log on locally using domain accounts. It only uses the local accounts database to authenticate user logons and assign resource permissions. When access permissions are given to workstation resources, they only can be given to users or groups contained within the workstation's accounts database. In the case of a shared resource on the workstation, a user that logs on to a domain must have an identical account ID and password within the workstation's account database to be given access. If he or she doesn't, the user will have to supply a valid account ID and password when attempting to initiate a connection to a shared resource on the workstation.

You can eliminate the administrative overhead that duplicate accounts create by adding the workstation to the network's account domain. Remember, the account domain is the Windows NT domain that contains the accounts for all network users. If users are permitted to log on to the workstation using their domain account, it will allow them to access the domain, trusting domain resources, and the workstation's resources without needing duplicate accounts.

If the Windows NT Workstation does not join the domain during its installation, you can join it to the domain later by following this procedure:

1. Log on to the workstation using an administrator's account. From Control Panel, click the Network icon to open the Network dialog box.

2. The default view is set to the Identification tab. Click the Change button located on this page to open the Identification Changes dialog box.

3. Mark the option button next to Domain in the Member of section of the dialog box. Then replace the default name of DOMAIN with the name of the domain the workstation will join.

4. If the administrator of the domain already has created a computer account for the workstation in the domain, click the OK button. If the administrator did not create the computer account, mark the box next to Create a Computer Account in the Domain. You then will have to supply a domain administrator's ID and password before the workstation is allowed membership in the domain.

5. If the workstation successfully joined the domain, a Network Configuration dialog box appears and displays a message welcoming you to the domain. Click the OK button to continue.

6. Click the Yes button in the dialog box prompting you to reboot the workstation.

Changes to the Workstation's Local Account Database

After the Windows NT Workstation joins the domain, the first thing that you'll notice is the extra selection box in the Logon Information dialog box. It enables you to specify a logon to the domain or to the workstation.

The workstation owner can then log on under the *workstations* Administrator account and give his or her domain user account membership in the workstation's administrator group. This allows the user to log on to the workstation using his or her standard domain account and yet have full administrative control over the workstation and its resources. To make this a little clearer, let's use an example.

The user with a domain account named JohnB has just installed an NT Workstation at his desk. During the installation, he specified that the workstation join the ADMIN domain. This is the company's account domain and it is the domain that JohnB regularly logs on to access domain resources. The domain's administrator had added a computer account for JohnB's Windows NT Workstation ahead of time, so the workstation was able to successfully join the ADMIN domain during installation.

After the workstation's installation, JohnB is now able to log on to the workstation using his domain account by specifying his domain account ID and password and selecting ADMIN from the domain box. This enables JohnB to access easily domain resources for which he has been granted access. He also can access resources located in trusting domains using this logon. He can't administer the workstation, though. His access to the workstation's administrative utilities is restricted to having no more rights than a standard user account.

To solve this problem, JohnB simply logs on to the workstation using the local administrator account. JohnB knows the administrator's password, because he set it during the workstation setup. Once successfully logged on as the administrator, he is able to execute the administrative utility User Manager and add his JohnB domain account to the local administrators group. The procedure is outlined as follows:

1. Log on to the workstation using the workstation's administrator account ID and password.
2. Run the User Manager utility and then double-click the Administrators group entry in the lower-half of the dialog box to open the Local Group Properties dialog box.
3. Click the Add button to open the Add Users and Groups dialog box.
4. Select the name of the domain in the List Names From drop-down list box.
5. Select the desired account from the Names window and click the Add button. The account name now is listed in the Add Names.
6. Click the OK button to return to the Local Group Properties dialog box. The Members window now reflects the domain account of the user as a member of the group.
7. Click the OK button to apply the changes and return to the User Manager utility's main window. Exit User Manager when finished.

Now when JohnB logs on to the workstation using his normal domain account, he will have administrative privileges on the workstation. This will allow JohnB to share resources, grant permissions, and set policy on the local workstation while still having his normal domain access.

You may have noticed something else that happened after the workstation joined the domain. The parent domain's administrators global group was added to the workstations local administrators group. This automatically gives the domain administrators their administrative access to any Windows NT Workstation that joins the domain.

This is similar to what happens during the setup of a trust relationship between two domains. The trusted domain's administrators global group is added to the trusting domains administrators local group. This again points out the similarity between a trust relationship and a workstation's domain membership.

Giving Access to a Workstation's Resources

The Windows NT Workstation can allow limited network access to the resources it may have available. As with a Windows NT Server, the Windows NT Workstation also can share directories and printer queues over the network. Unlike Windows NT Server, the number of inbound connections is restricted to no more than 10 concurrent connections at one time. Windows NT Workstation grants access to shared resources in the same way Windows NT Servers grant access to shared resources—by using share permissions. The workstation also is able to grant or deny access to files and directories using NTFS security if NTFS is implemented on the workstation's drives. Both share-level and NTFS-level access can be granted to accounts from the workstation's local account database and from the domain's account database.

Granting NTFS Permissions at the Workstation

The ability to apply NTFS permissions to the workstation's files and directories permits the workstation's owner to secure the workstation against unauthorized user access to any of the information contained on the workstation's drives. This can come in handy if several users have access to and use the same workstation.

NTFS permissions are applied on a Windows NT Workstation exactly the same way they are applied on a Windows NT Server. In the case of a workstation that is a domain member, accounts from the local accounts database or from the domain's account database can be granted access permissions. Windows NT Workstations that are not domain members only can give NTFS access permission to users or groups from their local accounts database.

Granting Share Permissions on the Windows NT Workstation

As with Windows NT Server, Windows NT Workstation also can share directories and print queues. And as with Windows NT Server, this is done exactly the same way by granting share permissions to users and groups. The ability to give access permissions to a domain user or group is dependant on the workstation being a member of a domain. As with NTFS permissions, share permissions only can be granted to a domain user or group if the workstation is a domain member. If the workstation does not belong to a domain (and is only a workgroup member), share access only can be delegated to a local workstation user or group accounts.

From Here...

Learning how to add a Windows NT Workstation to a domain and how this allows domain accounts to access the workstation's resources are the main goals for you to glean from this chapter. In the upcoming chapters, you take what you've learned in the previous chapters and apply it to a sample network installation and security setup.

- Chapter 10, "Planning the Master Domain," begins the planning phase of the installation example. You define the needs of a fictitious company and plan the security strategy that will be used to protect their network.

- Chapter 11, "Implementation Steps," gives you the opportunity to take what you've planned and implement the network's security configuration based on those requirements. This chapter focuses on security within the local domain's boundary.

- Chapter 12, "Setting Up Trust Relationships," expands on the local security implemented on the local domain to include other trusting domains and the resources they contain.

Setting Up an Example Master-Domain Model

Planning the Master Domain

This is the first chapter in the book's section that shows you how to set up a sample network installation. You'll see a lighthearted example of a company that wants to implement a network using Microsoft Windows NT 4.0 Server. As with most companies, they want a solution that meets their resource needs, one that offers maximum security, and one that is cost effective. The object of this chapter is to examine the security needs of the company and figure out the most effective solution. To do this, you must look at a few key areas.

First, take a look at the structure of the Orbit Company and its networking requirements. The goal of planning this is to make a detailed domain model to implement at Orbit. The general model decided on earlier is modified to include server designations, specific trust relationship properties, and user account policy information. ■

Company overview

A fictitious company named Orbit Rocket Design and Sales (henceforth referred to as "Orbit") wants to implement a new Windows NT network with connections to all their corporate offices. You must design a secure Windows NT network.

Domain action plan

Based on Orbit's list of requirements, make a determination on the domain model you are going to implement. The general details and extent of server participation within the domain model can be determined.

User requirements

The way users are allowed to interact with the company network is a big concern to Orbit's management team. Because of this, you must implement features of Windows NT that control user interaction on both a group and user level. Determine what user policies to apply to which network user accounts.

Other security considerations

Remote access and Internet use are some of the security requirements of the network. Orbit is flexible about allowing remote access to the network, but at the same time they want to maintain high security and accountability.

Company Overview

Orbit is a medium-sized company that employs 300 people at one central location. They design, construct, and sell rockets. Of the 300 employees, 200 are manufacturing personnel that do not currently require the use of a computer. About 100 of the employees do require the use of a personal computer. These 100 employees are spread throughout several different departments within Orbit. Here's a brief description of the different departments:

- *Administration* This department has about 20 employees, which includes management as well. They manage the company and set employee policy, and they want to access and configure all network systems, because they're the bosses. Much of the work they do is secret and confidential.

- *Rocket Design* These employees (typical rocket scientists) design the rockets and must be able to share information freely with one another. They also must have the ability to create and administer resources on their part of the network. This department has 60 employees, many of whom claim to have written complete operating systems from scratch.

- *Rocket Sales* Like most salespeople, these folks are on the road most of the time and must be able to access the network remotely. They need to easily access sales and marketing information on the network. These are typical sales types who have no concept of what a network resource is, nor do they care.

Orbit has decided that it's finally time to install a network system instead of relying on individual PCs at each person's desk. After all, they are a rocket company—they shouldn't be relying on floppy disks any longer to distribute information.

They need to have a highly secure network installed that enables them to store safely all their rocket design data. Because NASA could call any time for their assistance, they want to have the rocket specifications available online 24 hours a day. This information will be stored in a SQL Server database that will provide information to the entire design department. Other system requirements include servers that host application software, messaging servers, and remote access servers.

Additionally, the company foresees a real need to access and distribute information directly via the Internet. They want to bring the Internet to the desktop for all the employees. They would like salespeople on the road to have the ability to access not only the system but also the Internet from a remote location.

With this simple scenario in mind, list some of the system requirements that will directly affect the design of Orbit's Windows NT-based network. The list of design recommendations includes the following:

1. All user accounts must reside in a single user database.
2. The system must provide absolute security for the confidential information kept by administration.
3. Administrative personnel must be able to access and to control all the resources of the network.
4. The Design department must be able to administer their own portion of the network.
5. Remote access to the company network must be given to the Sales department.
6. Connectivity to network resources must be simple for the Sales department.
7. You must protect the resources of the network by limiting the ability of network superusers (our rocket scientists) to modify any network or system parameters.
8. A safe method of Internet access must be given to all users of the network.
9. All users of the system need to have some storage space on the network reserved for their personal use.
10. Common areas on the network must be established where files and programs can be exchanged.
11. The use of passwords will be required for any access to the network.
12. Because the information concerning rockets can be somewhat sensitive, you need to make sure users regularly change their network password.
13. Our rocket scientists are paid by the hour, so we'll also want to restrict the number of hours they can be logged on to the network.
14. Access to sensitive data belonging to Administration must be tracked.
15. Time-critical data for active experiments must be kept online at all times.
16. The security of the data contained on each network server must be ensured by the successful completion of regular tape backups.

Based on these general requirements, you can begin to think about the overall design of the domain. After you have a general idea of the way this domain model will work, you can start to focus on some specific strategies for securing the network.

Part
III

Ch
10

Domain and Server Criteria

OK, so what domain model is going to work the best? To answer that, let's first determine if any of the network requirements listed previously must have a specific domain model implemented.

Because you don't have 10,000 users at Orbit, the Multiple Master Domain Model can be immediately dismissed as one of the choices. Now, if you quickly review your requirement list, you see that the first item on the list specifies that all user accounts reside in a single user database. This narrows down our choices to either a single domain model or a master domain model. The complete trust model implies user accounts in more than one domain.

If you continue to look at the requirements, you see that administration wants to control the entire network, as stated in requirement number four. However, in requirement five, they also have determined that the Design department's portion of the network can be maintained by personnel within that department.

For this example, you could create a single domain and selectively assign special account permissions to different department members. However, using the master domain model is really the easiest way to give administrative personnel full control of everything, while allowing Design control over their resources.

The use of the master domain model implies the use of at least two domains. One domain will contain the user account information for every user on the network. This domain will be configured as the *trusted* domain in any trust relationships that you establish. The other domain will contain resources that network users must have access to. These domains will be the *trusting* domains on your network and will not contain any user accounts.

Now you're going to implement a master domain model with a primary account domain that will contain both user accounts and a variety of network resources. The other domain on the Orbit network will belong to Design. It will contain resources used exclusively by the rocket scientists and will participate in a one-way trust relationship with the account domain. The Design department will be allowed to administer the domain, although not exclusively. Administration will be able to manage fully the Design department's domain.

The security of any domain depends on having a backup copy of the security accounts database (SAM) available at all times. This is done by installing a Backup Domain Controller (BDC) on the domain to retain a copy of the SAM. This means you must provide at least two servers to act as domain controllers for each domain. Because we have determined that we will be using at least two domains, the total number of controllers required is at least four.

Summing up what's been established so far, you should come up with the following:

- A master domain model will be implemented.
- Two domains will participate in the domain model: an account domain and a resource domain.
- Administration will control both domains.
- Design will be able to control its resource domain.
- A one-way trust relationship will be established between domains with the accounts domain acting as the trusted domain.
- A minimum of four network servers will be required as domain controllers to provide redundancy for the security accounts database in both domains.

Now let's go on to look at the some of the user access requirements and what you'll need to do to meet the criteria.

User Access Requirements

Several areas of the network configuration will deal with establishing the user access policy requirements. The requirements set forth earlier necessitate the implementation of several controls that affect a user's ability to access the network.

First, you specified that a user must use a password when logging on to the network. This means the account policy of the network must be configured so that blank passwords are not permitted. Another requirement states that passwords must be changed on a regular basis. Both of these features are configurable using the Account Policy option in the User Manager for Domains program.

Our requirements also called for a personal area on the network for users where they could store information. This implies that we specify a user home directory in the user profile properties when adding an account to our user database. Another requirement limits the log-on hours available to the rocket scientists in the Design department. This too is a configurable user property available to you in the User Manager for Domains program.

One requirement that is more restrictive limits the Design department's ability to change or modify system and network configuration parameters. Although it's true that we want a few of the rocket scientists in Design to control file and print resource access in their domain, we don't want the rest of them having access to the various Windows NT administrative and configuration utilities. Likewise, you don't want the Sales team even messing with their desktop environment. To accomplish both of these goals we'll initiate the use of mandatory user profiles on the network using the System Policy editor.

Part

III

Ch

10

Internet access is a major user access requirement according to Orbit. They want to be able to access the Internet's vast resources without jeopardizing the local network. Several different approaches can be taken. One approach is the use of a segmented LAN as the Internet LAN. Any workstations (or servers) that need Internet access could be dual-homed. This is good if you only have a few machines that need access to the Internet, but it is inefficient if a large number of machines need to have Internet access. What's the point? They're all exposed anyway.

The next approach involves the use of a non-routable protocol on all machines except those that need access to the Internet. The machines needing Internet access get configured with the routable protocol TCP/IP. Once again, you have the same predicament—all the machines need access, so there's no point running a non-routable protocol on any of them.

An obvious choice would be the use of a firewall to provide the barrier needed between your local LAN and the Internet. This could be done using one of several third-party firewall products available. On the other hand, it easily could be done using the Microsoft proxy server product called Catapult. It would provide our network with a single protected point of contact to the Internet. This dual-homed machine is then specified in the client's browser software (such as Microsoft's Internet Explorer) configuration. Salespeople easily can connect via remote access and use the company's pipe to the Internet through the proxy server. In addition to the proxy server, Orbit also will implement a firewall server from a third-party vendor. Many types of firewall products are available, including both software- and hardware-based solutions. The combination of both the firewall and the proxy server will provide protection against most external types of security threats.

The last user-related requirement is that any activity involving sensitive files that belong to Administration is to be tracked and audited. Several options enable us to track usage. This can be done by enabling the audit policy for all file and object access or by tracking the use of user rights. It also can be done using file and directory auditing on the specific files and directories that are desired.

Here's a summary of the items you need to configure that are related to user access, as follows:

- Deny the use of blank passwords using the appropriate Account Policy option setting.
- Enforce the periodic change of user passwords using the appropriate Account Policy option.
- Specify a user home directory for each user account by modifying the appropriate user properties in User Manager for Domains.

- Use the Account Properties page in User Manager for Domains to restrict the log-on hours of Design employees.

- Use the System Policy Editor to create mandatory user profiles for both Design and Sales. The profiles will be assigned in the User Properties page during the user setup.

- Auditing of sensitive files will be initiated on specific directories using the file and directory properties page available in the Windows NT Explorer or "My Computer" utility.

- The configuration of a network proxy server for Internet access by clients. This involves minor configuration of the client's browser software, as well as the configuration of the proxy server.

The next items that must be considered deal with remote access and Internet access. Also, you have to consider the precautions that must be implemented to maintain the integrity and availability of the data contained on Orbit's file servers.

More Security Issues

The other security issues that need to be considered involve enabling the Remote Access Server service to give only a subset of users (Sales) the ability to make dial-up network connections. For an extra measure of safety, it is determined that the Remote Access Server (RAS) call back feature will be used to verify call origination.

The last requirements specify that critical on-line data be available at all times and that regular backups of the drive information become an administrative policy. To accomplish the first goal, you must consider two separate issues. What specific areas of the system are given fault tolerance, and then what type of fault tolerance will be implemented? The backup plan involves choosing a backup method and backup schedule.

The configuration of these other security features involves the following:

- Configure RAS privileges for Sales only (and the company execs, of course).

- Configure RAS for callback to the user whenever possible. This is not feasible for the Sales team that will be calling in from different locations. Any other RAS client must be configured for callback.

- Specify critical servers and provide fault tolerance to those servers in the form of mirrored drives (with duplexing).

- Create a tape backup schedule and designate the backup responsibilities for the network administrators.

You might be asking why we arbitrarily chose to provide fault tolerance in the form of mirrored drives. The reasoning is that mirroring provides a high level of performance and is easily recoverable in case of a drive failure. Orbit wants to save some money by not buying an expensive hardware-based array system. If Orbit were real, they might buy one. However, many companies can't. Fortunately, Windows NT provides the software-based mirroring and RAID tools that provide the same level of protection. And because this book is focusing on Windows NT security tools, we won't rely on a hardware-based solution for the example here. The choice of Windows NT software mirroring over RAID 5 is just because we want to be able to add fault tolerance to the boot partition of our server(s). This can't be done with the RAID 5 striping option in Windows NT.

Now take everything we've decided to implement and place it in a to-do list to use as a guide during the system implementation.

The Proposed System

The proposed system for Orbit incorporates all the security design features outlined in the previous sections of this chapter. Here's a list of the Windows NT security features that will be implemented on Orbit's Windows NT network:

- A master domain model will be implemented.
- Two domains will participate in the domain model—an account domain and a resource domain.
- The Administration will control both domains.
- The Design department will be able to control its resource domain.
- A one-way trust relationship will be established between domains with the accounts domain acting as the trusted domain.
- A minimum of four network servers will be required as domain controllers to provide redundancy for the security accounts database in both domains.
- Deny the use of blank passwords using the appropriate Account Policy option setting.
- Enforce the periodic change of user passwords using the appropriate Account Policy option.
- Specify a user home directory for each user account by modifying the appropriate user properties in User Manager for Domains.
- Use the Account Properties page in User Manager for Domains to restrict the log-on hours of Design employees.

- Use the System Policy Editor to create mandatory user profiles for both Design and Sales. The profiles will be assigned in the User Properties page during user setup.

- Auditing of sensitive files will be initiated on specific directories using the file and directory properties page available in the Windows NT Explorer or My Computer utility.

- The configuration of a network proxy server for Internet accesses by clients. This involves minor configuration of the client's browser software in addition to the configuration of the proxy server.

- Configure RAS privileges for only members of Sales (and executives, of course).

- Configure RAS for callback to the user whenever possible. This is not feasible for salespeople who call from different locations. Any other RAS client must be configured for callback.

- Specify critical servers and provide fault tolerance to those servers in the form of mirrored drives (with duplexing).

- Create a tape backup schedule and designate the backup responsibilities for the network administrators.

Part

III

Ch

10

You can take each of these items and break them down into specific tasks or design issues. Each of them can be planned before starting the installation of the system.

The first item on your list mandates creating a master domain model that consists of two domains (as per the second item on our list). The first domain will consist of user accounts and possibly a few user resources. The other domain will be strictly a resource domain. Start by choosing names for your domains, then draw a simple diagram of the proposed master domain.

Naming is sometimes the most difficult of all installation activities. The names should provide a limited amount of information as to what the domain's purpose is. For example, if you had an entire domain that contained nothing but servers for the Accounting department, you could choose a name such as "FINANCE" for the domain name. If you had a domain that contained only print servers, you could use the name "PRINTQUEUE" to identify it. Then again, you may not want to be so obvious about the domain's server membership or department affiliation. In this case, choose a name that is less descriptive. This same theory is true for server names also. You can use airport identifiers if you want to use a geographical domain-naming scheme. Just as long as it makes sense to your organization.

Orbit wants a domain-naming scheme that is easily understood and one that easily identifies the domain based on its departmental affiliation. Orbit has picked the following domain names: ADMIN for the administrative domain and DESIGN for the Design department's resource domain.

The next requirements stipulate that the user accounts must reside in a single "account" domain. All user accounts at Orbit will be maintained by Administration, so the ADMIN domain will be designated as the account domain. The DESIGN domain only will contain a limited number of administrative accounts.

The key administrative personnel want full control over the site, so they are placed in an administrative group on the ADMIN domain. Key personnel in Design need to be able to administer the DESIGN resource domain. They will be placed into a common global group and given administrative permission on the DESIGN domain once the trust relationship is in place.

The trust relationship will designate the ADMIN domain as the trusted domain, and the DESIGN domain will be designated the resource domain. Figure 10.1 shows the domain trust relationship that must be set up.

FIG. 10.1

The master domain trust relationship that will be implemented.

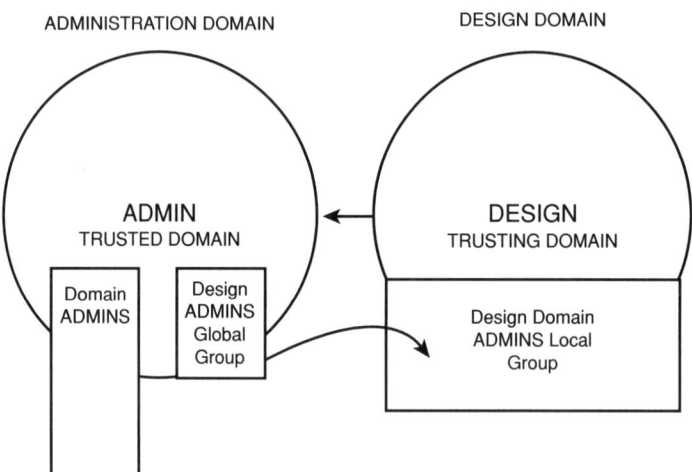

To round out the proposed model, define the servers you need to install and their placement within the domain structure. Server requirements for the ADMIN domain are:

- *Domain Controllers*   At least two servers must be used primarily as domain controllers. One server will be designated as the PDC, the other will be designated as the BDC. The name of the PDC is "ORBIT_PDC," and the name of the BDC is "ORBIT_BDC."

- *Application Server*   One server will be designated as an application server; this server's name will be "ORBIT_APPS." It will be installed into the ADMIN domain.

- *Remote Access Server*   The function of this server will be to provide remote access dial-in capability to Sales personnel. The name of this server will be "ORBIT_RAS" and it will be installed into the ADMIN domain.

- *Proxy Server*   User connectivity to the Internet will be provided by a proxy server. The name of this server is "ORBIT_INTERNET" and it will be installed into the ADMIN domain.

- *Messaging Server*   Orbit wants e-mail, so we'll install an MS Exchange server. The name of the server will be "ORBIT_MAIL," and it will be installed into the ADMIN domain.

Now for the server requirements of the DESIGN domain:

- *Domain Controllers*   The name of the PDC for the DESIGN domain is "DESIGN_PDC." The name of the BDC for the DESIGN domain is "DESIGN_BDC."

- *Database Server*   This is the Rocket Design department's critical server. It will be configured with mirrored drives and redundant power supplies. The name of this server is "DESIGN_DB1."

- *Rollover Database Server*   This will provide a complete physical backup for the original database server, should it be rendered inoperable. Database dumps will be performed at regular intervals to this server from the primary database server. It will be configured for the same mirrored fault tolerance. The name of this server is "DESIGN_DB2."

The other user related configuration parameters are straightforward from an administrative standpoint and will be covered in the course of the example installation.

From Here...

The groundwork has been laid for the installation of the network. You've seen the security requirements and built the needed controls into the network design. Now you can move on to the actual implementation steps beginning with a look at some of the upcoming topics:

- Chapter 11, "Implementation Steps," covers the setup of the servers in the example installation. After the servers have been set up, you'll start configuring the user accounts and groups.

- Chapter 12, "Setting Up Trust Relationships," shows you how to establish the trust relationship between the two domains in the example. Then, you grant the rights to the server using the domain relationship you've set up.

- Chapter 13, "Overview of Security and the Internet," examines the issue of integrating other BackOffice products into your network environment.

Part

III

Ch

10

Implementation Steps

Taking the installation requirements found in Chapter 10, "Planning the Master Domain," this chapter shows you how to implement them. In that chapter, you started a fictitious company named Orbit Rocket Design & Sales and created a security design based on the company's requirements. You learn some basic preparation that needs to be done before the first server installation takes place. The primary and backup domain controller installation is outlined, as well as fault tolerance and the proper replication of the security accounts database between the servers. ■

Preparing and installing domain controllers

Examine the preparation and installation of the primary domain controller for Orbit's Windows NT network.

Providing power protection

Study the configuration of the UPS service within Windows NT. This service is used with UPS systems that can signal the operating system via a serial cable link to a COM port. The service initiates the graceful shutdown of the system when certain conditions exist.

Fault tolerance protection

Learn about drive mirroring, a relatively inexpensive but reliable method of ensuring your drive systems are online and available to service requests.

Using the Domain Monitor Resource Kit utility

This is a tool you can use to monitor the synchronization of the controllers within a Windows NT domain. This tool enables you to monitor the local domain and any trusted domains that may be active on the network.

User and group account creation

You should consider the user and group account configuration issues prior to setting up domain trusts.

Preparing the Domain Controllers

The installation of the initial Windows NT domain controller marks the beginning of Orbit's new network. The implementation of security on the new network started during the planning phase when we determined the logical organization of the domain structure. At the same time, the user rights policy was determined and administrative roles were assigned. The planning phase also determined the type of fault tolerance that would be used on the Windows NT servers. It also specified the target server directories for tape backups and a backup rotation schedule.

With the planning phase complete, the security requirements now must be incorporated into the installation. You begin by installing the *Primary Domain Controller (PDC)* for the ADMIN domain.

Prepare the Server Area

Before you start the installation of the server software, you need to prepare the area where the server is to be kept. The location must provide adequate physical protection against both unauthorized access and environmental hazards. It is important that you provide a stable power source that can protect the server(s) from surges, brownouts, and even complete power loss.

Placing the servers in a locked room prevents unauthorized physical access to any of the domain controllers. The physical security of the servers is important and should not be overlooked. If the domain controllers are tampered with, the entire user accounts database may be compromised. The cost of supplying a secure area for a server is minimal compared to the loss of important company data.

Additionally, make sure the area the servers are to be located in has adequate ventilation and is protected from extreme hot or cold temperatures. Of course, operating temperature limitations vary for each device, but as a rule of thumb, if you're comfortable in the room, the equipment will be too. Most PCs don't require the installation of large air conditioning systems and do tolerate a fair amount of heat before they are adversely affected. This isn't to say that you should ignore the cooling requirements for the area, however. The larger processors that run in systems still need to be able to dissipate a lot of heat or the processor will indeed fail. Combining a proper heat sink for the processor(s) with a reliable fan assembly will help ensure that heat failure doesn't damage the processor.

Another environmental factor to consider is the grade of electrical power that is available to the servers. Usually, the power supplied by most electric companies is not regarded as computer-grade but rather utility-grade. Utility-grade power often spikes well above the normal limitations of delicate computer devices. Most PCs contain power supplies that convert the 120 volt AC power to 5 and 12 volt DC power that can be used by the system components. These DC power supplies only can tolerate a moderate amount of line spiking and dipping before the DC power supplied to the PC's components is affected. When the DC voltage applied to the system is varied, the computer may experience anything from corrupted data to damaged components.

The easiest way to prevent electrical problems is to provide the computer with adequate surge protection, line conditioning, or an Uninterruptible Power Supply (UPS). The degree to which you provide protection will depend on the computer and the information it contains. If the computer is used as a read-only application server that does not contain any critical data or sensitive information, it may be appropriate to use only surge suppression or line conditioning. On the other hand, if you have a server that contains critical, time-sensitive information that must be online 24 hours a day, you'll more than likely want to protect the server with a UPS system.

After you prepare a suitable area for the server system(s), it's time to install the PDC for the account domain.

Installing the Primary Domain Controller

The installation of the PDC for Orbit's new Windows NT network can be done using several different methods. Because the focus of this book is Windows NT security, it won't go into detail regarding the installation procedures involved. We will concentrate on the aspects of installation that are related to the security of the system, its resources, and the account database. Several excellent books that cover Windows NT Server installation are available from Que Publishing that are recommended reading for anyone wanting greater insight into the Windows NT installation process. An excellent choice is *Windows NT 4.0 Installation and Configuration Handbook* by Jim Boyce, ISBN 0-7897-0818-3.

Orbit's first server was installed as a PDC with a computer name of ORBIT_PDC in the Windows NT domain named ADMIN. The initial Windows NT Server installation formed the core of your account domain and created the security account database that eventually will be replicated to additional controllers as they are added to the Windows NT domain. After your server was installed you began the configuration of two items that help protect your new server against hardware failure. The first is the UPS system, and the second is the system's fault tolerance.

Guarding Against Electrical Problems with a UPS

The safest way to protect your delicate computer equipment is by using a reliable UPS system. Several vendors provide systems that are made specifically for computers acting as network servers. These systems only provide power in the event of complete blackout, but they also provide power to the computer that is free from spikes and dips. Also, most UPS systems that are sold for use with Windows NT enable the UPS system to shut down the server in the event of a complete power failure. A cable connection from the UPS to one of the computer's serial ports relays signaling information that can be used to gracefully shut down the system. This shutdown is performed in the event of an extended power outage that lasts beyond the capability of the UPS batteries. This saves the computer from abruptly being shut off and losing information if the batteries can't make it through the power outage. Configuration of the automatic UPS shutdown parameters often is accomplished using the optional software that can be purchased for use with most popular UPS systems. However, additional software may not be required.

If the UPS device includes a serial port connector, chances are that you can still program the system for graceful shutdown without having to purchase any optional UPS software. Of course the bells and whistles that the custom software provides won't be present, but the UPS still is able to signal the computer when a power outage occurs and to perform a normal shutdown of the Windows NT system. Advantages that accompany the vendor's custom UPS software are sometimes worth the additional expense incurred. The vendor software often enables you to monitor incoming line voltages and UPS operating conditions such as temperature.

Additionally, the vendor's software usually is able to log line activity and UPS load. The vendor software usually comes with any necessary serial cables that are needed to connect the UPS with the computer. However, if your UPS has a serial port, it can perform the basic shutdown process on the computer using the built-in UPS services provided by Windows NT. All you really need to do is supply the proper cable to connect the UPS with the computer's COM port.

The documentation that accompanies the UPS usually indicates whether a standard serial cable can be used to connect the UPS to one of the computer's serial ports. If a standard serial cable cannot be used, the documentation often gives the cable pin-out values, so that you can construct a proper cable.

Configuring the UPS parameters for Windows NT   If you decide to use the built-in UPS services within Windows NT, you'll need to know how to hook up your UPS to the computer's serial port, and you'll need to know how to configure Windows NT to recognize the UPS. The UPS vendor supplies the information needed to build a cable and connect the UPS to a computer. The UPS software is configured after installation using the Control Panel's UPS dialog box. The specific information you need to configure the Windows NT UPS service with the UPS device is obtained from the UPS installation reference. This information usually tells you which wires in the cable are used when the UPS signals the computer, and if the voltage on the wires is positive or negative. With this information, the

UPS service can be fully configured to issue shutdown-warning messages, and then complete the system shutdown process. To configure UPS parameters, follow the procedure listed here:

1. Refer to the UPS vendor's installation instructions to determine if the UPS unit must be pre-charged before its first use. If so, charge the unit according to the manufacturer's recommendations.

2. Refer to the UPS vendor's installation instructions to determine the proper serial cable configuration for the unit. Obtain the cable and connect the UPS to one of the Windows NT Server's available COM ports.

3. Log on to the Windows NT Server using an administrative account and open the Control Panel. Double-click the UPS icon to open the UPS dialog box shown in Figure 11.1.

FIG. 11.1

Use the Control Panel's UPS dialog box to configure the UPS parameters.

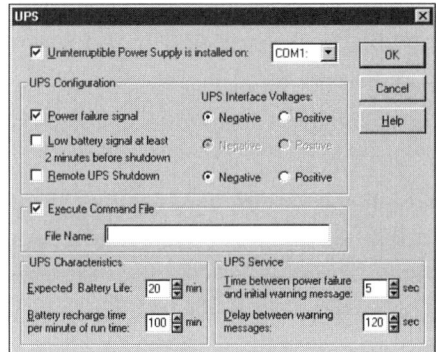

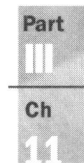

Part
III

Ch
11

4. Mark the box next to Uninterruptible Power Supply is installed on: and specify the COM port you hooked the cable up to in Step 2.

5. If your UPS is capable of sending a signal when the power fails, mark the box next to Power failure signal. The UPS serial port connection recognizes the CTS (clear-to-send) cable signal as the power failure signal and responds accordingly.

6. If your UPS is capable of sending a signal when the battery power is low, mark the box next to Low battery signal at least 2 minutes before shutdown. The UPS serial port connection recognizes the DCD (data-carrier-detect) cable signal as the battery low indication and responds accordingly.

7. Mark the box next to Remote UPS Shutdown if you want to conserve the battery power that remains in the UPS after the Windows NT Server has shut down. When this box is marked, the UPS disconnects power to the Windows NT Server after the shutdown process has taken place. The UPS serial port connection recognizes the DTR (data-terminal-ready) cable signal as the indication to turn off power to the computer.

8. Mark the appropriate option buttons to indicate the voltage polarity for each of the items you have marked during steps 5–7. The voltage type that is used for your specific UPS should be covered in the unit's documentation.

9. Mark the box next to "Execute Command File" if you want the UPS service to execute a file immediately before the shutdown takes place. The file can have any one of the following extensions: ".exe," ".com," ".bat," or ".cmd." The file must exist within the *%systemroot%*system32 folder or it doesn't execute. This file can be used to drop network connections, stop services, or perform any action that might be needed to ensure a smooth system shutdown. Note that this command must complete execution within 30 seconds or system shutdown will occur before the process has completed.

10. If the UPS can send a low-battery signal to the computer, skip ahead to Step 13.

11. Configure the settings in the UPS Characteristics portion of the UPS dialog box to indicate the how long the UPS device will be able to provide power to the system in the event of a total power loss. Specify the number of minutes the UPS documentation says the batteries will last for the specific load being placed on it by the server. Use the up and down arrow buttons to indicate the number of minutes next to the "Expected Battery Life:" entry.

12. The next configuration setting indicates how long the UPS device needs to charge by specifying a value next to the "Battery recharge time per minute of run time:" entry. Use the up and down arrows to select the proper number of minutes needed to recharge the unit. This information can be found in the UPS device documentation.

13. Specify the "Time between power failure and initial warning message:" and the "Delay between warning messages:" in the UPS Service portion of the dialog box.

14. Click the OK button when finished entering the UPS parameter to close the UPS dialog box.

15. Double-click the Services icon in the Control Panel to open the Services dialog box.

16. Scroll down the list of services to find and highlight the UPS entry. The startup method should be set to manual if this is a new installation. Click the Startup button to open the Service dialog box for the UPS service.

17. Change the startup type from Manual to Automatic and click the OK button to return to the Services dialog box.

18. To start the UPS service immediately, click the Start button. If you do not start the service at this time, it is started automatically the next time the system is restarted. Click the Close button to close the Services dialog box.

After UPS protection has been implemented, the Messenger and Alerter services can be used to notify Windows NT users of UPS-initiated shutdowns. The Event Log also records any power failures, power fluctuations, UPS service failures, and UPS service shutdowns.

Now that your system is protected against problems associated with electrical power, you need to add some redundancy to the Windows NT system in the form of fault tolerance for the mass storage devices located in the server.

Adding Fault Tolerance to the Server

During the planning of Orbit's network, it was determined that the servers would benefit from a fault tolerant configuration of the server's hard drives. Mirroring of the drives was selected as an alternative to a RAID 5 configuration, because the cost of hardware base array solutions was beyond Orbit's current budget. And the software-based RAID 5 striping (that Windows NT offers) is not capable of providing recovery of the boot partition.

However, the mirroring that the Windows NT Server operating system provides lets you mirror the boot partition and recover the system using a simple fault tolerant boot disk. This boot disk instructs the system to boot from the remaining good partition, permitting the system to operate at full speed until the system can be taken offline and the failed drive can be replaced. This method of protection does not offer the advantage of zero down time the way a hardware-based solution incorporating *hot-pluggable drives* (drives that can be replaced with the computer running) would. But it does have the advantage of providing good protection at a relatively low cost.

The major disadvantage to this scenario is the fact that the server eventually will need to be taken offline to repair, and then the task of synchronizing the remaining drive with the new drive will impact system performance until the rebuild is complete. The degree to which the system performance is impacted varies depending on the server load and the hardware involved.

Part

III

Ch

11

N O T E An advantage to some of the hardware-based fault tolerant drive devices is the capability to set the rebuild priority of the failed drive and to provide for an on-line *hot spare* to be available. A hot spare is a drive that remains powered and ready to take over for a failing drive should the situation arise.

The rebuild priority is used to specify how much disk time should be given to the system for the task of rebuilding the failed drive. While the array or mirrored set is in a failed condition, the fault tolerance on the drive may not exist. By setting a low priority, more disk time is given for file input-output tasks related to normal user activity. However, the drive array will remain in a non-fault tolerant state longer. Setting a high priority gives the task of rebuilding the failed drive more disk

continues

continued

time. This results in the failed drive being rebuilt faster and becoming fault tolerant sooner, but it decreases system performance for users accessing files on the array or mirror set.

The added advantage of an on-line hot spare is that it eliminates the need to physically replace the failed hard drive before the array or mirrored set is rebuilt. Once the system hardware detects a failed drive, it will activate the on-line spare and initiate the rebuild using the hot spare. This reduces the amount of time the system is vulnerable while in a non-fault tolerant state. ▪

To implement mirroring on Orbit's controllers, we installed two physical drives in each server. After Windows NT Server was installed, the remaining drive on the system is configured as a mirror of the first drive using the Disk Administrator utility. Then a fault tolerant boot disk is created. This disk is used to boot the system in the event the original drive containing the boot partition fails. You begin by going over the creation of the mirrored set, then you see how to create the fault tolerant boot disk.

Creating the Mirrored Drive Set   The first step in providing fault tolerance is the establishment of the mirrored drive set using the Disk Administrator utility. In the example shown here, two 500MB IDE hard drives have been installed in the computer. The Windows NT Server operating system has been loaded on the system's first hard drive. The second hard drive has not yet been partitioned and is reported as free space by the Disk Administrator.

Follow these steps to create a mirrored drive of the system's boot partition:

1. Log on as an administrator and run the Disk Administrator utility from the Programs/Administrative Tools menu.

2. The Disk Administrator displays the current disk information as shown in Figure 11.2.

FIG. 11.2
The unused area on the new drive is reported by the Disk Administrator as Free Space.

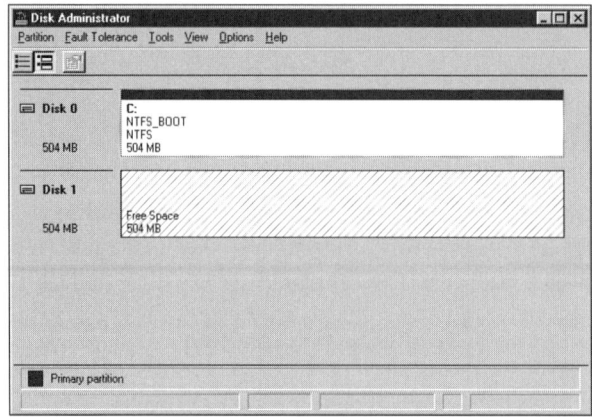

3. Click the original C: drive disk partition (located on Disk 0) with the mouse pointer. This bolds the outline of the original C: drive partition in the display window.

4. Hold down the <Ctrl> key and click the unpartitioned drive space on Disk 1. This bolds the outline of the free space located on the new hard drive (Disk 1) as shown in Figure 11.3. Both the original C: drive partition and the free space have bold outlines now.

FIG. 11.3

Select the free space to be mirrored.

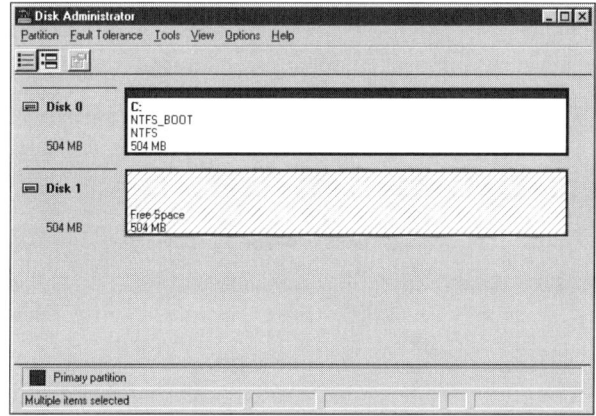

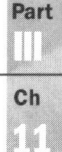

5. Select Establish Mirror from the Fault Tolerance drop-down menu. A Disk Administrator dialog box appears with information pertaining to fault tolerance on boot partitions. Click the OK button.

6. The Disk Administrator now indicates that Disk 0 and Disk 1 are a mirrored set as shown in Figure 11.4.

FIG. 11.4

The display now indicates that a mirrored set exists.

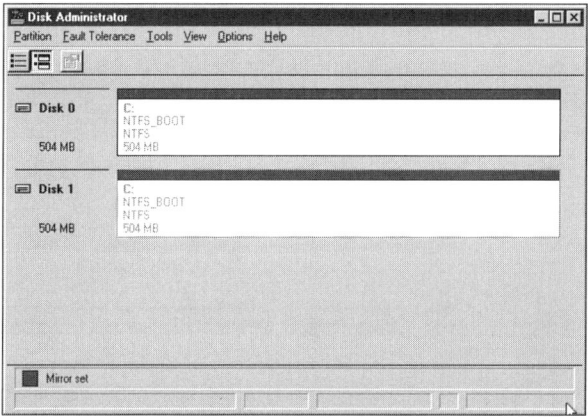

7. From the Partition menu select Commit Change Now and click the Yes button in the confirmation dialog box.

8. Click the Yes button at the next confirmation dialog box to restart the computer. An information dialog box appears recommending you to update your emergency repair disk with the new drive configuration information. Click the OK button to bring up the next informational dialog box that enables you to initiate a system restart. Click the OK button to begin the reboot process.

The system reboots at this time and begins the job of mirroring the new drive. The system will not be fault tolerant until the mirroring process has been completed by the system. If you open the Disk Administrator utility when the new drive is being mirrored, you'll see the new drive information indicated in the color red instead of black (see Figure 11.5). This indicates that the system is still in the process of mirroring the drives. The initialization of the mirrored set also is recorded in the Event Viewer's System Log with an entry when the process begins and another entry when the process ends.

FIG. 11.5
The Disk Administrator indicates the condition of the mirrored set.

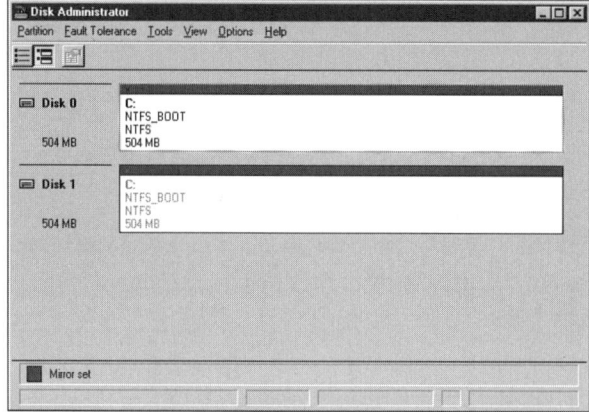

After the drives have been mirrored, the Disk Administrator utility will indicate the condition of the mirrored set as shown in Figure 11.6. When the mirrored set is fully synchronized the system will indicate the state of the set as "HEALTHY."

FIG. 11.6
The Disk Administrator indicates the synchronization is complete by replacing red text information with black text.

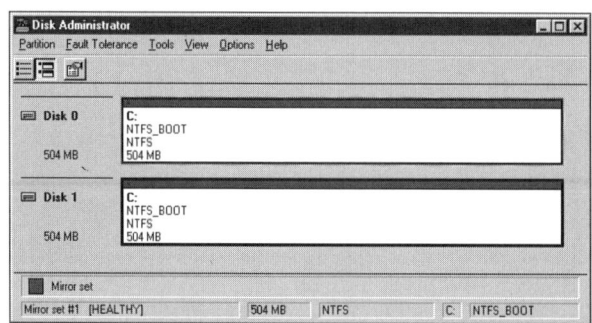

Now that the mirrored set is functioning, you need to do two things: The first thing is to update your system repair disk with the new drive configuration information. The second thing is to create a fault tolerant boot disk to use when the primary boot drive fails.

Updating the Repair Disk   You have changed the system's drive configuration and you now must update the information contained on the emergency repair disk. If you don't update this information, the repair disk may be useless when you need it.

The process to update the emergency repair disk is simple but can be a bit misleading. Because we have just changed the disk configuration on the server, we'll run through the steps required to create a valid emergency repair disk for the new disk configuration. To create a valid emergency repair disk, follow these steps:

1. Log on as an administrator and select Run from the Start menu.

2. Type "rdisk" in the Open text box and click the OK button. This displays the Repair Disk Utility dialog box shown in Figure 11.7.

FIG. 11.7
Use the Repair Disk Utility to update the drive configuration data on the emergency repair disk.

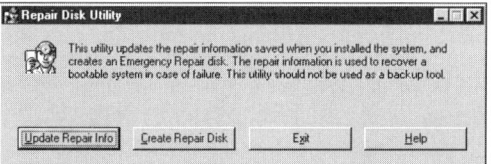

3. Click the Update Repair Info button. A dialog box appears informing you that the previous repair information will be deleted. Click the Yes button to continue the operation. The system then saves the configuration information to the systemroot\repair directory.

4. You are prompted to create a new emergency repair disk. Click the Yes button and you will be prompted to insert a diskette to use as the emergency repair disk.

5. Insert a floppy disk into the system's diskette drive and click the OK button. The disk will be formatted and the system's configuration information will be copied to it.

6. Click Exit to close the Repair Disk Utility.

If the administrator first does not update the repair information located in the system's systemroot\repair directory, the information placed on the emergency repair disk will not be valid for the new drive configuration. A repair disk created without first updating the repair information would contain data that pertained to the previous configuration and not the current configuration. Most likely, the repair disk would be useless if it was ever needed to restore a drive configuration.

Creating the Fault Tolerant Boot Disk   When you mirror the boot partition of your drive, the system still continues to boot from the original drive. This is referred to as the *primary* drive in the mirrored set because it is the drive the system still boots from. In the event the *secondary* drive failed, the system would boot as normal off the primary drive. The operating system would report the failure of the second drive while continuing to run its normal tasks. At an opportune time, the system administrator could take the system down and replace the failed drive. When the system came back up, the new drive could again be mirrored with the primary drive to re-establish fault tolerance.

The recovery procedure is different if the primary hard drive fails. When this happens, the system can no longer boot up from the first disk drive's *Master Boot Record (MBR)*. To overcome this obstacle we'll create a fault tolerant boot disk. This disk contains the boot files (NTDETECT.COM and NTLDR) required to get the system started. Once booted, the diskette's BOOT.INI file points to the secondary hard disk location where the rest of the system files can be found. This way the system can get itself going even though the primary drive and its MBR are missing.

First, you must create the boot disk by doing the following:

1. Format a floppy disk on the Windows NT Server from the command line or from the drive icon in My Computer or Explorer. The disk must be formatted on a Windows NT machine.

2. Copy the following files from the root directory on the Windows NT Server's boot drive to the floppy disk's root directory: ntldr, ntdetect.com, and boot.ini.

3. Additionally, if your system is running SCSI drives and you are not using the SCSI adapter BIOS, you'll have to copy the SCSI device drivers to the boot diskette. Each SCSI adapter has its own driver file (*.sys) that must be copied to the file named NTBOOTDD.SYS on the root directory of the diskette.

Now the boot.ini must be modified so that the system files can be found on the secondary drive. The original BOOT.INI file for a typical IDE drive is as follows:

```
[boot loader]

timeout=30

default=multi(0)disk(0)rdisk(0)partition(1)\WINNT
[operating systems]

multi(0)disk(0)rdisk(0)partition(1)\WINNT="Windows NT Server Version 4.00"

multi(0)disk(0)rdisk(0)partition(1)\WINNT="Windows NT Server Version 4.00
[VGA mode]" /basevideo /sos
```

In order to get the computer to load the operating system files from the secondary drive, you need to modify the Advanced RISC Computing (ARC) Path name in the BOOT.INI file. The ARC path name is used to define the location of the Windows NT system files on x86-processor-based computers and RISC-based computers. The modification to the ARC path name will differ depending on the types of drives you have installed in your system. That means if you have SCSI drives that do not use BIOS, the configuration of this path name will be different than if you're using IDE drives.

Let's take a look at the syntax of the different ARC path statements on an x86-based server:

```
multi (X) disk (Y) rdisk (Z) partition (W) \ <winnt_dir>
```

or

```
scsi (X) disk (Y) rdisk (Z) partition (W) \ <winnt_dir>
```

If the ARC path name used in the server's BOOT.INI file starts with the "multi (X)" syntax, it indicates that Windows NT should rely on the computer's BIOS to load the system files. In contrast, the "scsi (X)" syntax indicates that a device driver will be used to access the system partition and load system files. This device driver is the NTBOOTDD.SYS driver mentioned in Step 3 of the previous example. Actually, this device driver is a vendor-supplied Windows NT driver that has been renamed to NTBOOTDD.SYS and placed on the boot partition. For this example we're using the IDE drive, which always uses the computer's BIOS, and thus our BOOT.INI file from the Windows NT Server reflects "multi (X)" syntax.

With the "multi (X)" syntax, you only have to change the "rdisk" parameter in the ARC Path name to instruct your boot disk to load the system files from the secondary drive. The modified version of the BOOT.INI file for your example is given in the following:

```
[boot loader]

timeout=30

default=multi(0)disk(0)rdisk(1)partition(1)\WINNT
[operating systems]

multi(0)disk(0)rdisk(1)partition(1)\WINNT="Windows NT Server Version 4.00"

multi(0)disk(0)rdisk(1)partition(1)\WINNT="Windows NT Server Version 4.00

[VGA mode]" /basevideo /sos
```

The syntax needed to redirect the load of the system's files on your specific machine will be unique to your system configuration and hardware setup. More information on fault tolerance recovery techniques can be found in the following Que publications:

- *Special Edition Using Windows NT Server 4*, by Roger Jennings, ISBN 0-7897-0251-7
- *Windows NT Server 4 Advanced Technical Reference*, by John Enck, ISBN 0-7897-1167-2

Part
III

Ch
11

Configuring a Backup Domain Controller

As mentioned earlier, a Backup Domain Controller (BDC) is used as a means of fault tolerance for the security accounts database. Instead of having the database located on a single server, it can be replicated to one or more other servers. This keeps a live on-line copy of the database available at all times.

When a Windows NT Server is installed as a BDC within a Windows NT domain, it receives a copy of the security accounts database. You'll see Windows NT give you a notification that it is replicating the accounts database during the last part of the server installation process. It gives you the opportunity at that time to cancel the replication.

As with the database located on the PDC, the database located on the BDC can be used to authenticate users. Unlike the database located on the PDC, the database located on the BDC cannot be modified; only the database on the PCD can be modified. If the PDC happens to be offline for one reason or another, you will be unable to add, delete, or modify information contained within the account database. In order to modify the database, you'll have to bring the PDC back online or you'll have to promote a BDC to the status of PDC.

When the database located on the PDC is modified, directory synchronization updates the database copies on all BDCs located in the Windows NT domain. This is done automatically by the system whenever a change to the database occurs. However, if you have problems with account authentication (or resource access), you can initiate manual directory synchronization from within the Server Manager administrative utility.

Monitoring Directory Synchronization   The easiest way to monitor directory synchronization is by using the Domain Monitor utility included with the Windows NT Server Resource kit. The utility enables you to monitor the current domain and any trusted domains that might be present. If you suspect problems with a BDC, you can check its replication status using this utility.

N O T E   Unfortunately, the Windows NT Server Resource Kit for version 4.0 is not available via the Internet due to it size. However, you can obtain the Microsoft Windows NT Server Resource Kit CD-ROM by calling Microsoft and requesting the kit. You only are charged for shipping. They usually will ask you if you want the BackOffice Resource Kit CD-ROM put in the same shipment. If they don't, just request it, and if it's in stock they'll include it at no additional cost. ▪

After the first BDC on Orbit's new domain has been installed, install the resource kit's Domain Monitor to verify that the BDCs are all synchronized with the PDC. The Domain Monitor gives us a clear indication if all the servers within a domain are synchronized with each other or not. Figure 11.8 shows the Domain Monitor being used to watch the synchronization status of three separate domains. The domain synchronization status is indicated by the color of the icon that represents each domain. Green indicates that all the BDCs are synchronized with the PDC. A yellow icon indicates that some of the controllers in the domain are not synchronized with the PDC or they are offline. A red icon indicates that the PDC can't be found or is out of synchronization with the rest of the domain.

FIG. 11.8
The Domain Monitor gives you a clear indication of the domain's synchronization status.

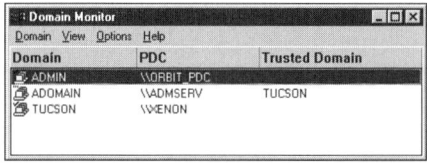

You can see that the green icons indicate the ADMIN and TUCSON domain controllers are synchronized completely with each other. However, the icon for the ADOMAIN is yellow, indicating that some of the controllers within that domain are not synchronized with the PDC. Double-clicking the ADOMAIN icon gives you the "Domain Controller Status on Domain ADOMAIN" dialog box shown in Figure 11.9.

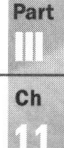

Part

III

Ch

11

FIG. 11.9
The Domain Monitor can give you detailed information regarding controller status.

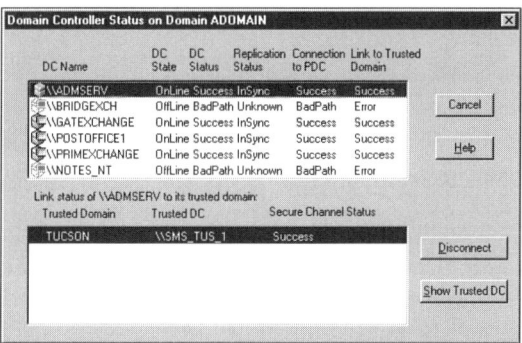

The monitor even can allow you to view the status of the secure channel link between controllers in the trusting domain and the controllers in the trusted domain.

User and Group Accounts

Creating group accounts on the accounts domain is an easy way to keep the administrative workload to a minimum when assigning access permissions to resources. Instead of trying to micro-manage individual user permissions, you can create a set of standard groups in your organization. Each of these groups will allow its members to have access to the specific set of domain resources to which the group account has been given access privileges.

A variety of built-in accounts are provided with Windows NT Server. These groups can be used, or you can create your own custom groups. Custom group accounts are created using the User Manager for Domains utility and are specified as being either a local or global group account. The global group can be given access permissions to trusting domain resources, while a local group is restricted to accessing resources from the local domain. The standard rule for configuring users and groups in Windows NT is "users into global groups, global groups into local groups." In smaller network domains, the additional step of adding users into global groups (instead of directly into local groups) may create more problems than it's worth. Although in larger network environments with multiple domains that include trust relationships, the use of the standard rule can save administrative overhead. And it works best if you can group the individual users into specific groups that are each allowed a specific set of access permissions. If everybody has different access requirements, the job of assigning access can be very cumbersome, to say the least.

From Here...

This chapter shows you a few of the items you can control that will provide greater security to your Windows NT Server installation. In the following chapters, here are some highlights you can look forward to:

- Chapter 12, "Setting Up Trust Relationships," looks at Orbit's domain environment and how it uses a separate resource domain that is controlled independently from within Orbit's design department.
- Chapter 13, "Overview of Security and the Internet," gives you information about how BackOffice products fit in with the Windows NT security model.
- Chapter 14, "Internet Security and BackOffice," examines the issues surrounding access to the Internet.

CHAPTER 12

Setting Up Trust Relationships

In Chapter 10, "Planning the Master Domain," you implemented a master domain model on Orbit's Windows NT network. This was done to enable resource domains to be created and controlled by individual departments at Orbit. This relieves some of the administrative burden from the Internal Support staff and gives the members of the Design department control over their own resources. Because trust relationships are non-transitory, you effectively can build a "security wall" that permits users' administrative roles in the DESIGN domain, while at the same time restricting any administrative authority for the same individuals in the accounts (ADMIN) domain, or for that matter, any other resource domains that may be created. ∎

Trusted domain setup

You begin the setup of Orbit's master domain with the configuration of the trusted domain. This is a simple process that enables you to establish quickly a trust relationship between the ADMIN and DESIGN domains.

Trusting domain setup

Configure the initial resource domain as the trusting member of the master domain. Because the trusted side of the relationship already was set up, the trust is completed by having the administrator of the resource (DESIGN) domain perform a few simple steps.

Verifying the trust

Several methods can be used to verify the operation's success. Explore a few of the methods available, including a utility available in the Windows NT 4.0 Server Resource Kit.

Using the trust relationship

Setting up the various group accounts that will be used in Orbit's master domain model is the next step to assigning network resources. First, create global groups in the ADMIN domain and add users to them. Then give the global groups from the ADMIN domain access to resources located within the DESIGN domain.

Configuring the Trusted Domain

The user and group accounts for Orbit's network users are first created on the ADMIN domain. A trust relationship is then established between the two domains. The trust relationship allows the assignment of further administrative duties to members of the Design department. Once assigned as an Administrator on the Design domain, the designated administrator can create shares and assign permissions to any of the users or groups located on the ADMIN or ACCOUNT domain.

To simplify the task of assigning permissions, the administrator or the ADMIN domain can create custom global user groups that contain only members of the Design department. The custom group can be given access to the DESIGN domain's resources by its appointed administrator, instead of that administrator assigning privileges to individual users. Although the assignment of access privileges to individual users can be done, it can increase the labor needed to maintain the DESIGN domain's access permissions. Therefore, we've decided to create a global group containing all the members of the Design department and to assign specific access privileges to this group for any resources located in the DESIGN domain.

Begin the process by establishing the trust relationship between the ADMIN and DE-SIGN domains. This is a simple procedure that can be completed in about a minute—and that's for both sides of the trust! The best way to configure the trust is first to configure the domain that will be the *trusted* domain. For Orbit's network, this means you configure the ADMIN domain's side of the trust relationship first. The reason for this is that the trust relationship can be verified and the resource (DESIGN) domain's Windows NT account can be created immediately after the resource (DESIGN) domain is configured. If the resource (DESIGN) domain is configured first, the trust cannot be verified immediately and may take up to 15 minutes before being completed. Follow these steps to configure the trusted domain:

1. Log on to the ADMIN (accounts) domain using and administrative account, and run the User Manager for Domain program.

2. Select Trust Relationships from the Policy Menu to open the Trust Relationships dialog box (see Figure 12.1).

FIG. 12.1
Configure the trust relationship with the User Manager for Domains utility.

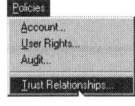

3. Click the Add button next to the Trusting Domains window to open the domain dialog box, as shown in Figure 12.2.

4. Enter the name of the trusting domain (DESIGN) in the Name field.

5. Enter a password that will be used by the administrator of the DESIGN domain to establish the trusting side of the relationship and confirm it.

FIG. 12.2

Specifying the trusting domain's name and selecting a password are the only requirements on the trusted domain side of the setup.

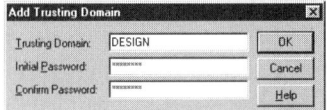

6. Click the OK button to close the dialog boxes and return to the User Manager for Domain main screen. Exit the program.

Now that the trusted domain has been set up, one of the ADMIN administrative staff can log on to the resource domain under the Administrator account and set up the other side of the trust relationship.

Configuring the Trusting Domain

Configuring the trusting side of the trust relationship is almost identical to setting up the trusted side. You simply provide the name of the trusted domain and the password that was designated during the configuration of the trusted domain's portion of the setup.

To set up the trusting side of the relationship, follow these steps:

1. Log on to the trusted domain using the Administrator account. You do this because it is the only account that should be on the resource domain at this time.

2. Run the User Manager for Domains program and select Trust Relationships from the Policy menu to open the Trust Relationships dialog box.

3. Click the Add button next to the Trusted Domains window to open the Domains dialog box.

4. Enter the name of the accounts domain (ADMIN) in the Name field. See Figure 12.3.

FIG. 12.3

Enter the name of the trusted domain and the password that was specified during the setup on the trusted domain.

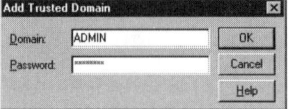

5. Enter the password that was designated during the setup of the Trusted domain in the password field. Then, click the OK button. You may receive a message indicating that the trust relationship could not be verified at this time and to watch the Event Viewer's System Log to monitor for the completion of the setup. Click the OK button to continue.

6. Click OK to close the Trust Relationship dialog box and return to the User Manager for Domains main screen. Exit the program.

Now that the trust has been configured on both sides, you need to determine if the trust actually has been established. This can be accomplished in several different ways. The simplest way is to check the Event Viewer's System Log for verification of the trust. Another way is to create a share on the resource domain and attempt to give access privileges to the Design department's global group that was created on the ADMIN domain. A third way is to use the Domain Monitor utility that's available in the Windows NT 4.0 resource kit. This utility monitors the synchronization of any domain, and it also can monitor the status of the secure channel link that exists between trusted and trusting domains. If the link has been established, the trust relationship is in place.

Confirming that the Trust Is Active

As stated, the trust relationship can be verified using different methods. The administrator easily can check the Event Viewer, or simply attempt to assign access privileges to one or more global groups from the ADMIN domain.

Another indication that the trust is in place shows up in the Logon screen on any Windows NT Server or Workstation that is a member of the DESIGN domain. In addition to being able to log on to the local DESIGN domain, the dialog box permits the user to select the name of the trusted domain ADMIN. Selecting the ADMIN name authenticates the user based on the security accounts database in the ADMIN domain and not the DESIGN domain. However, the same is not true for a user logging on to Windows NT Servers or Workstations that are members of the ADMIN domain. Because the ADMIN domain is the trusted domain, it only has a trusting domain. Users can't log on to a trusting domain from a trusted domain unless the trust is a two-way trust. In that case, the trusted domain also would be a trusting domain and would present the option of logging on to the other domain.

A clear indication that the trust has been established appears when the trusted domain's global groups and users can be assigned privileges to resources located on the DESIGN (trusting) domain. The option is given to specify the trusted domain's global group (and user accounts), in addition to any local group or user accounts that exist on the local (trusting) domain. In this situation you have no accounts on the resource (DESIGN) domain except for the built-in administrator's account. That's all you need in the domain, because it will provide the means to grant administrative authority to accounts on the ADMIN domain.

To permit selected members of the Design department to act as administrators of the DESIGN resource domain, you must create an additional global group in the ADMIN domain. This group will contain those users that have been designated as the administrators for the DESIGN resource domain. This global group will be added to the local Administrator's group located on the DESIGN domain. This permits those individuals the capability to assume the administrative responsibilities on the DESIGN domain, while at the same time preserving the central administrative staff's capability to oversee the entire domain structure if needed.

Granting Account Access in a Trusting Domain

Begin the setup of the administrative group for the DESIGN domain by creating a custom global group on the ADMIN domain. After that, you assign specific user accounts to the new global group. Let's begin by creating a new global group called Design Admins and assign user accounts to it.

1. Log on to the ACCOUNTS domain with Administrator privileges and start the User Manager for Domains utility.
2. Select New Global Group from the File drop-down menu to open the new Global Group dialog box.
3. In the Name field, type in the name Design Admins and click the Add member button (see Figure 12.4).
4. Select users from the Not Members of list in the right window and move them to the Members Of window by clicking the Add button.

FIG. 12.4

Adding the names of users to the global group is the first step.

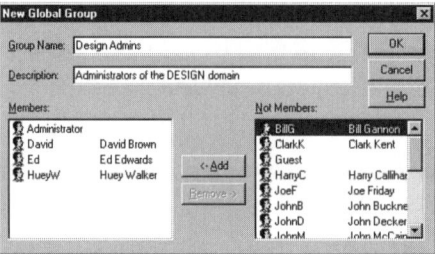

5. Click OK to exit the dialog boxes after moving the users' account names and return to the User Manager for Domains main screen. You should see the new global group (indicated with a globe icon) named "Design Admins" in the Groups (lower) portion of the main screen.

After the global group has been created and users added, it can be added to the local Administrators group on the DESIGN domain. This gives the members of the Design Admins group the ability to perform any further administrative tasks themselves. To add the Design Admins global group to the built-in Administrators group on the DESIGN domain, follow the procedure outlined in the following steps:

1. Log on to the DESIGN domain using the built-in Administrator account and run the User Manager for Domains utility.

2. Double-click the Local Administrator group entry located in the Groups section of the User Manager for Domain's main screen. This opens the global Group Properties dialog box.

3. Click the Add button to open the Members dialog box.

4. In the Domains drop-down list, select the ADMIN domain. The user accounts and global groups from the ADMIN domain now appear in the dialog box instead of users and groups from the local DESIGN domain (see Figure 12.5).

FIG. 12.5

Adding the Design Admins global group to the local administrators group is the next step.

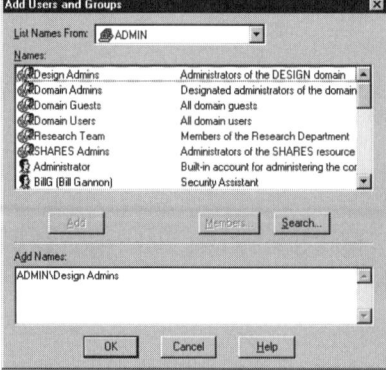

5. Select the global group Design Admins and click the Add button, then click the OK button to return to the User Manager for Domains main screen. Exit the program and log off the server.

Now any user that was added to the Design Admins global group on the ADMIN domain can log on to any Windows NT Server or Workstation in the DESIGN domain and create shares and grant access privileges to them. They actually can grant (or deny) resource access to any user or global group that exists on the ADMIN domain. They can grant access to any of the ADMIN domain's built-in accounts or to custom accounts as in the case of the global group that contains all the employees in the Design department.

For example, the new administrators of the DESIGN resource domain have created a printer queue that they want to allow the employees in their department access to. They don't want to give the whole company the ability to print to the queue, because they don't want to have the printer tied up by people who aren't in the department. They do want the company VIP's to be able to print to the queue because their offices happen to be close to the printer. This was no problem because the VIP's had been assigned to their own global group by the ADMIN administrator earlier.

To create the printer queue and assign access privileges, the DESIGN domain administrator follows these steps:

1. Log on using an ADMIN domain account that belongs to the Design Admins global group.

2. Click the Start button and select Printers from the Settings menu. This opens the Printers dialog box. Follow the steps the Wizard leads you through to install a new local printer. After the printer is installed, a new icon for it appears in the Printer dialog box representing the new printer.

3. Right-click the new printer icon and select Properties from the drop-down list.

4. Click the Sharing tab and then click the permissions button.

5. Select the Add button to open the Permission dialog box.

6. Select the ADMIN domain from the domain drop-down list. Select the groups named Design Users and OrbitVP, then click Add.

7. Click OK twice to close the properties page, and then exit the Control Panel.

Part
III

Ch
12

This same principle is used to assign access permissions to other printer queues, disk resources, and other services. For the duration, the only accounts on the system are contained within the ADMIN domain. This makes it easy to add users to the system and to assign them access privileges effortlessly. Also, it allows the total removal of a user account from the system just as easily.

From Here...

This chapter shows you how the trust relationship is established on a fictitious domain and how the trust is used to limit the amount of administrative burden. In the upcoming chapter you look at security beyond the realm of simple-share permissions.

- Chapter 13, "Overview of Security and the Internet," extends your view of security to other Microsoft products. These products are designed to integrate tightly with the security provided in Windows NT.

- Chapter 14, "Internet Security and BackOffice," begins the discussion on the measures that need to be taken when connecting to the vast expanse of the Internet. The trick is to maximize accessibility while at the same time taking care not to expose your network to the outside world.

Windows NT Security with BackOffice Products, the Internet, and Other Network Platforms

CHAPTER 13

Overview of Security and the Internet

The growth of the Internet has been explosive over the last few years. International Data Corporation (IDC) estimates that by the year 2000, there will be approximately 200 million Internet users, up from 35 million in 1995. It seems that everyone is rushing to get connected, and Windows NT's native support of all of the most popular Internet protocols makes it easy—you just load the TCP/IP protocol, install a router, get an Internet Service Provider, and before you know it, "Surf's Up!" However, connecting your systems to the Internet opens up a whole new can of worms that can lead to serious and possibly crippling security breaches. It's hard to imagine anything worse than being in the data center at 3:30 A.M. on a Saturday morning desperately seeking a clean backup to restore your network after a hacker has had his or her way with it. This chapter is your weapon against that nightmarish scenario. ■

Understanding NT's Internet support

Windows NT is Internet ready right out of-the-box. Learn the best way to implement and to secure Windows NT using its native Internet tools.

Protect yourself against Internet security risks

From a system administrator's perspective, the Internet is fraught with peril. Become aware of the many risks your TCP/IP networks face when connected to the Internet.

Learn and implement key security measures such as proxy servers and firewalls

As Internet usage increases, so do security breaches. Learn how proxy servers and firewalls create a nearly impenetrable barrier to hackers.

Plug holes in Windows NT security

No computer or operating system is airtight, and Windows NT is no exception. Build on the knowledge you acquired in earlier chapters to keep Windows NT secure when connected to the Internet.

Learn where to turn for additional security resources

The world of Internet security is ever changing—new holes are discovered and old holes are plugged. This chapter introduces you to several invaluable resources.

Internet Security Overview

Every single minute of every day, all over the globe, new computer networks and *hosts*, which are defined by the *Free Online Dictionary of Computing* as, "A computer connected to a network," join the online world. Hosts are being added to the Internet at an amazing rate (averaging about 94 percent for the last three years). According to Network Wizards' (www.nw.com) January 1997 Domain Survey, which tries to discover every Internet host by doing a complete search of the Domain Name System (DNS), 16,146,000 hosts were found, up from 9,472,000 in January of 1996.

 The *Free Online Dictionary of Computing (FOLDOC)* is one of the most useful technical resources on the Internet. I strongly encourage you to give it a try at **http://wagner.princeton.edu/foldoc/** .

After you are connected to the Internet, each of these 16 million hosts immediately becomes a potential target for intruders. As you probably know, the only completely secure system is one that has no network card, no hard disk, is not plugged in, and is physically secured in a vault somewhere. Obviously a system of this nature is not practical for any use. The alternative to this is a completely insecure system that is connected to the Internet and allows anonymous access to all its resources. While the latter system might be great in terms of usability, it's also not very practical, as anyone can steal its information and cause it to crash easily.

 One of the most contentious issues surrounding the Internet is the number of users. Because of its global reach and explosive growth, it's difficult to obtain accurate statistics. One good source for the latest statistics and demographics is CyberAtlas at **http://www.cyberatlas.com**.

With Windows NT's native support of TCP/IP and many built-in TCP/IP utilities and services such as FTP, Telnet, and HTTP, it's easy and cost effective to connect your Windows NT systems to the Internet. But before you install the TCP/IP protocol, buy a router and connect your network to the Internet—you need to have a thorough understanding of what you're up against in terms of keeping your corporate data secure.

If you are considering connecting your system to the Internet and you're worried about security, you should be! Before you even think about making the physical connection to the Internet, you should carefully research and plan your security policies and procedures to ensure that the security of your system cannot be easily compromised. RFC 1244, *The Site Security Handbook*, is an excellent guide and easily can be found on the Internet at **http://www.internic.net/rfc/rfc1244.txt**.

According to RFC 1244, "Setting security policies and procedures really means developing a plan for how to deal with computer security." An excellent approach for developing your plan is the "Basic Approach" suggested by Fites, Kratz, and Brebner in their 1989 Computer Science Press book *Control and Security of Computer Information Systems*. They propose that you should do the following:

- Identify what you are trying to protect.
- Know what you need to protect it from.
- Determine how likely the threats are.
- Implement measures that will protect your assets in a cost-effective manner.
- Review the process continuously, and improve things every time a weakness is found.

What Are You Trying to Protect?

Security is a series of trade-offs where you must balance security against usability and cost. Security is inversely proportional to usability and cost. As you make a system more secure, you make it more restrictive and more difficult to use. Hence, the cost of administrating and maintaining the system can go up significantly. Achieving the proper amount of security for your system is a delicate balancing act between protection and cost.

To balance effectively protection versus cost and usability, you need to determine just what exactly it is that you are trying to protect. For instance, if you are setting up a Web server for the CIA that will be connected to their internal network, security will be paramount because a hacker could gain access to information that could compromise national security. On the other hand, if you're a small local company that sells gum balls, your Web site security might take a back seat in importance to cost and effort.

An old saying for those in the security industry rings truer than ever today, "the cost of protecting yourself against a threat should be less than the cost of recovering if the threat were to strike you." The point here is that without knowing what you are trying to protect, it's darn hard to protect it.

Internet Security Threats

Although the Internet is an incredibly useful tool that can revolutionize the way you do business, it is fraught with security risks and the mere act of connecting your network to the Internet puts your network and your corporate data at significant risk of being compromised. At this point, if you have decided what you need to protect, let's examine what you need to protect it from. If you haven't been keeping up with the latest news in Internet

Part
IV

Ch
13

security, you might be quite surprised by both the frequency and success rate of security attacks on Internet systems.

Security Attacks on the Rise   According to the fourth annual Information Week/Ernst & Young Information Security Survey, awareness of the security problem is at an all time high, but the incidents of security breaches continue at an alarming rate. Last August, one of the most publicized and outrageous "hacks" to date was perpetrated on the U.S. Department of Justice. The department discovered that its Web site had been hacked and the original home page had been replaced with a new page containing a variety of electronic graffiti including swastikas, pictures of Hitler, and nudity. By September of 1996, the list of "hacked" Web sites included the British Conservative Party, the Nation of Islam, the American Psychoanalytic Association, the U.S. Air Force, and the CIA, whose site was renamed the Central Stupidity Agency.

If you'd like to see some of the hacked pages mentioned above, point your Web browser to **http:/ /www.2600.com** and follow the links. Complete re-creations of the Defense Department, CIA, and USAF hacks can be found there. It's a real eye-opener...

Testimony given by the General Accounting Office (GAO) to the Senate based on the 1995 Department of Defense study of computer penetrations helps to drive home this point. The department estimated that there were about 160,000 attacks on unclassified military computers in 1995; their own Defense Information Systems Agency study using penetration attacks on 38,000 unclassified systems suggested that about 65 percent of all such attacks on unclassified systems would succeed, but only a tiny percentage would be noticed and even fewer would be reported to higher authorities. Based on these studies, the GAO estimated that there might be as many as 250,000 attacks on U.S. government computer systems each year and other segments of the testimony suggested that about 120 countries are working on information warfare techniques that also could be applied to corporate espionage.

N O T E   The report noted above is available from the Government Accounting Office as document GAO/AIMD-96-84, Information Security: Computer Attacks at Department of Defense Pose Increasing Risks. ▨

Not all security violations are the result of a particularly brilliant intruder; many security incidents are the result of misconfiguration of the systems connected to the Internet. As system usage increases, it becomes more likely that security holes will be found. Additionally, increased usage most often leads to increased load on the system's administrators, which can lead to mistakes that open security holes.

The following is a "scary but true" example that clearly illustrates how critically important proper system configuration is. On May 23, 1996, a user discovered that AltaVista had indexed files in the root directory of an unsecured UNIX Web server. When she opened the site in her browser, she had root access on a system she had never heard of. Fortunately for the site managers, the user informed them and they immediately pulled the system off the Web.

In most cases where misconfiguration leads to insecure systems, it is not due to incompetence on the part of the systems administrators; it's due to the fact that they just don't know any better. For most administrators, there just aren't enough hours in the day to perform their day-to-day tasks, troubleshoot user problems, and stay abreast of all of the latest information regarding the ever changing field of Internet security. And just as importantly, that detailed security information is often hard to come by. The rest of this chapter covers the major security issues you face when connecting Windows NT systems to the Internet.

Hackers and Crackers   Sixteen million machines (and possibly the LAN's and WAN's to which they are connected) interconnected makes the Internet a target-rich environment for the attacks of wily *hackers* and *crackers*.

According to *The Free Online Dictionary of Computing* (see preceding Tip), a hacker is, "A person who enjoys exploring the details of programmable systems and how to stretch their capabilities, as opposed to most users, who prefer to learn only the minimum necessary." While a cracker is defined as, "An individual who attempts to gain unauthorized access to a computer system," these individuals are often malicious and have many means at their disposal for breaking into a system. Throughout the remainder of this chapter, I use the term *hacker* to generically refer to anyone who attempts to breach the security of another system.

When you are planning your Internet security, it's important to understand what you're up against in terms of the aptitude and attitude of hackers. The popular image of a hacker is a pimple-faced teenager with an old XT, a modem, a copy of *Phrack*, and too much time on his hands. However, there is a far more dangerous breed of hacker out there. One with years of programming and systems experience who knows all of the "back doors" and security holes. This hacker, often called an uebercracker (this term is coined from Nietzsche's *uebermensch*, is a man who has gone beyond the incompetence, pettiness, and weakness of the everyday man) can really wreak havoc on your systems and is extremely difficult to keep out.

Part

IV

Ch

13

N O T E   Ken Thompson, the father of UNIX, created one of the most devious and clever back doors yet discovered. In 1983, he revealed that many early versions of UNIX would allow Thompson access to the system even if he did not have an account. He inserted code into the C compiler that would recognize when the `login` command was being recompiled, then insert code that recognized a password chosen by Thompson. If the back door was discovered and removed, the compiler would add it when the login was recompiled, as well as the code to recognize itself and do the whole thing over again! The hack invisibly perpetuated itself, leaving the back door open with no trace in the source code.

The motivations for hacking also run the gamut from simple things such as trying to earn the respect of fellow hackers or the challenge and thrill of breaking into a "secure" system to steal corporate or military secrets for monetary gain. Naturally, the more motivated a hacker is, the better your defenses must be.

As you might expect, the attacks perpetrated by hackers are generally commensurate with their levels of experience and motivation. The pimple-faced teenager might use a mundane technique such as a *war-dialer*, while an experienced and accomplished hacker, such as the infamous Kevin Mitnick, resorts to using a combination of Internet protocols and services such as Finger, Telnet, and FTP to query a remote system, break-in, and steal the host's password file, which then gives the hacker the capability to log in using valid account names and passwords. Unfortunately, the more sophisticated the attack, the harder it is to prevent or detect. Table 13.1 shows some of the best resources.

   Hackers often seek the respect of other hackers and like to share their best "hacks." The good news is that the same resources that hackers use also can be used for reverse purposes and make excellent security resources for the beginner and the expert alike.

Table 13.1   Hacker's Resources Make Excellent Security Resources

Name	URL
Phrack Magazine	http://www.fc.net/phrack
2600	http://www.2600.com
Underground	http://www.underground.org
Hackerz.Org	http://www.hackerz.org/

Types of Attacks   Before you get into the specific steps you can take to protect your systems, you need to understand the types of attacks you are likely to face. There are two basic types of attacks hackers employ: *denial-of-service* and *intrusions* attacks.

Denial-of-service attacks are not designed to gain access to your system; they attempt to deny access to either a particular service, such as HTTP (Web services), or to the entire system.

This is normally accomplished by flooding the system with bogus requests for service, or by exploiting known holes and bugs that make the system hang or crash. A now famous example (it even has it's own Web page at **http://prospect.epresence.com/ping/**) of a denial-of-service attack is the aptly named "Ping 'O Death." By Pinging a remote system with the -l 65510 and -s 1 parameters (ping -l 65510 -s 1 <ip.address>), you can overload most any machine and cause it to crash.

T I P Fortunately, preventing the "Ping 'O Death" on Windows NT systems is relatively simple. A short term fix is to simply block ping at your firewall or through IP filtering (both of these topics are covered later in this chapter). For a permanent and less restrictive fix, Service Pack 2 for Windows NT 4.0 (available at **http://www.microsoft.com/ntserver/**) should fix this problem.

Intrusions are pretty much self-explanatory—the hacker attempts to gain access to your systems. If they are successful, they can do any number of things depending on the security measures you have implemented. Once an intruder gains access, they might do anything, such as upload a virus, steal confidential information, crash your system, or use your system as a springboard into other systems, making it much harder to track down the intruder. I've already mentioned some of the most famous intrusions that have been detected earlier in this chapter. With this basic understanding of the types of attacks you might face, let's examine how you can secure your system.

Securing Your Windows NT Systems for the Internet

The good news is that Windows NT's lack of native support for many of the most insecure Internet services helps to lighten your load. However, many of the same attacks that work on UNIX boxes also work on Windows NT.

Before you begin to examine Internet security concepts and issues, a quick review of Windows NT's native network security features is in order. Windows NT provides security in four basic areas:

- log-on authentication
- object security
- user rights
- auditing

Part
IV

Ch
13

When Windows NT's security features are configured correctly, they provide an extremely secure networking environment for corporate LAN's and WAN's.

Even with Windows NT's excellent network security features, you still run the risk of being hacked. The rest of this chapter examines the user rights and auditing of our basic approach to Internet security.

TCP/IP Architecture   The glue that holds the Internet together is the TCP/IP protocol suite. Before you adequately can defend your network against hacker's attacks, you need to have a basic understanding of the architecture of the TCP/IP protocol and its inherent weaknesses. TCP/IP is actually a protocol suite that consists of a number of protocols, each of which provide very specific functionality.

The TCP/IP protocol is a four-layer model written long before the seven-layer OSI model but is somewhat similar. Figure 13.1 illustrates how the TCP/IP protocol suite stacks up against the OSI networking model.

FIG. 13.1
The TCP/IP model compared to the OSI Model.

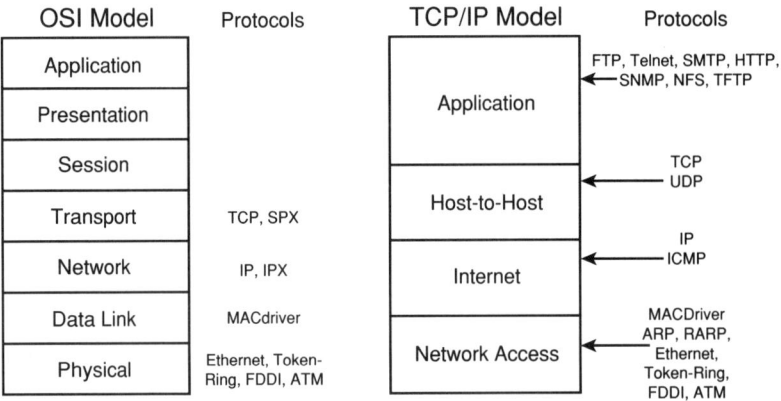

As you can see, there are a number of protocols that work together at different levels of the TCP/IP model to facilitate communications between hosts over a TCP/IP network, such as the Internet.

It all starts at the application level of the protocol, when an application such as FTP attempts to communicate with a remote host. FTP passes the IP address of the remote host, down through the Host layer (TCP), the Internet layer (IP), and then to the Network Layer (ARP) where it's passed onto the wire. When the request is received at the remote host, it's passed up through each corresponding layer until it reaches the FTP Service, where it's serviced.

Table 13.2 briefly summarizes the main TCP/IP protocols and services you are likely to use with TCP/IP and Windows NT.

Table 13.2 Common TCP/IP Protocols and Applications Used by Windows NT

Name	Type	Description
ARP	Network	Address Resolution Protocol is used to map a host's NIC address to its Internet address. ARP enables the Internet address to be independent of the NIC address.
FTP	Application	File Transfer Protocol enables a user on one host to transfer files to and from another host over a TCP/IP network.
HTTP	Application	Hypertext Transfer Protocol is the standard protocol used by Web servers to transfer HTML documents over IP networks.
ICMP	Network	Internet Control Message Protocol is an extension to IP that provides generation of error messages, test packets, and informational messages related to IP.
IP	Network	Internet Protocol is a connectionless, best-effort packet-switching protocol providing packet routing, fragmentation, and re-assembly.
RARP	Network	Reverse Address Resolution Protocol provides reverse function of ARP. RARP maps a NIC address to an IP address.
SMTP	Transport	Simple Mail Transfer Protocol is used to transfer electronic mail messages between hosts over TCP/IP.
SNMP	Transport	Simple Network Management Protocol is used to manage nodes on an IP network.
TCP	Transport	Transport Control Protocol, unlike UDP, is a connection oriented protocol that provides reliable communication, flow-control, multiplexing, and connection-oriented communication.
Telnet	Application	A protocol for remote log on that runs on top of TCP/IP.
UDP	Transport	User Datagram Protocol provides simple, connectionless transfer of datagrams over IP networks.

Part
IV
Ch
13

When communication takes place on a TCP/IP network, each protocol "talks" to its counterpart on the remote host through the use of sockets. A socket is a procedure that creates a virtual connection between hosts. Each socket has a socket address that consists of a port number and the local host's IP address. There are three basic types of sockets: IP sockets, TCP sockets, and UDP sockets. When communications take place between two hosts over IP, a socket is opened between the hosts, and a request containing the unique IP address of the remote host, as well as the port number of the service you are requesting, is sent. A port is nothing more than a channel that protocols can use to communicate with a specific service.

When you attempt to connect to a remote host, your request will consist of a unique IP address, the protocol type you are using (IP, TCP, or UDP), and the port you want to use. For example, if you are trying to Telnet in to a remote host, your request would contain the IP address of the remote host, the type of protocol you are using (TCP in this case), and the port that Telnet is watching on the remote host. If any of these variables are incorrect, a connection isn't made. Figure 13.2 illustrates a Telnet connection between two hosts on the Internet.

FIG. 13.2
A sample Telnet Session.

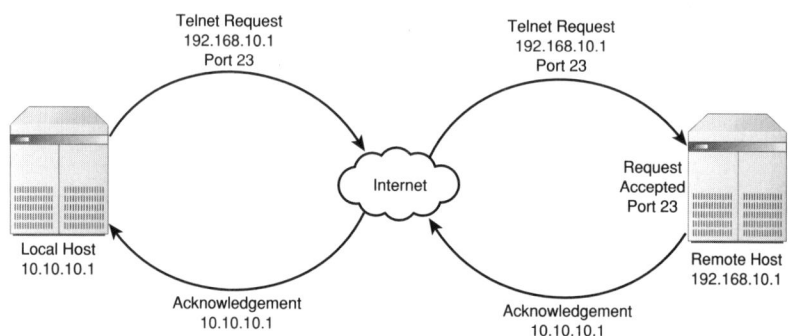

Since the early days of TCP/IP, many services have been assigned to specific ports for the sake of convenience and standardization. For example, SMTP services normally listen for requests on port 25, while HTTP listens for requests on port 80. On UNIX-based systems, ports are defined in the /etc/services file or the Network Information Service database. On Windows NT systems, ports are defined in <winroot>\system32\drivers\etc\services (<winroot> is the parent directory of your Windows NT installation, for example winnt40). Table 13.3 displays the most common predefined ports you are likely to work with when using Windows NT.

Table 13.3   Common, Predefined TCP/IP Ports

Service	Port	Alias
qotd	17	quote
ftp-data	20	
ftp	21	
telnet	23	

Service	Port	Alias
smtp	25	mail
time	37	timeserver
name	42	nameserver
whois	43	nicname
domain	53	nameserver
bootp	67	
tftp	69	
finger	79	
http	80	
pop3	110	postoffice
portmap	111	
nntp	119	usenet
ntp	123	ntpd ntp
snmp	161	snmp
snmp-trap	162	snmp
exec	512	
login	513	
shell	514	cmd
printer	515	spooler
nfs	2049	

TIP The Internet Assigned Numbers Authority (IANA) is the central registry for the predefined ports. You find currently assigned values listed in the Assigned Numbers document STD 2. You can find IANA on the Web at **http://www.isi.edu/div7/iana/**.

Now that you have a basic understanding of the architecture of the TCP/IP protocol suite, you are ready to learn how Windows NT supports TCP/IP. If you'd like to know all of the many intricacies of the TCP/IP protocol suite, the following books are excellent sources of detailed information on the TCP/IP protocol.

■ *Internetworking with TCP/IP Volume I,* Douglas E. Comer, Prentice Hall, 1991, ISBN:0-13-468505-9.

- *Internetworking with TCP/IP Volume II*, Douglas E. Comer and David L. Stevens, Prentice Hall, 1991, ISBN: 0-13-472242-6.

- *Internetworking with TCP/IP Volume III*, Douglas E. Comer and David L. Stevens, Prentice Hall, 1993, ISBN: 0-13-472222-2.

- *TCP/IP Unleashed*, Timothy Parker, Ph.D., Sams Publishing, 1996, ISBN:0672306034.

Windows NT and TCP/IP   Windows NT has excellent internal security that provides user log-on authentication, object security, user rights, and extensive auditing capabilities, all hallmarks of a highly secure system. But once you connect to the Internet, you open your Windows NT systems to many of the security flaws inherent in the TCP/IP protocol.

Luckily, right out of-the-box, Windows NT makes a more secure Internet platform than most flavors of UNIX. This is mostly because Windows NT does not natively support many of the most insecure Internet services, such as the Finger and Telnet services, and also because the Windows NT operating system was built from the ground up with tight security in mind. The fact that Windows NT stores user account information in a highly secure database (the Security Accounts Manager) as opposed to UNIX's plain text password file is a good example of this difference. Table 13.4 briefly compares Windows NT security with UNIX security.

Table 13.4   UNIX Security versus Windows NT Security

Feature	UNIX	Windows NT
User log-on required	Yes	Yes
Native encrypted log-on support	No	Yes
Native encrypted dial-up access	No	Yes
Directory access permissions	Yes	Yes
File access permissions	Yes	Yes—more granular than UNIX
File control lists	Some	Yes—all objects under the control of the operating system (OS) support access control.
Share permissions	Yes	Yes—in addition to file and directory permissions
Role-based access	Some	Yes
Security auditing	Yes	Yes—extensive auditing
Easy security configuration	No	Yes

As you might expect, the prerequisite for configuring Windows NT TCP/IP security is to install and configure the TCP/IP protocol. Once you have TCP/IP operational on your machine, you can take the first steps toward configuring your security implementation.

In order to configure your Windows NT systems for optimal security, you need to be aware of many of Windows NT's built-in security tools and features, as well as the many TCP/IP utilities that come bundled with Windows NT. Utilities such as *Telnet* make excellent probing tools that help you find and plug holes in your network. Table 13.5 lists the TCP/IP utilities that ship with Windows NT 4.0 along with a brief description of their purpose.

Table 13.5   Windows NT 4.0 TCP/IP Utilities

Command	Description
Arp	Displays and modifies the IP-to-Ethernet or Token Ring physical address translation tables used by Address Resolution Protocol (ARP).
Finger	Displays information about a user on a specified system running the Finger service. Output varies based on the remote system's OS.
FTP	(File Transfer Protocol) Transfers files to and from a computer running an FTP server service.
Hostname	Prints the name of the current host.
Ipconfig	Displays TCP/IP network configuration for the current host.
Lpq	This diagnostic utility is used to obtain status of a print queue on a computer running the LPD server.
Lpr	This connectivity utility is used to print a file to a computer running an LPD server.
Nbtstat	Displays protocol statistics and current TCP/IP connections using NBT (NetBIOS over TCP/IP).
Netstat	Displays protocol statistics and current TCP/IP network connections.
Nslookup	This diagnostic tool displays information from Domain Name System (DNS) name servers.
Ping	Verifies connections to a remote computer or computers.
Rcp	Copies files between a Windows NT computer and a system running Rshd, (Remote Shell Daemon). The remote computer also must provide the Rcp utility in addition to running Rshd.
Rexec	Runs commands on remote computers running the REXEC service. Rexec authenticates the user name on the remote computer before executing the specified command.
Route	Manipulates network routing tables on the current host.

Part
IV

Ch
13

continues

Table 13.5 Continued

Command	Description
Rsh	Runs commands on remote computers running the Rsh service.
Telnet	A terminal application that supports the Telnet protocol for remote log-on.
TFTP	(Trivial File Transfer Protocol) Transfers files to and from a remote computer running the TFTP service.
Tracert	Determines the route taken to a destination by sending Internet Control Message Protocol (ICMP) echo packets with varying Time-To-Live (TTL) values to the destination.

 You can find detailed usage instructions for the TCP/IP utilities in the TCPIP.HLP file in the Windows NT root directory. Alternatively, at the command prompt you can type any command with no parameters to see the valid parameters and an example of its usage. Figure 13.3 shows the command line help for the Ping command.

FIG. 13.3
The Ping command is a powerful tool with many options—learn it well.

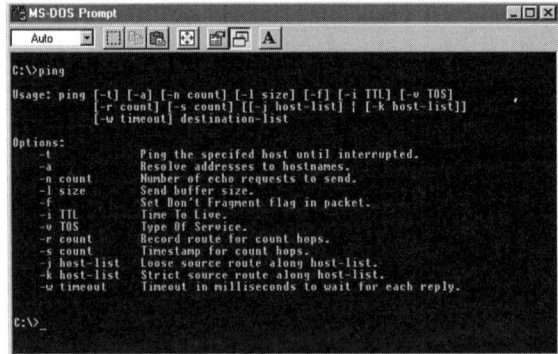

As you can see from Table 13.5, Windows NT provides nearly all of the most popular Internet client utilities. However, as I mentioned earlier, it doesn't natively provide a number of Internet services that are common sources of security breaches. The Internet services that are bundled with Windows NT are collectively called Internet Information Server and include an FTP Server, a Gopher Server, and an HTTP (Web) server.

The rest of this chapter examines the type of attacks hackers employ and what you can do to ensure the security of your Windows NT systems.

General Windows NT Security Measures   The vast majority of security holes that can be found on Windows NT systems running TCP/IP are related to misconfiguration. These holes easily can be exploited with minimal effort by a hacker. You might be surprised how much information you can gain about a remote system by using Telnet to query certain ports. Figure 13.4 displays a Telnet session with the port 21 (FTP) on my host. I have local echo enabled, so you can see what I'm asking the host to do (and how easy it is).

FIG. 13.4
See how easy it is to get information about a target?

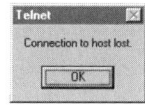

As illustrated previously, the MS FTP service is friendly; as soon as I connected to port 21, it offered the following:

> 220 samuel-1 Microsoft FTP Service (Version 3.0).

With minimal effort, I now know that the host's name is Samuel-1 and that it is running version 3 of the Microsoft FTP Service. Using the USER and PASS commands, I can actually log on anonymously to the host and then query the host for additional information. The SYST command tells me that the host OS is Windows NT 4.0 and the STAT command tells me a variety of additional information. The scariest part of all of this is that it doesn't take an ubercracker; you can learn these commands simply by connecting to the FTP port and typing HELP.

However, there are a number of basic network security items that just make good sense whether you are connecting to the Internet or not. For example, all systems should display a log-on message warning users that unauthorized access is not allowed and may be punishable by law. The good part is that by making your internal network more secure, you are by default making it more secure when it is connected to the Internet. This following section covers many simple issues that can substantially shore up your security.

Creating a custom log-on message is easy—you just add entries to the Registry. Start the Registry Editor (regedt32.exe) and select the following subkey:

HKEY_LOCAL_MACHINE\SOFTWARE\Microsoft\Windows NT\CurrentVersion\WinLogon.

You'll then need to add two new value entries as follows:

1. LegalNoticeCaption of type REG_SZ and then enter the text that will serve as the caption of the message box.

2. LegalNoticeText of type REG_SZ and enter the text that will be displayed as a warning message.

Doing this will display your message box each time a user logs on to the system.

Account and Password Security   Although Chapter 6, "User Account Security and Windows NT," covers many of the issues surrounding password selection and protection, it can never be stressed enough. Many security breaches are due to compromised passwords because the users were not informed on how to choose a secure password, were never required to change their password, were allowed to use a two-character password, or worse yet, no password at all! The following list summarizes some simple do's and don'ts for password selection that can help ensure that your passwords are secure:

- DON'T use a password shorter than six characters. The fewer characters the password contains, the easier it is to guess.
- DON'T use any part of your account name, as this is easily found on the Internet.
- DON'T use your spouse's, child's, pet's, or friend's names as they are also easy to find out and easy to guess.
- DON'T use any part of your real name. User accounts where the user uses their account name as the password is known as a *Joe* in the security industry. Joe accounts are easy for the user but present a serious security compromise.
- DON'T use any other information that is readily available about you, as this is the first thing experienced hackers try. For example, your social security number or your birthday.
- DON'T use any word that can be found in a dictionary or other list of words. Hacker's frequently employ programs that will attempt to try every word in the dictionary as a password.
- DON'T write your password down, and DON'T ever mail your password to someone else, no matter who they claim to be! A recent scam was for hackers to fake a mail message from the system administrator to an end-user requesting their password.
- DO use a password that contains mixed case, as this makes it much harder to guess.
- DO use a password that contains some combination of letters, numbers, and punctuation symbols.
- DO use a password such as X$2sC.8Zd9, which be very hard to guess and would certainly not be found in any dictionary, and even if the character combination was guessed, they have to get the case correct.
- DO change your password regularly (at least every 90 days) and DON'T use the same password twice.

Windows NT's user account polices can help you ensure that existing user accounts stay secure. Although users complain to the high heavens when they must change their password frequently, or when they can't use the six-character name of their wife for a password, it's important to ensure that your user accounts are secure. After you connect your system to the Internet, user accounts become a prime target for hackers. If a hacker can get a valid user account name and guess the password, they will gain access to your system and will have all of the rights and privileges granted to that user! Even worse is that it is difficult to detect this type of security breach.

Windows NT Account Policies can be very useful in helping to ensure that sensible restrictions are set for things such as user passwords, log-on times, user profiles, and account lockout procedures. Figure 13.5 displays the Account Polices window.

FIG. 13.5
The Account Policies window enables you to set global policies for your users.

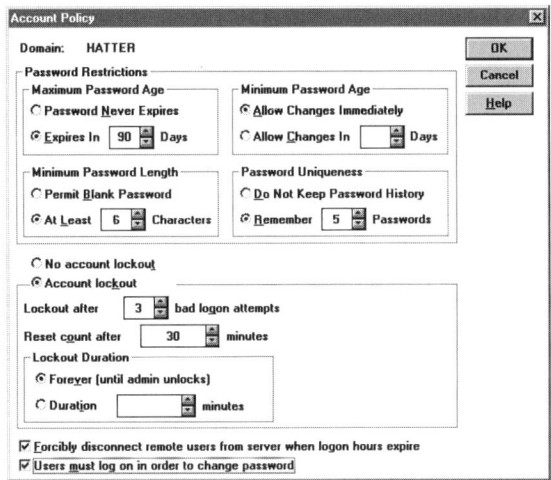

The Account Policies window contains many powerful and useful settings guaranteed to frustrate \hackers, but the single most important option is the Minimum Password Length option. It's imperative that you set a minimum password length so that users can't use a blank password. It's surprisingly easy to use a variety of well-known techniques to learn the names of a system's user accounts. If a hacker stumbles across a user with a blank password, they are into your system without even breaking a sweat. Most security experts recommend a minimum password length of six characters, but as with most things in the world of computers, more is better, and Windows NT supports passwords of up to 14 characters.

You also should use the Maximum Password Age option to ensure that users must change their password periodically; a time frame of 90 to 120 days is usually adequate. This ensures that if a hacker does obtain a password, it will eventually expire and they will lose access to the compromised account.

The Password Uniqueness option works hand-in-hand with the Maximum Password Age option. When this feature is enabled, it remembers a number of passwords for each user, forcing the user to choose a new password and thus ensuring that the user won't revert to a password that the hacker has already obtained.

You also should consider implementing Account lockouts. The capability to lockout an account is a powerful security feature, because it can be extremely frustrating for hackers (unfortunately, it may frustrate your users too…), making programs that attempt to log-on by guessing the password for an account ineffective.

Part
IV

Ch
13

Should you enable this feature, you can then determine how many bad log ons should be accepted (three attempts to log on should be plenty) within a given amount of time (this is specified by the value of the Reset count after x minutes field) before the account in question is locked out. Once an account is locked out, the user will not be able to log on even if he or she supplies the correct password for the amount of time specified in the Lockout Duration field. If your systems need to be ultra-secure, you might consider selecting Forever, which means that the account remains locked until an administrator unlocks it. For most systems, however, a 10 to 20 minute lockout period is sufficient.

The following example should illustrate the effectiveness of the account lockout in stopping hackers dead in their tracks. You configure your account policy to lock out any user account that has three bad log-in attempts during any 15 minute period. The lockout period is set to forever. A smart hacker with a packet sniffer gets your account name and the name of your host off the wire from an e-mail message you sent. She then tries to attack your system with a password cracking program that uses a dictionary of common words, but is foiled by Windows NT's accounts lockout feature. After the third invalid log-on attempt, the account is locked out, and when you call the administrator to have your account reset, it should make the administrator pause and consider that a security attack has taken place.

Another common security hole often overlooked is the availability of the default accounts created by Windows NT during installation. The Guest account really should be disabled. Although it has relatively limited access, a hacker could get in and download files such as the Security Accounts Manager, which they could then pick apart on another machine and then return with complete access!

If you feel that you really need a guest account, be sure to make the password hard to crack and limit the log-on times for the guest account to standard business hours. You also should be sure to enable auditing (more about auditing later in this section), and check the Security event logs to look for strange access times and behaviors.

Because of the far-reaching access granted to the Administrator account, it's extremely important to guard it. The following guidelines are some simple steps you can take to protect your Administrator account:

■ Rename your Administrator account! The administrator account usually is the first thing that hackers attack, because it is the the "skeleton key" of a Windows NT system. Make the name something obscure so that it's difficult to guess or recognize if a hacker gets in.

 T I P After you have renamed the real Administrator account, you might want to create another account named Administrator and grant it minimal rights and privileges to frustrate and befuddle hackers.

- Use the preceding password guidelines to make the Administrator's password extremely hard to guess, make it the maximum length (14 characters), and memorize it. For example, n*D74.Xj1$vP8g would be nearly impossible to guess.

- Don't have too many administrators—the more people who know the password, the more likely the account can be compromised. If the server you are connecting to is part of a Domain, use the other built-in groups to delegate authority.

- Always follow the principle of "least privilege." Only use the Administrator account when necessary. Remember that if you are connecting to a remote network, it's possible that someone with a sniffer could grab your password.

- Consider removing the Access this computer from network right from the administrator. Although this can be a hassle, it increases security.

Also, don't forget the other built-in groups such as Account Operators, Server Operators, and especially Backup Operators. Remember that users who have been assigned to the Backup Operators group can read and possibly right (restore right) any file in any directory. If a hacker can gain access through an account that has the backup or restore rights, or is a member of the Backup Operators group, you could be in trouble!

You should use the User Manager's User Rights options to ensure that these groups have no more access than necessary and that people are assigned to them judiciously. Again, remember the principle of least privilege.

File System Security   As you know, Windows NT supports Microsoft's highly secure New Technology File System (NTFS), which is detailed in Chapter 7, "New Technology File System (NTFS) Security." There are several ways you can use NTFS to increase the security of your systems that are connected to the Internet.

First and foremost, you should ensure that any systems directly connected to the Internet are running NTFS so that hackers not only have share permissions to contend with, they also must deal with the directory and file permissions that NTFS provides. Once the partitions have been formatted for NTFS, be sure that you thoroughly check the permissions and that you keep the principle of least privilege in mind. That way if a hacker does gain access, they will be hard pressed to access sensitive data.

Another somewhat obvious tactic is to ensure that there is no sensitive data stored on any machine that has a direct connection. If all of your other "ducks are in a row" in regards to security, there will be virtually no way for an intruder to access sensitive data.

Although it can be a real nightmare from the administrative and maintenance points and certainly is not the best way to utilize your disk space, another good tactic is to use multiple partitions on your system to keep data separate. For instance, you can install the OS on one partition, the Web server on another, the Web server's data directories on yet

Part
IV

Ch
13

another partition and so on. This makes it difficult for a hacker who finds a hole to use it to gain access to other parts of the system.

You also should take ample precautions to protect the registry from unauthorized access. Not only can a hacker gain a wealth of information from reading the registry, if they can edit it they can essentially perpetrate a denial-of-service attack by changing its settings, and this can be very, very difficult to detect. In fact, most administrators would assume Windows NT needed to be re-installed and do so. Then the hackers regain access and change it again...

As a final note, you also should consider deleting TCP/IP utilities that are installed on the server by default, such as FTP, Telnet, and Finger. Although these utilities might occasionally come in handy for diagnostic purposes, you are running a risk by having these programs on your server. For example, if an intruder can gain access and run any of these utilities, they will appear to be coming from inside your network, which might allow them to circumvent other security measures you have in place, such as a proxy server or firewalls (which are discussed later in this chapter).

Auditing As you are probably aware by now, Windows NT provides extensive auditing capabilities (Windows NT's auditing capabilities are discussed in more detail in Chapter 2, "An Overview of Microsoft Windows NT Security"), and this can prove to be an invaluable aid for ensuring the integrity of your systems.

For any systems connected directly to the Internet, you should consider enabling all of the auditing features. Although it will add some overhead in terms of performance and disk space, it will allow you to track virtually everything that happens on the machine. If this is not desirable or feasible, you should (as a bare minimum) enable the features shown in Figure 13.6.

FIG. 13.6

Audit Policies help you maintain system integrity by tracking user activity.

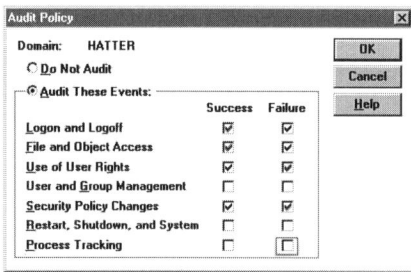

Once you have enabled auditing, you can use the Security Log view in the Event Viewer to see what users are up to. Figure 13.7 displays the Security Log from my Windows NT Server, Samuel-1.

FIG. 13.7

The Security Log details user activity for Audit Policy events you elect to track.

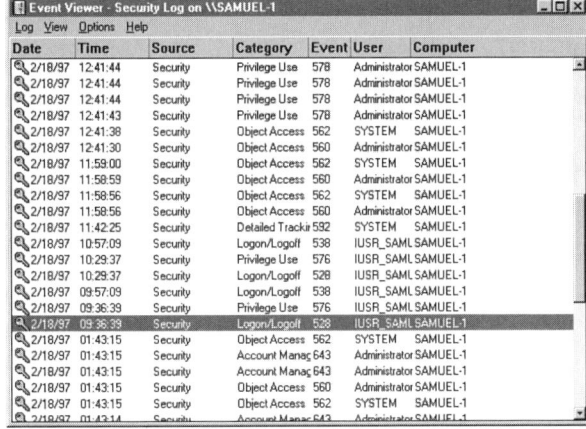

As you can see in Figure 13.7, starting at 9:36 A.M. on 02/18/97, there were several success audits logged for the default IIS user (IUSR_SAMUEL-1, we'll cover this later in the chapter). To see exactly what the event was, you can double-click it and view the detailed information as displayed in Figure 13.8.

FIG. 13.8

The Event Detail window can shed additional light on any particular event.

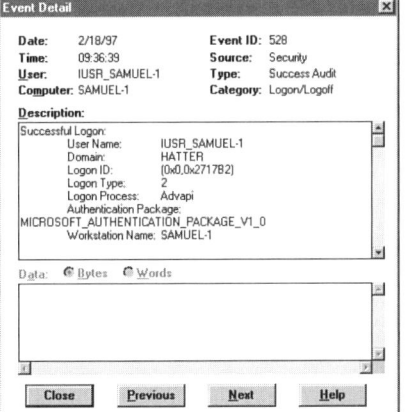

Auditing and logging work hand-in-hand to help you keep track of what people are trying to do on, or more importantly, TO your system. You can look at the extensive log-in features IIS provides later in this chapter.

TCP/IP Specific Security Options   Connecting any system to a TCP/IP network makes it more susceptible to compromise, and Windows NT 4.0 is no different in this respect. Although special precautions must be taken to ensure the security and integrity of systems running the TCP/IP protocol, Windows NT 4.0 makes this significantly easier than other *Network Operating Systems (NOS)* because of the many built-in features it includes and its extensibility. This section covers what you need to know and what you need to do to protect your TCP/IP networks.

Native TCP/IP Filtering   As I mentioned earlier in this chapter, Windows NT was built from the ground up with security in mind, and with each subsequent release of Windows NT, Microsoft has improved upon its native security capabilities. Windows NT 4.0 now supports some native TCP/IP filtering capabilities that can help ensure the security of your system. Naturally, the prerequisite for using these features is that the TCP/IP protocol is installed and running.

At this point, there's a need to address the concept of trusted networks versus untrusted networks. To use Windows NT's native TCP/IP security, launch the Control Panel, and double-click the Network icon, which opens the Network window. You can then click the Protocols tab and select TCP/IP from the list of installed protocols that will open the Microsoft TCP/IP Properties window. If the IP Address tab is not on top, click it and then click the Advanced button, which displays the Advanced IP Addressing window. At the bottom of this window, click the Enable Security checkbox to enable TCP/IP security, and then click the Configure button, which displays the TCP/IP Security window shown in Figure 13.9.

FIG. 13.9
The TCP/IP Security window allows you to permit or deny access to various protocols and ports.

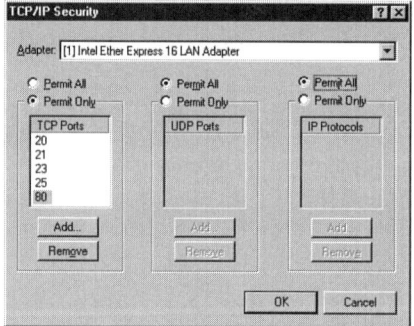

This is a powerful new feature that can act as a "poor man's firewall." It enables you to perform relatively extensive filtering of TCP/IP protocols and port requests, which is one easy way to deny a hacker's access to your network. To configure TCP/IP security for the selected machine, select the network adapter to which you want to apply filtering. If you have more than one NIC installed in your computer, verify that you have selected the correct one, or you accidentally filter the wrong packets and deny access from your trusted users.

After you have selected the correct card, you can start to configure filtering for TCP/ IP and UDP. For each of the listed protocols, you have two basic choices: Permit All or Permit Only.

■ Permit All allows all communications to pass through to the server for the selected protocol.

■ Permit Only allows you to choose which ports will accept connections and pass packets through to the server.

By default, Permit All is selected for each protocol. If however, you want to filter requests directed to specific ports, simply select the protocol to filter and click the Add button, which launches the Security Add dialog box, shown in Figure 13.10.

FIG. 13.10
The Security Add dialog box enables you to specify individual ports to permit.

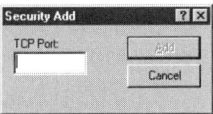

You simply enter in decimal format the port number that you want to enable and click the Add button. If you later decide to disable a port, simply select it from the list and click the Remove button. Disabling ports is a powerful and important step toward securing your network for two reasons: The first reason is that some services give away information about your system that makes it easier for a hacker to break in (remember how friendly the TCP/IP service was?). The second reason is that unneeded but enabled ports often become the target of denial-of-service attacks called *SYN-Flood* attacks.

N O T E Speaking of disabling ports, The Computer Emergency Response Team (CERT **http://www.cert.org**) strongly recommends that you disable unneeded ports to bolster your network security. ▪

Here's how SYN Flooding works, how you can detect it and what ports you should disable to help prevent these attacks. In a SYN-Flood attack, a network request (called a SYN) is sent to the target computer using a bogus IP address, a technique known as IP Spoofing. The hacker sends as many of these as possible to tie up as many resources as possible on the target computer.

When the target receives the request, it designates resources to service the new connection and then responds with an acknowledgment of the request called a *SYN-ACK*. Because the SYN-ACK is returned to a bogus address, no response is received and the target computer will continue to attempt to send the SYN-ACK.

According to Microsoft, Windows NT 3.5x and 4.0 machines retransmit the SYN-ACK five times by default. Each time a retransmission takes place, the time-out value is doubled and begins at three seconds. By the fifth retransmission, the machine will wait 48 seconds for a response. If no response is received, the machine waits another 96 seconds before deallocating the resources set aside for the connection. A total of 189 seconds have elapsed before those resources are released.

You can use the netstat command to check the current status of your connections and to see if you might be under a SYN-Flood attack. Just drop to the command prompt and type in **netstat -n -p tcp**, which displays all the connections from your machine. If a large number of connections are in the SYN_RECEIVED state, it is possible that the system is under attack.

The good news is that the hacker perpetrating this attack cannot gain access to the system—the bad news is that there is a limit to the number of connections that can be in the SYN_RECEIVED state for most every TCP/IP protocol stack. When a port's limit is reached, the target machine usually responds by resetting all further connection requests until the allocated resources are freed.

Microsoft has identified this problem on both Windows NT 3.5x and 4.0 machines. If you are running Windows NT 3.5x, you can download a fix from **ftp://ftp.microsoft.com/ bussys/winnt/winnt-public/fixes/usa/nt351/hotfixes-postsp5/syn-attack**. If you are running 4.0, simply get Service Pack 2.

In order to provide maximum security, only enable the specific ports that your applications and services need. In particular, do not enable any UDP ports less than 900, except those for the specific services that you need; FTP, for example. In particular, the echo (7) and chargen (19) ports for the UDP protocol should not be enabled. They are rarely used and are prime targets for SYN-Flood attacks.

Another less well-known threat is the use of Windows nbtstat command. This command discloses sensitive information about your system, such as your Domain name and your server's NetBIOS name. Even worse, if the Windows NT system is running IIS, that is disclosed as well as the anonymous user account for IIS. This is obviously a bad thing.

The good news is that it's relatively simple to stop users on the outside from using Nbtstat to probe your systems. Simply disable UDP ports 137 and 138, and TCP port 139 at your router or firewall. This prevents these requests from being passed through to the internal network, but allows Nbtstat to function properly internally.

And, as if that isn't enough to worry about, yet another hole exists through Windows NT's RPC services. A user can Telnet to port 135 on a Windows NT 3.5x or 4.0 server, enter 10 random characters, a return, and disconnect. This causes CPU utilization to jump to 100 percent. While a simple reboot eliminates this problem, it can be a major pain and seriously affects system performance.

This same attack also is known to befuddle services listening on two other ports, namely 53 and 1031. If DNS server services is running on port 53, this attack makes it hang, and you'll need to restart it. Likewise, if you're running IIS, attacking port 1031 hangs IIS, requiring a restart of the services.

Fortunately, this is a well-known problem that Microsoft addresses in Service Pack 2.0 for Windows NT (see **http://www.microsoft.com** for more information). If you are not using services that listen on these ports for external users, you can disable them at the firewall (more about firewalls in the next section) as well.

Advanced Internet Security: Firewalls   Even if you take all of the precautions discussed up to this point, your network may still be vulnerable to attack from an uebercracker. In order to provide the maximum level of protection, you need to consider the ultimate in Internet security (and expense)—*firewalls*.

By now, you most likely have heard all the buzz surrounding the darlings of Internet security—firewalls. But if you've never worked with one before, you're probably wondering just what it is and how it can help you secure your network. This section helps you understand what they are and shows you how they can add tight security.

Let's start by defining a firewall. According to *Webster's Dictionary*, a firewall is defined as "A wall constructed to prevent the spread of fire." In relation to Internet security, a firewall is a system (hardware, software, or both) placed between your network and the Internet that monitors all inbound and outbound network traffic and allows only authorized traffic (as defined by local security policies) to pass through based on security rules defined by the administrator. Additionally, it should ensure that IP addresses on the trusted network are invisible to the untrusted network—in this case, the Internet.

Before you examine the types of firewalls and strategies for using them, you need to define two terms that are commonly used when discussing this technology: *trusted* networks and *untrusted* networks.

Concerning a firewall, a *trusted* network is the internal, secure network that you are trying to protect with the firewall. The *untrusted* network is the outside, unsecure network (the Internet, in this case) that you are trying to protect your trusted network from.

Also, a basic firewall system needs to be easy to use. In particular, adding rules to firewall software should be easy and, more importantly, examining and understanding previously entered rules also should be easy. Figure 13.11 displays a basic firewall implementation.

Part

IV

Ch

13

FIG. 13.11
The firewall acts as
a military checkpoint,
allowing only
authorized traffic
to pass.

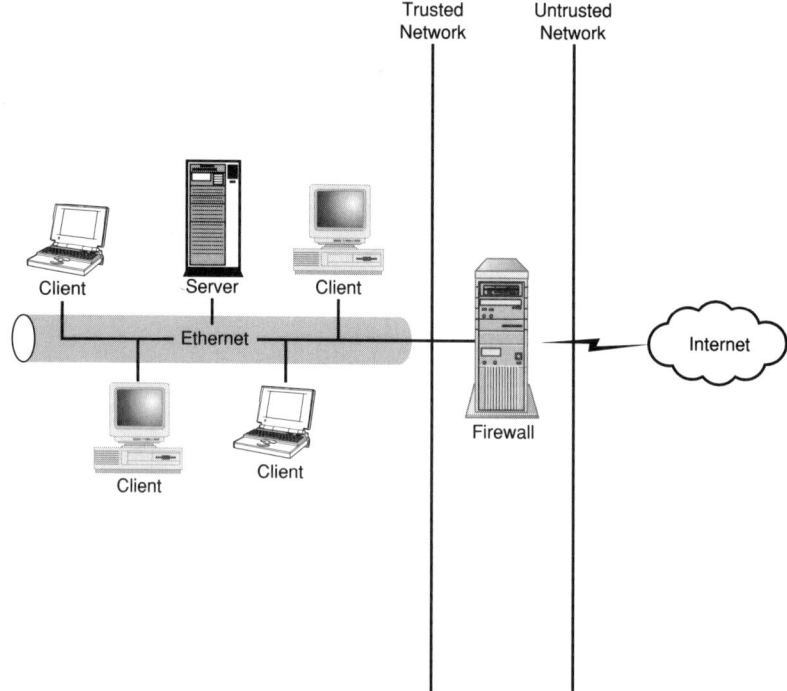

While there are three basic types of firewalls, their functionality is beginning to overlap, and thus the distinction between them is starting to blur. The three basic categories of firewalls are:

- Network Level (Packet-Filtering Routers)
- Application Level (Proxy Servers)
- Hybrid Firewalls

Now you're ready to take a look at the three basic types of firewalls.

Network Level Firewalls   Network Level firewalls are really nothing more than packet-filtering routers operating at the IP level. They are placed between your trusted network and the Internet (untrusted network), and a single IP interface is given to each. The primary function of a Packet-Filtering Router is to check the source address, destination address, and the requested port in each packet. The following example illustrates this point:

   1. A router is configured with a set of filter rules, such that any requests coming from the untrusted network with an IP address in the range 8.8.8.1 through 8.8.8.254 are not allowed to pass through to the trusted network.

2. A host on the Internet with the IP address 8.8.8.8 attempts to send a packet to a host in the trusted network.

3. The router receives and compares the data in the packet with the access control policy.

4. The router determines that this packet should not be allowed to pass through to the trusted network and discards the packet. In most cases, the access attempt is written to a log file.

Naturally, there are pros and cons associated with Network Level firewalls. The pros are that these firewalls are usually fast and transparent to your end-users. The cons are that it's fairly easy to use *IP spoofing* to fool the router and make it believe that packets coming from the untrusted network are really coming from the trusted network. In addition, most routers provide rather limited logging and alerting features.

N O T E *IP Spoofing* is a technique hackers use to fool firewalls so they can gain access to your network. It generally involves writing a program that changes the packet header of an IP packet so that the source and destination address appear to be originating from inside the trusted network and thus slip through. ▨

 Not all routers are created equal when it comes to packet-filtering capabilities. Before you purchase a router for a firewall solution, be sure that it can provide the level of filtering you need and that it has antispoofing and antisource routing capabilities.

The are four basic types of Network Level firewalls:

- ▨ Router
- ▨ Bastion Host
- ▨ Screened Host
- ▨ Screened Subnet

Bastion Host Firewall   According to *Webster's Dictionary*, a bastion is defined as "A fortified area or position." Relative to firewall technology, a *bastion host* is a computer with at least one connection to the untrusted network and one connection to the trusted network. The bastion host performs packet-filtering on a request for services coming from or going to the trusted network. If a host on the untrusted network is granted access to the trusted network, all traffic from that host is allowed to pass through. Figure 13.12 shows the bastion host architecture.

FIG. 13.12

A bastion host firewall provides protection from requests on the untrusted network.

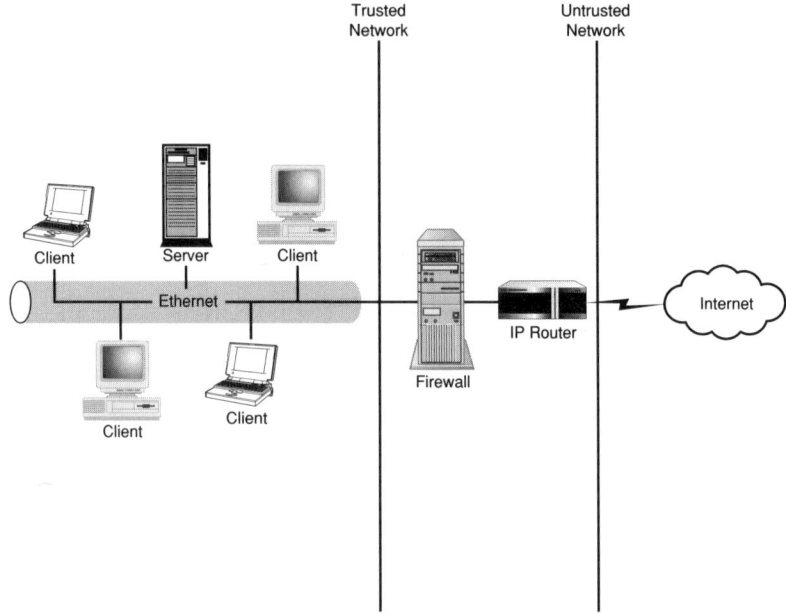

Because a bastion host primarily provides packet-filtering style security, they are generally used as a foundation for more sophisticated firewall solutions.

Screened Host Firewall   A *screened host* firewall adds an additional level of security by adding a router between the untrusted network and the bastion host. The router is configured with a set of filter rules that grant or deny access to packets targeted for hosts on the trusted network. If a packet passes the initial screening done by the router, it then is passed on to the bastion host for additional scrutiny. Figure 13.13 displays a typical screened host firewall configuration.

A screened host firewall not only adds an additional layer of security, it can increase performance because the initial filtering is handled by a fast router, and it also allows the filtering logic to be less complex on the bastion host.

Screened Subnet Firewall   In terms of network-level firewalls, it's hard to beat the security provided by a *screened subnet* firewall. The screened subnet firewall builds upon the screened host firewall concept by adding at least one additional router and possibly additional bastion host machines separated on different subnets. Figure 13.14 shows a screened subnet firewall.

Using the screened subnet model, the bastion hosts provide a secured "bridge" over the "demilitarized zone" network to a subnet of the trusted network. Because the trusted network never passes IP traffic directly with the untrusted network, the untrusted network cannot see IP addresses inside the trusted network.

FIG. 13.13

The router in a Screened Host performs preliminary packet-filtering.

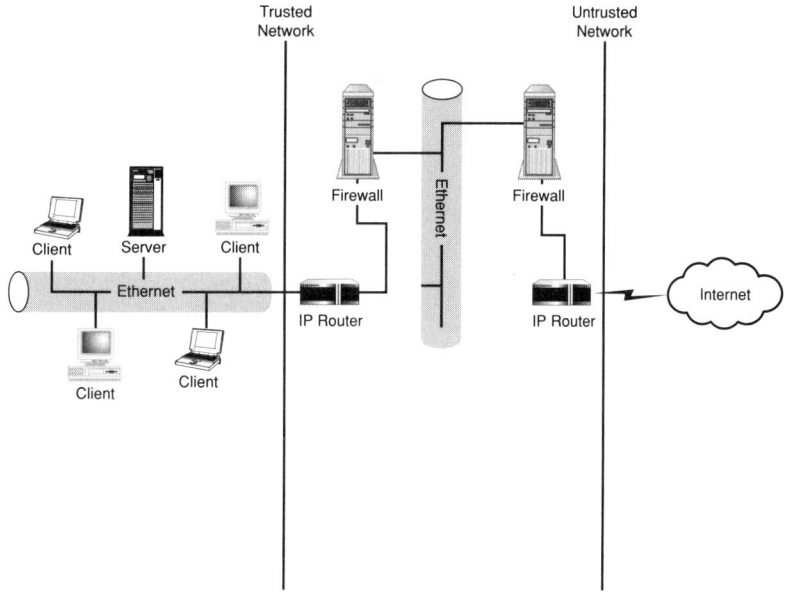

FIG. 13.14

The screened subnet firewall is actually a network of screened hosts.

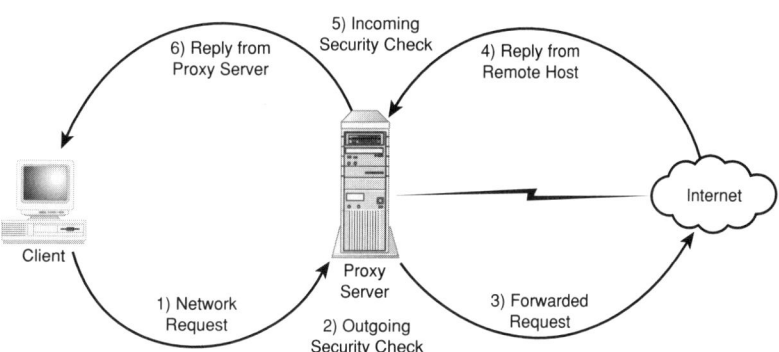

Keep in mind that while this model provides excellent security, it can be very costly both in terms of the expense of the hardware and software and in the amount of time and highly-skilled labor required to configure properly a screened subnet firewall.

Pseudo-Firewalls   If you are on a tight budget and can't afford to spend a lot of money on a more elaborate solution, you can create a *pseudo-firewall* to help pump-up your Internet security. A pseudo-firewall prevents Internet users from gaining access to your trusted network by blocking unauthorized access to Windows NT's native SMB/NetBIOS protocol services used for file and print sharing.

The basic premise of the pseudo-firewall technique is to run the NetBEUI for all internal communications and TCP/IP for external communications over the Internet. Although this is a relatively cheap and easy solution, it is designed primarily for small LAN's, because NetBEUI is designed for small workgroups of no more than 200 users and is not routable.

Creating a pseudo-firewall is easy, you simply install the NetBEUI protocol and the TCP/IP protocol on all of the workstations in the trusted network. You then ensure that the gateway machine (the machine connected to the Internet) is running the TCP/IP services, while the clients only run the TCP/IP client software (which allows them to access Internet services such as FTP, Telnet, and HTTP) through the gateway.

This is accomplished by binding and unbinding the communication layers between the NetBEUI and TCP/IP protocols. You can view and change the bindings by launching the Network Applet from within the Control Panel. When the Network dialog box appears, click the Bindings tab to display the Network Bindings dialog box shown in Figure 13.15.

FIG. 13.15

The Network dialog box enables you to enable and disable network bindings.

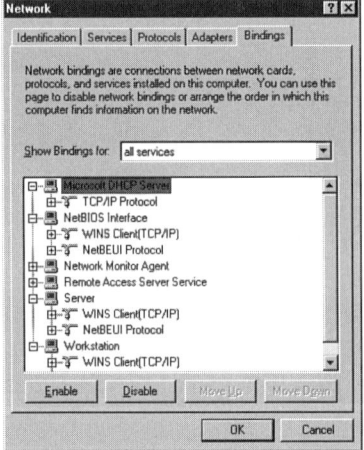

You need to disable the session bindings for:

NetBIOS	->	TCP/IP
Workstation	->	TCP/IP
Server	->	TCP/IP

and enable the session bindings for:

NetBios	->	NetBEUI

| Workstation | -> | NetBEUI |
| Server | -> | NetBEUI |

and enable the transport bindings for:

| NetBEUI | -> | Your Network Adapter Card |
| TCP/IP | -> | Modem RAS Connection |

Once you have made these changes, simply reboot the machine and it will be secured from unauthorized access from external IP users.

 TIP If you are required to run TCP/IP on your internal network, consider using IP address ranges defined for private networks (i.e., 10.0.0.0 - 10.0.0.255) on the trusted network. Because most routers won't pass packets to the addresses, you are secured from unauthorized access. A proxy server (discussed in the following section) can be implemented to provide access to the untrusted network.

Application Level Firewalls   Application Level firewalls also are known as *proxy* servers. What is a proxy server? According to *Webster's Dictionary*, proxy is defined as "authority or power to act for another" and that's just what proxy servers do, —they act on behalf of a user on the trusted network to retrieve data from the untrusted network.

A proxy server is a firewall that sits between the trusted network and the untrusted network and services the TCP/IP request on the client's behalf. The proxy server protects the trusted network by disallowing traffic to pass directly between the two networks and by hiding the IP addresses on the trusted network.

When a user on the trusted network makes a request targeted at a remote host on the untrusted network, the request is passed to the proxy server. It determines (based on a set of configurable rules, such as the source address and the destination address) if the request should be serviced. If the request is valid, the proxy server masks the address of the client with its own address (or some other address you supply) and retrieves the re-quested data, which is then returned to the user. The best part is that minus the small performance overhead, this process should be completely transparent to the user.

A proxy server also can filter packets and as a rule of thumb, tends to provide more detailed logging and tighter security than a network-level firewall because it tracks users, applications, and packet information. Because an application-level firewall understands the application being used, it also can implement protocol-specific security; for example, an HTTP proxy might be configured to permit outgoing HTTP and block incoming HTTP.

An application-level firewall could be multiple servers acting as host and proxy, or it could be one machine with two network cards installed. In order to ensure the proper

Part

IV

Ch

13

configuration and placement of a proxy server, it should be done by an expert. Figure 13.16 displays a simple proxy server architecture.

 T I P Microsoft's Internet Access Server is an excellent proxy server/firewall solution that is tightly integrated with Windows NT's native security architecture.

FIG. 13.16
A Proxy Server can make an excellent firewall.

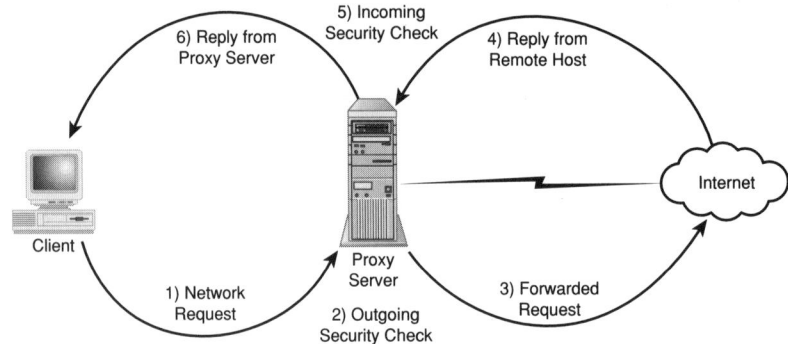

There are three basic types of network-level firewalls:

- Proxy Server Host
- Dual-Homed Gateway
- Circuit Gateway

Dual-Homed Gateway A *dual-homed gateway* is a "never the twain shall meet" concept. The dual-homed gateway is a host computer sitting between the trusted and untrusted networks that effectively blocks *all* TCP/IP traffic between the two networks, because routing is disabled between the NIC's that connect each segment. All data is exchanged only through applications running on the host, providing a highly secure environment.

Configuring a Dual-Homed Gateway is simple. Just follow these steps:

1. Install and configure two NICs in your server.
2. Connect one NIC to the trusted network and one to the untrusted network (Internet).
3. Install the TCP/IP protocol and bind it to both NICs.
4. From the Control Panel, start the Network applet and click the Protocols tab and select the TCP/IP properties.
5. Select the IP Address tab which will list the names of each of the installed NICs; be sure to provide the correct IP address, subnet mask, and default gateway for each.

6. Repeat this procedure under the WINS Address tab; if the untrusted network simply provides a path to an Internet router, configuring WINS for the NIC on that network is unnecessary.

7. Finally, select the Routing tab and ensure that Enable IP Forwarding is deselected. If you leave this setting enabled, it negates the security provided by the dual-homed gateway because IP packets will be able to pass through to the trusted network.

After you configure the Dual-Homed gateway, applications on the untrusted network can access applications (and their data) on the dual-homed gateway, and applications on the trusted network can access applications and data on the dual-homed gateway. However, no packets are ever passed between the two networks. Figure 13.17 depicts a dual-homed gateway.

FIG. 13.17
With a news forwarder, a dual-homed gateway can safely read and post to Usenet groups.

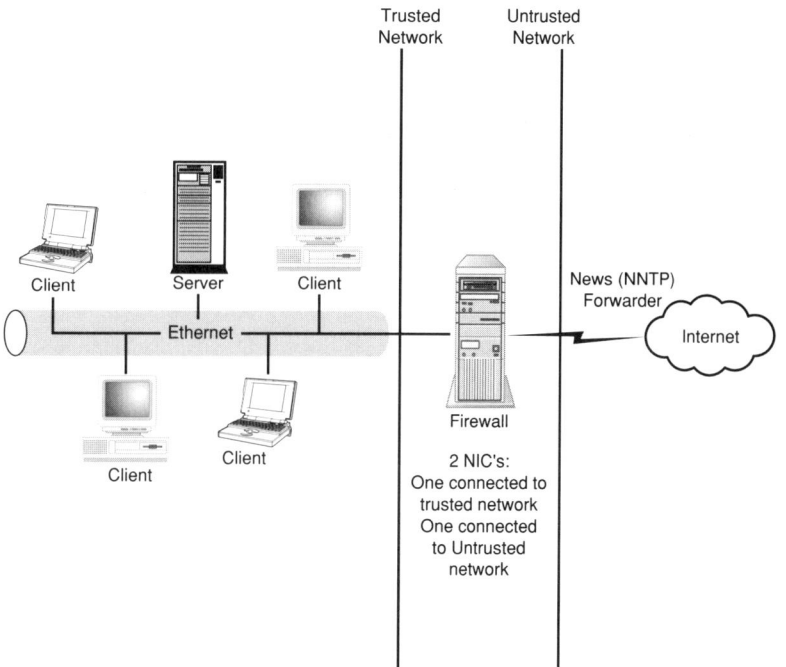

In most cases, a dual-homed gateway uses an application forwarder (mail forwarder, news forwarder) to provide proxy-like functionality. For example, when the mail forwarder receives a request, it validates the request and then forwards it to the untrusted network.

Part
IV

Ch
13

Circuit Gateway Firewall   A *circuit gateway* firewall provides communication between a client application (such as Telnet) and network resources by using TCP ports. Because Circuit Gateways usually only support TCP/IP applications, they can pose problems for any other applications and can add significant overhead if special application interfaces are needed.

Hybrid-Firewalls   Some firewalls use an architecture known a *stateful inspection,* which is essentially a cross between a network-level firewall and an application-level firewall. Stateful inspection works like packet filtering but provides better security because it examines application-level information within IP packets, such as the source and destination IP addresses, the port, the type of request, and keeps track of a connection's context. Stateful inspection is a powerful technique because it can verify that a request directed at a specific port, SMTP (tcp port 25) for example, is actually an SMTP connection and not a hacking attempt.

General Firewall Considerations   Once you have selected the proper firewall architecture for your network environment and security requirements, there are some general guidelines you should follow regardless of the firewall you implement. They are as follows:

- Remember the principle of least privilege. Configure your firewall to block every-thing and then allow access to only those packet types and ports required to support the applications (for example, FTP, Telnet) that you need.

- Be sure to filter the ports used for NetBIOS traffic, 137 UDP, 138 UDP, and TCP 139. Filtering these ports will disallow traffic flow between NetBIOS and TCP/IP.

- Bind only TCP/IP to the NIC connected to the Internet, and if the host directly connected is running Windows NT, disable IP routing so your internal network is isolated from the Internet.

- Keep any information that needs to be accessed from the untrusted network between your firewall and your Internet router.

- Choose an IP address pool for your trusted network that is likely to be in use on the Internet. Because existing routes point to the other network, it eliminates the chance of the routes pointing to your network.

- Run only the services that you absolutely need. The fewer services running, the less likely mistakes or security holes will allow your security to be exploited.

In addition to the basic requirements previously listed, The National Computer Security Agency (NCSA) has devised a rather rigorous testing and certification plan for firewalls. Before you purchase a firewall, I'd strongly recommend that you read this document, which can be found at **http://www.ncsa.com**.

Firewall Vendors Table 13.5 lists a variety of firewall and proxy server vendors.

Table 13.5 Firewall Vendors

Company	Contact	Product
Check Point	www.checkpoint.com	FireWall-1
Digital Equipment Corporation	www.dec.com	AltaVista Firewall
McAfee Associates	www.mcafee.com	PCFirewall
Microsoft	www.microsoft.com	Internet Access Server
Network-1 Software	www.network-1.com	FireWall/Plus for Windows NT
Raptor Systems	www.raptor.com	Eagle NT
Secure Computing	www.sctc.com	Sidewinder Security Server

From Here...

According to the NCSA, security is not a one-time event. It is a continual process, and this is especially true when talking about Internet Security. It is an ongoing and evolving process, and you must remain constantly vigilant, both in testing your systems and in learning about new technologies. As technology changes, so do the methods hackers use. It's a constant battle, and ignorance is the worst security problem of all.

Now you know the basic issues you must address to ensure the security of your Windows NT systems (and the networks to which they connect) when connecting to the Internet, including basic TCP/IP architecture and services, Firewalls, Internet Mail Connector for Exchange Server security, and Internet Information Server security.

This chapter only scratches the surface of Internet security; in fact, entire books have been written on this subject. For more detailed information on Internet security, check out the following books:

- *Actually Useful Internet Security Techniques*, Larry Hughes, New Riders, ISBN: 1562055089.
- *Internet Firewalls and Network Security*, Hare & Siyan, New Riders, ISBN: 1562056328.
- *Internet Security : Professional Reference*, Atkins, Buis, Hare, New Riders, ISBN: 1562055577.

Part
IV

Ch
13

For more information on the Windows NT security concepts discussed in this chapter, see the following chapters:

- Chapter 2, "An Overview of Microsoft Windows NT Security," provides a comprehensive overview of Windows NT security and is an excellent place to start.

- Chapter 4, "Windows NT Domain Concepts," explains the intricacies of the Windows NT domain model.

- Chapter 6, "User Account Security and Windows NT," explains how Windows NT uses the Security Accounts Manager, user names, and passwords to authenticate users.

- Chapter 7, "New Technology File System (NTFS) Security," shows you how to secure your directory structure and the files it contains from intruders.

CHAPTER 14

Internet Security and BackOffice

The Microsoft BackOffice suite is a set of complementary applications built upon the Windows NT Server framework that provides unprecedented power, connectivity, and security for enterprise-wide information storage, processing, and distribution.

With the recent inclusion of Internet-enabled applications such as Microsoft Exchange Server and Internet Information Server, Internet connectivity, messaging, and information publishing has never been easier! However, just by virtue of connecting to the Internet, you are opening up your systems to a number of potential security holes. This chapter helps you shore up your defenses when connecting BackOffice applications to the Internet. ■

What is the Microsoft BackOffice suite?

Microsoft's BackOffice suite is an incredibly powerful bundle of enterprise applications that provide extensive Internet connectivity and capability right out-of-the box. Learn what these tools are and how they can help you.

Understand and use Internet Information Server (IIS)

Internet Information Server is the keystone of BackOffice's Internet capability. Understanding the services it provides are key.

Securing Internet Information Server's Web server service

IIS's Web server service is a robust, full-featured Web server that ships with Windows NT and enables you to get your company on the Web with minimal effort.

Securing Internet Information Server's FTP server service

Like the Web Server service, the FTP service is powerful, easy to use, and best of all it's FREE. Learn the tips and tricks you need to know.

Securing SQL servers

Microsoft SQL server, when combined with IIS' Web service, is a potent combination for Web publishing. See how to ensure the security of your SQL servers connected to the Internet.

Microsoft BackOffice: One Big Happy Family

Microsoft BackOffice is a suite of world-class products built upon the foundation of Windows NT Server and designed with synergy and security in mind. Each product leverages the capabilities and functionality of the other products to provide seamless integration and unparalleled power. The current release of BackOffice, version 2.5, includes the following:

- Windows NT Server 4.0, which includes Microsoft Internet Information Server 3.0, Microsoft Index Server 1.1, and FrontPage 1.1.
- Microsoft Exchange Server 5.0.
- Microsoft SQL Server 6.5.
- Microsoft SNA Server 3.0.
- Microsoft Systems Management Server 1.2.

While each of the included applications can stand on their own and are competitive in their own right, Microsoft has leveraged the tight integration, seamless connectivity, and complimentary nature of the applications by selling them as a suite—a tried-and-true model proven through the incredible success of Microsoft Office.

Microsoft BackOffice enables you to create, manage, and publish online information, communicate with customers, and build a line of business applications. The BackOffice family is designed to meet the complex and varying needs of businesses of all sizes and shapes. Additionally, BackOffice includes an integrated installation utility that helps you select the proper options for your site.

Let's take a quick, 10,000-foot aerial view of the individual applications before we examine the unique security considerations each one presents.

N O T E The products that are part of the BackOffice suite are changing constantly. For the latest information regarding BackOffice, see **http://www.microsoft.com/ backoffice**.

Windows NT Server 4.0

As you know by now, Windows NT Server 4.0 is Microsoft's latest incarnation of its popular 32-bit *Network Operating System (NOS)*. Windows NT is a robust, scalable, and secure NOS that provides basic file sharing, printing, and workstation connectivity ser-vices. It also serves as a powerful and extensible application server upon which BackOffice applications can be built.

Microsoft Internet Information Server 3.0

Over the last couple of years, Microsoft has made a concerted effort to "Internet-enable" their applications. Microsoft Internet Information Server (IIS) is the culmination of this effort, and it is included with Windows NT Server 4.0.

IIS provides basic Internet functionality, including the following:

- Full-featured Web server.
- *File Transfer Protocol (FTP)* Support.
- Gopher support.
- Support for the *Common Gateway Interface (CGI)*.
- Support for Active Server Pages, which makes posting dynamic content quick and easy.
- Built-in search engine (Microsoft Index Server).
- Easy Integration with other BackOffice applications, such as SQL Server.
- A secure platform that supports log-on validation, ACLs, SSL 2.0, SSL 3.0, and PCT.

IIS is an excellent platform for publishing information to the Internet, as well as for building a corporate Intranet. When combined with Index Server and SQL Server, it provides one of the most full-featured and secured systems available today.

Microsoft Index Server

Microsoft Index Server is a component of Windows NT Server version 4.0 that works hand-in-hand with IIS to allow you to perform full-text searches and retrieve virtually any type of information through a Web browser. It includes support for Hypertext Markup Language (HTML), text, and naturally, all Microsoft Office documents in their native format. It is a powerful addition to the BackOffice family and allows your organization quick and easy access to all of the documents stored on your intranet or Internet site.

Microsoft Exchange Server 5.0

Microsoft Exchange Server 5.0 is an industrial strength, client/server messaging and groupware solution that was designed to replace the Microsoft Mail product line. In addition to seamless integration with its sibling, Exchange Server, it provides the following features:

- Directory architecture based on X.500 specification.
- Native Windows NT security.

Part
IV

Ch

- Digital signatures and encryption provided by Key Management component.

- Connectors provide easy and effective connectivity to other messaging systems such as the Internet, X.400, MS-Mail and cc:Mail.

- Directories can be synchronized between Microsoft Mail 3.x or cc:Mail and Exchange.

- Exchange Client runs on all Microsoft operating systems.

- Microsoft Schedule+ delivers powerful, user-friendly calendaring and scheduling features.

- Exchange 5.0 now has POP3 support.

- Microsoft *Exchange Forms Designer (EFD)* provides simple application development capabilities.

Microsoft SQL Server 6.5

Microsoft SQL Server is a mature, full-featured relational database management system (RDBMS) that is designed around the Windows NT Server framework. Its many features include the following:

- Transaction processing and distributed transactions.

- Stored procedures.

- Data replication to heterogeneous ODBC subscribers.

- Referential integrity.

- Dynamic Locking.

- Web Assistant enables you to generate HTML from SQL Server databases.

- Isolation of business rules.

- A secure platform that takes advantage of Windows NT security.

- Supports industry standards, including ANSI SQL-92 and FIPS 127-2.

- Graphical administration tools.

Microsoft SNA Server 3.0

Microsoft SNA Server provides connectivity to IBM AS/400 and IBM mainframe computers. Clients running MS-DOS, Windows, Windows for Workgroups, Windows NT, Macintosh, UNIX, or OS/2 can use SNA Server to "see" host computers, which allows organizations to leverage legacy data.

Microsoft Systems Management Server 1.2

Microsoft Systems Management Server (SMS) allows network and system administrators to administer centrally an entire network. This includes the administration of each node and the software on all computers. Specifically, SMS is designed to support the following:

- Hardware and software inventory management.
- Automated software installation and distribution.
- Remote system troubleshooting by enabling an administrator to control the keyboard, mouse, and screen of any computer on the network that's running MS-DOS or a Windows operating system.
- Network application management.
- Network protocol analysis.

SMS simplifies the administrative tasks associated with these important functions.

BackOffice Security Overview

Microsoft BackOffice provides robust network security because it is fully integrated with the Windows NT Server model. It provides the following advantages:

- The administrator has complete control over users' access and privileges to any and all applications through the User Manager for Domains application.
- Users only need one account and password to log on to any of the BackOffice applications.
- Passwords are encrypted as they are transmitted over the network.
- Knowledge of security on Windows NT can be leveraged across the entire product suite.

While native Windows NT security is sufficient for most installations, many of the BackOffice products provide additional security features, such as data encryption and digital signatures that significantly can bolster your security. Coupling BackOffice's additional security features with the native security that Windows NT provides makes for a secure environment.

However, connecting BackOffice systems to the Internet exposes you to new security concerns that require additional planning and security measures. Let's examine how to secure your BackOffice products when connecting to the Internet.

Part
IV

Ch
14

Security and Exchange Servers Acting as SMTP Hosts

Over the last decade or so, electronic mail (e-mail) has become one of the most ubiquitous and mission-critical services that organizations provide to users. The phenomenal growth of the Internet, which largely has been fueled by e-mail, is driving the requirement for many businesses to get connected to the Internet.

Microsoft Exchange Server is an excellent client/server messaging platform that takes advantage of Windows NT's native security to provide a powerful, robust, and secure messaging environment for your trusted network that includes digital signatures and encryption. Additionally, Microsoft Exchange Server provides easy administration and seamless integration with all of the most popular e-mail systems and protocols such as cc:Mail, MS-Mail, *Simple Mail Transfer Protocol (SMTP)*, and X.400.

There are two basic ways to use Exchange Server with the Internet:

- Sending Internet Mail through the *Internet Mail Connector (IMC)*.
- Providing Exchange client access over the Internet.

Each of these options presents a number of security challenges that you'll explore in this section.

Using the Internet Mail Connector   The *Internet Mail Connector (IMC)* is the Microsoft Exchange Server component that enables Exchange users to send and receive SMTP messages. It adheres to RFC 821, which defines the SMTP server-to-server protocol and RFC 822, which defines the message format and supports file attachments through both *Multipurpose Internet Mail Extensions (MIME)*, defined in RFC 1521 and UUENCODE, defined in RFC 1154.

> **N O T E**   RFC stands for Request For Comments, which according to FOLDOC are "One of a series, begun in 1969, of numbered Internet informational documents and standards widely followed by commercial software and freeware in the Internet and UNIX communities. Few RFCs are standards but all Internet standards are recorded in RFCs."

Additionally, the IMC provides SMTP transport, message routing, translation, and delivery functions. It can be configured as an SMTP client, an SMTP server, or both. When configured as a server, the IMC waits for incoming messages from other SMTP hosts. As a client, it initiates a connection to an SMTP host so that it can transfer outgoing messages.

You'll need to familiarize yourself with the Internet Mail Connector's Properties dialog box and its many tabs to configure it correctly and securely. To access the IMC's Properties dialog box, start the Exchange Administrator and in the left pane, double-click

Connections. Then in the right pane, double-click Internet Mail Connection. Figure 14.1 shows the IMC's Properties dialog box.

FIG. 14.1

The Internet Mail Connector Properties dialog box is the key to configuring your IMC.

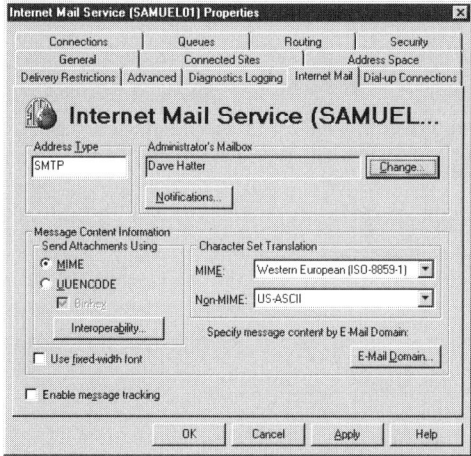

Before you can use the Internet Mail Connector, there are several things you'll need to do. First, you must have the TCP/IP protocol installed and configured on the Exchange Server. Second, you need to know whether you are using *Domain Name Service (DNS)* or not.

If you are using DNS, you need to know the IP address of your DNS server so that the IMC can query it to resolve names to IP addresses. You also need to add an A or Address record to DNS so that the addresses in a mail message can be resolved and messages can be routed to the proper host. For example, if the host name is SAMUEL01, the domain name is Hatter.com, and the IP address is 8.8.8.1, you enter the following A record to DNS:

        Samuel01.hatter.com   IN   A   8.8.8.1

You also should consider adding an MX or mail exchanger record to DNS. This often results in faster name resolution on DNS queries. Using the same information in the preceding example, the MX record looks like this:

        Samuel01.hatter.com   IN   MX   10   8.8.8.1

If you are not using DNS, you need to update the local Hosts file (found in <winroot>\ system32\drivers\etc) on the Exchange Server to specify the IP address and domain name of all of the SMTP hosts to which you will transfer mail. Also, you need to update the hosts file on all remote hosts that will transfer mail to this Exchange Server. The

Part

IV

Ch

14

following is an example of the entry you need to make on a remote host to transfer mail to the Exchange server named Samuel01:

Samuel01.hatter.com

After you complete these tasks, there are a few additional things you need to do to complete your Exchange Server configuration. The following is a list of these procedures:

- Create an Address Space.
- Configure Site Addresses.
- Assign an Administrator's Mailbox.
- Choose to Deliver all messages to a single host or to deliver messages by using DNS.

Upon completion of these tasks, you'll have the minimum configuration needed to use the Internet Mail Connector. Next, you should take time to examine the three most common IMC configuration scenarios.

Common Internet Mail Connector Configuration Scenarios   There are three basic ways to implement the Internet Mail Connector, as follows:

- Exchange routes mail directly to the Internet.
- Exchange routes mail through an existing SMTP Host.
- Other systems route SMTP mail through Exchange.

Regardless of the configuration that is best for your organization, you need to familiarize yourself with the Connections tab of the Internet Mail Connector Properties sheet shown in Figure 14.2.

FIG. 14.2

The Connections tab allows you to configure routing options.

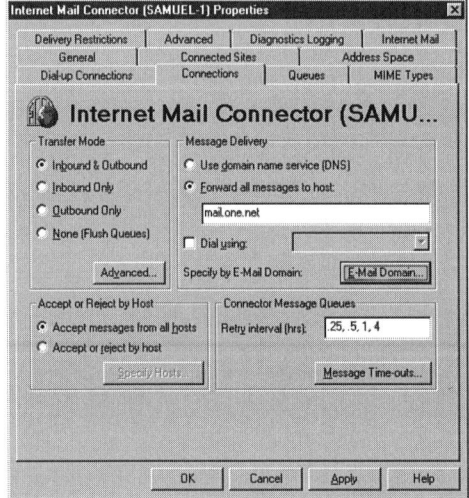

Now let's take a look at how each scenario works. You should be thinking about your particular system and what would work best, as you review each method.

Exchange Routes Mail Directly to the Internet It's easy to configure Exchange and the Internet Mail Connector so that Exchange becomes your SMTP host, sending and receiving mail directly from the Internet. In this scenario, when a message is bound for a remote host, the Internet Mail Connector can use either an internal or external DNS server to resolve names and deliver mail to the specified SMTP servers, or the IMC can use the local hosts file to resolve the IP addresses of the remote host. Figure 14.3 illustrates this scenario.

FIG. 14.3
Exchange Server with
an internal DNS
Server routing mail
directly to the
Internet.

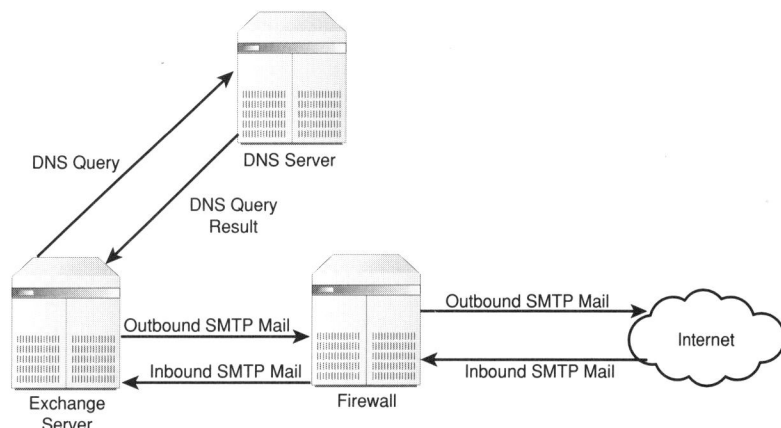

Exchange Routes Through an Existing SMTP Host In many organizations, SMTP mail systems have been implemented prior to Exchange. In this scenario, you configure the IMC to receive inbound mail and to route all outbound mail through an existing SMTP host (see Figure 14.4).

You set up this scenario the same way you set up the first scenario, with one difference: In this scenario, the Internet Mail Connector Connections forward all mail to the specified SMTP host, which then delivers the mail. You can accomplish this through the Internet Mail Connector Connections property page. Select Message Delivery and forward all messages to one host, and then enter the IP address of the SMTP host.

FIG. 14.4
Exchange Server
routing Internet mail
through another SMTP
server.

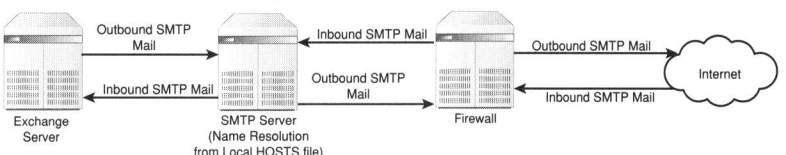

Part
IV

Ch
14

Other Systems Route SMTP Mail Through Exchange   The third option is to have an Exchange Server route all Internet mail for other Exchange and SMTP servers in your site. In this scenario, you have all of your other hosts pass mail to the Exchange Server, which resolves external addresses and routes the mail. You can see this scenario in Figure 14.5.

FIG. 14.5
Exchange Server routing all SMTP mail to the Internet.

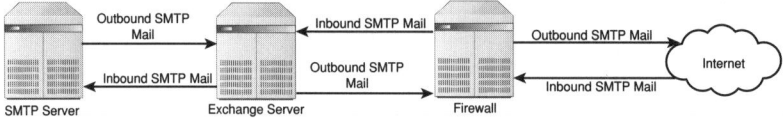

Before you even think about installing the IMC and connecting your Exchange Server to the Internet, you must consider security. E-mail, by virtue of its incredible success, is one of the most tempting targets for hackers. Take a look at how you can secure your Internet mail with Exchange.

SMTP Related Security Risks   E-mail systems are not only at risk from the types of attacks we have previously discussed, such as a malicious intruder who corrupts system files or a SYN-Flood attack on port 25 (the default SMTP port); they also can fall prey to certain mail oriented attacks such as:

- *Data Theft/Tampering*   By *sniffing* packets or intercepting messages in transit, an attacker could read and possibly even modify data.

- *Mail Forgery*   A hacker forges e-mail messages so that they appear to have come from someone/somewhere else.

- *Denial of service*   A hacker can tie-up your system or network by flooding it with mail messages (frequently referred to as *Mail Bombing*) that fill up the queue and consume precious CPU cycles and network bandwidth.

- *Viruses*   Modern e-mail makes it easy to send file attachments that an unsuspecting user may execute and thereby infect their systems.

Internet Mail Connector Security Features and Considerations   As with Windows NT, Microsoft built Exchange Server from the ground up with security in mind, and the Internet Mail Connector is no exception. For example, its store-and-forward, client/server model uses proxying by design, so a separate proxy server is unnecessary when Exchange is configured properly.

You can take advantage of Exchange's many built-in security features (configured through the IMC's Properties dialog box shown earlier in Figure 14.1), and you can implement firewall technology to increase the security of your SMTP messages and your Exchange

Server when connecting to the Internet. Some of the most useful techniques are listed here, as follows:

- Build a Network Level firewall that acts as a screening router between the untrusted network and the Exchange/IMC server, and build another screening router between the Exchange/IMC server and the trusted network. Remember to allow TCP connections to and from port 25.

- Install Exchange and the IMC on a dual-homed gateway or a bastion host that routes mail between your organization and SMTP hosts on the Internet. Make it a dedicated mail server with no user mailboxes.

- Reject messages by IP address. The IMC accepts incoming connections from any IP address by default. If your IMC only communicates with specific SMTP hosts, configure it to reject connection attempts from other IP addresses. This makes it difficult for hackers to get in from the Internet. Figure 14.6 shows the Connections tab of the Internet Mail Connector Properties page.

- In the Accept or Reject by Host section, click the Accept or reject by host option button and then click the Specify Hosts button to add hosts that you can and cannot receive messages from.

- Transfer modes. Select the transfer mode in the Connections property page. The Internet Mail Connector can be set up to accept inbound messages, send outbound messages, or both. This feature also is accessible from the Connections tab.

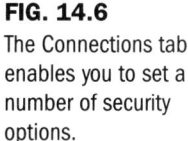

FIG. 14.6
The Connections tab enables you to set a number of security options.

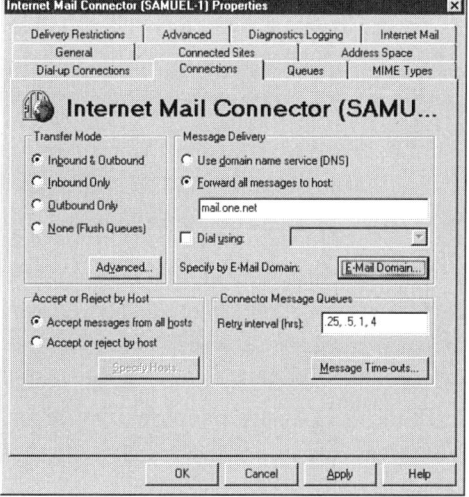

Part
IV

Ch
14

■ Set message size limits. The IMC can be configured to limit the size of incoming and outgoing mail messages. If an incoming message exceeds the size limit, the IMC discards any remaining data. This can help prevent or lessen the impact of a mail-bombing attack.

■ Set delivery restrictions. You can restrict which users in your organization have permission to send mail through the Internet Mail Connector.

■ Configure one IMC for outgoing mail that only initiates connections and one for incoming mail that only accepts connections from a trusted host.

■ Unbind unneeded services from your NICs. TCP/IP is the only protocol you will need to bind to the NIC connected to the Internet.

■ Use NTFS for the Exchange Server's file system. NTFS provides secure access to the SMTP messages that are written to disk.

■ Message Tracking. You can take advantage of the message tracking capabilities in Microsoft Exchange Server to locate messages across Internet Mail Connectors.

■ Diagnostic Logging. The Windows NT Event log provides basic event logging. Protocol logging is helpful for troubleshooting IMC problems but can impact performance.

You also will want to familiarize yourself with and take advantage of the security features found on the Security tab of the Internet Mail Service Properties dialog box. Using this feature, you can create a Windows NT user account that has very limited access in your network which can then be used for all outbound SMTP connections. Once you have created the account, on the Security tab, enable the Secure Outbound Connections check box and then enter the information for the account you created. Figure 14.7 illustrates how to do this.

If you communicate with multiple external domains, you can use the Specify by e-mail domain button to set a secure account for each domain. You also can enable Show in each message to make it show in a mail message that is an Internet message.

Exchange Client Access over the Internet   Another way to use Exchange Server with the Internet is to allow users to access their Exchange Server over the Internet. The Exchange Server uses *Remote Procedure Calls (RPCs)* to communicate with the Exchange Server, so it's easy to configure this option. However, allowing clients to access the Exchange Server over the Internet is somewhat more risky than allowing only SMTP connections.

FIG. 14.7
The Security tab allows you to ensure the security of outbound connections.

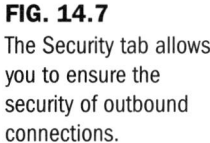

Internet Mail Service (SAMUEL01) Properties

| General | Connected Sites | Address Space |

Delivery Restrictions | Advanced | Diagnostics Logging | Internet Mail | Dial-up Connections

Connections | Queues | Routing | Security

Internet Mail Service (SAMUEL...

☑ Show in each message whether that message came from the Internet

☑ Secure outbound connections

Default Windows NT account for all connections

Windows NT account: SMTP

Windows NT domain: HATTER

Password: ××××××

Confirm password: ××××××

Specify by e-mail domain: [E-Mail Domain...]

[OK]   [Cancel]   [Apply]   [Help]

The Exchange Server uses Windows NT's Security Accounts Manager database to authenticate all RPCs, so only an Exchange client with a valid Windows NT account and the appropriate access rights can log on and gain access to a mailbox or folder. But, enabling RPC access to the server that holds user mailboxes means opening a hole in your security, because you must enable additional TCP/IP ports. A mistake in configuration could allow an attacker to gain access to the Exchange Server, compromising mailboxes and public folders. Let's look at how you can configure this access correctly and securely.

Exchange Client's RPCs are directed at port 135, which is the Windows NT RPC End-Point Mapper service. Once connected to this port, the End-Port Mapper tells the Exchange client which port numbers to use for access to the Exchange Server directory and information store.

Because the ports are assigned dynamically, if you use Windows NT's native filtering capabilities, or if you're using a packet-filtering router as a firewall, you will have problems getting connected. However, you can force Exchange Server to use fixed ports for RPCs. You simply add two REG_DWORD values called TCP/IP port to the registry that contains the port number you opened in your packet filter. For the directory, the value should be under the following key:

Part
IV

Ch

14

- HKEY_LOCAL_MACHINE\SYSTEM\
  CurrentControlSet\Services\MSExchangeDS\Parameters\TCP/IP port.

  For the information store, the value should be under the key below:

- HKEY_LOCAL_MACHINE\SYSTEM\
  CurrentControlSet\Services\MSExchangeIS\ParametersSystem\TCP/IP port

You then configure your packet-filtering router to allow TCP connections to port 135 (the RPC End-Mapper Service), and you are ready to commence with Exchange Client communications over the Internet.

To further enhance the security of an Exchange Client connection over the Internet, you can enable RPC encryption on the client to completely secure the client/server communication. To configure your Microsoft Exchange client for encrypted RPC communication do the following:

- Select Tools, Services which will display the Services dialog box.
- Select the Microsoft Exchange Server service and click the Properties button.
- In the Microsoft Exchange Server dialog box, click the Advanced tab to see the options displayed in Figure 14.8.

FIG. 14.8

The Advanced tab enables you to configure network security for Exchange clients.

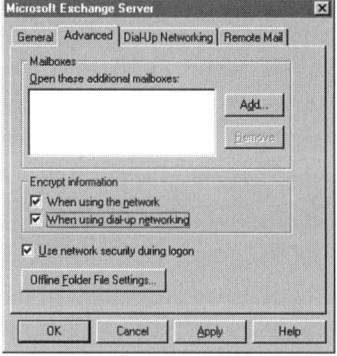

In the Encrypt Information section, you can click "When Using the Network" and "When using dial-up networking" to encrypt RPC's communications.

 T I P If you plan to use the Internet for Exchange Client connectivity, you must specify the server name in such a way that it can be resolved over the Internet. You'll need to specify the fully-qualified domain name of the server, such as aegis.definiti.com or you can use an IP address such as 10.10.10.10.

Exchange Server Advanced Security   Out-of-the box, Microsoft Exchange Server provides a very secure messaging platform, but if you need ultra-high security for your mail messages, you can implement Advanced Security. Unfortunately, for advanced security to be effective, the sender and the recipient both must be using Exchange Server as their mail platform and must be certified by the same Key Management server. What this means is that you can use this technology to secure your Internet mail to non-Exchange users, or users who are not using advanced security.

However, you can use this powerful technology to secure your mail messages transmitted to other Exchange users if you use the Internet as a conduit to connect your Exchange client to your Exchange Server. Here's how it works.

Microsoft Exchange Server Advanced Security is based on public/private key technology and involves both the Exchange Server and the Exchange Client. It provides two additional security features: data encryption and digital signatures.

N O T E   Exchange Server supports the *Data Encryption Standard (DES)* that is based on a 56-bit key and was developed by the U.S. Government and the CAST encryption algorithm, which can use a 40-bit or a 64-bit key. According to existing government regulations, DES and 64-bit CAST only can be used in North America.

Encryption is the process of using a public key to convert plain-text (your mail message) into ciphertext (scrambled gobbledy-gook) that only can be decrypted by the intended recipients with the appropriate key. In an Exchange environment using Advanced Security, a message is encrypted when sent and decrypted when received.

A digital signature is a generated code based on the message contents and appended to the mail message. When the recipient receives the message, the process is reversed (known as verifying) and if the two codes are equal, it indicates that the data has not been corrupted and that it came from the given sender. As with encryption, a message is signed when sent and verified when received.

In order to make this possible, Exchange uses keys to sign and encrypt messages. Each Exchange mailbox receives two pairs of keys; each pair contains a public and private key. One pair is used for encrypting and decrypting messages while the other pair is used for signing and verifying messages.

The public encryption key is used to encrypt a message, and the recipient's private encryption key is used to decrypt the message. The private signing key is used to sign a message, and the public signing key is used to verify the sender of the message, as well as verify that the contents of the message have not been altered in transit.

Part

IV

Ch

14

To use the Advanced Security features of Exchange Server, you must configure an Exchange Server as a Key Management server that becomes responsible for the following services:

- Creates public and private encryption keys.
- Certifies public signing and encryption keys.
- Stores backup copies of private encryption keys and public signing keys.

N O T E Private keys are stored on the user's local disk in an encrypted security file with the .EPF extension.

Once private encryption keys and public signing keys are generated for users, they are stored in the Key Management server's key management database, which also is encrypted, making it very difficult for the security of the keys to be compromised.

Additionally, each public key must be certified by the Certification Authority component of the Key Management server. A key is certified to indicate that it is a valid, secure key and then is bound to the user's mailbox.

N O T E Each user configured for advanced security has two certificates: an encryption certificate that contains the user's public encryption key and a signing certificate, which contains the user's public signing key.

Once the Key Management server is configured and running correctly, you'll need to enable advanced security for your users, which can be done either by the administrator through the Exchange Administrator interface, or individually by each user through the Exchange client software.

N O T E For more information on Exchange Server Advanced Security, see Chapter 3 in the *Microsoft Exchange Server Concepts* manual and Chapter 6 in the *Microsoft Exchange Server Planning Guide.* You will also find the *Microsoft Exchange Server Administrator's Guide* very helpful.

Security and the Internet Information Server (IIS)

Microsoft Internet Information Server (IIS), included with Windows NT Server 4.0 (also available at **www.microsoft.com**), is a powerful and popular member of the BackOffice family that enables you to get your organization "serving up information" on the Internet with a minimum of effort (see Figure 14.9). IIS includes the following features:

- World Wide Web Service (HTTP)

- FTP Service

- Gopher Service

- Internet Service Manager

- Internet Database Connector

- Microsoft FrontPage

- Graphical Administration Interface

FIG. 14.9

The IIS Service Manager's interface is powerful and easy to use.

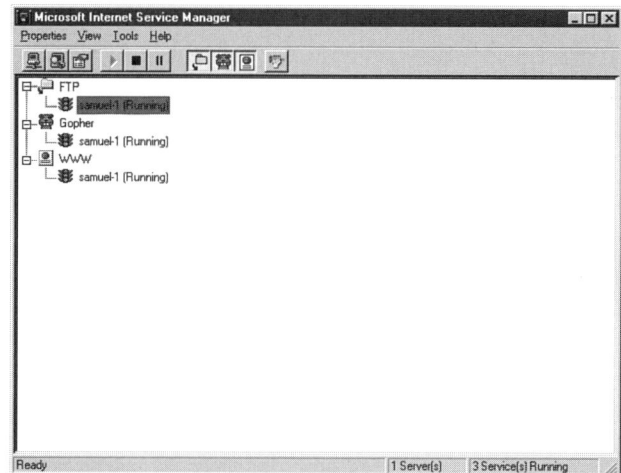

As with the entire BackOffice suite, IIS was built from the ground up around the Windows NT architecture. It runs as a set of Windows NT Server services, allowing it to leverage the Windows NT features such as Performance Monitor, Server Manager, User Manager, the Security Accounts Manager, and Auditing.

However, security remains a key issue that must be addressed to ensure the integrity of your data. IIS meets the challenge with authentication, access control, and audit capabilities that are both ample and robust, because IIS is built upon the foundation of the Windows NT server operating system. In addition, it includes Secure Sockets Layer support to keep secure communications private by encrypting the conversation between IIS and all browsers that support SSL.

Hackers know that most Web and FTP sites allow anonymous access (meaning that anyone can gain access and have limited permissions) and are often configured incorrectly so that security holes exist. What you need to do to ensure that IIS keeps your network and data secure from hackers follows.

Part
IV

Ch
14

Using Existing Windows NT Security to Secure IIS   As noted earlier, IIS provides security through the Windows NT security model, which means that user accounts and groups defined in the Security Accounts Manager database will determine what users can do once they are connected to the IIS machine. It's critically important for you to check not only existing account rights and permissions, but also to restrict the rights and permissions of the accounts used for Anonymous access.

By design, IIS' three services share many of the same security options, so we'll cover those that are shared together. The options that are specific to each service are covered individually later in this section. Figure 14.10 illustrates how all of the IIS services handle a service request.

FIG. 14.10

Internet Information Server's security model.

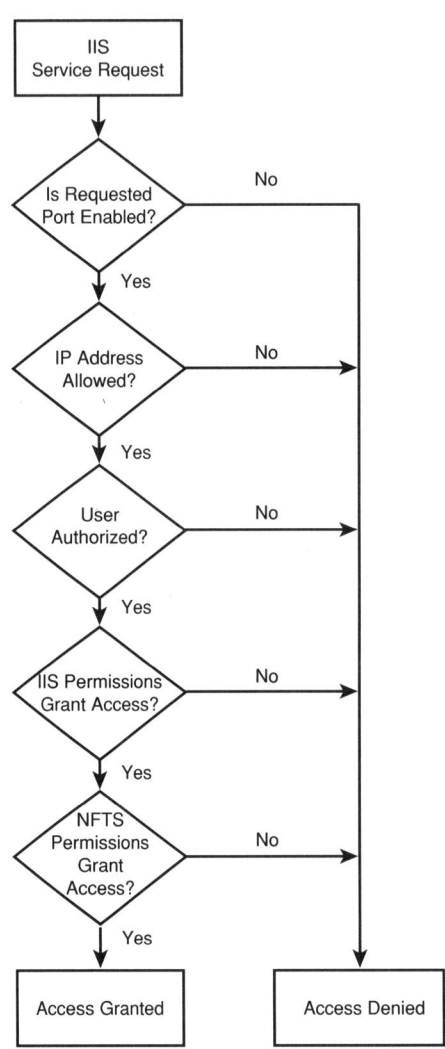

Logging All of the IIS Services support extensive logging capabilities, and it's important to enable logging so you can keep an eye out for suspicious activity, to determine what content should stay and what should go, and for capacity planning. Figure 14.11 displays the contents of a daily log file.

Enabling logging is easy and the events of each service are shared in a common file. To enable logging, open the IIS Manager, and double-click the server for which you want to start logging, which displays its Properties dialog box. Then click the Logging tab that displays the options shown in Figure 14.12.

FIG. 14.11
The IIS log files contain a plethora of valuable information about each request.

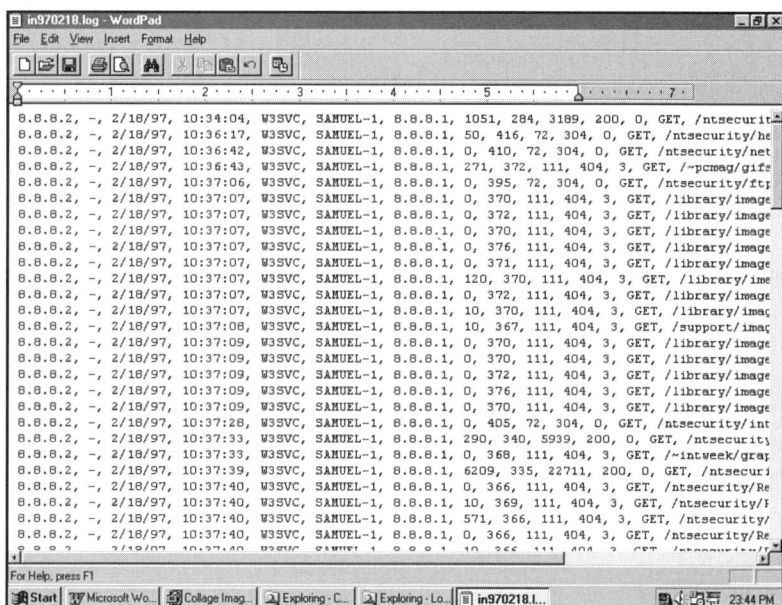

FIG. 14.12
The Logging tab enables you to configure the level of logging you need for each service.

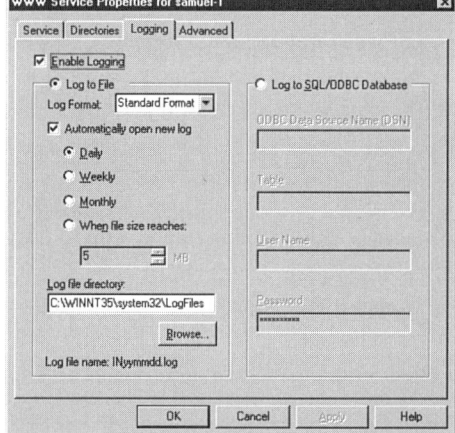

Part
IV

Ch
14

This tab is fairly straightforward—you just click the Enable Logging option. You then can opt to log to a text file, a SQL database, and how often the log files should start anew.

 TIP   When you first set up your server, configure Daily Logging so you can see results each day. Over time, you can determine what the proper logging options are for your installation.

Advanced Options   The IIS also supports simple filtering through the Advanced tab of a services' Properties dialog box. You can use the Advanced Options tab to limit or grant access to the Web Server by IP Address. Figure 14.13 displays the Advanced tab of the WWW Service Properties dialog box.

FIG. 14.13

The Advanced tab enables you to perform access control by filtering certain IP addresses.

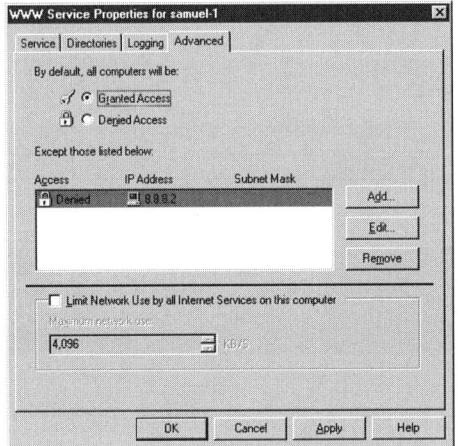

Enabling By default all computers will be granted access (which is the default) allows you to use the Add button to add specific IP addresses or ranges of addresses to which access should be denied. In Figure 14.13, you can see that all computers except 8.8.8.2 will be allowed access.

Alternatively, if you want to enforce tight security, you can choose By Default all computers will be denied access and then define a list of hosts by IP address that should be able to access this machine. This is a powerful and useful tool that can help ensure the security of your site, and it should not be overlooked.

Advanced Security for IIS   As with Exchange Server, the Internet Information Server provides several advanced security features that enable you to provide extremely secure communication. They are Secure Sockets Layer (SSL) version 2.0 and 3.0, which provide data encryption, server authentication, and message integrity for a TCP/IP connection; and *Private Communications Technology (PCT)* 1.0.

The goals of both SSL and PCT are to keep communication secure by doing the following:

- Ensure Private Communications over the Internet
- Verify identity of both clients and servers on the Internet
- Control access to information and resources
- Ensure software accountability and integrity

Secure Sockets Layer   *Secure Sockets Layer (SSL)* is a protocol developed by Netscape Communications Corporation and submitted to the World Wide Web Consortium (W3C) as a standard for secure communications over the Internet. When a client supporting SSL (Internet Explorer 2.0 and 3.x and Netscape 3.x) connects to a server that supports SSL, a "handshake" takes place during the TCP/IP connection that performs authentication and determines the level of security that will be used during communication.

After the connection is established, SSL then encrypts and decrypts the data passed by the application protocol being used. All the information in both the request and the response are fully encrypted, including the *Uniform Resource Locator (URL)* the client is requesting, data submitted through a form (such as your address or credit card numbers), any authentication information (user names and passwords), and all the data returned from the server to the client.

SSL is layered beneath application protocols such as HTTP, and SMTP is layered above the connection protocol TCP/IP. Figure 14.14 shows where SSL fits in the TCP/IP architecture.

FIG. 14.14
The SSL protocol rides between the application protocol and the transport protocol in the TCP/IP model.

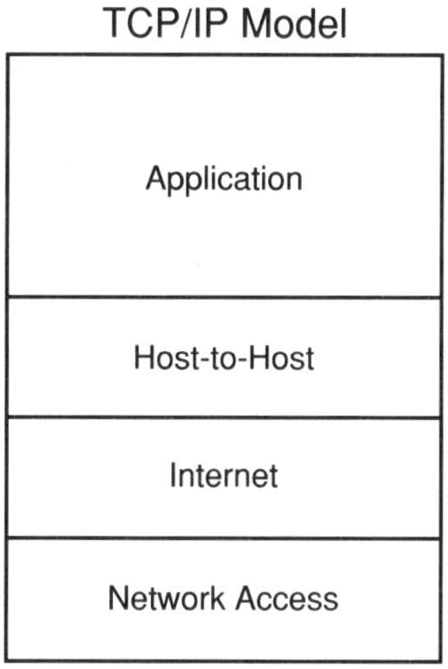

TCP/IP Model

| Application |
| Host-to-Host |
| Internet |
| Network Access |

Part
IV

Ch

14

Microsoft Internet Information Server supports the *HyperText Transmission Protocol Secure (HTTPS)* access method. Although SSL can provide virtually unbreakable encryption, SSL-encrypted transmissions are slower than unencrypted transmissions. So, to prevent performance degradation for your entire Web site, consider using only SSL for virtual folders that deal with highly sensitive information, such as a form submission containing credit card information.

 TIP You can enable SSL security on the root of your Web site (\InetPub\Wwwroot by default) or on one or more virtual folders. Once SSL is configured and enabled, only SSL-enabled clients are able to communicate with the SSL-enabled WWW folders.

Enabling SSL security on a Web server requires the following steps:

1. Use Key Manager to generate a key pair file and a request file.
2. Obtain a certificate from a certificate authority.
3. Install the newly obtained certificate on your server.
4. Activate SSL security on a Web service folder.

 TIP Microsoft recommends that you use separate directories for secure and public content. For example, C:\InetPub\Wwwroot\Secure and C:\InetPub\Wwwroot\Public.

Generating a Key Pair for IIS   The good news is that generating a key pair for IIS is pretty easy, as the Key Manager component is integrated into the new IIS interface. You can either double-click the Key Manager icon in the IIS submenu, or you can click the Key Manager icon on the Internet Service Manager tool bar, which displays the Key Manager dialog box shown in Figure 14.15

After you have launched the Key Manager applet from the Key menu, click Create New Key, which displays the dialog box shown in Figure 14.16.

Simply fill in the requested information and when the form is complete, click OK. You then are prompted to retype the password you entered to confirm it. Your new key is generated, and a dialog box appears to explain what you need to do to obtain a certificate.

After reading all of the information, you need to save your new key, choose Commit Changes Now from the servers menu and when prompted to save changes, choose OK. Your new key will appear in the Key Manager window under the name of the computer for which you created the key. By default, a key is generated on your local computer, although you can create the key on another computer.

N O T E   Do not use commas in any field, as they are interpreted as the end of that field, and they generate an invalid request without warning.

FIG. 14.15
The Key Manager interface is easy to use.

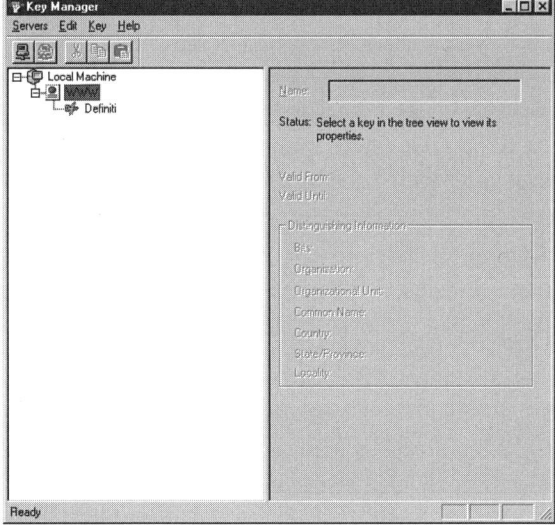

FIG. 14.16
The Create New Key and Certificate Request dialog box creates a new key and a file that you can use to request a valid certificate.

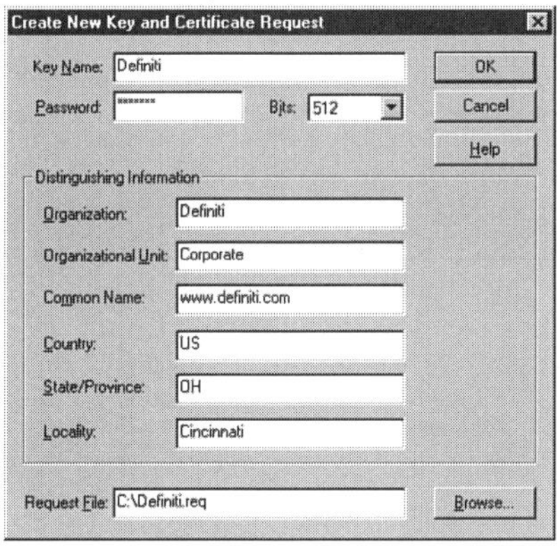

You are now ready to request a certificate from a third-party certificate authority.

Obtaining a Certificate The key generated by Key Manager is not valid for Internet use until you obtain a certificate for it from a Certificate Authority, such as VeriSign. Send the certificate request file to the Certificate Authority to obtain a valid certificate. Until you do so, the key exists on its host computer but cannot be used. To obtain a digital certificate, visit the VeriSign Web site at **http://www.verisign.com/microsoft/** and follow the instructions given there.

Installing Your New Certificate When you have received your digitally signed certificate, you'll need to install it in the Key Manager. From the Key Manager, select the key pair that matches your signed certificate (or click the hand holding a key icon on the toolbar), and from the Key menu choose Install Key Certificate.

Part
IV

Ch
14

N O T E If you are hosting multiple Web servers with the Virtual Server capability of IIS, you'll need to specify an IP address of a particular server while installing your certificate. Otherwise, the same certificate is applied to all virtual servers created on the system. ▨

You need to select the certificate file from the list and click Open, which causes the Key Manager to prompt you for the password that you used in creating the key pair. At this point, the key and the new certificate are combined and stored in the registry of the server. Choose Commit Changes Now from the Server menu and click OK when prompted to commit changes, and then you are finished!

Enabling SSL   Once you have applied the certificate, you must enable the SSL feature from Internet Service Manager. SSL can be required on any or all virtual folders in your Web site. It is configured on the Directories property sheet of the WWW Service Properties sheet. To require SSL communications, double-click the WWW service in the Internet Service Manager, which displays its property sheets, then click the Directories tab, which displays the property sheet shown in Figure 14.17.

FIG. 14.17

The Directories tab of the WWW Service Properties sheet makes it easy to configure SSL security.

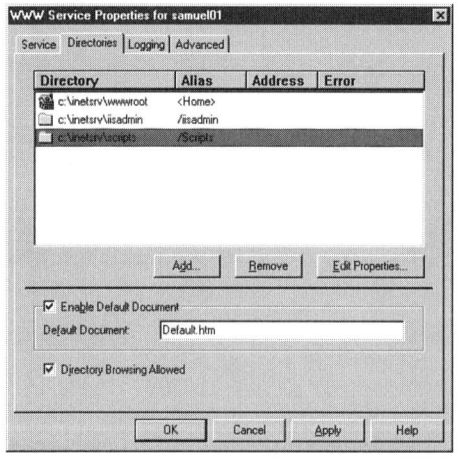

N O T E If you enable SSL, any URLs that point to documents on a SSL-enabled WWW folder must use **https://** instead of **http://** in the URL. Any links using **http://** in the URL will not work on a secure folder. ▨

From the Directories property sheet, choose the folder that requires SSL security and click Edit Properties, which displays the Property sheet shown in Figure 14.18.

From the Directory Properties dialog box for any directory that should support SSL, select the Require secure SSL channel option, and then click OK, and all requests for access to that directory will require SSL.

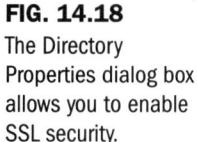

FIG. 14.18

The Directory Properties dialog box allows you to enable SSL security.

Private Communications Technology The Private Communications Technology (PCT)protocol secures communications on the Internet through features such as privacy, authentication, and mutual identification. According to Microsoft's Web site, PCT enhances SSL because it solves serious security problems with SSL. Additionally, PCT enhances authentication and protocol efficiency by separating authentication from encryption. This allows applications to use authentication that is significantly stronger than the 40-bit key limit for encryption allowed by the U.S. government for export. Microsoft's implementation of PCT is backward-compatible with SSL.

PCT provides secure communications between two applications (a client and a server), as well as authentication. PCT necessarily requires a reliable transport protocol such as Transmission Control Protocol (TCP)for data transmission and reception.

PCT is protocol-independent; an application protocol such as FTP can ride transparently on top of the PCT protocol, which makes it easy to use. A PCT communications session begins with a handshake phase that authenticates the client to the server (and optionally vice-versa) and negotiates an encryption algorithm based on certified public keys. Once the client and server agree, all data is encrypted using the session key negotiated during the handshake. Additionally, PCT verifies the integrity of messages using a hash function-based *Message Authentication Code (MAC)*.

The PCT protocol is completely compatible with SSL, and servers implementing both protocols can distinguish between PCT and SSL clients because PCT uses a different handshaking method. Some of the many organizations supporting PCT are Cylink Corporation, FTP Software Inc., Internet Shopping Network, NetManage Inc., OpenMarket Inc., Spyglass Inc., and Starwave Corp. For more information on PCT, please visit **http://www.microsoft.com/intdev/security**.

Part
IV

Ch
14

General IIS Security Tips In addition to the features and issues we've already covered, there are some additional things you can do to ensure the security of your network when using IIS to publish information to the Internet at large. They are the following:

- Create separate partitions for the system partition and each of the IIS services so that a hacker cannot gain access easily to the entire machine from a hole-in-one service.

- Use NTFS for all partitions of the machine and make sure that the user rights are set correctly.

- Put the IIS server in its own Domain and set up a one-way trust with your accounts domain. If a hacker can get the information for a valid account, that account won't grant access in your user domain.

- Use separate accounts for each of the Internet services (if you plan to run more than the Web server). This makes it easier to track what users are doing.

- Check and then double-check the rights and permissions assigned to the accounts designated for Anonymous access. Assign the minimum permissions a user will need, normally this will be read.

- Store only non-confidential information on your IIS machine and put it outside the firewall. This will ensure that if its security is compromised, the hacker will still have to breach the firewall.

- Use Windows NT Server's TCP/IP filtering on the server, only allow connections to the ports you need for IIS's services. For example, if you intend only to run the Web server, only enable port 80.

- If users will be accessing the server with any accounts other than the "Anonymous" account, be sure to require authentication via an encrypted password!

Now let's take a look at some of the service-specific security issues and settings.

Security and the Web Server The World Wide Web Server included with IIS is a powerful, full-featured tool that stacks up well against its competition. It is optimized for performance and runs as a service under Windows NT Server, providing fast, easy, and secure Web publishing on virtually any scale, from a small corporate Intranet to the global Internet user base with a minimum of skill and effort.

The IIS Web Service includes the following features:

- Virtual Directories, which make publishing documents on remote servers easy.

- Extensive, comprehensive logging capability, which enables you to track what users are doing, as well as analyze usage and plan capacity.

- Integration with Windows NT administrative tools such as Performance Monitor and Event Viewer.

- Full CGI capability.

- Full Internet Server Application Programming Interface support.

- Virtual Server capability, allowing multiple Web sites to be hosted on one Windows NT Server. For example, two Web sites, **www.acme.com** and **www.xyz.com** appear to be different sites, but they really are hosted on the same server.

- Integrated Windows NT security that can be configured to require User ID's and passwords for user authentication before protected documents can be accessed.

- Support for the SSL, which provides transparent encryption for Internet communications.

- Easy configuration and management through the Internet Information Server Manager application.

How the Web Server Works   When a user with a Web browser attempts to gain access to content on your Web server, they enter an URL that tells the browser how to get the information being requested. The browser then initiates a conversion with the Web server. The following is a brief synopsis of what happens during this process:

1. A user enters the URL **http://www.definiti.com** and presses enter.
2. The browser then attempts to resolve the URL entered to an IP address by querying a DNS.
3. If the domain name is found, DNS returns the IP address and the browser attempts to connect to port 80 on the identified host.
4. If the host accepts Anonymous requests (most do) and the requested document is not stored in a secured partition, the server returns the requested document. If Anonymous access is not allowed, or the requested document has been secured, the user is required to enter a valid user ID and password.
5. The browser renders the document for the user based on the HTML tags in the document. If graphics are included, they are downloaded separately.

Securing the Web Server   To ensure the security of your Web site and its content, as well as the security of your network and its resources, there are some things you should do that are above and beyond those we have already mentioned if you plan to set up a Web site.

Part

IV

Ch

14

N O T E   Because the configuration of the three services provided by IIS is very similar, this book covers the Web server in detail and then only examine the differences in the FTP and Gopher servers.

User and Password Authentication   First and foremost, you need to understand the significance of "Anonymous" access and take precautions to ensure that the account you create for anonymous access has the appropriate permissions. To configure the type of access users will have to your Web server, from the IIS Manager, double-click WWW to expand your Web server(s) and double-click the Web server, which displays the WWW Service Properties dialog box (shown in Figure 14.19).

FIG. 14.19

The WWW Service Properties property sheet makes it easy to control access to your Web site.

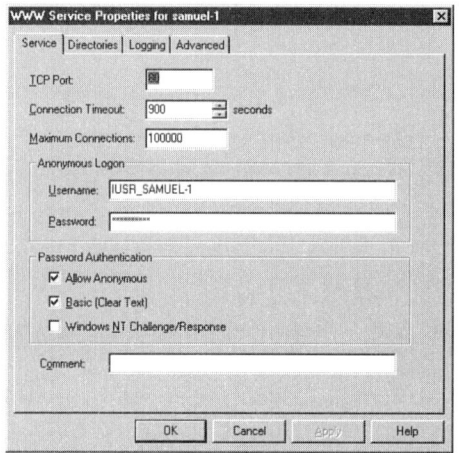

As you can see in Figure 14.19, there are a number of options you can set for the Web Server service. For most installations, the default options are fine. However, there are two critical settings that will determine what level of access users will have to the Web site: Anonymous Logon and Password Authentication.

If you want to allow access to the general public, be sure you allow Anonymous Access. By default, when IIS is installed, a new user account is created in your user database with the name IUSR_ and the name of the server it's installed on. For example, IUSR_SAMUEL-1 if the server's name is SAMUEL-1. When the account is created, it is given limited access rights, and is added to the groups Domain Users, Guest, and Everyone.

Additionally, the IUSR_ account is granted the right to Log on Locally. All Web users must have this right, because their request is passed to the Web Server service, which uses their account to log on, which then allows Windows NT to assign the appropriate access rights.

If you want all users to be authenticated based on a specific user account and password, you can simply clear the Anonymous Logon option, which will require each user to enter a valid User ID and password before they are able to access resources on the server. This has the added benefit (if you have logging enabled) of seeing who is accessing the Web server and what they are doing.

The other key setting that determines the security of your site is the type of password authentication you want to use, which is determined in the Password Authentication section. For maximum security, you can enable the Windows NT Challenge/Response option, which encrypts your User ID and password before transmission, ensuring the security of the account information across the wire. Unfortunately, only Microsoft Internet Explorer 2.0 and above support this functionality.

If you need to support a mixed environment of browsers, choose Basic (Clear Text), which sends the user name and password as easily readable text. If you choose this option, IIS displays the dialog box shown in Figure 14.20 to warn you that this is a less secure method.

FIG. 14.20

IIS's warning message about Clear Text authentication.

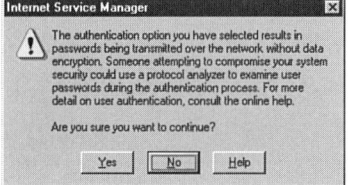

Virtual Directories Configuring the directories that the Web server can see and the appropriate level of access also is an important step toward ensuring the security of your site.

When you first install IIS, by default, it creates a directory called InetPub (older versions were installed InetSrv) for itself and then creates root directories for each of the Internet services it provides. The Web server's root directory (by default) is wwwroot, which is where your home page should be by default. You then can use the Directories tab to add new directories for storing additional content. For example, you might create a subdirectory under wwwroot for all of your graphics.

When you add a new directory, you can define five levels of access: Read, Execute, Require Secure SSL Channel, Enable Client Certificates, and Require Client Certificates, as shown in Figure 14.21.

Part

IV

Ch

14

FIG. 14.21

The Directories Properties tab enables you to set tight security options on each directory.

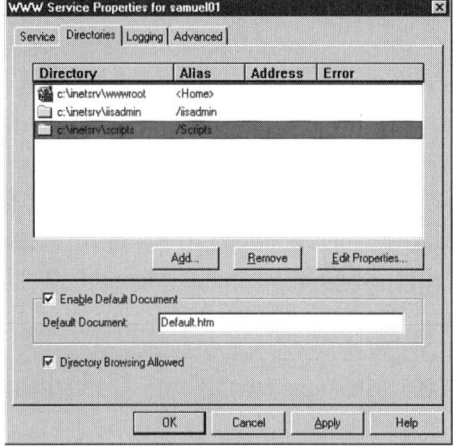

To allow Web users to view the content of files in a directory, enable the Read option. If the users are using CGI scripts or other programs, enable the Execute option, which enables them to run programs; however, enabling Execute without read access doesn't enable users to view the contents of a directory. This is important if you have a directory that contains scripts; users should be able to run a script only when called directly through the browser—they should not be able to go in and look around to see what they can run!

The other three options—Require Secure SSL Channel, Enable Client Certificates and Require Client Certificates—all pertain to advanced security features that require additional software. See the earlier section on Advanced Security and IIS.

Web Server Security Tips   If you are running the Web server, there may still be a few small security holes for you to fill, even if you take all of the precautions covered so far. The following is a list of some general things you should do when providing Web services:

- Disable mappings for .bat and .cmd files. It may be possible for a hacker to run executable programs on the Web server if they can get to these files. You can do this by turning off read permissions in any directory that contains scripts.

- Always store your scripts and data in different directories, and be sure that the directories containing scripts have only execute access.

- Disable Directory Browsing Allowed. This feature, when enabled, presents a browser with a hypertext list of files in a directory, allowing a hacker to meander through the files in a directory.

- Avoid using Remote Virtual Directories. Be sure to install all of the executables for IIS, as well as all data, on the same machine and use NTFS to secure it. When a user attempts to access documents from a remote directory, the user name and password entered on the properties page always will be used, possibly circumventing access control lists.

- Be careful when writing and implementing CGI scripts. Skilled hackers may be able to use poorly written CGI scripts to gain access to your system.

- Be sure to enable logging and look for suspicious activities such as failed logons in the log and the Event Viewer.

- Remember the principle of least privilege. If you are planning only to run the Web server, enable only port 80 on the Web server host.

- Thoroughly test your Web server—try to find and plug any holes. Better yet, have trusted, knowledgeable colleagues try to breach your security.

- As an additional resource, check the NCSA Web Site Certification Program documentation at **www.ncsa.com/webcert/sgl_site.html** for guidelines to make your Web server secure.

Security and the FTP Server   The FTP Service included with IIS is a powerful addition to your Internet arsenal, providing features such as Anonymous Logon and virtual directories. It provides a proven interface for uploading, downloading, and manipulating files on the FTP server regardless of their format. While much of the functionality of the FTP server provides overlaps with the Web server, it is the only IIS service that allows users to transfer files to your server over the Internet

Securing the FTP Server   For the most part, configuring FTP security is similar to the Web Server service. You can enable logging and filter access by IP address and configure user log-on authentication. There are a number of things you should do when implementing the FTP service to ensure the security of your network. The following sections form a a checklist of security items you should consider and implement.

User and Password Authentication   Just like the Web Server, users can be permitted to log on Anonymously. You need to take precautions to ensure that the account that you create for anonymous access has the appropriate permissions. Configuring access to your FTP server is pretty easy. From the IIS Service Manager, double-click FTP to expand your FTP server(s). You can then double-click the FTP server, which displays the FTP Service Properties dialog box (shown in Figure 14.22).

Part

IV

Ch

14

FIG. 14.22

Configuring FTP access control is easy through the FTP Service Properties.

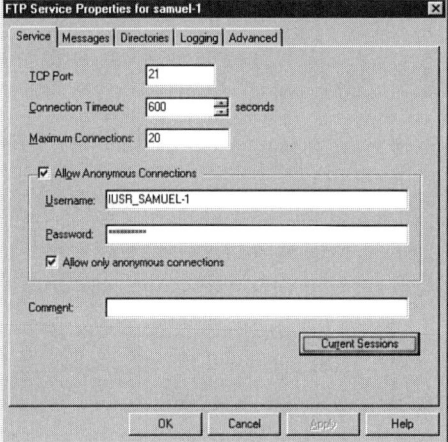

Like the Web server, you can configure the FTP server to allow anonymous log on, or you can require users to log on with a valid account.

> **CAUTION**
>
> Remember that user names and passwords will be transmitted to the FTP Server service in the clear (not encrypted), which means that someone with a network sniffer could trap this information and compromise your security!

If you want to allow access to the general public, enable the Allow Anonymous Connections option, and choose the IUSR_ account created when IIS was installed. If you want users to be authenticated based on a specific user account and password, you can clear the Allow Anonymous Connections option, which will require each user to enter a valid User ID and password before they are able to access any resources on the server.

While requiring a valid account has the added benefit (if you enable logging) of seeing who is accessing the FTP server and what they are accessing, you inadvertently could allow a hacker to gain valid account information. You need to weigh this option carefully.

You also can enable the Allow only anonymous connections to ensure that users cannot log on with an account other than the account specified for Anonymous Logon.

 Get familiar with the Current Sessions button on the FTP Service Properties sheet. It tells you which users are connected to the FTP server, when they connected, and for how long they have been connected.

Virtual Directories   Configuring the directories on the FTP server is pretty much identical to the Web server service. Be sure that users cannot get access to directories above the FTPRoot directory and that permissions are set correctly for FTP directories.

FTP Messages   The FBI suggests that any system containing data that needs to be secured should have a warning message telling hackers that only authorized users are allowed to access the system. This is done because in the past, most systems had a Welcome message and hackers used the Welcome message as a legal loophole, claiming that because they were welcomed to the system, it must be OK for them to go on in and explore.

To configure the welcome and exiting messages for your FTP server, choose the Messages tab on the FTP Server Services properties sheet, shown in Figure 14.23.

FIG. 14.23
The FTP Server has a number of message options.

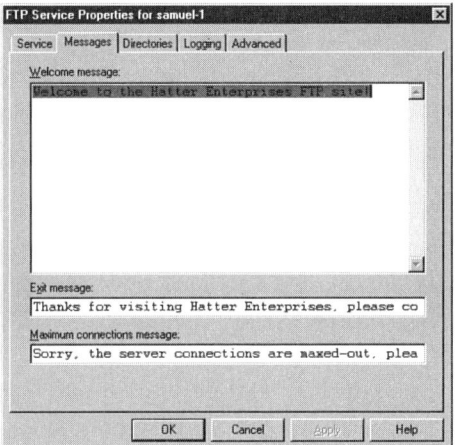

You can enter a welcome message that displays when a user establishes a connection to your FTP server and an exit message that displays when the user terminates the session. You also can have a Maximum connections message that displays when the maximum number of connections is reached on the server.

FTP Server Security Tips   The following is a list of some general things you should do to provide security when running FTP services:

■ Remember that users can change directories on the FTP server. Be sure that they cannot get into directories above the FTPRoot directories, and use NTFS to ensure the security of your server.

- Avoid using Remote Virtual Directories. When a user attempts to access documents from a remote directory, the user name and password entered on the properties page will always be used, possibly circumventing access control lists.

- Be sure to enable logging and look for suspicious activities such as failed logons in the log and the Event Viewer.

- If you only are planning to run the FTP server, enable only ports 20 and 21 on the FTP host.

- Thoroughly test your FTP server and try to find any holes. You also can have a trusted, knowledgeable colleague try to break in.

Security and the Gopher Server   Gopher is a distributed document retrieval system that provides a menu of documents that may be a plain text file, sound, image, submenu, or other Gopher object type. The primary functionality Gopher provides has been largely supplanted by the Web.

Securing the Gopher server is much like securing the FTP and Web services. The primary difference is that the Gopher server allows only Anonymous login.

Security and Publishing SQL Server Data with IIS

World Wide Web technology is cool and powerful, but static Web sites become "cobweb sites" quickly. The capability to easily and effectively publish data from legacy and client/server databases is becoming increasingly important, and Microsoft has made it easy.

Microsoft has come to the table with two tools to publish data from SQL Server (or any ODBC database). They are the following:

- *Internet Database Connector*   An excellent tool for dynamically manipulating SQL data. It is included with IIS.

- *SQL Server Web Assistant*   Enables you to publish SQL data on a schedule. It ships with SQL Server 6.5.

These tools help you solve two key business problems: how to publish database information on a Web page, and how to allow users to submit queries and input data using a Web browser instead of a custom database front-end.

From a security standpoint, as with all its siblings in the BackOffice suite, SQL server is built upon the Windows NT Server foundation and can take advantage of the native security it provides. Also, when you connect a SQL Server to the Internet, there are some special things you should consider to ensure the security and integrity of your data. You can examine those items closely throughout the remainder of this chapter.

N O T E If you elect to serve up SQL Server data on the Web, you'll need to purchase a special
license pack called the SQL Server Internet Connector. This is required whether the
Web server is IIS or a third-party product; whether the Web server runs on Windows NT Server or
another operating system; whether the Web server is on the Internet or on your company's
intranet; or whether the access is performed by a service such as IDC or methods such as
Common Gateway Interface (CGI) scripts. ▤

Security and the Internet Database Connector with SQL Server The *Internet Database
Connector (IDC)* is a cool and powerful new integral feature of Microsoft Internet
Information Server (see Figure 14.24). It is designed for SQL programmers with little
HTML experience. The IDC uses standard SQL queries, making it easy to create Web
page content dynamically from a database. Each request for a Web page causes a query
to be executed, and HTML is then dynamically generated using the query results.

FIG. 14.24
The Internet Database
Connector makes it
easy to access SQL
Server data.

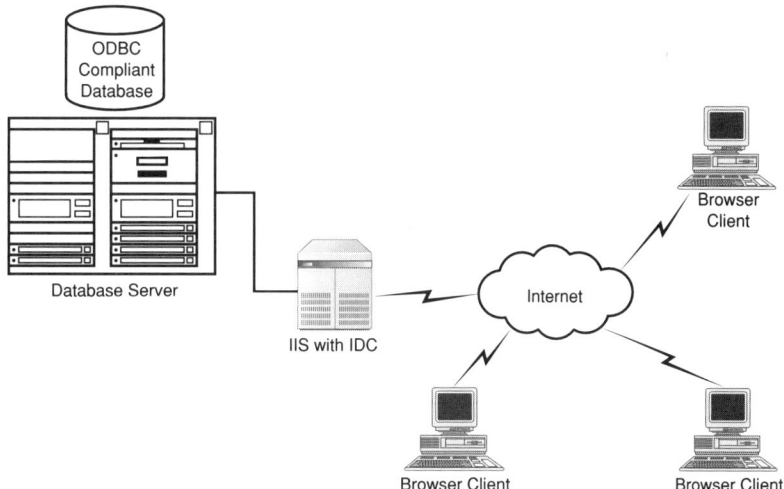

An IDC application consists of two documents: an .IDC file that contains the query information, and an .HTX file that is a standard HTML file with special syntax for referencing
the query results. When a user requests an IDC document, the associated query is run
and the HTML page displays the results.

To use the Internet Database Connector, simply complete the following steps:

▤ You need to purchase Microsoft SQL Server Internet Connector which is an add-on
product for customers connecting a Microsoft Internet Information Server or any
equivalent third-party Web server to Microsoft SQL Server. It allows an unlimited
number of Internet and intranet connections to a single Microsoft SQL Server.

Part
IV

Ch
14

- Install IIS on a Windows NT Server computer running TCP/IP.

- Use a text editor to create the .HTX file containing HTML code and the .IDC file containing the name of the ODBC data source, SQL statements that manipulate information, and a reference to the .HTX file.

- Create a Web page with a link that references the .IDC file. When the user clicks this link, IIS notifies the IDC about a request. The IDC checks the appropriate .IDC file to locate the ODBC data source, sends the SQL statements, and receives the results, which are then merged with the .HTX file to create a new Web page that is served up to the user.

You're ready now to use the IDC to manipulate SQL Server data. First, consider how you should secure your databases. Naturally, you need to start by ensuring that you take all of the normal security measures needed for connecting a Windows NT Server to the Internet, such as the following:

- Using NTFS partitions

- Granting users minimum levels of access required to complete daily tasks

- Enforcing password and log on policies

- Auditing

- TCP/IP filtering

- Firewalls and proxy servers

When all of the Windows NT Server security measures are in place, you can use the following list of items to increase the security of your SQL Server data:

- Users must have permission to access the .IDC and .HTX files in order to manipulate data. If you grant anonymous access, the IUSR_computername account, or the account specified for anonymous access, must have permission to access these files.

- An .IDC file lists a user name and optionally, a password, which must be valid for the SQL Server database you want to access. If the .IDC file doesn't contain a user name and password, the user name and password from IIS are passed through to the SQL Server database.

- Running SQL Server and IIS on the same machine enables you to use Integrated SQL Server security to pass encrypted user names and passwords for database access. However, if you are using integrated SQL Server security, you don't need to provide a user name and password in the .IDC file.

- Remember that Windows NT user names must strictly adhere to SQL Server integrated security name rules. Underscores, dollar signs, and pound signs are not permitted, which means that the default account IUSR_computername cannot be used for SQL Server access.

Security and the SQL Web Assistant IIS   The SQL Server Web Assistant configures SQL Server periodically to publish data to the Web either by scheduling a task or creating a trigger. At the scheduled time, or when the trigger is tripped, the Web Assistant automatically creates Web pages by inserting SQL query results into an HTML table.

According to Microsoft's Web site, "The SQL Server Web Assistant is the perfect tool for generating intermittently updated HTML documents." Rather than executing a query that causes a Web page to build dynamically, users access a static page that was previously built by the Web Assistant. This method is much faster than having a Web page generated dynamically, and SQL Server manages the currency of the content without further user intervention.

N O T E   The SQL Server Internet Connector is required in conjunction with any Microsoft or third-party Web server, CGI, BGI, or ISAPI application that connects to a SQL Server.

To use SQL Server Web Assistant you need to do the following:

- Install and configure SQL Server 6.5.
- On a 32-bit SQL client, launch the SQL Server Web Assistant and create a new query from the Query screen.
- Use the Scheduling screen to schedule the frequency of the query.
- Create a file name and add formatting and options to the HTML file that will be generated. You can use the File Options and Formatting screens to accomplish this.

Once you have completed the configuration, at the scheduled time, or when a the specified trigger value changes, SQL Server will re-execute the query and build a new HTML file based on the results.

From Here...

As mentioned in Chapter 13, "Overview of Security and the Internet," security is not a one time event—it is a continual process. You should ensure the security of your corporate data by testing your site every time you install a new application or change security settings. It also would be a good idea to test it on some regular basis just to verify its integrity.

In this chapter, you learned how to secure your Microsoft Exchange Server, Internet Information Server, and SQL Server by using the Internet Database Connector and SQL Web Assistant.

For more information on the security concepts discussed in this chapter, see the following chapters:

- Chapter 2, "An Overview of Microsoft Windows NT Security," provides a comprehensive overview of Windows NT security and is an excellent place to start.
- Chapter 4, "Windows NT Domain Concepts," explains the intricacies of the Windows NT domain model.
- Chapter 6, "User Account Security and Windows NT," explains how Windows NT uses the Security Accounts Manager, user names, and passwords to authenticate users.
- Chapter 7, "New Technology File System (NTFS) Security," shows you how to secure your directory structure and the files it contains from intruders.
- Chapter 13, "Overview of Security and the Internet," explores the many facets of securing Windows NT for Internet access.

CHAPTER 15

Windows NT Integration with NetWare and Other Network Operating Systems

With the growing popularity of Windows NT in the marketplace, it is important to understand the issues surrounding the integration of Windows NT into existing network infrastructures. Windows NT is rapidly gaining marketshare from competitors such as Banyan, Novell, and the number of UNIX vendors in the market today. Integration into a UNIX environment is discussed later in the book. Another place Windows NT is showing up is as an upgrade from peer-to-peer operating systems such as LANtastic, or even the peer-to-peer networking services offered by Windows 95. Security in mixed operating system environments can create some challenges not found in a homogenous Windows NT environment. This chapter discusses the integration of Windows NT into a LANtastic, Banyan, and Novell NetWare network. It also examines some of the security issues to watch out for during this integration. ■

Common cross-platform security issues

No matter what Network Operating System you use, there are some common security issues that should be explored. This chapter explains the most common ones.

Maintaining security in a mixed environment

When Windows NT is integrated into mixed network environments, the security considerations extend beyond the Windows NT operating system.

Windows NT and peer-to-peer operating systems

Peer-to-peer operating systems have their own specific security issues. Adding Windows NT to the environment can create additional considerations.

Windows NT and Banyan VINES

The first network operating system to introduce the concept of directory services, Banyan VINES has a number of services that can ease the introduction of Windows NT.

Windows NT and Novell NetWare

Novell NetWare is one of the most popular network operating systems on the market. As a result, integrating Windows NT and Novell NetWare is common.

Common Cross-Platform Security Issues

One of the critical issues to consider when dealing with cross-platform security is the problem of password synchronization. Depending on how Windows NT is deployed in your environment and the types of clients you employ, this synchronization of passwords can be tricky to implement. In some instances, such as Banyan's StreetTalk for Windows NT, Windows NT servers and Banyan VINES servers coexist in the same directory tree. Passwords for accessing any resource on a Banyan VINES or Windows NT server are the same. This is because the user is accessing the directory tree, not an individual server. The directory service maintains the access control for any resources in the tree. In a case where users are accessing a Novell NetWare 3.12 server and a Windows NT Domain, password expirations might need to be manually synchronized and users trained to manu- ally change passwords to ensure they remain synchronized, because presently there is no easy way to synchronize those passwords.

Another issue to consider when dealing with cross-platform security issues is the problem of maintaining multiple passwords. Take a case where a user is accessing a company-wide Windows NT Domain. Additionally, the department has a Banyan VINES server that hasn't been migrated to Windows NT yet. Because department servers are frequently maintained by department personnel, there is no easy way to synchronize password ag- ing, and password requirements can vary from the corporate system to the department server. How are the multiple passwords maintained, particularly when you add an e-mail password, a password to access the Internet, a mainframe password, and so on? In far too many instances, these multiple passwords are maintained by writing them on a note and sticking it to the side of the monitor.

A related issue along these lines is user ID synchronization. It becomes difficult for a user to securely track a number of different user IDs to access different operating systems within the company. For example, if the corporate Domain user ID standard is the first seven letters of the last name and first initial, as in CrensonC or HarrisH and the department server uses IDs such as TedN or JohnW, there can be an extra learning curve for new employees, as well as additional support costs maintaining multiple standards. The best way to handle these issues is through a sensible, well-maintained, updated, and enforced standards policy. Ideally this would be a company-wide standard, and it should be pretty rigorously enforced. This cuts down on the "passwords stuck to the monitor" syndrome and makes it easier for the end users to access multiple systems.

Another issue surrounding cross-platform security is providing access to multiple sys- tems. In some instances, providing end users with the most convenient access to multiple systems can cause a serious compromise in security. An example of this is the use of the Windows NT Gateway Services for NetWare in a Novell NetWare 3.12 environment. Windows NT Gateway Services for NetWare is discussed in greater detail later in the chapter, but the reason this can be problematic is that any user who is accessing the NetWare volume accesses it with the same rights as any other user. This means there is no way to granularize the user rights to any data stored on that volume; Jack the temporary hire has the same access as Jill the District Manager.

Yet another concern is *password caching*. If password caching is used, it means that the client workstation takes the passwords input by the end user and stores them somewhere on the hard disk. While this can save the user from having to type passwords repeatedly, it also means that anyone knowing the end user's ID can access network resources. Another problem with cached passwords is that they are stored on the hard disk. This means anyone who knows where to look can access the stored passwords. If they are stored in clear text, it is as simple as printing the file to get a list of that user's passwords. If they are encrypted, there are a number of shareware or freeware programs available on the Internet for decrypting those passwords. No good hacker's tool kit is missing a decryption tool these days.

A final issue with security in a mixed network environment is the varied levels of security each type of network provides. Some networks allow clear text passwords, while others do not. If users are synchronizing their passwords, and one of the operating systems passes clear text passwords, anyone with a shareware packet analyzer can compromise your entire network. Also, as the number of different types of systems proliferates, the number of special security issues inherent to each multiplies. If there is an issue with Banyan VINES and a specific IP socket, the network support and security people need to be aware of it and need to be able to patch it or work around it. Keeping track of all the issues for each operating system in a network can be a real support headache.

Additionally, the patch for a security issue that affects all the systems will need to be addressed differently. An example would be the packet spoofing issue that arose a couple of years ago. This was a case where it was found that by using a packet analyzer and some custom code, user sessions could be "hijacked" by spoofing the server into believing the unauthorized user was in fact an authorized user, with all the applicable permissions and capabilities. The patch for that issue in Novell NetWare was a series of NetWare Loadable Modules. In Windows NT that patch would have been in the form of a Service Pack or a Hot Fix. For Banyan, the patch would have taken yet another form. Being able to quickly address these issues in a multiple operating system environment is a constant challenge to corporate support personnel everywhere.

Maintaining Security in a Mixed Operating System Environment

Integrating Windows NT with other operating systems is relatively simple from a security standpoint. Windows NT supports the common security models, including passwords, file access, share access, and user profiles. The key to ensuring that Windows NT security is compatible with other systems is to develop a consistent, enforceable security policy for all systems. If password aging is set to 90 days for NetWare, the password aging for the Windows NT Domain shouldn't be 45 days. If a VINES password has to be at least seven characters, don't allow Windows NT passwords to be two characters in length. The best way to ensure your policy is usable is to use the three C's—be sure the policy is Clear, Communicated, and Checked. In order for people to follow a policy for any operating system, it must be clear. Encourage feedback on the policy from the administrators as well as some of the more technical end users. The best security police on earth is no good if end users are not aware of it.

One company had pages and pages of security policies in its Security Director's desk. The network administrators at branch offices had no idea what the policies were. As a result, many man hours went into reconfiguring servers throughout the country when the organization moved to a centralized support model. It turned out the Security Director had only sent the directives to a couple of key MIS managers, and they were never disseminated to the field. Simply communicating these directives would have saved a lot of time and money, as the central support people spent weeks bringing the branch offices up to the levels specified in the security directives.

Password security can be a significant issue when dealing with multiple systems. As discussed before, you should not allow clear text passwords if possible. Discourage the use of password caching.

When integrating Windows NT into existing environments such as Banyan VINES or Novell NetWare, both systems allow Windows NT servers to be integrated directly into the directory. In order to maintain the integrity of the existing infrastructure, it is critical that the Windows NT server is implemented carefully, by someone with the technical skills to complete the integration successfully. Don't hesitate to use outside consultants, or to borrow expertise from other departments to ensure that the implementation is successful. This integration is not a good place to start on-the-job training, especially where maintaining security is an issue. Another thing that helps with these types of implementations is to try it in the lab first. In many companies time constraints or lack of equipment can prevent the testing of these types of implementations, but this testing is strongly recommended whenever possible.

LANtastic and Windows NT Compatibility

A discussion of the specifics of LANtastic and Windows NT integration deserves a look at peer-to-peer operating systems in general. In a peer-to-peer network, each workstation in the network shares its resources with the other machines in the network. A collection of these machines is known as a *workgroup*. These machines share resources such as printers, modems, files, or CD-ROM drives. Figure 15.1 is an example of a typical four-computer workgroup, with resources such as hard disks, printers, and so on.

FIG. 15.1

Sample peer-to-peer network.

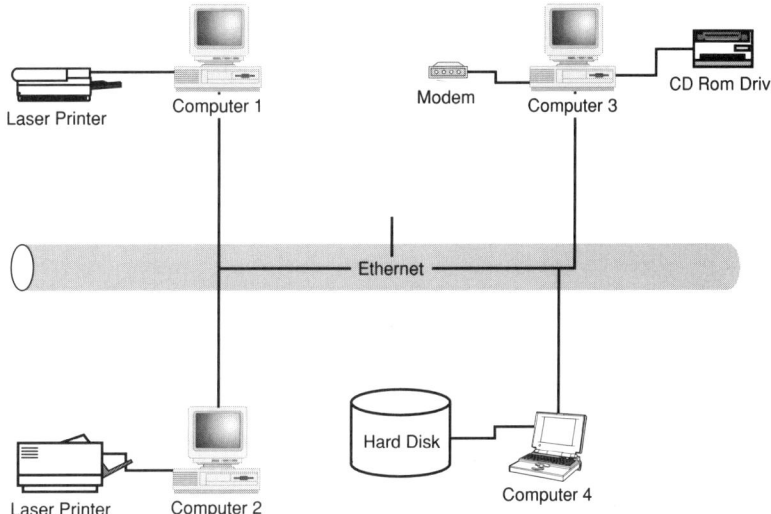

Laser Printer Computer 1   Modem   Computer 3   CD Rom Drive

Ethernet

Hard Disk

Laser Printer Computer 2   Computer 4

In the preceding example illustrated by the peer-to-peer figure, any of the machines in the workgroup would be able to access the hard disk of Computer 4. Likewise, Computer 1 could make its printer available to anyone in the Workgroup.

Now that you have a basic understanding of how peer-to-peer operating systems work, let's talk about some of the drawbacks of using a peer-to-peer operating system.

N O T E This applies to any peer-to-peer configuration, from Windows for Workgroups to Windows NT to Artisoft's LANtastic. ▦

The major security issue surrounding peer-to-peer operating systems is that because any user can make portions of their workstation available on the network, they have, in effect, a file server on their desk. This means you have put your end user in the position of being a systems administrator. And if your end user is a person who enjoys "experimenting" with the configuration of their PC, you can have some significant security concerns.

The potential for someone to accidentally allow access to areas that should remain secure or even to allow people to write data where it doesn't belong can be an embarrassment or worse. What happens if Sheila from Human Resources accidentally shares all the personnel files for the MIS Department? When Bill finds out how much the new guy makes, your boss will have the joy of participating in salary negotiations while you are looking for work. And let's not even think about what happens when Tim the temporary employee stores XXX JPEG files on the CEO's hard drive, and one of those files has a virus. Lots of people will be looking for work after that happens!

One additional challenge that peer-to-peer operating systems can cause is data integrity. Because of the distributed nature of data and resources in a peer-to-peer environment, ensuring that data is backed up regularly can be quite a challenge. Using a tape drive and reliable backup software in conjunction with a rigorous testing of the backups can alleviate this issue. The biggest problem with this scenario is the user that inadvertently turns off his or her PC when backups are scheduled, or the laptop user who is at home sick when you need the file that is on their D: drive. A good design can go a long way towards minimizing these problems.

Not to make it sound as if peer-to-peer operating systems are an inherently bad thing— when implemented correctly, peer-to-peer operating systems can be extremely secure, cost-effective, and a flexible solution for a department or small business. Many consider peer-to-peer operating systems ideal for a small office (25 users or fewer) where the cost and support overhead of a server-centric Network Operating System (NOS) make peer-to-peer look attractive. However, the 25-user number varies heavily from consultant to consultant. Some refuse to install more than 10 users in a peer-to peer-architecture, while others happily allow them to grow as large as possible. It is generally agreed that anything over 100 users is definitely too large for a peer-to-peer implementation.

You've learned about peer-to-peer operating systems in general; let's study the most popular in the field. Artisoft's LANtastic product is by far the most popular peer-to-peer operating system on the market today, boasting over five million users (discounting the peer-to-peer capabilities inherent in Windows for Workgroups, Windows 95, and Windows NT). Products such as Novell's Personal NetWare have been dropped over the past few years, leaving LANtastic the only major peer-to-peer operating system vendor on the market. In fact, Artisoft licensed the NetWare 4.x software for inclusion in their product line. Some of the features Artisoft brings to the table include modem and Internet access sharing, speed and ease of use, as well as being an all-in-one solution for sharing files and printers among Windows 95, Windows 3.x, and DOS PCs.

To successfully integrate Windows NT into this environment, there are a couple of things that must be considered. First, is the long range plan to migrate from peer-to-peer to a more server-centric model? Many would consider Windows NT a replacement for many LANtastic implementations. This replacement would require a Windows NT implementation to be designed and implemented. Users would be migrated from the peer-to-peer design to a login to the Windows NT Workgroup or Domain. Data also would need to be migrated from the distributed machines and placed on the centralized server. This simplifies access control and backup. In this model, LANtastic could be maintained for sharing resources such as printers and local CD-ROM drives, while Windows NT acts as a department or organization file server.

In the case of Windows NT and LANtastic coexisting in the same environment, the key to integrating the two is entirely in the client. Windows NT is not presently a supported operating system in a LANtastic network. So for Windows NT and LANtastic to coexist, the clients need to be either Windows 95 or Windows for Workgroups, which are capable of loading multiple clients. Given the many advantages of Windows NT over LANtastic, this situation generally arises as an intermediate step during the migration to Windows NT.

Working with Banyan VINES Security

Banyan VINES is a NOS that has its roots firmly planted in UNIX System V. Building on UNIX's excellent protocol support and scalability, Banyan added StreetTalk, a robust directory naming and messaging service. Boasting over 4 million users on some of the largest networks in the world, Banyan's StreetTalk directory service has long been the anchor of Banyan's networking strategy. The latest release of VINES, version 7.0, offers a number of enhancements to this mature operating system, most notably a new administrative tool, called StreetTalk Explorer, which simplifies the administration of file and print sharing, security, and the management of resources across heterogeneous networks including Windows NT and Novell NetWare. Banyan also has a number of directory services-enabled applications, such as backup and messaging that further enhance their NOS offerings. Because security is the topic of this book, however, it is the StreetTalk directory service.

StreetTalk Directory Service Structure

Banyan's StreetTalk directory service was the first distributed directory service on the market. According to Banyan, who first introduced the idea of directory services around ten years ago, it is in its third generation and is years ahead of its competition. Novell introduced their Novell Directory Services only a couple of years ago. Microsoft, the other major player in the NOS arena, has adopted and discarded several different strategies for implementing a true directory service but has yet to replace the Windows NT Domain architecture. The StreetTalk directory service enabled Banyan to capture a number of major WAN implementations, including the United States Marine Corps.

Why is a directory service important, particularly in the context of security? A true distributed directory service offers a greater measure of control than other methods on the market. In StreetTalk, each object in the network has a unique StreetTalk name, such as Dave Hatter@Marketing@Ajax Construction Company, or LaserJet IV@Dispatch@Ajax Construction Company. These unique names give StreetTalk a hierarchical directory structure, which means that Sales would be a logical grouping of objects below Ajax Construction Company in the StreetTalk directory. StreetTalk stores all of the users or devices information in its directory, which is a distributed database of objects. Every device in the StreetTalk network is an object with specific attributes, such as location in the network, security attributes, description fields, as well as any attributes specific to that particular object.

For example, a user might have different attributes than a printer or a server. The power of this is that instead of needing to know that the Sales server is at IP address 10.44.55.66, you just log in to the StreetTalk directory, and access Sales Server@Sales@Ajax Construction Company. This also simplifies administration of the network, particularly from a security standpoint. An administrator now has a single point of administration. No longer does a company with a number of locations need administrators at each location. This gives Corporate MIS much greater capability in designing and implementing policies and standards to enhance their Corporate security. Also, fewer administrators means fewer people with the powers of the administrator.

When an administrator of a VINES network needs to add a user, they assign the user an ID that is an object in the StreetTalk directory. This object is assigned a unique name, such as Henry Jones@Headquarters@Ajax Construction Company. This object is then assigned a host of attributes, including password, security access, phone number, location, and so on.

The other advantage which needs to be emphasized to really bring the advantages of a directory service home is the concept of a single point of log in to the network. What this means is that a user needs only to remember a single user ID and password. In architectures such as Novell's NetWare 3.x, every time a user wanted to access a resource on a different server, they had to have a user ID and password on that server. With

Windows NT, you log on to a Domain, which is a flat structure. All users and printers exist on the same level in a Domain. This can complicate administration if there are large numbers of users and printers to be managed.

Another value to the VINES single point of log in is that it is a single point of log in from anywhere on the network. If a user is a member of a Global Area Network, when they log in to the VINES network, they have access to the same resources whether they are in Bombay or Baltimore, Singapore or St. Martin.

Windows NT as a Banyan VINES Client

When integrating Windows NT and Banyan VINES, Banyan's first method of access was to enable Windows NT as a client in the Banyan StreetTalk network using their Enterprise Client for Windows NT client software. Today, Windows NT versions 3.51 and 4.0 are valid clients for a VINES network. All that is required is the 32-bit client software, and a user at a Windows NT machine is able to access VINES resources seamlessly as a client. Banyan has spent a great deal of time making these clients robust and feature-rich. Some of the features presently available with this client include full access to the VINES environment, including the StreetTalk directory structure, file and print services, messaging services, and VINES management utilities, such as StreetTalk Explorer, as well as support for multiple processors.

An additional feature of the client that is particularly useful when dealing with security is support for password synchronization between VINES and Windows NT log ins. But as robust as this client support is, there are not many people that would consider this true integration of the two operating systems, because it requires either ignoring Windows NT's server capabilities or setting up a Workgroup or Domain network in addition to the VINES network. A more useful integration tool introduced by Banyan is StreetTalk Access for Windows NT File and Print.

StreetTalk Access for Windows NT File and Print

StreetTalk Access for Windows NT File and Print enables Banyan VINES users seamless access to Windows NT resources. When Banyan realized that Windows NT was being introduced into existing VINES networks more and more, they realized it was to their benefit to add access to Windows NT resources from the VINES network. They also realized that the easiest way to get their existing user base to accept this was to make these resources available without requiring administrators to reengineer their existing networks to make it possible. From this idea came the StreetTalk Access for Windows NT.

Some of the advantages StreetTalk Access makes available to VINES users include the capability to define unlimited VINES services against the underlying Windows NT servers, which eliminates the need to create and maintain a Windows NT Domain or any Domain user accounts, as well as all the original advantages of the distributed StreetTalk directory service. These include a single point of log on, hierarchical organization of resources, and the security features of Banyan's security architecture, which allows rights to be assigned object-by-object to the file level. But the next obvious step in this progression was to eliminate the need for the VINES operating system altogether. Because the power of the system was the StreetTalk directory service, why not make that available on the Windows NT operating system? Thus Banyan StreetTalk for Windows NT was born.

Banyan StreetTalk for Windows NT

First introduced in the fall of 1996, StreetTalk for Windows NT is the first directory service that runs natively on a Windows NT server.

N O T E   Novell has announced plans to implement a native Windows NT version of their Novell Directory Services, scheduled to be released by the end of 1997. This product differs from the Banyan StreetTalk Access for Windows NT in the location of the StreetTalk directory.   ■

StreetTalk Access made Windows NT resources available from the VINES StreetTalk directory, which was stored on the VINES servers. StreetTalk for Windows NT moves all those services directly to the Windows NT operating system. This eliminates the need for the design, implementation, and support of the Windows NT Domain structure, allowing administrators to harness the power of Banyan's hierarchical security and authentication services. Other features include full interoperability with StreetTalk for VINES, and support for NTFS and FAT file systems, including support for long file names, integration into the standard Windows NT support tools, Event Monitor and Performance Monitor, and support for the new StreetTalk Explorer administration tool, which further simplifies the setup and support of the StreetTalk directory. This service, if deployed correctly, can enhance Windows NT security and scalability, easing a lot of the overhead associated with Windows NT Domain support.

Concerning specific security issues in a mixed Windows NT and Banyan VINES environment, it obviously depends on the implementation of the integration. If Windows NT is a client on the VINES network, it really isn't a mixed environment. Standard VINES security policies would be effective in guarding this type of network when used in conjunction with a solid password policy. VINES security would include things such as only assigning user objects the access they need, ensuring that employees who are no longer with the organization have been removed from StreetTalk, and that security policies are clear, communicated, and checked. (Yes, those are the three Cs discussed earlier.)

In an environment where the StreetTalk Access for Windows NT File and Print software is used, it is particularly important to ensure the software is configured properly. Consider the type of environment being discussed. This is probably an existing VINES network that is interested in making Windows NT services available to their established user community. If you assume the VINES network is configured properly from a security perspective, the greatest place for a security breach will be the software linking VINES and Windows NT. It is most likely to be where administrators are the least familiar, and because no Domain architecture is needed, it is also the place where access to Windows NT resources could be inadvertently or maliciously granted. This is a good place for extensive testing of security policies and configurations.

The final configuration is using the Banyan StreetTalk for Windows NT software. Oddly enough, this takes us back to the first scenario, where Windows NT is used as a client. The key security issues are in the configuration of the StreetTalk directory structure. In fact, this wouldn't be considered a true mixed environment. It is really a Windows NT network, where the use of Domains has been replaced by a third-party directory service. Once again, pay attention to the three Cs—ensure that your implementation follows the recommended StreetTalk security measures, and you should have a secure network.

Using Windows NT Gateway Services for NetWare

Novell's NetWare and IntranetWare NOS software is arguably the leading network operating system on the market today. For the sake of brevity we will refer to these operating systems collectively as NetWare. Novell's market dominance, boasting over 55 million users, is one of the reasons that Microsoft has been targeting Novell networks for their Windows NT server product line. One of the ways that Microsoft provides for integrating Windows NT and Novell NetWare is Microsoft's Gateway Services for NetWare. This service enables a Windows NT server to provide access to NetWare resources for all the Windows NT users in a Windows NT Workgroup or Domain. This is accomplished by the Windows NT server opening a single connection to a NetWare server or Novell Directory Services and then making the NetWare resources available to any number of Windows NT clients. Figure 15.2 provides a graphical representation of this architecture.

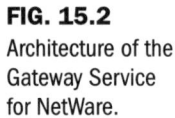

FIG. 15.2

Architecture of the
Gateway Service
for NetWare.

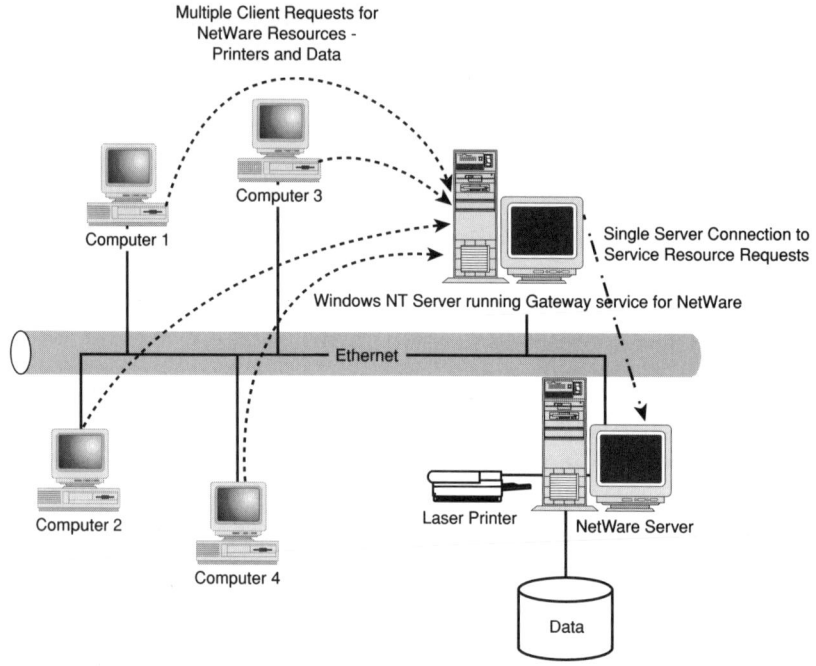

There are a couple of issues that should be mentioned before you start into the installation and configuration of the Gateway Services.

First, there is performance. Because Windows NT is using a single connection to provide this access, if a large number of users are trying to connect to the NetWare resources, such as printers or volumes, performance can suffer dramatically. The way that Windows NT provides this access is by translating the *Server Message Block (SMB)* protocol, which is the protocol used by Windows NT and its clients, to a *NetWare Core Protocol (NCP)* request that is forwarded to the NetWare server. This translates into additional overhead for any of these connections.

A second issue is that this connection uses a single server connection. This is considered by many to be a violation of the NetWare licensing agreement. The intention of the NetWare connection licensing is one connection per user. The Windows NT Gateway Services for NetWare service neatly sidesteps this agreement.

A third issue is the fact that all the Windows NT clients share a single NetWare log-in account. This means that everyone in your Windows NT Domain that has access to the NetWare resources has the same access as any other user. There is no way to restrict access of certain resources to certain users. For instance, if your Accounting Department kept all of its data on a NetWare volume and some of the users were in the Windows NT Domain, the only way to give those users access to the data is to grant access to all the users accessing NetWare. If you are sharing a NetWare printer with your entire building, everyone in the building now has access to the payroll data. This is generally a bad idea.

For these reasons, the most common use for this service is as an intermediary step in a migration from Novell NetWare to Windows NT. It is an excellent utility for this purpose, if used correctly.

Installing Gateway (and Client) Services for NetWare

Let's take a quick look at exactly how to install and configure Gateway (and Client) Services for NetWare. There are two parts to installing and configuring Gateway Services. First, take a look at what needs to happen from the NetWare side. In order for Gateway Services to function, there needs to be a way for the Windows NT server to log on to the NetWare server or Novell Directory Services. The first thing Gateway Services needs is a user account to access the NetWare resources. You will take an in-depth look at creating these accounts in the NetWare 4.x environment. Because NetWare 3.x is rapidly becoming a legacy system, that environment is touched on in less detail.

Preparing NetWare for Gateway Services

To get NetWare 4.x ready for Gateway Services, you need to take the following steps:

1. Create a new user.

   To create a user account under NetWare 4.x, load the NetWare Administrator utility. This is located in the PUBLIC subdirectory of the SYS: volume of your NetWare server and is named NWADMIN.EXE. With NetWare 4.11, there is a 32-bit version of this utility in the WIN95 subdirectory located under PUBLIC. This version is named NWADMN95.EXE. The SYS: volume is mapped to the Z: drive by default.

   N O T E In order for you to create these objects, you must be logged in as a user with Create rights to the container where these objects will reside.

   Navigate through the tree until you reach the container you want for creating the Gateway Services objects. Select Object, Create and select the User object (see Figure 15.3).

FIG. 15.3

Select User to create a new User object. Be sure you are in the proper NDS context for creating the User.

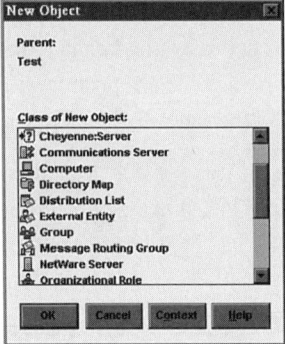

This opens the Create User dialog box (see Figure 15.4). Fill in the Login Name (Windows NT) and Last Name (Gateway) and select Define Additional Properties. Fill in properties as dictated by your standard user ID requirements. One thing to keep in mind is that if you enable password aging, you will need to manually change the password when it expires. Gateway Services does not presently contain a mechanism for automating this. You then need to adjust the Gateway Services log-in information accordingly. The less secure alternative is to disable password aging. While this is not recommended for security reasons, there are environments where this would be acceptable. Select OK and return to the main screen.

FIG. 15.4

When creating the user object for the Windows NT Gateways Services, be sure to remember the rights granted to this user will be the rights granted to anyone using Gateway Services. Be careful not to grant too many rights.

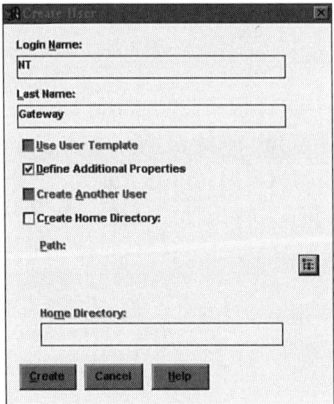

N O T E   While Windows NT is a terrific log-in name for an example in a book, choosing something a little less obvious is strongly recommended, preferably something unrelated to its use. If your naming convention is Last Name, First Initial, make the Windows NT account something anonymous such as WilsonW, or SmithB. If you use some other naming convention, make the account something that appears anonymous when viewed with the rest of your IDs. ▮

2. Create the Windows NT Gateway Group.

Select Object, Create and select the Group object. The Create Group (see Figure 15.5) dialog box opens up. Select the Define Additional Properties check box and then select Create. This opens up the properties for the newly created Windows NT Gateway Group Object.

FIG. 15.5

Select Group to create a new Group object. Remember, the Group must be named NT Gateway.

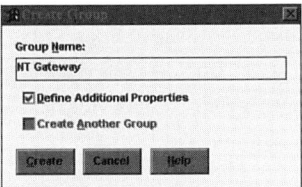

From here you need to select Members and put the Gateway Services user ID in the group. Use Rights to Files and Directories to assign file access. For any printer access, go to the Print Queue object and add the group Windows NT Gateway to the user's property (see Figure 15.6).

FIG. 15.6

When creating the group object for the Windows NT Gateways Services, be sure to remember the rights granted to this group are the rights granted to anyone using Gateway Services. Be careful not to grant too many rights.

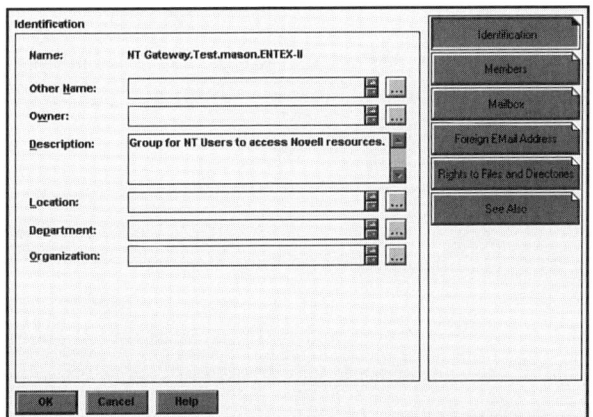

To get NetWare 3.x ready for Gateway Services, follow these steps:

1. Create a new user.

To create a user account under NetWare 3.x, load the DOS utility SYSCON.EXE, located in the PUBLIC subdirectory of the SYS: volume of your NetWare server. The SYS: volume is mapped to the Z: drive by default.

N O T E   In order to create this User and Group, you should be logged in as Supervisor or an equivalent. ▨

From the Available Topics menu, select User Information, and press enter. This brings up a list of users. Press Insert and then type the user name in the box it opens. If your naming convention is Last Name, First Initial, make the Windows NT account something anonymous such as WilsonW, or SmithB. If you use some other naming convention, make the account something that appears anonymous when viewed with the rest of your IDs. Press enter to create the user. You are asked to create a user directory. Follow whatever standards you presently use to determine the necessity or location of this directory.

Select the user you just have created from the Users List and press enter. This opens the User Information box, and shows you the list of all the information you can change for that user. Set this user up just as you would a regular user, keeping in mind that all your Windows NT users potentially will be sharing this account through Gateway Services. One thing to keep in mind is that if you enable password aging, you will need to manually change the password when it expires. Gateway Services presently does not contain a mechanism for automating this. You then need to adjust the Gateway Services log-in information accordingly. The less secure alternative is to disable password aging. While this is not recommended for security reasons, there are environments where this is acceptable.

2.   Create the Windows NT Gateway Group.

From the Available Topics screen, select Group Information. This brings up the list of groups. Press Insert and type **NTGateway**. This name is a requirement of Gateway Services. Press enter to create the group. Select the newly created group from the list and add the user you created in the previous step to the group. Assign rights to files and directories to the group as needed. If you need access to printers, use the standard 3.x utilities to give the group Windows NT Gateway access to the printer.

Installing Gateway Services in Windows NT

There are a few more steps involved in getting Gateway Services installed in Windows NT. However, if you are familiar with installing Windows NT services, this is a relatively simple task. Be sure you are logged in as Administrator before you begin the installation. Also, be sure to remove any other NetWare client software that might be loaded, such as the Client32 for NetWare, or the Microsoft NetWare Client. Because the Gateway Service is providing NetWare connectivity, having additional clients can cause problems.

1. Select Start on the Taskbar and open the Control Panel. It is located under Settings.

2. After the Control Panel is open (see Figure 15.7) select the Network icon.

FIG. 15.7

Select the Network icon. Be sure to close any other applications, as a reboot of the systems will be necessary after the changes are made.

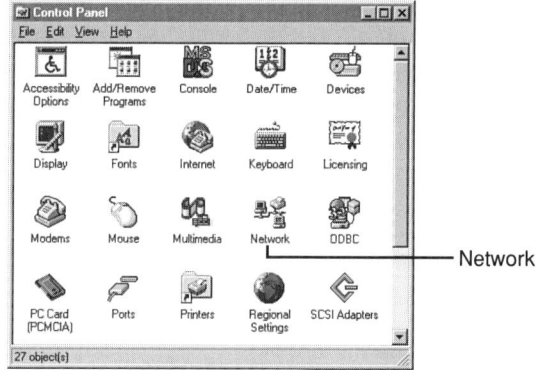

Network

3. From the Network dialog box (see Figure 15.8) select the Services tab, and click Add.

FIG. 15.8

Remember, whenever you install a new service, you should reinstall the latest Windows NT Service Pack.

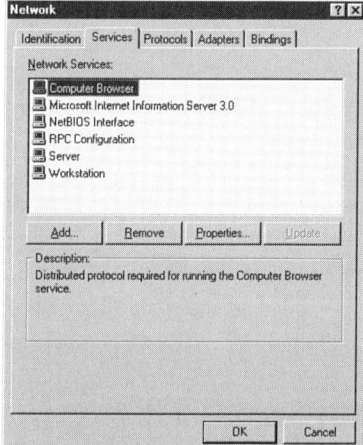

4. From the list of available services (see Figure 15.9) select the Gateway (and Client) Services for NetWare and click OK. Windows NT asks for the path to the installation files (see Figure 15.10), which is generally your CD-ROM drive path, in the directory i386. If your installation files are in a different location, either type or browse to the appropriate path.

FIG. 15.9

Be sure to have your Windows NT media available for the installation. Windows NT will prompt you for it.

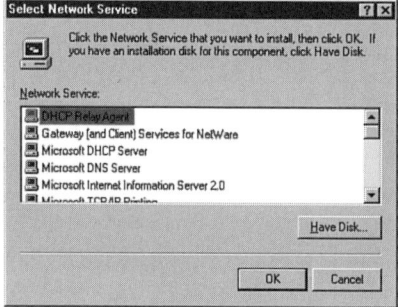

FIG. 15.10

If misplaced media is a problem at your office, it is sometimes a good idea to copy the i386 subdirectory (or appropriate subdirectory for non-Intel servers) for installations like this. If you have done this, type in the proper path to the installation files.

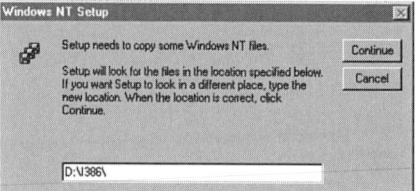

N O T E If you have multiple adapters in your machine, you need to assign unique Internal IPX Addresses to each card (see Figure 15.11) in case you want to use your server as an IPX router. It is critical that these numbers be unique not only between cards, but also unique to your Novell network. Don't select the same number as your production server's internal IPX address or you will start seeing network problems. ▩

FIG. 15.11

This error is seen on servers with multiple Network Interface Cards. It is caused by the fact that the server could act as an IPX router. Don't be concerned if you do not see this dialog box on your installation.

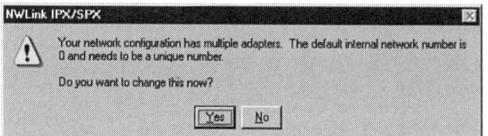

These addresses are set in the NWLink IPX/SPX Properties dialog box (see Figure 15.12). Select the General tab and set an address on each card. If you want to enable IPX/SPX routing, select the Routing tab and check the RIP Routing box.

FIG. 15.12

If you are prompted to change the IPX address, or your company has an addressing convention, change the address from 0 to something appropriate. Otherwise, the default should work.

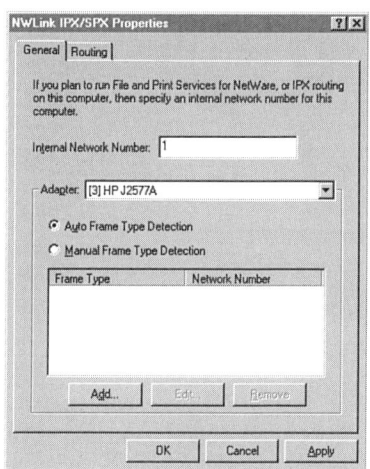

5. Once the installation is complete, the server asks to be rebooted. (See Figure 15.13.) Select Yes and let the server reboot.

FIG. 15.13

If you need to close applications before the server reboots, you can select them on the Taskbar and close them.

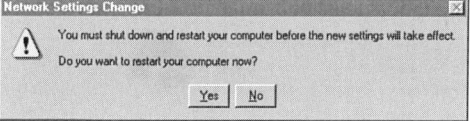

6. When the server is back up, the Control Panel should open automatically, unless you manually closed it before rebooting the server. If it is closed, reopen it using the directions above. To configure the Gateway Service, select the GSNW icon by double-clicking (see Figure 15.14). This opens the Gateway Service for NetWare dialog box (see Figure 15.15). If you are working in a NetWare 3.x environment, fill in the preferred server in the top section. If you are in a NetWare 4.x environment, fill in the preferred tree and the appropriate context for the user object you created. Complete the rest of the options as appropriate.

FIG. 15.14

Unlike many Windows NT Services, Gateway Services for NetWare creates its own icon in the Control Panel.

Gateway Services for NetWare

FIG. 15.15

Using either the NDS or NetWare 3.x information, customize the Gateway Services to connect to your NDS Tree or NetWare 3.x file server.

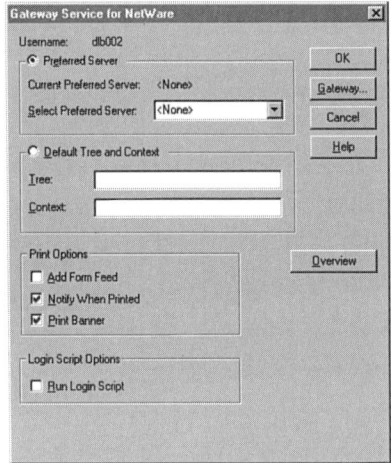

7. To complete the configuration, select Gateway from the Gateway Service for NetWare dialog box. This opens the Configure Gateway dialog box and enables you to complete the configuration (see Figure 15.16). Fill in the user and password you created in the earlier steps, and create the shares for either volume or printers in the box at the bottom of the screen. Windows NT Permissions for the NetWare resources are also assigned in that area.

FIG. 15.16
Using the User you created, and the context it was created in (NetWare 4.x), customize the Gateway Services to communicate with your NetWare server(s).

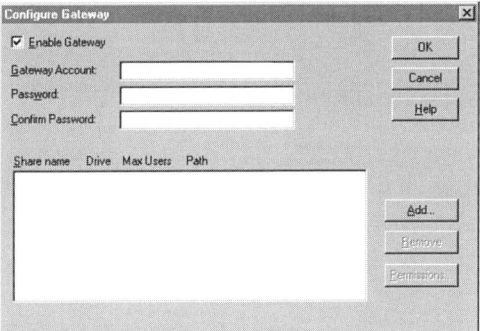

Security Issues Surrounding the Gateway Service for NetWare

As you saw earlier in the chapter, there is one major security issue surrounding the use of the Gateway Service for NetWare. There is no way to grant specific rights to specific users. Gateway Service for NetWare uses a single account and a single group to access the resources of the NDS tree or NetWare server. This means that anyone granted the rights to use any of these resources has the rights to use all the resources. This can be a major issue if there is any confidential data still stored on the NetWare server when the Gateway Service for NetWare is installed. Be careful when this service is used. It is very useful during a migration but has some extreme limitations surrounding flexible access.

Migration of NetWare Users to a Windows NT Environment

Gateway Services for NetWare is considered by some to be a good intermediate step in a migration from NetWare to Windows NT. It enables you to set up your Windows NT infrastructure while still providing some level of access to legacy data and services still residing on the NetWare network. After you have completed the design and implementation of Windows NT and you're ready to get rid of NetWare, or even if you are not a big fan of intermediate steps and want to migrate immediately, what is the best way to do it?

Windows NT 4.0 ships with a utility called the Windows NT Server Migration Tool for NetWare, which enables you to migrate NetWare servers directly to Windows NT Server. The Migration Tool allows the flexible transfer of user and group accounts, volumes, folders, and files while enabling you to specify passwords on the migrated accounts, maintain the existing NetWare rights, and generate comprehensive logs of precisely what occurred during the migration. One particularly useful feature is the capability to run test migrations, so you aren't left with surprises during the real thing.

NetWare Directory Service and Windows NT Domains

One of the major differences between Novell's 4.x network operating system (NOS) and the Windows NT network operating system is the way they handle user IDs and network access. Windows NT uses a Domain model (or in the case of large or distributed environments a multiple Domain model) to support clients with a single point of log on to the network. This is a flat database that is stored on Primary or Backup Domain Controllers, which are Windows NT servers that perform Domain authentication. Novell NetWare, on the other hand, uses a distributed, hierarchical database to store its directory information, known as *Novell Directory Services (NDS)*. The NDS is the foundation of Novell's networking strategy, and they are betting the survival of their operating system on it. Let's explore this in a bit more depth.

Novell Directory Service

Before examining the finer points of Novell's NDS, you need to know about the latest version of NetWare, Novell's flagship operating system. In an attempt to jump aboard the Internet furor sweeping the corporate environment, Novell is making an attempt to position their latest release of NetWare, renamed IntranetWare, as the premier operating system for Internet and intranet connectivity, support, and development. Bundling the core operating system with a Web server, a Multi-Protocol Router, and an IPX to IP gateway; enabling NDS to be browsed by a Web Browser, and announcing support for the new Internet *Lightweight Directory Access Protocol (LDAP)*, Novell seems to be making every effort to regain some of the ground they have lost to Windows NT in recent months.

NDS is the heart of the NetWare 4.x and IntranetWare NOS. NDS gives you seamless access to all authorized network resources from anywhere on the network using a single login. NDS is a distributed, hierarchical database for storing all the objects on your network. Users, volumes, printers, and file servers are the commonly thought-of devices, but new advances with NDS now enable applications, fax servers, and eventually Windows NT Servers and Workstations to become part of the NDS structure.

Other advantages that NDS makes available include an easy way to organize network resources. Resources can be grouped in NDS by physical location, department, ZIP code, or any combination your company finds useful. Also, because of the distributed nature of NDS, the entire structure can be centrally managed. Changes made at a central management site are quickly replicated throughout the network, allowing for greater control and accountability as well as reduced support costs.

Some other features IntranetWare and NDS make available are a new host of integrated management tools, including a new 32-bit version of NetWare Administrator and a new application called Partition Manager, used exclusively to maintain the partitions of the NDS database. Between the capability to granularize access to the file attribute level for anyone on the network, as well as the C2 certification Novell received for its trusted network design, and password encryption standards, security under NDS is excellent. Clear text passwords are a thing of the past with IntranetWare.

The other major NDS initiative that Novell is undertaking presently is an all-out effort to make NDS the directory service for all operating systems. Recent announcements surrounding NDS include a commitment to port NDS to Windows NT as a native service by the end of 1997, the adoption of NDS by a number of major UNIX players, including Sun and HP, and finally an announcement that Novell is licensing NDS for free. It will be interesting to see where Novell takes the product over the next year.

Workstation Access to NetWare Servers

The key to any NOS is how users access it. Here you can see how to get a workstation, be it DOS, Windows 3.x, Windows 95, or Windows NT access. Keep in mind that access is also available from UNIX, OS/2, and Macintosh clients, but those topics are outside the scope of what this covers.

Windows NT Workstation and Server Access

Let's quickly touch on how to access a NetWare server from Windows NT. There are basically three ways to access NetWare resources from Windows NT. First is through the use of Gateway (and Client) Services for NetWare, which are discussed in depth earlier in this chapter.

Second is through the use of the Windows NT NetWare Client. Under Windows NT 4.0, this is a robust, 32-bit client that is loaded from the Windows NT installation media under the Network Icon of the Control Panel. This enables Windows NT to seamlessly access resources in either NetWare 3.x or 4.x networks. The NDS tree is selected and browsed in the same way as the Windows NT Domain, and drives can be mapped through Windows Explorer, much in the way shares are accessed in a Windows NT Workgroup or Domain. Log-in scripts can be run or not, as selected in the client configuration, and most of the other standard NetWare client attributes can be set as well. The one interesting feature in this client is the pass through capabilities for log on and password. When you press Control+Alt+Delete in the typical Windows NT log-on method, if the user ID and password are the same as the user ID and password for NetWare, the log-on to NetWare happens automatically. This is a robust and stable client, and it deserves serious consideration if access to a NetWare network is a requirement.

The final way to access a NetWare network is by using IntranetWare Client for Windows NT. This client has some new features that make its capabilities a bit more interesting in a NetWare environment than the Microsoft client. The first thing this client does is insert itself between the log-in screen and the Windows NT authentication mechanism. It does this without impacting the security of the log-in process. When you press Control+ Alt+Delete after this client has been installed, you immediately authenticate against NDS as well as the Windows NT account database. Another interesting feature of this client is the capability to use NDS automation tools such as the Novell Application Launcher (NAL) and the Automatic Client Update (ACU) utility. NAL allows administrators to make application objects in the NDS. Users are granted access to applications through the NDS structure and run the application without needing to know where it is, where to map the drives, and how to set up their environment.

In fact, applications on the network can be moved from one server to another, and the only thing that needs to be updated is the Application object in NDS. The ACU utility enables administrators to script client updates from either the NDS log-in script, user requested updates, or the Windows NT Schedule Facility. This can greatly ease the administrative overhead associated with keeping client software up-to-date as well as standardized across an enterprise.

At this time, the Microsoft client is adequate for providing access to the network, but the Novell client has a number of attractive enhancements with many more promised in the future. Novell recognizes Windows NT's popularity in the marketplace and seems determined to ensure that it makes a terrific client for a NetWare network.

Windows 95 Client Access

Much like Windows NT, there are a number of ways to access a NetWare server from Windows 95. The first is to use the Gateway Services for NetWare connectivity. As mentioned before, this is a good choice while migrating to Windows NT.

A second method for connecting is loading the VLMs, which are discussed in detail in the next section. This is generally a poor method for accessing NetWare resources, because the VLMs are 16-bit applications, and Windows 95 is a 32-bit operating system. This means that VLMs can be finicky and unstable in a Windows 95 environment.

The next method for accessing NetWare servers is the Windows 95 Client for NetWare Networks, provided by Microsoft as part of the Windows 95 operating system. This client is fine for a NetWare 3.x environment but is not NDS-aware, so it's of little use in a NetWare 4.x environment.

The fourth and most feature-rich client is the Novell NetWare Client 32. This 32-bit client provided by Novell, while struggling in early releases, has become a robust, reliable client for Windows 95. Fully NDS aware, this client is available for download from Novell and installs through the use of an installation application, rather then through the Control Panel as the Microsoft client does. This client enables you to configure how log-in scripts run, printer-capture characteristics, as well as a host of advanced features that allow a great deal of fine tuning of the client. This is probably the best NetWare client on the market for Windows 95.

Troubleshooting Problems with Cross-Platform Security

OK, now that you are all experts in cross-platform security, what do you do when you are having problems? And what sorts of problems can you expect to see?

Password synchronization problems are probably the biggest headache in this environment. Users will change a password on one system, not realizing that it doesn't change the password on all systems, and then call for support when they can access one server and not the other. This issue can usually be cleared up with good user manuals and network orientation. In too many companies, your introduction to the network consists of a piece of paper with a user ID and password. While this certainly is sufficient to get the user on the network the first time, it doesn't address issues such as the one just discussed. If you don't have the personnel to conduct training, create a FAQ (Frequently Asked Questions) compiled from your most common Help Desk calls, and distribute it. Make it available on your intranet, so people can look up answers to their questions on their way to check the company's stock price or hit their favorite comics page.

What do you do if someone tries to gain illegal access to your systems? In a cross-platform environment, do you have the tools, personnel, and skills to even tell if someone has been doing things they shouldn't? The reason this can be an especially tricky issue in a cross-platform environment is that auditing capabilities and security tools vary from operating system to operating system. The key to this is to be alert. Are you getting a large number of calls from people whose files have been deleted or altered? Do you notice people on the system at hours they wouldn't ordinarily be there, or are they logged in from two machines, or machines they wouldn't ordinarily use? Keep an eye on your network, do an audit now and then, some scheduled, some unscheduled. Many Fortune 1000 companies even bring in security consultants who specialize in external auditing. If security is critical to your environment, you might want to investigate this option as well.

From Here...

The best bit of advice is be consistent in your policies, be sure they are being implemented, and be sure your personnel have the skills, training, and experience to ensure everything is being implemented properly. Most of the problems you'll see in this arena are not technical; instead they are procedural or political. Be alert and stay on top of the condition of your network, and things should run smoothly.

The following chapters will provide more information on securing your Windows NT environment.

- Chapter 13, "Overview of Security and the Internet," shows you how to handle security if your Windows NT Network is connected to the most mixed environment there is, the Internet.

- Chapter 16, "Allowing Macintosh Clients Access to Windows NT Resources," shows you how to let Macintosh clients get access to resources in your Windows NT network.

- Chapter 17, "Integration of Windows NT with a UNIX Environment," explains how to handle Windows NT if you are integrating into a UNIX environment.

Allowing Macintosh Clients Access to Windows NT Resources

Making Windows NT Server resources available to Macintosh clients and building on the integration of Windows NT server with other operating systems is the subject of this chapter. The Apple Macintosh has long been a major player in the desktop operating system market, and although sales have been on the decline of late, it is still a significant presence in the desktop market. The introduction of Macintosh clones has further bolstered the Macintosh operating system (os) presence. This chapter discusses what the Windows NT Server Service for Macintosh provides for the Macintosh environment, as well as installing the service, working with the users, volumes, and making printers available to the Macintosh clients. ∎

Windows NT services for Macintosh features

An overview of just what Windows NT Services for Macintosh can provide to Macintosh Clients. This includes the authentication mechanism and file permissions.

Security considerations with the Macintosh clients

Issues to be aware of when working in a Macintosh environment, particularly while accessing a Windows NT server.

Setting up Windows NT services for Macintosh

The installation and configuration of Windows NT Services for Macintosh.

Setting up the Macintosh client software

The Macintosh client software addresses the most significant security issue of Macintosh connectivity—clear text passwords. This chapter explains how the problem is addressed and how to install the client software.

Features of the Windows NT Services for Macintosh

Microsoft's Windows NT Server Services for Macintosh is a set of services designed to enable seamless access to Windows NT servers from Apple Macintosh clients. This service is broken into two main parts: File Server for Macintosh and Print Server for Macintosh.

The File Server portion of the service enables Macintosh users to access and store files on a Windows NT server. The File Server also enables Macintosh and PC clients to share files. Files that have a common application in the Macintosh and PC world such as Microsoft Word can open the same file stored on the server, whether it was stored by a Macintosh client or a PC client. The File Server also provides the user permissions translations, enabling Macintosh clients to take advantage of the security of the NTFS file system. One thing to note prior to installing the Services for Macintosh service is that it requires an NTFS partition to allow Macintosh clients file access. This partition can be created after the service is installed but must be created before logging Macintosh clients onto the server.

After the NTFS partition is available, File Server for Macintosh provides a transparent translation from the Macintosh permissions to the Windows NT permissions, and vice-versa. The following tables cover exactly how that translation occurs. Table 16.1 compares the permissions available in the Macintosh environment to the equivalent NTFS permissions in Windows NT. Table 16.2 compares the permissions from Windows NT to the Macintosh equivalents.

Table 16.1 Macintosh to Windows NT Permissions Translation

Macintosh Permission	Windows NT Equivalent Permission
See Files	Read
See Folders	Read
Make Changes	Write and Delete
Cannot Move, Rename, or Delete	Removes the Change and Delete permissions

Table 16.2 Windows NT Permissions to Macintosh Equivalents

Windows NT Permission	Macintosh Permission
Read	See Files and See Folders
Write and Delete	Make Changes

There are a couple of other idiosyncrasies to be aware of from a security perspective when working with Macintosh clients. A Macintosh user assigns rights similarly to a UNIX environment, and Macintosh users only can assign rights by Owner, User/Group, or Everyone. It is not possible to assign rights to a file or to a folder with multiple users or groups. Also, unlike Windows NT file security, where the most restrictive policy is the one enforced, Macintosh permissions allow the most rights when rights are assigned in multiple ways. That probably isn't incredibly clear; I'll show you a couple of scenarios.

In Scenario 1, Barney is a Windows NT user and has rights to the Sales folder. That means Barney should be able to read any files in the folder, but not change or delete them. The group Everyone, which Barney is a member of, has Read, Change, and Delete permissions to the same folder. Anyone in this group can read, change, or delete any files in the folder. In the Windows NT security model, Barney would have the most restrictive of the two permission levels; that is to say, he would have Read permission only. This is very different than Scenario 2, a Macintosh user.

In this scenario, Betty is a Macintosh user and has See Files and See Folders rights to the Sales folder. This would be the Macintosh equivalent to Barney's Read permissions in the preceding scenario. The group Everyone, which Betty is a member of, has See Files, See Folders, and Make Changes to the same folder. Because Betty is accessing the folder from a Macintosh client machine, she would have See Files, See Folders, and Make Changes, because the Macintosh security model allows the most permissive of the security levels to take precedence. From a Security perspective, the Windows NT model is preferable.

Once Services for Macintosh is installed, Macintosh-style permissions can be set on any of the Macintosh volumes by using File Manager. There will be a Macfile entry on the toolbar. This functionality is not carried over into the new Explorer interface, so WINFILE.EXE will need to be executed.

The second part of the Services for Macintosh is the Print Server for Macintosh. As its name implies, this piece of the service allows Macintosh clients to print to any Windows NT printer and to spool jobs to existing AppleTalk printers. Spooling is handled by configuring the Windows NT Server to connect to the AppleTalk printer and then advertise it on the network. Macintosh users print to the printer advertised by the Windows NT Server, and Windows NT handles spooling the jobs to the appropriate printer. The exact mechanism for this is discussed later in the chapter.

Some of the other features Services for Macintosh makes available to Macintosh clients, as well as to administrators of Windows NT Servers with Macintosh clients include secure login, remote connectivity using the Remote Access Service, integrated GUI administration tools, and support for AppleTalk Phase 2 routing. AppleTalk routing means that a

Windows NT Server has the capability to act as a *seed* router for the Macintosh network, providing zone names and network numbers. This is particularly useful in environments where the Windows NT server may be replacing the existing Macintosh server and router.

Additional Security Considerations When Integrating Macintosh Clients

There are a few additional considerations when working with Windows NT security and Macintosh clients. The first thing to be aware of is that when the Windows NT Services for Macintosh service is installed and configured, Macintosh clients are authenticated to the Windows NT Server exactly the same way as PC clients are. Services for Macintosh translates the Macintosh user ID, passwords, and permissions so that the security of the server is never compromised. This allows Windows NT to maintain the same level of security no matter what client is used to access the system. Another thing which people who are familiar with the Macintosh password model will find interesting is that clear text passwords are no longer required. One of the largest issues surrounding the security of Macintosh client is that the default Macintosh client uses clear text passwords. What this means is that any hacker with a decent sniffer program can take a look at the traffic on the wire, and if he or she times it right, can have as many Macintosh passwords as he or she can pack on a floppy. This is generally considered a server security issue.

Services for Macintosh fixes this issue. Services for Macintosh ships with authentication files for the Macintosh client, which are copied to a Macintosh accessible volume when the service is installed. We will discuss installing and configuring this feature later in the chapter; at this point, let's just say that it removes the need for clear text passwords and allows an administrator to require encrypted passwords from all client workstations. One other feature Services for Macintosh provides is the capability to password each Macintosh volume individually. To be honest, because this restriction is not carried over to the PC clients, this is of limited use. But it is available if the additional level of security is required.

How to Set Up the Macintosh Services

Before you get into the step-by-step installation of Services for Macintosh, let's take just a minute to discuss preparing for the installation. There are a few pieces of information which will prove invaluable during the installation that can be determined before installing and configuring the service. Get a sheet of paper, or an Excel spreadsheet, or a Lotus form, and determine the following items:

1. What is the name of the Macintosh server to be? The Services for Macintosh can be configured to broadcast the name of the Windows NT Server, or can broadcast something entirely different. If the Windows NT Server's name is something obscure such as USROCB004, you might want to set the AppleShare name to something a little more user friendly like Bob, or Sales Server. If you are an extremely security-conscious company, names which identify the purpose of the server are not recommended. In a slightly more relaxed environment, security can be maintained and user ease increased with the friendlier naming conventions.

Part
IV

Ch
16

2. What will the name of the AppleTalk zone be? Will the server broadcast into an existing zone, or should it broadcast its own? Are there any zones at all? If this is a new installation, you might want the Windows NT Server to act as the seed router for the Macintosh network, providing all the zone names and numbering. These concepts appear a little later in the chapter. This would also be a good time to determine the zone numbering convention. Consult with your company's documentation standards, or if none exists, now might be a good time to start designing and documenting standards.

3. Make a preliminary decision as to how the volumes will be configured and named. Will there be one large Macintosh volume, or a number of little ones? Will you use volume passwords? Who can access what, and how will you ensure PC and Macintosh permissions are secure from operating system to operating system?

4. This is also a good time to record information like the network interface card(s), amount of RAM, Windows NT Server name, amount of hard disk space (both total and available), and amount of memory. Also the install date, name of installer, and location of the equipment. Ideally, you have a server log book next to the server from the original installation of the networking operating system (NOS), so you can record the changes you are making. If this is the original installation of the NOS, now is an excellent time to start your log book.

5. One final thing I am fond of verifying is that my third-party backup software will back up the Macintosh files stored on my server. Windows NT Backup should have this capability, but it is a good idea to verify this fact before putting critical Macintosh data on the file server.

Once you have gathered this information, you're ready to install the service.

Installing the Microsoft Windows NT Services for Macintosh

1. From the Task Bar, select Start, then Settings, and finally Control Panel (see Figure 16.1).

2. From the Control Panel, select Network (see Figure 16.2).

FIG. 16.1

To install any of the Windows NT services, including Services for Macintosh, you need to open the Control Panel.

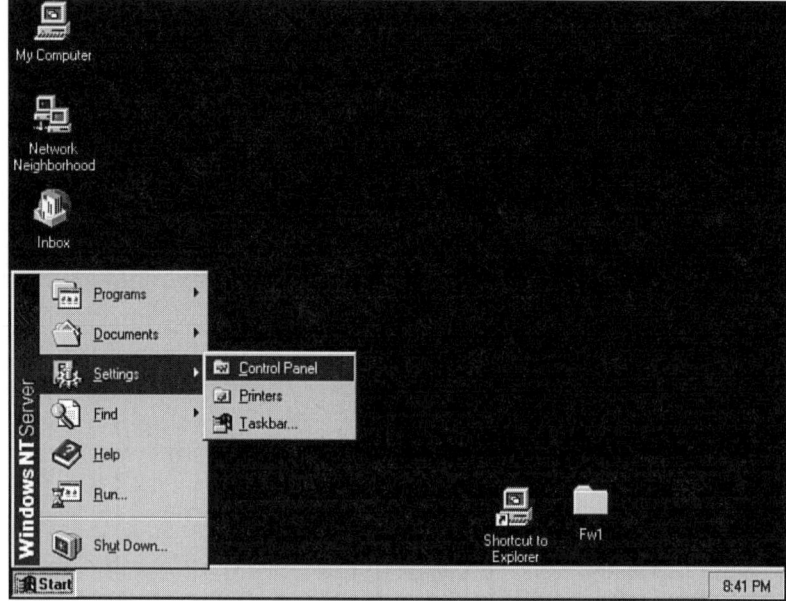

FIG. 16.2

Services for Macintosh are installed from the Network portion of the Control Panel. It is a good idea to close any other applications because you will need to reboot the server after the service is installed.

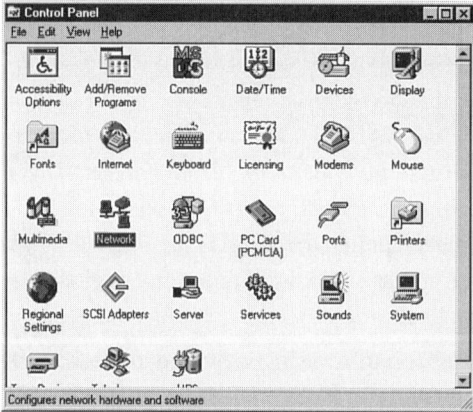

3. Select the Services tab and then select Add.

4. From the list of services, select Services for Macintosh and click OK (see Figure 16.3).

5. Type the path to the Windows NT Server distribution files when prompted. All the Services for Macintosh files are copied to the hard disk and the appropriate Registry changes are made.

FIG. 16.3

Remember, you should always reinstall the latest Windows NT Service Pack after installing network-related services.

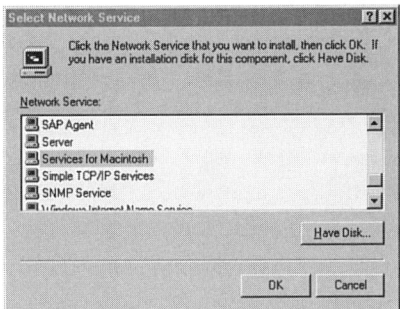

6. In the Network dialog box, click Close. You should be given a message that tells you how to configure the networking portion of the service (see Figure 16.4). Following this message, the AppleTalk Protocol Configuration dialog box appears (see Figure 16.5). Use this section to select a new zone, a different network, or to enable AppleTalk routing as your circumstance requires. The information gathered prior to installation is invaluable at this point.

7. Restart the computer for the changes to take effect.

FIG. 16.4

When configuring Services for Macintosh, it is important to have the correct naming and addressing of any existing Macintosh networks. This ensures you access to the server from a Macintosh after installing the service.

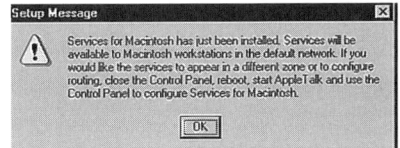

FIG. 16.5

While configuring AppleTalk routing, remember that if you have an existing AppleTalk network, your Windows NT server probably doesn't need to act as a seed router.

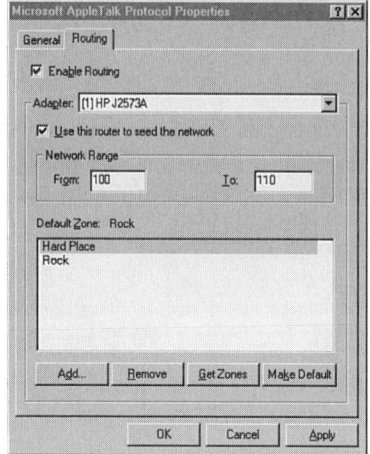

Setting Up the Macintosh Client Software

As promised, let's now discuss connecting to the Windows NT Server from the Macintosh, which should be very familiar for any Macintosh users, and copying the Microsoft authentication files to the Macintosh client. Microsoft Authentication is an AppleShare extension that allows for a secure, encrypted login to the Windows NT Server. It also allows users with accounts in multiple domains to specify a domain to log in to. This is done by entering Domain Name\User ID in the Name box of the login. To get the authentication files installed, follow these steps:

1. Select the Chooser from the Macintosh Apple menu.

2. Select the AppleShare icon, and then the AppleTalk zone in which Windows NT Server is broadcasting.

3. Select the appropriate Windows NT Server. This obviously should match the name you told your Windows NT Server to broadcast to the Macintosh clients. Be sure to choose a unique name for the server. Then click OK.

4. Log in as a Registered User, or as a Guest by selecting the appropriate option button. For the most secure method, the Guest account should be disabled, and all users should be required to log in as a Registered User. Click OK when your choice has been made.

5. The Microsoft UAM Volume, which is installed by Services for Macintosh, should appear in the window. Select it and click OK. You are now logged in and have a volume mounted. You can close the Chooser.

6. The Microsoft UAM Volume appears on the Macintosh desktop. Double-click it to get the Microsoft UAM Volume window to open.

7. Select the AppleShare Folder which appears in the Window and copy it to the System Folder on the client hard disk. This can be done by clicking the folder and dragging the folder from the UAM Volume to the System Folder on the local hard drive. Keep in mind that the System Folder contains all the extensions that the Macintosh needs to operate. If your Macintosh is a client on a different network, such as Novell or Banyan, there may be other UAM extensions on the hard drive. If you are prompted to overwrite an existing AppleShare folder, copy the Microsoft UAM file from the network directly into the AppleShare folder on the client machine. This prevents accidental overwriting of other vendor's UAM files.

8. Reboot the Macintosh.

When the Macintosh completes its restart, Microsoft authentication is available to the client. If the use of clear text passwords is disabled on the file server (a highly recommended practice), Microsoft authentication will be the only way a Macintosh client will be able to access the server.

Resource Configuration of Macintosh Volumes

There are a number of things that you can do to configure resources with Macintosh Volumes. This process encompasses most of the configuration options available when working with Macintosh file resources. All resource configuration is done through an option in File Manager called MacFile. This must all be done through File Manager, because MacFile is not an option with Explorer. From MacFile you can create and delete Macintosh-Accessible Volumes, set and change permissions and passwords on the Macintosh Volumes, change the volume name, and even limit the number of concurrent users for that particular volume. One of the critical things to do as you set this up is to translate your existing security policies to a format which can be implemented under the MacFile utility. It is critical to maintain as much consistency between security policies as possible between all the client platforms.

Creating a Macintosh Volume on the Windows NT Server In order for Macintosh users to access the server, you need to create Macintosh-accessible volumes for them to use. To create and assign permissions to a Macintosh Volume, follow these steps:

1. Run Winfile.exe. The Macintosh Volume Configuration utilities are installed in File Manager by the Services for Macintosh. These utilities are not available in the Explorer.

2. Select the MacFile menu option. Under that option, choose Create Volume.

3. When the Create Macintosh-Accessible Volume dialog box appears, you can either click OK to accept the default options, or you can enter a volume name, which the Macintosh users will see at the login. You also can specify the other options, which

are a new path, a volume password, any security options you want to configure, and user limits.

4. If you want to configure the user permissions on the volume, click Permissions. The dialog box that opens offers you the three standard Macintosh permissions, which were discussed at length earlier in the chapter. To complete the configuration, click OK.

There are a couple of additional things to remember as you start implementing your Macintosh Volumes. To the Macintosh clients, these servers appear to be AppleShare file servers. The volumes appear to be standard Macintosh volumes, and things such as files and folders are created and manipulated from the Macintosh interface just as they would be if they were stored on the Macintosh hard disk. It is generally a good idea to do as much of the file and folder manipulations as possible from the Macintosh client operating system. This ensures that files copied or created have the correct characteristics, and you don't run as much of a risk of inadvertently damaging or deleting important information. This rule actually carries over to any operating system that is emulating AppleShare, including Novell NetWare of Banyan Vines. Always try to do your Macintosh file maintenance from a Macintosh interface. It saves time, frustration, and confusion for you and your users.

Printer Access

No network is complete without the capability to print. As discussed earlier, Services for Macintosh installs two services when it is installed. The first, File Server, was discussed at length previously. The second service is the Services for Macintosh Print Server. This service has three advantages for your users. First, Macintosh users can print PostScript jobs to any printers connected to the Windows NT Server. To the Macintosh user, these printers appear like the standard LaserWriter. For those of you not familiar with the standard Macintosh printing features, Macintosh prints all documents in the PostScript format. PostScript is a language/file format that allows Macintosh applications to talk to the printer. Any file which is printed from a Macintosh is printed in PostScript format. In the past, if you had an HP LaserJet III and it didn't have the PostScript option installed, a Macintosh would not be able to print to it. Services for Macintosh removes this limitation.

Print Server for Macintosh also makes AppleTalk printers available to PC users. This is particularly useful because you don't need duplicate printers for a mixed population of Macintosh and PC users. The Windows NT Server uses the Print Server for Macintosh to capture the AppleTalk Printers. PC users can then print to, and check the status of, jobs they have printed to the AppleTalk printer. These features can save you a significant amount of money, as well as spare you from complaining PC users if the Macintosh users have a better printer, or vice-versa.

Yet another benefit of this service is the capability of Windows NT to provide printer spooling. In the traditional Macintosh printing model, each Macintosh can directly access any AppleTalk printer, because the printers were just plugged into the network, broadcasting their services. That meant that whenever a Macintosh user sent a job to the printer, it would send as much of the job as the printer's memory could handle, and then it would have to wait until a page printed and cleared buffer space before it could send more data. This had a major impact on performance, because even a Macintosh Classic can send data across the network faster than a LaserJet can print one page of a document. By allowing Macintosh users to spool their jobs to the server, the server is the only device which is waiting for the printer to become available, so the end user is back to work as soon as all the data has been sent to the server, and the server, which is designed for this type of activity, continues processing the job. One other benefit of this capability is that the service can spool PC clients, as well as Macintosh clients. Everyone gets back to work faster once this is set up and running.

Part
IV

Ch
16

Let's briefly observe how this service works, and then walk through setting up a Macintosh printer on a Windows NT Server. After Services for Macintosh is installed, installing and configuring printers is very similar to what you'd normally do using Windows NT Server. However, there is one additional consideration—you must take the AppleTalk zones into account. The print server and file server absolutely must appear in the same zone. In most instances, this is the way people configure their printers, but in case your company uses a printer zone or some other creative method for organizing the logical appearance of your printers on the network, you need to be aware of this limitation.

One other feature you should know about before creating your printer is how to capture an AppleTalk printer from Windows NT. When you set up a printer on the AppleTalk network to be used with Services for Macintosh, you can decide whether to capture the printer, giving Windows NT complete control over the printer and preventing anyone or anything else from printing directly to the printer. This can be attractive to administrators who like to keep tight control over the way their network is used. A captured printer requires that all jobs be spooled through the Windows NT Server, adding overhead to the server but freeing up a lot of clients from waiting for the printer to accept the entire job. One advantage of not capturing the printer is that if the server is having a problem with the printer, Macintosh clients can still print directly to the printer across the network.

Now you can actually create a Macintosh printer. You can create your printer using the Add Printer wizard that ships with Windows NT. To create a printer, you need to do the following:

1. From the Start menu, choose Settings and then choose Printers.
2. Click Add Printer in the Printers dialog box.

3. Let the wizard guide you through the creation of the printer. The wizard prompts you for a printer name, correct printer driver, and the printer ports. Be sure to share the printer, so users can actually access it.

4. If the printer is on the network, choose Add Port, then select AppleTalk Printing Devices from the Printer Ports list. Click OK.

5. From the Available AppleTalk Printing Devices window, select the appropriate zone and printer.

You have now successfully installed and captured an AppleTalk Printer.

From Here...

You have seen how the different features of the Microsoft Windows NT Services for Macintosh enable a Windows NT Server to make volumes accessible to Macintosh users, how it can be used to share files and printers between Macintosh and PC users, and how it can be used to augment the security available with Macintosh logins. In short, the Services for Macintosh allows Macintosh clients to be full participants in a Windows NT network, with all the capabilities available to a PC client.

The following chapters provide more information on securing your Windows NT environment in conjunction with other operating systems.

- Chapter 13, "Overview of Security and the Internet," shows you how to handle security if your Windows NT Network is connected to the most mixed environment there is—the Internet.

- Chapter 15, "Windows NT Integration with NetWare System and Other Network Operating Systems," teaches you how to securely integrate Windows NT in a mixed operating system environment.

- Chapter 17, "Integration of Windows NT with a UNIX Environment," shows you what to do if you are integrating into a UNIX environment.

Integration of Windows NT with a UNIX Environment

With an installation base of millions and almost three decades of maturity, UNIX represents one of the most popular operating systems ever created. As Microsoft Windows NT's popularity continues to grow, system administrators find themselves integrating the two systems more and more frequently. While Windows NT was originally touted as the UNIX killer, it is becoming more and more evident that the legacy of UNIX applications isn't going away any time soon. UNIX also is the most popular server operating system on the Internet. Industry-savvy administrators (such as the ones reading this book) will leverage the strengths of each operating system and provide their organizations with a smooth-running, securely integrated computing environment. ■

Introduction to TCP/IP

This section gives you a quick overview of what TCP/IP is and why it is an important part of integrating Windows NT and UNIX.

Installing TCP/IP in Windows NT Server

If you want to connect to a UNIX system, you absolutely need to have TCP/IP installed. You also see some of the TCP/IP routing features of Windows NT.

Common TCP/IP security issues

Identify some of the more common security issues with the TCP/IP protocol.

Taking the next step in your Windows NT and UNIX integration

Additional methods for integrating Windows NT into a UNIX environment, including using applications, such as Telnet, FTP, Web browsers, and mounting volumes using *Network File System (NFS)*.

Introduction to TCP/IP and How It Works

The *Transmission Control Protocol/Internet Protocol (TCP/IP)* suite provides the backbone of UNIX networking. TCP/IP is a public domain protocol that was originally designed to provide extremely reliable communication over an inherently unreliable network—the *ARPAnet (Advanced Research Projects Administration)*. The ARPAnet was originally developed by the Department of Defense in the 1970s as a research network to allow labs to communicate throughout the United States. The ARPAnet is also the precursor to today's remarkably popular Internet. In fact, TCP/IP is not only the protocol of choice for the Internet, but it is also rapidly becoming the protocol of choice for industry-leading *Network Operating Systems (NOS)*.

The release of version 4.0 of Windows NT has significantly improved its support of TCP/IP by introducing or enhancing features such as *Domain Name Service (DNS)*, *Dynamic Host Control Protocol (DHCP)*, and TCP/IP routing. Windows NT's IP routing also supports the *Routing Information Protocol(RIP)* for dynamic routing table updates. Novell has committed to making its NetWare and IntranetWare protocols independent in the near future, and it has announced initiatives to tie its *Novell Directory Services (NDS)* to DNS and DHCP. For the past couple years, Novell has offered comprehensive IP routing as an add-on product, but it has bundled the product with its new IntranetWare product. Both companies (Novell and Microsoft) also offer Web servers, which rely on TCP/IP as a transport protocol. And UNIX has been running predominantly on TCP/IP since the creation of the operating system.

Each computer on a TCP/IP network is normally assigned a unique 32-bit (4 bytes) number known as an *IP address*. IP addresses separate each byte with a period, also known as dotted decimal notation (such as **206.98.128.2**). This addressing scheme allows the IP portion of TCP/IP to identify a specific computer or host within many networks. The IP addresses are generally classified as being Class A, Class B, or Class C, according to the value of the first byte (206 in the example).

In Class A addresses, the network portion of an IP address is the first byte, and the host is the remaining three bytes. In Class B addresses, networks are identified by the first two bytes; hosts by the final two bytes. The first three bytes of Class C addresses represent the network; the final byte specifies the host. If you look at Table 17.1, you can identify the IP address **206.98.128.2** as a Class C address. A network that uses this address range will have a theoretical limit of 256 hosts.

Table 17.1 IP Address Classifications

Range Decimal	Range Binary	Class	Theoretical Maximum Hosts
0-127	00000000-011111111	A	16,777,216
128-191	10000000-101111111	B	65,536
192-223	11000000-110111111	C	256

Additional IP Addressing Information

The maximum number of hosts is called "theoretical" because of the conventions currently used in assigning IP addresses. Guidelines stipulate that 0, 1, and 255 should not be used for any of the four bytes in an IP address. These values are used for other purposes. Also, RFC 1597 provides three sets of IP addresses for private networks that do not plan to connect to the Internet.

10.0.0.0-10.255.255.255 (Class A)

172.16.0.0-172.31.255.255 (Class B)

192.168.0.0-192.168.255.255 (Class C)

Another special IP address is 127.0.0.1. This address points to the current host and can be used to determine if there is a problem on a TCP/IP network.

Part
IV
Ch
17

This is only a brief overview of TCP/IP. If you are interested in more information on how Microsoft Windows NT's TCP/IP implementation works, take a look at *Networking with Microsoft TCP/IP, Second Edition*, ISBN 1-56205-713-8, published by New Riders Publishing. It is an excellent reference for Windows NT and TCP/IP. Chapter 14, "Internet Security and BackOffice," also has some additional TCP/IP information.

Installing TCP/IP on Windows NT

As discussed previously, UNIX relies on TCP/IP to communicate with its clients and other hosts. If you are going to integrate Windows NT into this environment, you need to have TCP/IP loaded on your server.

Requirements for Installation

Before you jump into the installation, make sure you have the following information:

- *You need an IP address for each of the interface cards in your server.* For simplicity's sake, assume there is a single interface card in your machine.

N O T E   If you are using Dynamic Host Control Protocol (DHCP) to dynamically assign IP addresses on your network, this information is not needed. One security issue to keep in mind when using DHCP: If you use DHCP and you assign rights based on IP subnet, users can access resources just by plugging into a different subnet. For example, if users on subnet 10.1.1.x are allowed Internet access based on a firewall configuration, and users on 10.4.4.x are not, a user on 10.4.4.x can get access by plugging into the 10.1.1.x subnet. In addition, anyone who can get access to a connection on your network automatically gets a valid address—and any access that it entails.

- *You need to know what your subnet mask is.* A subnet mask is used to identify what portion of your IP address is the network address, and what portion of the address is the host address. Let's assume you are working in the typical Class C environment, which makes your subnet mask **255.255.255.0**.

N O T E   Some environments make use of what is known as "variable length subnetting" to more efficiently utilize the addresses. This results in the subnet mask being something other than 255. This is one of the more complex features of IP addressing that will not be covered in this chapter.

Due to the shortage of IP addresses for use on the Internet, a new IP addressing standard has been developed. The IPV6, a new addressing scheme, provides addressing for the Internet for the foreseeable future. (For more information, check RFC-1883, available at **http://ds.internic.net/ rfc/rfc1883.txt**.)

- *You need the address of the gateway.* This is generally the router that enables your LAN segment to communicate with the rest of the network. In smaller offices where there is a single segment, this information is not necessary, because there will be no router in which to point.
- *You need the address of the Domain Name Service (DNS) server (this is optional, but strongly recommended).* The DNS server provides name-to-address resolution for any of the machines on the network that are included in its table. If you don't currently use DNS, this information can be omitted.

Here's how DNS works: On the DNS server, you have a table of names and addresses. Pick your research workstation, aptly named "Marsha," which has an address of **10.14.55.233**. In the table there is an entry that says "Marsha **10.14.55.233**." If you type in "Telnet Marsha," your machine looks at the address and realizes the "Marsha" is not a valid IP address. It queries the DNS server and asks if the DNS server has the address of "Marsha." The DNS server responds with the correct address and the connection is made.

CAUTION

One security note about DNS. If you really want to secure your hosts, don't publish a list of DNS table entries. If that list is available, anyone can get to a log-in prompt just by entering the name from the list. To secure your environment, you should give only the DNS names to users who need to access the system. Also, if you are connected to the Internet, be sure your DNS information isn't being replicated to the Internet. It's like giving a burglar the address of your house—hackers love it, but security people don't.

Part
IV

Ch

17

Installing TCP/IP on Your Server

Now that you know what information you need, install TCP/IP on your server.

1. From the task bar, choose Start, Settings, Control Panel.
2. From the Control Panel, select Network (see Figure 17.1).

FIG. 17.1
Remember, you should always reinstall the latest Windows NT Service Pack after installing new protocols.

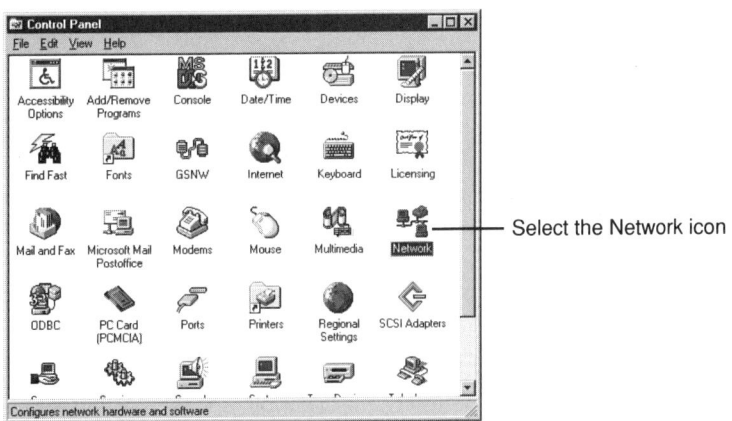

Select the Network icon

3. Select the Protocols tab and then click <u>A</u>dd.

4. From the list of services, select TCP/IP Protocol and click OK (see Figure 17.2). You will be asked if you want to use DHCP to dynamically assign IP addressing. Click Yes or No depending on your configuration.

FIG. 17.2

Remember, you should have confirmed whether your network addressing uses DHCP prior to installing TCP/IP.

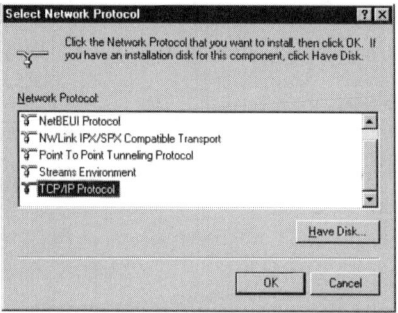

5. Type the path to the Windows NT Server distribution files when prompted. All of the TCP/IP files are copied to the hard disk and the appropriate Registry changes are made.

6. In the Network dialog box, click Close. A dialog box prompts you to enter the information you gathered with your checklist (see Figures 17.3 and 17.4). You also are asked if you want to configure the WINS portion of the setup for this adapter. Check with your network administrator to find out what your standard is. A final feature in this configuration is the capability to enable IP Forwarding (see Figure 17.5). Only use IP Forwarding if you have an overwhelming need to have your Windows NT Server act as an IP router. This is useful if you have two segments that are connected by your server and you need to provide IP connectivity between the two. If you do not need to provide routing, or you are not sure, leave the box unchecked. You always can select it later, and inadvertently installing unplanned IP routers can have a detrimental effect on your routing infrastructure.

7. Restart the computer for the changes to take effect.

FIG. 17.3
Unless you have a registered IP address, you should use one of the reserved IP address ranges as shown in the figure. These are discussed earlier in the chapter.

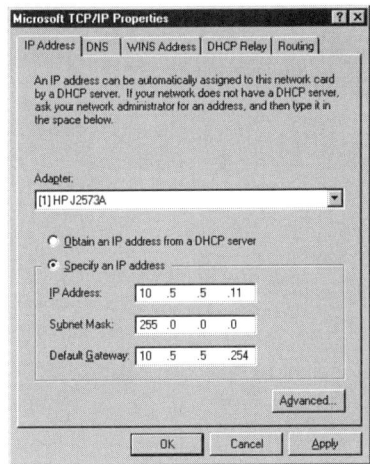

FIG. 17.4
Most UNIX environments take advantage of DNS to provide name resolution. If your network does not, the DNS service included in Windows NT Server 4.0 is easy to set up.

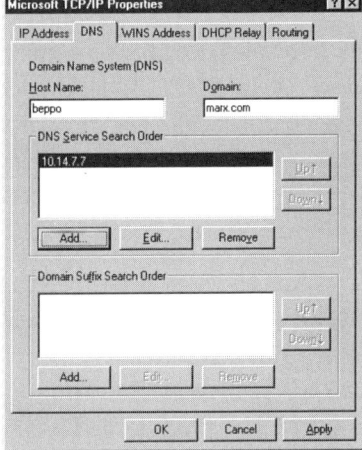

FIG. 17.5
Be careful that you understand your IP routing environment before you enable IP Forwarding. Adding routers to IP networks can cause significant problems in your routing infrastructure.

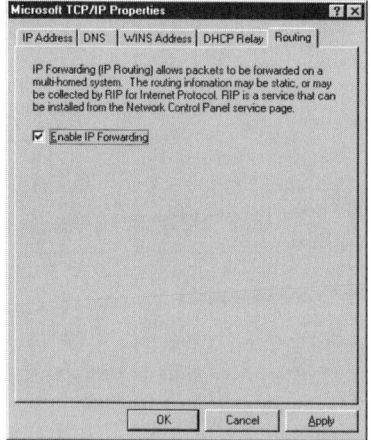

Simple UNIX Integration

The Windows NT TCP/IP installation includes two programs that are well-known to most UNIX users: Telnet and *File Transfer Protocol (FTP)*. Telnet provides a virtual terminal connection to a Telnet server, and FTP permits basic file transfers from an FTP server. The server implementation for each is provided with almost every variation of UNIX. While an FTP server is provided with Windows NT, terminal access to your Windows NT computer requires a Telnet server. Here are the applications in brief, as follows:

■ *Telnet Client* The Telnet client enables you to access UNIX systems from your Windows NT environment. This is very useful for system maintenance, accessing applications with a character-based interface, or doing file maintenance on your account. To take advantage of many of the new client/server applications, you really need to install an X Terminal application, which is discussed later in the chapter.

■ *FTP Client/Server* The FTP client enables you to transfer files to and from your computer by accessing an FTP server in either ASCII or binary format. In the early days of the Internet, this was how a lot of information was exchanged. Lists of public FTP servers were circulated throughout the "Net" as people shared information, games, utilities, and graphics. FTP is still used in conjunction with many of the Web browsers to allow you to download from a Web page. By loading the FTP server on your Windows NT server, you give users the capability to read and write files to your Windows NT server. When you configure this application, be very careful with your permissions. Disable the anonymous logon and make sure that you require passwords. Clear text passwords should be avoided whenever possible—they are very vulnerable to the network analysis tools used by many hackers.

Extending Your UNIX Integration

FTP and Telnet give you basic connectivity, but what can you do to enhance your integration into a UNIX environment? Let's talk about some types of applications that will make this integration a bit more useful.

Telnet Server

The "Microsoft Windows NT Server Resource Kit," available from Microsoft, contains a Telnet server for Windows NT server. If you are interested in a third-party Telnet server, a company called Pragma Systems offers one that works very well. (These companies are listed at the end of the section.) "Why a Telnet server?" you might ask. If your administrators are used to working from the UNIX command line, the ability to access Windows NT from a Telnet connection can be useful in easing the transition. With a Telnet server, your administrators can edit configuration files, start and stop services, rename, delete, or move files, as well as any other command-line functions Windows NT supports.

Part

IV

Ch

17

Network File System

The *Network File System (NFS)* is a file system that allows UNIX file systems to be mounted by remote systems. This is similar to a Windows NT share. This capability is not inherent to Windows NT, but can be added by using products from WRQ, Hummingbird Communications, or NetManage.

The NFS file system does have some inherent security issues, so when configuring it from the UNIX host, keep the following points in mind:

- First, avoid giving NFS access to the root of the file system. This is for the same reason that you should never share from the root of a drive in Windows NT. If you make the file system available from the root, you potentially give access to the UNIX system file subdirectories. This can cause any number of problems, including access to the password files, corrupted utilities, Trojan horses, or any number of other system problems.

- Second, as in everything, be restrictive in the permissions you allow users to the file system. Assign permissions as needed, and avoid giving large numbers of users access, unless absolutely necessary. It's easy to use a group to give access, and it is usually okay if done properly. Occasionally, systems administrators may get lazy and use large groups to assign access. This inadvertently can open security holes in your system.

■ Finally, because NFS is vulnerable to spoofing (this technique is discussed in Chapter 14, "Internet Security and BackOffice"), reduce your vulnerability by restricting access to ports 111 (the RPC port) and 2049 (the NFS port) from networks outside of your own. This includes the Internet, as well as any other external connections such as business partners, customers, or even subsidiaries if necessary. Blocking these ports significantly reduces your exposure to unauthorized NFS mount commands.

X Terminal Access

The latest method for accessing applications on UNIX systems are X Terminals. They enable users to access UNIX systems, or if the right software is loaded, Windows NT systems from a *Graphical User Interface (GUI)*. You could spend a couple chapters discussing "X" applications, but it really falls outside the scope of this chapter. Some vendors that sell X Terminal emulation packages include Attachmate, Hummingbird Communications, NetManage, and WRQ.

Vendors Listed in this Chapter

Microsoft Press
http://www.microsoft.com

Microsoft Windows NT Server Resource Kit ISBN: 1-57231-344-7

WRQ
http://www.wrq/com

X Terminal and NFS software

Hummingbird Communications
http://www.hummingbird.com

X Terminal and NFS software

NetManage
http://www.netmanage.com

X Terminal and NFS software

Attachmate
http://attachmate.com

X Terminal software

From Here...

The following chapters provide more information on securing your Windows NT environment in conjunction with other operating systems.

- Chapter 14, "Internet Security and BackOffice," shows you how to handle security if your Windows NT network is connected to the most diverse network environment there is—the Internet. This chapter also contains in-depth information on the TCP/IP suite of protocols and applications.

- Chapter 15, "Windows NT Integration with NetWare and Other Network Operating Systems," shows you how to securely integrate Windows NT in a mixed operating system environment.

- Chapter 18, "An Overview of the *Department Of Defense Trusted Computer System Evaluation Criteria*," and Chapter 19, "The Implementation of C2-Level Security with Windows NT," discuss the Department of Defense security models, as well as the C2 Security Classification. This information helps you understand what a truly secure system is, and how to measure the quality of your security configuration.

Part

IV

Ch

17

Implementing Department of Defense Security Criteria in a Windows NT Environment

An Overview of the Department of Defense Trusted Computer System Evaluation Criteria

Until now, you've concentrated your efforts on the mechanics of Windows NT security. Windows NT's architecture and Security Model have been covered in detail, and you should understand how the Local Security Authority (LSA) in conjunction with the Security Account Manager (SAM) helps to protect your system. To solidify your education in computer security, we'll leave Windows NT-specific information to delve briefly into the reasoning responsible for its security implementation. Then, you can implement C2-level security on your own Windows NT system. ■

Evolution of security controls

The National Computer Security Center (NCSC) prepares documents on computer security and evaluates and rates products based on their conformance with published standards. Their efforts assist public and private organizations in protecting sensitive information.

The Orange Book

Better known as the Orange Book, DOD 3200.28-STD is part of the NCSC's Rainbow Series, a group of documents devoted to computer security. The Orange Book provides standardized classifications for evaluating security controls in computer systems.

System classifications and security levels

The Orange Book divides security levels into four categories: D, C, B and A, with D being the lowest.

An explanation of the MLS environment

Multilevel Security, introduced in Division B, offers airtight security.

Evolution of Security Controls

Computer security has been a concern for over 30 years. In October 1967, a defense department group known as the Defense Science Board began searching for ways to protect information. Almost three years later in February 1970, they presented a report, "Security Controls for Computer Systems," that made several policy and technical recommendations to minimize the chances of classified material being compromised. In 1972, the Department of Defense issued Directive 5200.28 as an answer to the policy recommendation made by the Defense Science Board by establishing requirements and controls for protecting sensitive information processed on computer systems. Following this policy change, computer security research and development was carried out by the Air Force and other agencies. The advancements made by the Air Force, Advanced Research Projects Agency (ARPA, now famous for ARPANet, which was the beginning of the Internet), and a few government contractors led to the Department of Defense Computer Security Initiative, which concentrated on computer security issues.

Around the same time as the Defense Department's Computer Security Initiative started in 1977, the National Bureau of Standards (NBS) got involved. The NBS held invitational workshops dealing with computer security issues. These meetings led to a paper recommending answers to the problems in determining criteria for computer security evaluation. Soon after this report, the MITRE Corporation started working on computer security evaluation criteria. Computer security experts studied the result of MITRE's work. Then, in 1981, the Department of Defense Computer Security Center was formed to expand on earlier efforts and foster computer security in both the public and private sectors. In August 1985, the Defense Department's Computer Security Center's name changed to the National Computer Security Center (NCSC). Today, the NCSC evaluates product security levels of operating systems, network components, and security subsystems using the Trusted Product Evaluation Program (TPEP). Both the NCSC and TPEP are units within the National Security Agency (NSA).

The Rainbow Series

Today, the NCSC publishes documents on computer security. The entire collection of documents is affectionately known as the Rainbow Series because of the color of their covers. Table 18.1 lists the "colors of the rainbow," as well as their titles.

Table 18.1   The Rainbow Series

Color	Title
Amber	*A Guide to Understanding Configuration Management in Trusted Systems*
Bright Blue	*Trusted Product Evaluation Questionnaire*
Blue	*Introduction to Certification and Accreditation Concepts*
Bright Blue	*Vendor Guide to Trusted Product Evaluations*
Bright Orange	*A Guide to Understanding Security Testing and Test Documentation in Trusted Systems*
Brown	*A Guide to Understanding Trusted Facility Management*
Burgundy	*A Guide to Understanding Design Documentation*
Dark Lavender	*A Guide to Understanding Trusted Distribution in Trusted Systems*
Forest Green	*A Guide to Understanding Data Remanence in Automated Information Systems, September 1991, Version 2*
Green	*Department of Defense Password Management Guideline*
Hot Peach	*A Guide to Writing the Security Features User's Guide*
Light Blue	*A Guide to Understanding Identification and Authentication in Trusted Systems*
Light Blue	*A Guide to Understanding Object Reuse in Trusted Systems*
Light Pink	*A Guide to Understanding Covert Channel Analysis of Trusted Systems*
Light Yellow	*Guidance for Applying the Department of Defense Trusted System Evaluation Criteria in Specific Environments*
Neon Orange	*A Guide to Understanding Discretionary Access Control in Trusted Systems*
Orange	*Department of Defense Trusted Computer System Evaluation Criteria*
Pink	*Rating Maintenance Phase Program Document Version 2*
Purple	*Guidelines for Formal Verification Systems*
Purple	*Trusted Database Management System Interpretation of the Department of Defense Trusted Computer System Evaluation Criteria*
Purple	*A Guide to Procurement of Trusted Systems: An Introduction to Procurement Initiators on Computer Security Requirements*

Part

V

Ch

18

continues

Table 18.1   Continued

Color	Title
Purple	*A Guide to Procurement of Trusted Systems: Language for RFP Specifications and Statements of Work—An Aid to Procurement Initiators*
Purple	*A Guide to Procurement of Trusted Systems: Computer Security Contract Data Requirements List and Data Item Description Tutorial*
Purple	*A Guide to Procurement of Trusted Systems: How to Evaluate a Bidder's Proposal Document—An Aid to Procurement Initiators and Contractors*
Red	*Trusted Network Interpretation of the Department of Defense Trusted Computer System Evaluation Criteria*
Silver	*Trusted UNIX Working Group (TRUSIX) Rationale for Selecting Access Control List Features for the UNIX® System, 7*
Teal Green	*Glossary of Computer Security Terms*
Turquoise	*A Guide to Understanding Information System Security Officer Responsibilities for Automated Information Systems*
Venice Blue	*Computer Security Subsystem Interpretation of the Department of Defense Trusted Computer System Evaluation Criteria*
Violet	*Assessing Controlled Access Protection*
Yellow	*A Guide to Understanding Trusted Recovery in Trusted Systems*
Yellow	*Technical Rationale Behind the Guidance for Applying the Department of Defense Trusted Computer System Evaluation Criteria in Specific Environments*
Yellow-Green	*Guidelines for Writing Trusted Facility Manuals*

The NCSC's documents come in three forms: standards, interpretations, and guidelines. The focal point of many of the NCSC's documents is the Trusted Computer System Evaluation Criteria (TCSEC), or the Orange Book. The Orange Book is the NCSC standard on computer security evaluation. Because of its importance, the Orange Book is covered in detail later.

Interpretations Interpretation documents restate the evaluation criteria based on the type of system being evaluated. Specialized interpretations allow the general requirements contained in the Orange Book to be applied not only to current types of systems, but to systems that will be developed in the future. Rather than totally restating requirements for each individual system type, the design of the Orange Book is such that it can be used as a foundation on which security requirements can be built. Interpretations of the Orange Book provide a simple, yet elegant method of constructing these requirements.

Interpretations are NCSC official statements explaining how to apply the Orange Book's requirements to a particular situation. For example, the Red Book, *Trusted Network Interpretation of the Department of Defense Trusted Computer System Evaluation Criteria*, restates each of the Orange Book's requirements in the context of a networked environment. In addition to the Red Book, there are two other specialized explanations of the Orange Book. These are the *Computer Security Subsystem Interpretation of the TCSEC*, (the Venice Blue Book) and the *Trusted Database Management System Interpretation of the TCSEC*, or Purple Book.

Guidelines NCSC Guidelines are just that—guidelines. They are not standards, nor are they interpretations. These guidelines offer further insight into the requirements stated in the Orange Book, or one of its interpretations. These guidelines range from site management to applying the TCSEC in specific environments.

The guidelines provided by the NCSC offer security-enhancing suggestions that can be applied to almost all organizations. For example, the Green Book, the *Department of Defense Password Management Guideline*, discusses authentication issues. Administrators can use this document as a basis for establishing their local policy on password management and can feel confident their procedures are thorough.

NCSC guideline documents also provide information on product evaluation and insight on certain aspects of the TCSEC. The Bright Blue Book, the *Vendor Guide to Trusted Product Evaluations*, outlines the evaluation process. The documentation that must accompany a request as well as the steps in evaluation are included to assist companies in assembling the necessary documentation. This ensures that all vendors have the information they need prior to having their product evaluated.

The Orange Book

The *Department of Defense Trusted Computer System Evaluation Criteria*, better known as the Orange Book, provides standardized methods for determining the security level of a particular system. Almost all other documents provided by the NCSC exist because of the Orange Book. Although the Orange Book originally was designed to evaluate government systems, it is now used to measure security for virtually all computer systems.

The Orange Book's security levels are grouped by divisions and classes. Divisions are the broadest category and range from A to D. Division A represents the highest degree of security, while division D is the lowest. Within divisions C and B, additional tiers are represented by classes. Division C has two classes, C1 and C2, with C2 providing greater security than C1. Division B has three levels: B1, B2, and B3. As in division C, a higher class depicts heightened security. Within the separate classifications, the Orange Book presents its criteria in the form of Control Objectives. Control Objectives simply categorize security requirements into related groups. The Control Objectives used by the Orange Book are Security Policy, Accountability, and Assurance.

Security Policy

A Security Policy simply is a statement detailing how information will be accessed and distributed over a system. This Control Objective stems from the inability to accurately define "computer security." As pointed out in the Orange Book, "a given system can only be said to be secure with respect to its enforcement of some specific policy." The Security Policy Control Objective can be expressed in terms of its Mandatory Security Policy, Discretionary Security Policy, and Marking. Mandatory Security bases the access to information solely on a combination of a user's clearance and the information's designated sensitivity level. As long as the user has the proper clearance, access is granted. Discretionary Security couples Mandatory Security with "need-to-know" requirements. Not only must a user have the proper clearance, he or she must have been given explicit permission to view, use, and modify the data. Discretionary Security facilitates information departmentalization. Marking deals with a system's capability to not only label information based on its sensitivity level, but also to maintain that label.

Accountability

The Accountability Control Objective deals with individual accountability. Before a user can be held accountable however, they first must be identified and the stated identity authenticated in a reliable manner. Identification and authentication are central to almost all other security measures. Unless a user's identity can be verified reliably, their clearance cannot be determined and the entire Security Policy, be it Mandatory, Discretionary, or any combination thereof, breaks down. Also classified in Accountability, Auditing depends on proper user identification. Audit data assists authorized personnel in tracking actions that could compromise the system's security.

Assurance

The third Control Objective, Assurance, deals with guaranteeing that the security implementation is working exactly as intended. Assurance includes Life-Cycle Assurance and Operational Assurance. Life-Cycle Assurance primarily deals with how the organization designs, develops, and maintains the system. In contrast, Operational Assurance's concerns focus on ensuring that the system's execution adheres to its stated Security Policy.

System Classifications and Security Levels

The classifications and levels outlined by the Orange Book have three major purposes, each of which is interdependent. First, they provide a guideline for users to determine realistically the security level of their system. Once their current level of security accurately has been determined by using a standardized method, organizations can more accurately address the remaining issues for achieving their desired security level. Second, they provide manufacturers with a guide to determining controls that should be implemented according to the desired level of security. Finally, the Orange Book's security levels can serve as specifications for procurement. By using a standard, the playing field is divided into distinct levels that allow not only government agencies, but also private enterprise and individuals to determine accurately which product fulfills their need.

Pick a Color, Any Color...

The beginning of each classification includes the actual summary from DOD 5200.28-STD Appendix C. Following that summary, I've included explanations and notes that should offer a little more insight, along with a list of evaluated products. The summaries and notes, however, cannot replace the actual documentation. A copy of the Orange Book and the other Rainbow documents can be obtained by sending a request to:

INFOSEC AWARENESS, ATTN: Y13/IAOC
DEPARTMENT OF DEFENSE
9800 SAVAGE ROAD
FT MEADE MD 20755-6000

You also can call (410) 766-8729 or better yet, visit their Web site at **http://www.radium. ncsc. mil /tpep/**. At the time of this writing, the NCSC is providing a single copy at no charge— a price that's hard to beat! If you're reading this book, security is obviously important to you, so I encourage you to obtain the Rainbow Series.

Division D

Division D, also known as the "Minimal Protection" division, is a "catchall" for evaluated products that do not meet the requirements for higher security divisions. The key word in the previous sentence is "evaluated." Being categorized as Division D does not mean the product will not assist an organization with security; it simply means that all of the security features of higher levels have not been implemented in that product. Table 18.2 lists some Division D products.

Table 18.2 D Evaluated Products

Company	Product
Fischer International Systems Corp.	Watchdog PC Data Security
Okiok Data, Limited	RAC/M and RAC/M II Version 3.3

In order to help clarify what being evaluated as a Division D product means, take Okiok Data, Limited's RAC/M and RAC/M II, for example. It provides a number of security features such as user identification, authentication, auditing, access control to certain system resources, and encryption, along with several other features, for personal computers running MS-DOS and Windows. However, it is not as secure as a C Division product. For certain environments, this product may be the perfect solution. Basically, while the Evaluated Products List from the NCSC is a tool to assist groups in selecting products related to security, it should not be the only tool used.

Division C

Division C, also known as Discretionary Protection, contains two classifications, C1 and C2. Systems qualifying for this level provide for need-to-know access along with accountability and basic auditing.

Class C1 In layman's terms, the C1 of Division C meets discretionary security requirements because it provides a separation of users from data through access control restrictions, ensuring that users can protect sensitive data from disclosure and destruction.

N O T E The NCSC no longer tests systems for a C1 rating; because C1 remains in DOD 5200.28-STD, it was included in this chapter.

In a C1 system, each user must be allowed a method of specifying other users, or groups of users, allowed to access their data. C1-level systems require users to identify and authenticate themselves prior to performing any actions. Once reliably determined, the user's identity can be used to account for their actions on the system. Any form of authentication can be used as long as the data used to verify the identity is protected from unauthorized access. The most common methods of identification and authentication, however, are User Names and Passwords.

To certify that the system's functions work properly, C1 systems provide either hardware, software, or some combination, providing organizations a means of assuring their operation. Systems also are tested for obvious methods of unauthorized entry.

Another important part of C1 systems is the documentation. Vendors must provide information on the system's security features, how to use them, and how they interact with one another. Additionally, a system administrator's manual that details functions and privileges that require close control, test plans, and procedures showing how the system was tested, as well as the results of those tests and the manufacturer's philosophy of security is included.

Class C2 C2 class systems are a step up in the Orange Book hierarchy and build on the foundation of the C1 specification. The C2 systems provide tighter security than C1 systems by enforcing more granular access of control policies, auditing all security related events, and better resource isolation. Currently, there are 12 products, nine Operating Systems, and three Trusted Applications that have been evaluated level-C2. Table 18.3 lists the operating systems while Table 18.4 lists the Trusted Applications.

Table 18.3 C2 Evaluated Operating Systems

Company	Product
Data General Corp.	AOS/VS II Release 3.01
Data General Corp.	AOS/VS II Release 3.10
Digital Equipment Corp.	OpenVMS VAX Version 6.0
Digital Equipment Corp.	OpenVMS VAX Version 6.1
Digital Equipment Corp.	OpenVMS VAX and Alpha Version 6.1
IBM	AS/400 with OS/400 V2R3M0
IBM	AS/400 with OS/400 V3R0M5
Microsoft	Windows NT 3.5 (Service Pack 3)
Tandem Computers, Inc.	Guardian-90 w/Safeguard S00.01

Table 18.4 C2 Evaluated Trusted Applications

Company	Product
Informix Software, Inc.	INFORMIX-OnLine/Secure 4.1
Informix Software, Inc.	INFORMIX-OnLine/Secure 5.0
Oracle Corp.	Oracle7

Part
V

Ch
18

Beyond the simple access controls in C1, C2 systems either allow or disallow object access all the way down to a single user. Another important requirement is how C2 systems deal with object reuse. C2 systems protect objects, such as memory, by not allowing more than one process to access it and making sure the object's data cannot be read when it's released back to the system.

While a C1 system may or may not provide audit-trail capabilities, C2 systems are required to furnish extensive auditing. Once a user has been authenticated, their unique identification is used for each object access. C2 systems must be able to create, maintain, and protect the data created from audits. Audit trails only can be viewed or destroyed by authorized users. The C2 requirements dictate that systems be able to record several types of events, including identification and authentication, objects being introduced or deleted from a user's address space, actions performed by operators and administrators, and other security related events. For each event recorded in the audit trail, the system must include the date and time, unique user identification, and whether or not the event succeeded. For object introduction and deletion events, the system also must include the object's name. System administrators can select which events and which users to audit.

Division B

Also known as Mandatory Protection, Division B contains three classifications. In addition to C2 requirements, Division B introduces an informal statement of the security policy model, security labels, and mandatory access control over all objects. This division also is where Multi-Level Security (MLS) is introduced.

Class B1 Classification B1 builds on the specifications of the earlier, less secure classifications, and it introduces sensitivity labels to the list of requirements. Each object within the system must be associated with a sensitivity label. When combined with the user's identification, these labels provide the system with mandatory access-control information. Should objects already not associated with a label be introduced into the system, an appropriate label is requested, then assigned by an authorized user. Although similar to object access based on user grouping, sensitivity labels, combined with discretionary access, provide thorough control of sensitive information. Not only must a user be given permission either explicitly or by group membership to view certain data, they also must have security clearance that is at least equal to the security clearance of the data to be viewed.

When exporting data, sensitivity labels may or may not be maintained, depending on the device. When exporting to single-level devices or devices using a single-security level at any one time, sensitivity labels do not have to be maintained. Should the device be multi-level, or capable of securely processing data of two or more security levels, sensitivity labels also are exported and must reside on the same physical medium in the same form as the data, be it human or machine readable.

Tables 18.5, 18.6, and 18.7 list a number of B1-compliant operating systems, network components, and trusted applications.

Table 18.5 B1 Evaluated Operating Systems

Company	Product
Amdahl Corp.	UTS/MLS Version 2.1.5+
Digital Equipment Corp.	SEVMS VAX Version 6.0
Digital Equipment Corp.	SEVMS VAX Version 6.1
Digital Equipment Corp.	SEVMS VAX and Alpha Version 6.1
Digital Equipment Corp.	ULTRIX MLS+ Version 2.1 on VAX 3100
Harris Computer Systems Corp.	CX/SX 6.1.1
Harris Computer Systems Corp.	CX/SX 6.2.1
Hewlett Packard Corp.	HP-UX BLS Release 8.04
Hewlett Packard Corp.	HP-UX BLS Release 9.0.9+
Silicon Graphics, Inc.	Trusted IRIX/B Release 4.0.5EPL
Unisys Corp.	OS 1100 Security Release I
Unisys Corp.	OS 1100/2200 Release SB3R6
Unisys Corp.	OS 1100/2200 Release SB3R8
Unisys Corp.	OS 1100/2200 Release SB4R2
Unisys Corp.	OS 1100/2200 Release SB4R7

Table 18.6 B1 Evaluated Network Components

Company	Product
Cray Research, Inc.	Trusted UNICOS 8.0
Harris Computer Systems Corp.	CX/SX with LAN/SX 6.1.1
Harris Computer Systems Corp.	CX/SX with LAN/SX 6.2.1

Part
V

Ch
18

Table 18.7 B1 Evaluated Trusted Applications

Company	Product
Informix Software, Inc.	INFORMIX-OnLine/Secure 4.1
Informix Software, Inc.	INFORMIX-OnLine/Secure 5.0
Oracle Corp.	Trusted Oracle7

Class B2 A B2 class system is very secure; in fact, the government goes as far as saying that a B2 system is "relatively resistant to penetration." Classification B2 requires mandatory access control for all objects through subject and device labeling. Subject sensitivity labels inform users when their associated security level changes and allows them to display a subject's sensitivity label. For example, when a user leaves a document to view another document having a higher or lower sensitivity label, the system informs the user of the new document's security level. While viewing that same document, the user may at any time request the document's sensitivity level.

Device labels, on the other hand, allow for minimum and maximum security levels to be placed on all attached devices. By using device labels, administrators can control which devices are suitable for specific security levels. Should a printer's physical location be in an unsecured office, the system administrator can specify that only nonsensitive information be printed on that specific printer.

B2 also introduces covert channels. The term *covert channel* refers to a method where one process communicates data to another process in a way that violates the system's security policy. Each element in a covert channel must know how to access the channel and interpret signals from the other. The information sender usually executes at a high security level, while the receiver runs at a lower level.

There are two different types of covert channels: timing and storage. A *timing covert channel* is one where the receiver observes the length of time the sender takes to perform operations, based on predetermined codes. *Storage covert channels* are those where the sending process modifies an aspect of the system that causes the receiver to either fail or succeed (which may mean for the receiver to write a 0 or a 1). The information then is passed from the sender to the receiver bit-by-bit with each successive operation.

The five products listed in Tables 18.8 and 18.9 meet all of the requirements imposed on Classification B1 systems.

Table 18.8 B2 Evaluated Operating Systems

Company	Product
Trusted Information Systems, Inc.	Trusted XENIX 3.0
Trusted Information Systems, Inc.	Trusted XENIX 4.0

Table 18.9 B2 Evaluated Network Components

Company	Product
General Kinetics Corp.	VSLAN 5.0
General Kinetics Corp.	VSLAN/VSLANE 5.1
General Kinetics Corp.	VSLAN/VSLANE 6.0

Class B3 Class B3, also known as Security Domains, calls for more attention to detail than its predecessors, and it's very secure. Reference monitors are used for the first time to track object usage. Trusted paths, introduced in the B2 class, are expanded upon. Table 18.10 lists B3 evaluated operating systems.

Part
V

Ch
18

Table 18.10 B3 Evaluated Operating Systems

Company	Product
Wang Federal, Inc.	XTS-200 STOP 3.1.E
Wang Federal, Inc.	XTS-200 STOP 3.2.E
Wang Federal, Inc.	XTS-300 STOP 4.1
Wang Federal, Inc.	XTS-300 STOP 4.1a

Division A

The highest level of protection found in the Orange Book specifications is Division A, also known as Verified Protection. Currently, Division A contains only one classification—A1. While A1 systems functionally are equivalent to class B3 systems, additional security is provided by extensive analysis and design of the system architecture, ensuring that the Trusted Computer Base is correctly implemented. This includes a formal model of the security policy, a formal top-level specification (FTLS) of the design, and it requires more stringent configuration management. In most cases, these systems will have a Systems Security Administrator. Table 18.11 lists some A1 evaluated network components.

Table 18.11   A1 Evaluated Network Components

Company	Product
The Boeing Company	MLS LAN
Gemini Computers, Inc.	Gemini Trusted Network Processor

An Explanation of the Multi-Level Security Environment

As mentioned earlier, Multi-Level Security, or MLS, is a requirement of Division B-compliant systems. MLS extends and enhances Division A and B systems by allowing information with varying sensitivities to be simultaneously stored and processed in a system with users of varying security levels while preventing users from accessing unauthorized information.

The MLS significantly can enhance the efficiency and effectiveness of a highly secure system, because it eliminates the need to have several different systems to ensure the security and integrity of sensitive data. Previously disconnected systems now may be interconnected using MLS technology to ensure security, which allows users who once had to access the data they needed through several workstations the capability to do so through one secure workstation. Hence, this makes it easier for an organization to minimize costs and effort to maximize productivity.

There are five basic components of an MLS system: Hosts, Guards, Workstations, Networks, and Databases, defined as follows:

- *MLS Hosts*   The platform for applications such as data bases, decision support systems, and communication systems.
- *MLS Guards*   Act as secure bridges across boundaries between systems operating at varying security levels.
- *MLS Workstations*   Provide users access to systems operating at different security levels from a single access point.
- *MLS Networks*   Provide security when interconnecting single-level and multilevel components with sensitivity labels and network security services for data being transferred between the systems.
- *MLS Data Bases*   Act as a repository for multiple levels of related data. This allows users of varying security levels to access a shared set of data based solely on their individual access level.

From Here...

As you can see, the *Department of Defense Trusted Computer System Evaluation Criteria* is rigorous. The fundamental security aspects outlined in the Orange Book can be applied not only to government systems requiring mandated security levels, but to other organizations as well. Understanding the security objectives in the different divisions helps administrators identify shortcomings in their current policies. In the upcoming chapter, you learn how to configure your Windows NT computer for C2-level security. Also, refer to the following chapters for related information:

- Chapter 2, "An Overview of Microsoft Windows NT Security," contains general information about how security works in Windows NT.

- Chapter 3, "Windows NT Operating System Architecture," explains how the various components work together.

- Chapter 6, "User Account Security and Windows NT," explains mandatory access control.

- Chapter 19, "The Implementation of C2-Level Security with Windows NT," is where you actively apply the information given in this chapter to your own system.

Part
V

Ch
18

The Implementation of C2-Level Security with Windows NT

The Department of Defense Class C2-security definition

Before you can make your Windows NT system meet C2-security requirements, however, a thorough understanding of each requirement is necessary. Each C2 requirement is explained along with the NCSC evaluation team's findings.

How to meet C2 requirements with Windows NT

The steps required to make your system C2 secure are explained in detail as are the default C2-security features of Windows NT. Additionally, you learn how to the secure the file system and operating system as well as how you can use the C2 Configuration Manager to make your system C2 secure.

As you learned in Chapter 18, "An Overview of the *Department of Defense Trusted Computer System Evaluation Criteria*," the *Department of Defense Trusted Computer System Evaluation Criteria* provides standardized security measurements useful with virtually all computer systems. Under the proper conditions, Windows NT adheres to level C2 as outlined by the Orange Book. In this chapter, you review the requirements of C2 security, then adjust Windows NT's settings so that our system meets C2's provisions. ■

The Department of Defense Class C2 Security Definition

The National Computer Security Center (NCSC) report number CSC-FER-95/003 (for more information, see **http://www.radium.ncsc.mil/tpep/epl/entries/CSC-EPL-95-003.html**), dated April 29, 1996, contains the Final Evaluation Report of Windows NT Workstation and Server version 3.5 with U.S. Service Pack 3. While this document painstakingly details the results of the NCSC's evaluation of Windows NT at great length (over 200 pages!), the entire report cannot be included in this chapter. Instead, a brief overview is provided.

The Windows NT Evaluated Platforms

Windows NT 3.5 was evaluated using three different systems: Compaq Proliant 2,000, Compaq Proliant 4,000 (**http://www.compaq.com**), and the DECpc AXP/150 (**http://www.digtal.com**). Memory capacities ranged from 16M to 512M.

Each of the Compaq Proliants used Intel Pentium processors (90 and 100 MHz). The Proliant 2,000, which has a capacity of two processors, and Proliant 4,000, up to four processors, were each configured as shown in the following listing:

- Tri-Flex EISA System Board
- SVGA 1024×768×4 Video Adapter
- 32-bit FAST SCSI-2 Controller
- 1.5 GB SCSI-2 Hard Drive
- 2.5 GB SCSI-2 Hard Drive
- CD-ROM
- 3.5" 1.44M Floppy Drive
- 2/8 GB DAT Drive
- 101 Keyboard
- 3 Button Mouse
- HP LaserJet IV

The DECpc configuration is next:

- 150 MHz DEC CPU
- Compaq Qvision SVGA Video Adapter
- Adaptec 1742 SCSI Controller

- 535M SCSI Hard Drive
- CD-ROM
- 3.5" 1.44M Floppy Drive
- 101 Keyboard
- 3 Button Mouse
- HP LaserJet IV

Although the platforms used in Windows NT's evaluation mainly are known as network servers, the NCSC evaluated them as stand-alone units. Also, the DECpc ROM Console Firmware must be version 3.5 or later.

Discretionary Access Control Discretionary Access Control (DAC) secures information by allowing access based not only on a user's identity, but his or her need to know. For example, a Windows NT system using NTFS enables object owners to detail access in terms of groups or all the way down to a single user. Windows NT's DAC facilities enable finer control of access than available on other systems.

Remember the requirements for a C2-level system? Well, just in case you don't, here they are again. According to the Orange Book, "The Trusted Computer Base shall define and control access between named users and named objects (e.g., files and programs) in the ADP system." In layman's terms, this means that the operating system must provide the capability to control access to all system objects based on individual user names, group membership, or both. It also must ensure that only explicitly authorized users can grant access to other users.

Windows NT controls object access by using *Access Control Lists*, otherwise known as ACLs (ACLs are covered in detail in Chapter 3, "Windows NT Operating System Architecture"). These ACLs enable authorized users to control object sharing in accordance with C2 requirements. Each ACL contains an ACL header and *Access Control Entries (ACE)*. The header contains information on the size and number of ACEs stored in the ACL, while the ACE contains the access information. Windows NT has two types of ACLs: Discretionary Access Control Lists and System Access Control Lists.

Discretionary Access Control Lists (DACL) control object access. DACLs have two types of ACEs: AccessAllowed and AccessDenied. The AccessAllowed ACE is used to grant access to a user or group of users, while the AccessDenied ACE is used expressly to deny access to a user or group of users. *System Access Control Lists (SACL)* handle auditing control on object access. The SACL has a single ACE, SystemAudit. SystemAudit is used to control auditing access generation.

The only way access permission is granted to an object is by changing the DACL of that object. Only users with WriteDAC access to the object can modify the DACL of that object. This ensures that only authorized individuals, namely the Administrator(s), can allow others access to that object. Through its use of these ACLs, Windows NT adheres to the discretionary access requirement.

Object Reuse   The C2 specification also calls for strict security around the reuse of system storage objects. In order to accomplish this, the operating system must revoke all authorizations to an object before it is allocated from the system's pool of unused objects. It also must ensure that *no* information, even if it has been encrypted, is available to a user through a prior user's session of actions.

Windows NT does a good job of handling object reuse and does so in three basic ways:

1. The object header and body are initialized to the correct new values.
2. Object memory is zeroed.
3. The most recently written object can only be read.

The method of handling object reuse varies depending on the type of object. For executive subsystem objects, when the Object Manager initializes the fields of the header, any previously used memory is completely overwritten. Prior to mapping Protected Server objects to the address space of the process, the Memory Manager zeros all allocated memory that will be used by the object.

Identification and Authentication   The C2 specification calls for the operating system to require user identification and authentication (normally through the use of passwords) before any action can be performed and any data can be accessed. It also mandates that user authentication data be protected from unauthorized users and that each user's actions be identified and logged.

Windows NT requires each user to identify themselves with a unique username, which is represented internally by a *Security Identification (SID)*. This SID is totally unique and cannot be reassigned—even if a username is deleted and then added back. Authentication is carried out by the *Local Security Authority (LSA)* via a password. All passwords are stored in an encrypted form in the *Security Accounts Manager (SAM)* database.

Audit   As mentioned, a C2-level operating system must have the capability to log all system activities and to access the system objects it is protecting. It also must ensure that the audit log is protected from unauthorized access and destruction. Here is a list of the types of events that can be logged:

- Using identification and authentication mechanisms
- Introducing objects into a user's address space; for example, a user opening a file
- Deleting objects

- Administrator's and Security Officer's actions
- Any other security related events

For each event recorder in the log, the following items must be tracked: the date and time of the event, user name, type of event, and success or failure of the event. If the event is a log-on event, the origin of the event must be logged. Additionally, the administrator should have the capability to audit selectively the actions of any user based on the user name.

Windows NT's audit system is made up of the LSA, the *Security Reference Monitor (SRM)*, Event Logger and Event Viewer. All audit information is protected by a DACL, which only can be accessed by administrators. Table 19.1 lists the auditable events in Windows NT.

Table 19.1   Auditable Events in Windows NT

Event Type
System Restart
System Shutdown
Authentication Package Loading
Registered Log-on Process
Audit Log Cleared
Number of Audits Discarded
Logon Successful
Unknown Username or Password
Time Restricted Logon Failure
Account Disabled
Account Expired
Invalid Workstation
Logon Type Restricted
Password Expired
Failed Log-on
Logoff
Open Object
Close Handle
Assign Special Privilege

Part
V

Ch
19

continues

Table 19.1 Continued
Event Type
Privileged Service
Privileged Object Access
Process Created
Process Exit
Duplicate Handle
Indirect Reference
Privilege Assigned
Audit Policy Change
Domain Changed
User Changed
User Created
User Deleted
Global Group Member Removed
Global Group Member Added
Local Group Changed
Local Group Created
Local Group Member Removed
Local Group Member Added
Local Group Member Deleted

System Architecture   The architecture of any C2-compliant system must maintain a protected domain for its own execution, ensuring that processes and data within the protected domain are free of external tampering. These system resources also must be subject to access control and auditing. Windows NT protects all system resources. Attempted access to any resource is auditable and must pass access control measures.

System Integrity   Another requirement of the C2-security specification is that the system must have hardware and software features that periodically can test and validate that the system is operating correctly and securely.

The System Integrity testing requirements primarily are dependent on the hardware being used. However, upon request, Microsoft may be able to provide software to test the hardware platform.

Security Testing   As you might imagine, to be evaluated as C2, extensive security testing must be done during development and evaluation, which must be done on an ongoing basis to ensure continued system integrity and to eliminate possible security holes.

Microsoft tested the functionality of the protected servers running in user mode, the executive running in kernel mode, and the Win32 API. Separate tests were used on the major security-relevant areas of Windows NT, such as object access, object reuse, and privilege use. The evaluation team found their testing philosophy to be thorough.

User's Guide to Security Features   In order to be evaluated as a C2 operating system, the vendor must provide at least one chapter in user documentation detailing the security mechanisms in the operating system (OS), how they are used, and how they work together to ensure system integrity.

Windows NT includes a Security Features Users Guide (SFUG) that describes procedures such as logging on, changing passwords, locking and unlocking the computer, and how to use a screen saver. It also describes how discretionary access control works on files and directories, along with file and directory ownership in Windows NT.

Trusted Facility Manual   In addition to user documentation, a Trusted Facility Manual must be provided. This manual is aimed at system administrators and teaches the administrator what security facilities exist and how they should be implemented when running a secure system. Also, it must contain the procedures needed to implement auditing.

The Windows NT Trusted Facility Manual (TFM) adheres to the Trusted Facility Manual requirement. It describes the privileges and groups that should be controlled, how to examine and maintain the security logs, and descriptions of the administrative tools included with Windows NT.

As part of the documentation required to meet the C2 specifications, the vendor must provide the evaluators with a document describing how the system was tested and the results of the testing. Windows NT's test documentation adheres to C2 requirements.

Design Documentation   As a final bit of the extensive documentation required to meet C2 requirements, the vendor must provide documentation explaining how the security philosophy is translated into the operating system architecture. If the operating system is modular in nature, the documentation also must explain how the interfaces between the modules are protected.

Windows NT's documentation adheres to the Design Documentation requirement.

Other Orange Book Security Considerations   In addition to meeting the requirements for C2-level security, certain aspects of Windows NT qualified for even higher security levels, up to B2 in some areas. The components of Windows NT that meet B2 evaluation requirements are as follows:

B2 Trusted Facility Management   One of the many requirements that must be met in order for an operating system to be evaluated as a B2 system is that it must support separate operator and administrator functions. Windows NT includes the capability for administrators to grant certain rights to individual users. This allows organizations to dictate the actions that individuals can perform. This capability, coupled with the built-in groups, makes Windows NT conform to the B2 Trusted Facility Management criteria.

B2 Trusted Path   Another requirement for evaluation as a B2 system is a trusted communication path between the system and its users for initial log on and for user authentication. Additionally, the log-in path only can be initiated by a user, never by the system itself.

The secure log-on sequence, CTRL+ALT+DEL, also known as the Secure Attention Sequence, ensures that identification and authentication information is sent only to the WinLogon server. This sequence allows Windows NT to conform with the B2 Trusted Path requirement.

As you have seen, Microsoft has placed a tremendous amount of effort into making Windows NT a secure operating system. Now that you have a thorough understanding of C2-level security and how Windows NT meets the requirements, you can use the C2 configuration manager to increase the security of your computer.

How to Meet C2 Requirements with Windows NT

The simplest way to implement C2 security on Windows NT is with the Windows NT Resource Kit, and more specifically with the C2 Configuration Manager. This section shows you what you need to know about the C2 Configuration Manager to implement C2 security for your Windows NT installation.

The C2 Configuration Manager

The C2 Configuration Manager supplied with the Windows NT Server 4.0 Resource Kit makes implementing C2-level security almost too easy. It looks at your system's configuration and points out almost everything that must be changed to bring you within C2 compliance. Figure 19.1 displays the C2 Configuration Manager.

FIG. 19.1
The C2 Configuration
Manager.

File Systems

Recall that Division C, classification 2 calls for Discretionary Access Control. Although
Windows NT does support other file systems such as FAT, NTFS is currently the only file
system supported by Windows NT that offers Discretionary Access Control. Should your
system have any non-NTFS partitions, clicking the C2 button selects them for conversion
the next time your system boots.

Operating System Configuration

For your system to reach C2 security, Windows NT must be the only operating system
installed. While the C2 Configuration Manager does not uninstall other operating systems,
it can make them unavailable when the system boots. This is done by telling the OS
Loader to wait before starting Windows NT. If your operating system options are not C2,
double-clicking the item opens the dialog box in Figure 19.2.

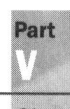

Part
V

Ch
19

FIG. 19.2
Operating Systems
dialog box.

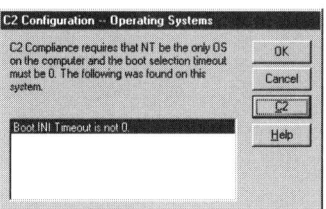

Click the C2 button, then click OK. A message box appears and informs you that you are
not able to select another operating system at startup. Clicking OK updates BOOT.INI.

OS/2 Subsystem

The OS/2 subsystem enables Windows NT to run OS/2 character mode applications. The
C2 requirements, however, dictate that the OS/2 subsystem must not be installed in order

for Windows NT to be required. This is mainly because OS/2 was not designed to meet C2-security requirements (see Figure 19.3).

FIG. 19.3
Uninstalling the OS/2 Subsystem.

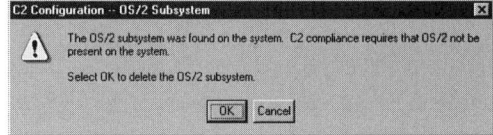

POSIX Subsystem

The Portable Operating System Interface based on the UNIX (POSIX) subsystem enables Windows NT to execute 32-bit POSIX applications. These applications are character based and run in a console window. Because of the POSIX UNIX-based security, it cannot be installed on a C2-secure Windows NT platform. Double-click the POSIX subsystem item to open the dialog box in Figure 19.4.

FIG. 19.4
Uninstalling the POSIX subsystem.

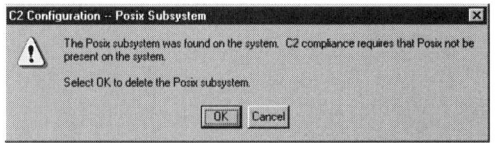

Selecting the OK button brings up a message box requesting confirmation. Click OK again to remove the POSIX Subsystem. Should you decide to reinstall the POSIX Subsystem at a later time, simply copy the file PSXSS.EXE from your Windows NT CD-ROM into your %SystemRoot% directory.

Security Log

The Accountability Control Objective for C2 requires that the system creates, maintains, and protects from modification, unauthorized access, or destruction of an audit trail the access to the objects the system protects. By default, Windows NT overwrites events in the Event Viewer after they are seven days old. Double-click Security Log to bring up the dialog box in Figure 19.5.

FIG. 19.5
Security log settings for C2.

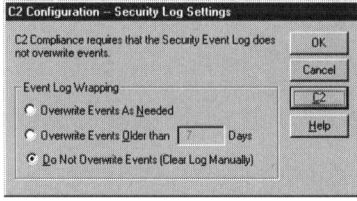

Select the option button beside "Do Not Overwrite Events (Clear Log Manually)," then click OK.

Halt-on-Audit Failure

In the normal Windows NT setup, even if the Event Viewer is configured to not overwrite any events, should the log's size exceed the maximum size set by an administrator, the system keeps functioning. While this may be convenient at times, the system stops auditing. This means any policy violations or attempted violations go unrecorded. To bring your audit settings within C2 requirements, double-click the item (see Figure 19.6).

FIG. 19.6
Halting on Audit
Failure.

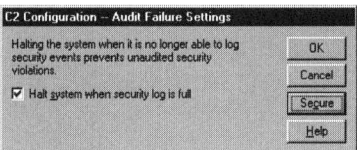

Select "Halt system when security log is full," then click OK. Your audit settings are now within C2 requirements.

Display Log-on Message

While not a C2 requirement, having the system notify users at logon that the system they are entering stores sensitive information and that you are willing to prosecute them for violating your security policy may or may not deter a would-be hacker. However, it can be essential when attempting to prosecute a hacker for violations. To specify a log-on message, double-click the item shown in Figure 19.7

Part
V

Ch
19

FIG. 19.7
Displaying a log-on
message to all users.

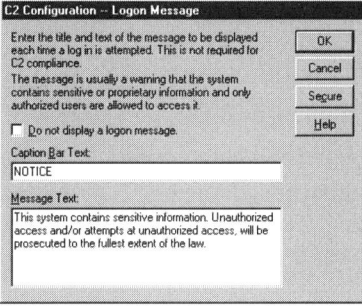

Specify the message box caption and the message you want displayed, then click OK.

Last Username Display

As you undoubtedly have noticed, Windows NT automatically displays the last user to log on to the system at a particular computer. While convenient at times, automatically providing one-half of the Identification/Authentication information to others could prove to be one-half too much. Although not required for C2 security, disabling this item is a good idea (see Figure 19.8).

FIG. 19.8

Disabling the Last Username Display.

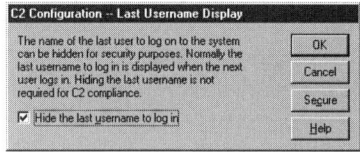

Select "Hide the last username to log in" then click OK.

Shutdown Button

When a user is entering a username and password, Windows NT provides him with a means of shutting down the system prior to authentication (see Figure 19.9). Most computers are turned on for a reason. Personally, I prefer only for myself or another administrator to decide when one of my computers is going to be shut down.

FIG. 19.9

Remove the shutdown button from the log-on dialog.

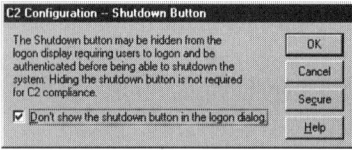

Select "Don't show the shutdown button in the logon dialog" then click OK.

Password Length

Windows NT's default configuration allows for passwords to be blank. For security to work, however, the Authentication portion of Identification/Authentication must exist. C2-security mandates that passwords are not blank. Double-clicking Password Length enables you to change the default setting (see Figure 19.10).

FIG. 19.10
Changing the minimum password length.

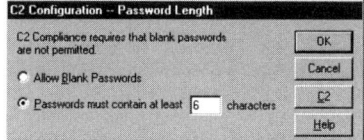

Click the C2 button then OK.

N O T E Changing the minimum password length does not affect passwords currently on the system. ■

Guest Account

One of the first things I always do when setting up Windows NT is disable the Guest account. If your system needs to be secure, especially C2 secure, your Guest account needs to be disabled also. Double-click Guest Account to open the dialog box in Figure 19.11.

FIG. 19.11
Disabling the Windows NT Guest Account.

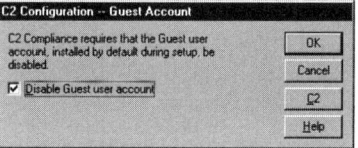

Select the check box "Disable Guest user account," then click OK.

Networking

As I mentioned earlier in this chapter, Windows NT's C2 certification was on a stand-alone computer. Before your system can be C2 secure, you need to uninstall all network hardware and software on your system (see Figure 19.12).

Double-clicking the Networking item in the Configuration Manager brings up a dialog box. Clicking OK in this dialog box takes you to the network setup where you can uninstall network protocols, adapters, and so on.

Drive Letters and Printers

Controlling a system's resources is central to security. This not only means access control, but installation control as well. Double-click this item to view the dialog box in Figure 19.13.

Part
V

Ch
19

FIG. 19.12

Double-click the Networking item to uninstall network hardware and software.

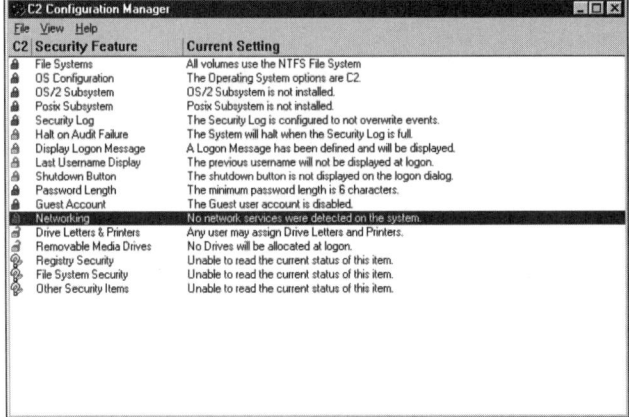

FIG. 19.13

Drives and Printers.

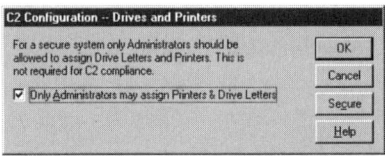

Select the "Only Administrators may assign Printers and Drive letters" check box, then click OK.

Removable Media Drives

Although this feature is not required to make Windows NT 4.0 meet the C2 security requirements, it does help to ensure the security of your system. The C2 Security Manager enables you to *allocate* removable drives (e.g., floppy disks and CD-ROMs) upon logon, which prevents an application started by another user from accessing these drives and more importantly, the data they contain while you are logged on. Figure 19.14 displays your choices for allocating removable drives in Windows NT 4.0.

FIG. 19.14

Allocating removable drives.

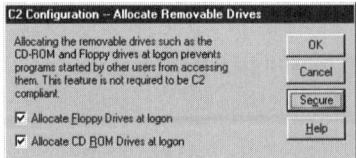

Registry Security

As you know, the Windows NT registry contains virtually all of your system's configuration information. Should your registry become damaged, it's conceivable that you could lose everything, including your job, wife, kids, cat, and so on. Double-clicking Registry Security opens the dialog box in Figure 19.15.

FIG. 19.15

Setting the Registry's security.

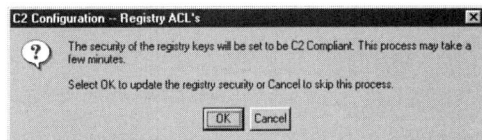

Selecting the OK button sets up an ACL for your registry. When the registry permissions have been set, a confirmation dialog displays indicating the operation is complete.

The specific keys and permissions defined in the file C2REGACL.INF are shown in the following list:

HKEY_LOCAL_MACHINE\SOFTWARE

HKEY_LOCAL_MACHINE\SOFTWARE\Classes

HKEY_LOCAL_MACHINE\SOFTWARE\Classes*

HKEY_LOCAL_MACHINE\SOFTWARE\Description

HKEY_LOCAL_MACHINE\SOFTWARE\Description*

HKEY_LOCAL_MACHINE\SOFTWARE\Microsoft

HKEY_LOCAL_MACHINE\SOFTWARE\Micorosft*

HKEY_LOCAL_MACHINE\SOFTWARE\Program Groups

HKEY_LOCAL_MACHINE\SOFTWARE\Secure

HKEY_LOCAL_MACHINE\SOFTWARE\Windows 3.1 Migration Status

The C2 Configuration Manager sets the security on each of these keys granting the proper access to individuals and groups. C2REGACL.INF provides a legend that enables you to view each key's permissions. Although you may be tempted, do not change this file. Any changes could not only effect your machines operation, but possibly could open security holes in your system.

Part
V

Ch
19

File System Security

File system security is arguably the most important item on the Configuration Manager's list. Even systems not containing sensitive information have required files. The files on a secure system are normally the whole reason the system is secured. Double-click the File System Security item to open the dialog box in Figure 19.16.

FIG. 19.16
Setting the File
System Security.

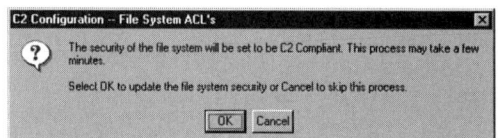

Clicking OK sets the permissions required for C2 security. When the Configuration Manager has finished, a confirmation dialog box appears. Click OK to continue.

C2NTFACL.INF contains the permissions the Configuration Manager sets on certain directories and files on your system. They are as follows:

> %SystemDrive%\
>
> %SystemDrive%*.*
>
> %SystemDrive%\IO.SYS
>
> %SystemDrive%\MSDOS.SYS
>
> %SystemDrive%\BOOT.INI
>
> %SystemDrive%\NTDETECT.COM
>
> %SystemDrive%\NTLDR
>
> %SystemDrive%\AUTOEXEC.BAT
>
> %SystemDrive%\CONFIG.SYS
>
> %SystemDrive%\TEMP\!
>
> %SystemDrive%\USERS\!
>
> %SystemDrive%\USERS\DEFAULT\!
>
> %SystemDrive%\WIN32APP\!
>
> %SystemRoot%\!
>
> %SystemRoot%*.*
>
> %SystemRoot%*.INI
>
> %SystemRoot%\LOCALMON.DLL
>
> %SystemRoot%\PRINTMAN.HLP

%SystemRoot%\REPAIR\!

%SystemRoot%\SYSTEM*.*

%SystemRoot%\SYSTEM32*.*

%SystemRoot%\SYSTEM32\AUTOEXEC.NT

%SystemRoot%\SYSTEM32\CMOS.RAM

%SystemRoot%\SYSTEM32\CONFIG.NT

%SystemRoot%\SYSTEM32\MIDIMAP.CFG

%SystemRoot%\SYSTEM32\PASSPORT.MID

%SystemRoot%\SYSTEM32\CONFIG

%SystemRoot%\SYSTEM32\CONFIG*.*

%SystemRoot%\SYSTEM32\CONFIG\DEFAULT.LOG

%SystemRoot%\SYSTEM32\CONFIG\SAM

%SystemRoot%\SYSTEM32\CONFIG\SAM.LOG

%SystemRoot%\SYSTEM32\CONFIG\SECURITY

%SystemRoot%\SYSTEM32\CONFIG\SECURITY.LOG

%SystemRoot%\SYSTEM32\CONFIG\SYSTEM

%SystemRoot%\SYSTEM32\CONFIG\SYSTEM.ALT

%SystemRoot%\SYSTEM32\CONFIG\SYSTEM.LOG

%SystemRoot%\SYSTEM32\CONFIG\USERDEF

%SystemRoot%\SYSTEM32\DHCP\!

%SystemRoot%\SYSTEM32\DRIVERS\!

%SystemRoot%\SYSTEM32\OS2\OSO001.009

%SystemRoot%\SYSTEM32\OS2\DLL\DOSCALLS.DLL

%SystemRoot%\SYSTEM32\OS2\DLL\NETAPI.DLL

%SystemRoot%\SYSTEM32\RAS

%SystemRoot%\SYSTEM32\RAS*.*

%SystemRoot%\SYSTEM32\REPL\!

%SystemRoot%\SYSTEM32\REPL\EXPORT

%SystemRoot%\SYSTEM32\REPL\EXPORT*.*

%SystemRoot%\SYSTEM32\REPL\EXPORT\SCRIPTS

%SystemRoot%\SYSTEM32\REPL\EXPORT\SCRIPTS*.*

%SystemRoot%\SYSTEM32\REPL\IMPORT

Part
V

Ch
19

%SystemRoot%\SYSTEM32\REPL\IMPORT*.*

%SystemRoot%\SYSTEM32\REPL\IMPORT\SCRIPTS

%SystemRoot%\SYSTEM32\REPL\IMPORT\SCRIPTS*.*

%SystemRoot%\SYSTEM32\SPOOL\!

%SystemRoot%\SYSTEM32\SPOOL\DRIVERS\W32X86\1

%SystemRoot%\SYSTEM32\SPOOL\DRIVERS\W32X86\WINPRINT.DLL

%SystemRoot%\SYSTEM32\WINS\!

The exclamation point (!) tells the Configuration Manager to include all files and subdirectories below the specified directory as well as the specified directory itself. As with the registry settings, do not edit this file.

Other Security Items

Unfortunately, not all required configuration changes can be made from the C2 Configuration Manager. Double-clicking Other Security Items brings up the dialog box with four choices. The four items shown must be configured to complete your C2 implementation. The Power-On Password varies from system to system, so please consult your manual for instructions. The User Manager for Domains must be replaced with the standard User Manager program, and the accounts on your system should be configured as outlined in the Windows NT C2 Security System Administrator's Guide.

From Here...

This chapter covers the Orange Book's C2 requirements in detail and examines the individual, corresponding features of Windows NT. Understanding the requirements and how Windows NT conforms with C2-level security helps administrators concerned with security. Additionally, you used the C2 Configuration Manager to implement C2-level security on your system. Even on systems not requiring C2-level security, with the Configuration Manager, subtle holes in your security policy can be filled.

Index

Symbols

! (exclamation point), 446
16-bit VDM, 74-87

A

access
  control entries, 68
  masks
    DELETE, 84
    GENERIC_EXECUTE, 84
    GENERIC_READ, 84
    READ_CONTROL, 84
    SYNCHRONIZE, 84
    WRITE_DAC, 84
    WRITE_OWNER, 84
  objects, controlling, 431
  permissions, assigning (NTFS), 197-203
  privileges, assigning (DESIGN domain), 283
Access
  Control Entries, *see* ACEs
  Through Share Permissions dialog box, 131
accessing
  anonymous access, 350
  domain resources, 243-245
  files, NTFS permissions, 187-188

network resources, 29
  remote, 53
resources
  interactive logons, 175
  remote logons, 175-183

UNIX systems with X-Terminals, 408
workstations, 238-239
  resources, 245-246

Account
  button, 105
  Information dialog box, 235
  Policy dialog box, 105

accountability, Orange Book (Rainbow Series) control objective, 418

accounts
  access
    granting in trusting domains, 281-283
    printer queues, assigning, 283
  administration, domains, 95
  Administrator accounts, 304-305
  Administrator user, 161
  anonymous access, 350
  computer, memory requirements, 98
  domains, 119-123, 252

global, 161-165
global group, memory requirements, 98
group, creating, 275-276
Guest, 161, 304
IIS FTP Server, authentication, 353
IIS Web service, authentication, 350-351
interdomain trust, 134
  viewing, 135
local, 161-165
local group, memory requirements, 98
lockouts, 303
network security, 22-23
policies, 28
  Account lockouts, 303
  defining, 27
  least privilege, 305
  Maximum Password Age, 303
  Password Uniqueness, 303
resource permissions, network security, 23
share level security, 160-161
SIDs (Security ID), 166-168
user, 45-46, 101-114, 160-168, 161-165
  administrator accounts, 161-162

MACMILLAN COMPUTER PUBLISHING USA

A VIACOM COMPANY

Technical - - - - Support:

If you need assistance with the information in this book or with a CD/Disk accompanying the book, please access the Knowledge Base on our Web site at **http://www.superlibrary.com/general/support**. Our most Frequently Asked Questions are answered there. If you do not find the answer to your questions on our Web site, you may contact Macmillan Technical Support **(317) 581-3833** or e-mail us at **support@mcp.com**.

Check out Que® Books
on the World Wide Web
http://www.quecorp.com

As the biggest software release in computer history, Windows 95 continues to redefine the computer industry. Click here for the latest info on our Windows 95 books

Make computing quick and easy with these products designed exclusively for new and casual users

Examine the latest releases in word processing, spreadsheets, operating systems, and suites

Desktop Applications & Operating Systems

que®

new Users

what's new?

Windows 95

Internet
And New Technologies

The Internet, The World Wide Web, CompuServe®, America Online®, Prodigy® —it's a world of ever-changing information. Don't get left behind!

Que's Publishing Areas

Calendar of Events

DEVELOPER AND EXPERT USERS

Find out about new additions to our site, new bestsellers and hot topics

ZD ZIFF-DAVIS PRESS

Que's Top 10 Titles

Macintosh & Desktop Publishing

In-depth information on high-end topics: find the best reference books for databases, programming, networking, and client/server technologies

A recent addition to Que, Ziff-Davis Press publishes the highly-successful *How It Works* and *How to Use* series of books, as well as *PC Learning Labs Teaches* and *PC Magazine* series of book/disc packages

Stay on the cutting edge of Macintosh® technologies and visual communications

Find out which titles are making headlines

With 6 separate publishing groups, Que develops products for many specific market segments and areas of computer technology. Explore our Web Site and you'll find information on best-selling titles, newly published titles, upcoming products, authors, and much more.

- Stay informed on the latest industry trends and products available
- Visit our online bookstore for the latest information and editions
- Download software from Que's library of the best shareware and freeware

Complete and Return this Card
for a *FREE* Computer Book Catalog

Thank you for purchasing this book! You have purchased a superior computer book written expressly for your needs. To continue to provide the kind of up-to-date, pertinent coverage you've come to expect from us, we need to hear from you. Please take a minute to complete and return this self-addressed, postage-paid form. In return, we'll send you a free catalog of all our computer books on topics ranging from word processing to programming and the internet.

Mr. ☐   Mrs. ☐   Ms. ☐   Dr. ☐

Name (first) ☐☐☐☐☐☐☐☐☐☐   (M.I.) ☐   (last) ☐☐☐☐☐☐☐☐☐☐☐☐☐

Address ☐☐☐☐☐☐☐☐☐☐☐☐☐☐☐☐☐☐☐☐☐☐☐☐☐☐☐☐

☐☐☐☐☐☐☐☐☐☐☐☐☐☐☐☐☐☐☐☐☐☐☐☐☐☐☐☐

City ☐☐☐☐☐☐☐☐☐☐☐☐☐☐   State ☐☐   Zip ☐☐☐☐☐☐☐☐

Phone ☐☐☐☐☐☐☐☐☐☐   Fax ☐☐☐☐☐☐☐☐☐☐

Company Name ☐☐☐☐☐☐☐☐☐☐☐☐☐☐☐☐☐☐☐☐☐☐

E-mail address ☐☐☐☐☐☐☐☐☐☐☐☐☐☐☐☐☐☐☐☐☐☐

1. Please check at least (3) influencing factors for purchasing this book.

Front or back cover information on book .... ☐
Special approach to the content .... ☐
Completeness of content .... ☐
Author's reputation .... ☐
Publisher's reputation .... ☐
Book cover design or layout .... ☐
Index or table of contents of book .... ☐
Price of book .... ☐
Special effects, graphics, illustrations .... ☐
Other (Please specify): _____ ☐

2. How did you first learn about this book?

Saw in Macmillan Computer Publishing catalog .... ☐
Recommended by store personnel .... ☐
Saw the book on bookshelf at store .... ☐
Recommended by a friend .... ☐
Received advertisement in the mail .... ☐
Saw an advertisement in: _____ ☐
Read book review in: _____ ☐
Other (Please specify): _____ ☐

3. How many computer books have you purchased in the last six months?

This book only .... ☐   3 to 5 books .... ☐
2 books .... ☐   More than 5 .... ☐

4. Where did you purchase this book?

Bookstore .... ☐
Computer Store .... ☐
Consumer Electronics Store .... ☐
Department Store .... ☐
Office Club .... ☐
Warehouse Club .... ☐
Mail Order .... ☐
Direct from Publisher .... ☐
Internet site .... ☐
Other (Please specify): _____ ☐

5. How long have you been using a computer?

☐ Less than 6 months   ☐ 6 months to a year
☐ 1 to 3 years   ☐ More than 3 years

6. What is your level of experience with personal computers and with the subject of this book?

	With PCs	With subject of book
New	☐	☐
Casual	☐	☐
Accomplished	☐	☐
Expert	☐	☐

Source Code ISBN: 0-7897-1213-x

7. Which of the following best describes your job title?

Administrative Assistant .... ☐
Coordinator .... ☐
Manager/Supervisor .... ☐
Director .... ☐
Vice President .... ☐
President/CEO/COO .... ☐
Lawyer/Doctor/Medical Professional .... ☐
Teacher/Educator/Trainer .... ☐
Engineer/Technician .... ☐
Consultant .... ☐
Not employed/Student/Retired .... ☐
Other (Please specify): _____ ☐

8. Which of the following best describes the area of the company your job title falls under?

Accounting .... ☐
Engineering .... ☐
Manufacturing .... ☐
Operations .... ☐
Marketing .... ☐
Sales .... ☐
Other (Please specify): _____ ☐

9. What is your age?

Under 20 .... ☐
21-29 .... ☐
30-39 .... ☐
40-49 .... ☐
50-59 .... ☐
60-over .... ☐

10. Are you:

Male .... ☐
Female .... ☐

11. Which computer publications do you read regularly? (Please list)

_____
_____
_____
_____
_____
_____
_____
_____
_____
_____

Comments: _____
_____
_____

Fold here and scotch-tape to mail.